SPRUNG FROM SOME COMMON SOURCE

CONTRIBUTORS

Robert Austerlitz

Garland Cannon

J. C. Catford

Søren Egerod

Shiela Embleton

Marija Gimbutas

Joseph H. Greenberg

Carlton T. Hodge

Winfred P. Lehmann

Saul Levin

Samuel E. Martin

Roy Andrew Miller

Robert L. Oswalt

Edgar C. Polomé

Jaan Puhvel

Alexis Manaster Ramer

Merritt Ruhlen

Vitaly Shevoroshkin

Sprung from Some Common Source

INVESTIGATIONS INTO THE PREHISTORY OF LANGUAGES

92-1676

Edited by
Sydney M. Lamb and E. Douglas Mitchell

Stanford University Press, Stanford, California

Stanford University Press
Stanford, California
© 1991 by the Board of Trustees of the
Leland Stanford Junior University
Printed in the United States of America

Library of Congress
Cataloging-in-Publication Data

Sprung from some common source :
investigations into the prehistory of languages /
   edited by Sydney M. Lamb and E. Douglas Mitchell.
      p. cm.
   Includes index.
   ISBN 0-8047-1897-0 (alk. paper):
     1. Language and languages—Origin.
   2. Language and languages—Classification.
   3. Indo-European languages—History.
   4. Oriental languages—History.
   I. Lamb, Sydney M.   II. Mitchell, E. Douglas.
   P116.S65   1991
   401'.2—dc20   90-46495
                                          CIP

∞ This book is printed on acid-free paper

To Murray B. Emeneau
Sanskritist, Dravidianist, Indologist,
Linguist, Teacher, Gentleman

Contents

Contributors   ix

Introduction   1
Sydney M. Lamb and E. Douglas Mitchell

PART I:
SIR WILLIAM JONES AND HIS LEGACY   9

The Process of Linguistics   11
Winfred P. Lehmann

Jones's "Sprung from Some Common Source": 1786–1986   23
Garland Cannon

PART II:
INDO-EUROPEAN IN CONTEXT   49

Whence the Hittite, Whither the Jonesian Vision?   51
Jaan Puhvel

Indo-European Religion and the Indo-European Religious
Vocabulary   67
Edgar C. Polomé

Deities and Symbols of Old Europe and Their Survival in the
Indo-European Era: A Synopsis   89
Marija Gimbutas

PART III: THE SEARCH FOR
RELATIVES OF INDO-EUROPEAN   123

Some Problems of Indo-European in Historical Perspective   125
Joseph H. Greenberg

Indo-European and Afroasiatic   141
Carleton T. Hodge

Full and Other Key Words Shared by Indo-European and
Semitic   166
    Saul Levin

Some Recent Work on the Remote Relations of Languages   178
    Vitaly Shevoroshkin and Alexis Manaster Ramer

PART IV: LINGUISTIC GENEALOGY
IN EUROPE, ASIA, AND AMERICA   201

Far Eastern Languages   205
    Søren Egerod

The Classification of Caucasian Languages   232
    J. C. Catford

Recent Research on the Relationships of Japanese and Korean   269
    Samuel E. Martin

Genetic Connections Among the Altaic Languages   293
    Roy Andrew Miller

The Amerind Phylum and the Prehistory of the New World   328
    Merritt Ruhlen

PART V: METHODS IN GENETIC
CLASSIFICATION OF LANGUAGES   351

Alternatives in Long-Range Comparison   353
    Robert Austerlitz

Mathematical Methods of Genetic Classification   365
    Sheila Embleton

A Method for Assessing Distant Linguistic Relationships   389
    Robert L. Oswalt

Index   405

Contributors

ROBERT AUSTERLITZ, a native of Rumania, came to the United States at the age of 15. He is Professor of Linguistics and Uralic Studies at Columbia University, where he has taught since 1958. He has been a visiting professor in Germany, Sweden, and Finland, as well as at several universities in the United States. His research has concentrated on Uralic languages and various languages of northeast Asia including Gilyak, which have long resisted the attempts of linguists to find genetic affiliations.

GARLAND CANNON, a Professor in the Department of English at Texas A&M University, has also held visiting positions at the University of Washington, M.I.T., Kuwait University, Oxford, and Cambridge. He has done fieldwork on Thai, Spanish, Persian, Arabic, and Russian. He has published extensively on the structure and history of the English language. An authority on the history of linguistics and especially on the life and work of Sir William Jones, he is the author of seven books, including *Oriental Jones: The Life and Mind of Sir William Jones* (1985).

Professor IAN CATFORD, a native of Edinburgh, became interested in phonetics upon seeing Shaw's *Pygmalion* at the age of 14. Educated in Edinburgh, London, and Paris, he taught at the University of Edinburgh before going to the University of Michigan as Professor of Linguistics and Director of the English Language Institute in 1964. In addition to phonology, his research has centered on the languages of the Caucasus, an area characterized by extreme phonetic complexity of consonants. His books include *Fundamental Problems in Phonetics* and *Practical Introduction to Phonetics*.

SØREN EGEROD, a leading expert on the languages of Asia, recently retired as director of the Scandinavian Institute of Asian Studies and Professor of East Asian Languages at the University of

Copenhagen. He studied Classical Philology and Sanskrit at the University of Copenhagen before turning to Sinology and general linguistics, and he did postdoctoral research and teaching at the University of California, Berkeley, before returning to Copenhagen as a Professor. He has done extensive fieldwork on Asiatic languages and is a fluent speaker of Chinese and Thai.

Professor SHEILA M. EMBLETON, who teaches Linguistics at York University in Toronto, combines expertise in historical linguistics with professional skills in mathematics, an area regrettably omitted from the toolkits of most linguists.

MARIJA GIMBUTAS, born and educated in Lithuania, received her Ph.D. and did postdoctoral studies in Germany before coming to the United States in 1949. She is Professor of European Archeology and Indo-European Studies at UCLA. As an expert on the archeology of Europe and the Near East, she has uncovered the changing states of European culture before, during, and after the spread of the Indo-Europeans. Among her several books are *The Gods and Goddesses of Old Europe* (1974) and *The Language of the Goddess* (1989).

JOSEPH GREENBERG, Ray Lyman Wilbur Professor Emeritus of Social Science at Stanford University, has combined linguistics and anthropology in his teaching and research and has become one of the most renowned and honored figures of his time in both fields. Among his best-known contributions are those in the areas of linguistic typology and the genetic classification of languages. His classification of African languages, greeted as revolutionary and controversial when it appeared in several parts beginning in 1949, has now become the generally accepted standard. More recently he has made similarly comprehensive proposals for other parts of the world, including the Americas (see Merritt Ruhlen, this volume). His current research relates Indo-European to other linguistic families of Europe and Northern Asia.

CARLETON HODGE, Professor Emeritus of Linguistics at Indiana University, is an expert on the very diverse Afro-Asiatic language family, which extends from Semitic in the northeast through Egyptian and Berber in North Africa, to Cushitic, Omotic, and Chadic in sub-Saharan Africa. As the relationships among these branches are considerably more remote than those among the branches of Indo-

European, the search for evidence linking them is far more difficult. Even more difficult is his recent and current area of research, which attempts to find a common source for Afro-Asiatic and Indo-European.

WINFRED P. LEHMANN, Louann and Larry Temple Centennial Professor Emeritus in the Humanities at the University of Texas (Austin), is also Director of the Linguistics Research Center at that University. A scholar of international renown whose work has been recognized with numerous honors from the United States and abroad, he has written widely in Germanic and Indo-European linguistics as well as in general linguistics.

SAUL LEVIN, Professor in the Department of Classical and Near Eastern Studies at the State University of New York at Binghamton, is an expert on ancient languages of the Mediterranean area, including Latin, Greek, and Hebrew.

SAMUEL E. MARTIN is Professor of Linguistics at Yale University, and he has served several times as a visiting professor at the University of Hawaii. His research has centered on Japanese and Korean and, along with Roy Miller, he has presented evidence in a series of publications for a distant genetic relationship between these two languages, previously thought to be genetic isolates.

ROY ANDREW MILLER taught linguistics and Japanese at Yale University for several years before going to the University of Washington, where he recently became Professor Emeritus. An expert on Japanese, Korean, and Altaic with thorough grounding in the methods of historical linguistics as developed in the context of comparative Indo-European studies, he currently resides in Honolulu.

ROBERT OSWALT moved into linguistics after several years as a professional chemist. Now retired and living in Kensington, California, he taught for several years at the University of California, Berkeley, after receiving his Ph.D. in linguistics there. His research has concentrated on the Pomo languages of Northern California.

EDGAR POLOMÉ received his Ph.D. from the Université Libre de Bruxelles and is Professor of Germanic, Oriental, and African Languages and Linguistics at the University of Texas. He specializes in

African languages but has a specialist's erudition in several related fields as well, including Indo-European and ancient religions. He is the author of *Swahili Language Handbook* and *Language in Tanzania*.

JAAN PUHVEL is a Professor of Classics and Indo-European Studies at UCLA. A native of Estonia, he was trained in Indo-European linguistics at Harvard, where he was a Junior Fellow. A master of Indo-European languages and cultures, he concentrates on Hittite. His recent books include *Comparative Mythology* and a multi-volume *Hittite Etymological Dictionary*.

ALEXIS MANASTER RAMER, Associate Professor of Computer Science at Wayne State University, received his Ph.D. in Linguistics from the University of Chicago and taught Linguistics for a few years at the University of Michigan, where he worked with Vitaly Shevoroshkin. In his research in historical linguistics, he has worked both on remote relationships and on reconstruction of the common source of the Uto-Aztecan languages of North and Central America. He also does research in phonology and in mathematical and computational linguistics.

MERRITT RUHLEN, a former student and research assistant of Joseph Greenberg, is an expert on language classification whose domain covers the entire world. He is particularly interested in long-range groupings. He is the author of *A Guide to the World's Languages, Volume 1: Classification* (Stanford, 1987).

VITALY SHEVOROSHKIN was one of a group of Russian linguists actively investigating distant linguistic relationships before he emigrated to the United States in 1974. He taught in the linguistics department at Yale for a few years before assuming his current position as Professor at the University of Michigan in 1979. He remains one of the most active of the scholars working on distant relationships.

SPRUNG FROM SOME COMMON SOURCE

Introduction

The year 1986 marked the two-hundredth anniversary of an address by Sir William Jones to the Asiatic Society in Calcutta. In his address, Jones declared that Latin, Greek, and Sanskrit must have "sprung from some common source," which probably was also the origin of Gothic, Celtic, and Persian. These words have often been credited with sparking the burst of scholarly activity in comparative linguistics that became one of the major currents in European intellectual life of the nineteenth century, and the address has thus been considered a milestone in the history of linguistics.

In observance of this anniversary, the Department of Linguistics and Semiotics of Rice University sponsored the Symposium on Genetic Classification of Languages, held in March 1986 in Houston. This volume contains selected papers from the symposium, several of them in revised form, for the authors were urged to revise their papers after the symposium to take account of arguments expounded in the other papers and to reflect the lively discussions that took place. It notes the progress of the last 200 years and proposes new ideas in the hope of stimulating future work, just as the address of Sir William Jones had done two centuries earlier. In keeping with this aim, the contributors to this volume adopted a broad outlook, both by looking at genetic relationships outside of Indo-European (IE) and by looking beyond the grammar and phonology of IE and into the mythology, religion, and culture of the Indo-Europeans.

Sir William's celebrated proposal is really two proposals: The first, of course, is the hypothesis of a genetic relationship among certain languages, notably Latin, Greek, and Sanskrit, and we now know that the family does indeed include not only Gothic, Celtic, and Iranian, as he suggested, but also the Slavic and Baltic groups of languages, together with Hittite and other lesser known branches. The second proposal is the notion of common origin as an explanation for observed similarities among languages, the hypothesis that the languages must have "sprung from some common source, which perhaps no longer exists."

The anniversary of Sir William's address seemed to us an appropriate time to bring together some of the world's leading investigators in the area of genetic classification of languages. For several decades after that address, linguistics progressed vigorously: new branches were added to the Indo-European family, their "common source" was partially reconstructed, and theories of linguistic change were developed and refined. But in more recent decades the excitement in IE studies has waned and conservatism has set in, in part because of the onset of theories that examine language synchronically, in part because some influential scholars have been reluctant to look beyond the now traditional genetic boundaries and have been critical of a few of their colleagues who have not shared that reluctance. This small but growing minority of linguists has been seeking to uncover common sources more remote in time even than Proto-IE, and investigators of languages of other areas of the world have also been discovering remote genetic relationships, using methods that—like their findings—sometimes differ from those that had become comfortable over the years.

A fitting celebration of the bicentennial, we decided, would be a symposium that would inject some new vitality into comparative linguistics, with a focus on Indo-European. In organizing the symposium and in planning this publication, we sought to recognize some of the more innovative workers in historical linguistics and to encourage others who may be hesitant to let their full creative powers loose in a field that was in danger of stifling itself from an excess of caution. It is of course impossible to enliven any scholarly field without arousing controversy, but we took the risk of doing so as the price of ensuring a fitting commemoration of Sir William's landmark contribution.

As suggested above, it is our intention that this volume take account of the progress of the last 200 years while encouraging innovative future work. For the sake of the latter objective we adopted a broad outlook, looking beyond comparative Indo-European linguistics in two ways: first, by looking at genetic relationships outside of IE, with a focus on the possible relatives of IE, and, second, by looking beyond the grammar and phonology of IE into the mythology, religion, and culture of the early Indo-Europeans.

We have also sought some balance in the form of a cautionary note and a warning to those who might tend to exceed their evidence in constructing genetic groupings of languages. Professor

Robert Austerlitz took upon himself the burden of arguing against unrestrained "lumping," and he suggests in his paper that we explore some alternatives to genetic affiliation as explanations of observed similarities among disparate linguistic groups. As a specialist in the Uralic language family, Austerlitz is particularly well suited to this role, for Uralic figures very prominently in questions of deeper relationships not only of Indo-European but of many other groups. Uralic has been connected by various investigators not only with IE but also with Altaic (whose existence as a genetic unit is itself doubted by many, including Austerlitz), Dravidian, Japanese, Eskimo-Aleut, Penutian, and other groups, all of which would have to be considered related to each other under the family-tree hypothesis if all are related to Uralic.

The volume begins with a pair of introductory pieces, one of them a broad general introduction by the renowned Indo-Europeanist and general linguist Winfred Lehmann, the other a study of the work and influence of Sir William Jones by Garland Cannon, one of the world's leading students of his life and career.

Part II, appropriately enough, focuses on Indo-European, but with attention not just to the IE languages and their common source but also to the culture of the Indo-Europeans. In addition Marija Gimbutas takes us one step further, by offering archeological insight into the culture of "Old Europe," the culture of the peoples who were there before the Indo-Europeans.

The volume then branches out, in Part III, to examine some recent work on various hypothesized relationships of IE to other linguistic stocks, some of them far-reaching and controversial. Perhaps this is the area that Jones himself would find most interesting if he could return to the Earth today.

The comparisons with possible relatives of IE inevitably focus on such potential cousins as Uralic, Altaic, and Kartvelian. Part IV thus goes on to survey the comparative linguistics of the areas to the northeast and east of Indo-European. Here we include also Merritt Ruhlen's study of certain implications of Joseph Greenberg's new classification of the American Indian languages, *Language in the Americas*, which was still in press at the time of the symposium.

Part V, finally, contains three papers concerned with methods of investigation. First, Robert Austerlitz presents the cautionary note previously mentioned. Readers who believe that some current investigators are going too far too hastily in positing distant genetic relationships will doubtless welcome the piece warmly. Sheila Embleton presents an account of some techniques that can be used to refine lexicostatistical studies. And Robert Oswalt describes a computer program for developing and testing hypotheses of distant genetic relationships among languages.

The symposium also enjoyed some presentations that for various reasons have not been included in this volume. The Dravidian family of India is increasingly being compared with families that are also proposed as relatives of IE, and Bhadriraju Krishnamurthi presented a comprehensive survey of the Dravidian family. Mary Ritchie Key presented an innovative proposal for research on diachronic aspects of semantic features aimed at the discovery of patterns of semantic change. She suggested that such exploration can lead to a more systematic and more reliable means of determining how much and what kind of semantic latitude to allow when conducting lexical comparisons among languages and families whose hypothetical genetic relationships have yet to be established. Key's procedure is based on tabulating and classifying examples of semantic change, using accepted etymologies in established language families, in order to arrive at a framework that can then be applied in new lexical comparisons, especially in long-range comparison.

Two other papers dealt with two of the many possible connections that have been proposed for Uralic. Stephen Tyler reviewed some of the evidence for a connection between Uralic and Dravidian, and Otto Sadovszky presented evidence for the geographically surprising (but, as he pointed out, explainable) hypothesis of a connection between Uralic and Penutian. For both of these hypotheses, the brief presentations at the symposium could not do justice to the controversial and rather bulky evidence that has already been presented elsewhere. In the case of the Uralic-Dravidian connection, Tyler's earlier paper, published in *Language*, vol. 44 (1968), was followed by more extensive comparisons in Elli Marlow's University of Texas dissertation, "More on the Uralo-Dravidian Relationship: a Comparison of Uralic and Dravidian Etymological Vocabularies" (1974); and Illich-Svitych compared Dravidian with IE, Uralic, Afro-Asiatic, Kartvelian, and Altaic (see the paper by Shevoroshkin and Manaster-Ramer in Part III of this volume). The Uralic-Penutian hypothesis is supported, insufficiently in the view of many, in a series of papers by Sadovszky. Both hypotheses would require a more detailed presentation of evidence than is feasible in this volume. Both also raise once again the important question of *degree* of relationship with respect to the various other proposals involving Uralic, not the least of which is that connecting it with IE. Thus, for example, Sadovszky's hypothesis is consistent with the view that Greenberg's

Amerind (discussed by Ruhlen in Part IV) is related to his Eurasiatic (discussed in Part III) or to the Nostratic of various Russian linguists. That view was supported by Shevoroshkin at the symposium, but Sadovszky proposed that the connection of Uralic to Penutian is closer than that. As with so many previous comparative studies, the question of relative degrees of relationship is crucial; genetic classification is concerned not so much with the simple binary (yes-or-no) question of whether two languages or groups are related, as with the question of degree of closeness or distance in comparison to other possible relatives.

Short, relatively formal presentations, not included in this volume, were given by Carol Justus and William Christie, and several informal discussions were offered by the various presenters and formal discussants, the latter of whom included Justus, Christie, Raimo Anttila, and Mark Kaiser.

The final discrepancy between the list of contributors to this volume and the roster of presenters at the symposium is that Alexis Manaster-Ramer, who at the last minute had to cancel his participation in the symposium, is nevertheless the co-author of the revised version of the paper presented at the symposium by Vitaly Shevoroshkin.

It will be clear from the foregoing that some of the ideas presented in this volume will be found controversial, particularly those involving possible distant genetic relationships. The field of historical linguistics currently suffers from the curious phenomenon that new proposals of possible genetic relationships tend to be met not with the interest that welcomed Sir William's proposal but with resistance, even with moral indignation. Those who are thus indignant insist that the only way to discover the existence of genetic relationships is by means of regular phonological correspondences, and it is commonly also held that comparisons leading to the positing of such correspondences should be done on a binary basis, two languages or groups at a time.

But Jones's comparison of three languages—Latin, Greek, and Sanskrit—would then have violated this principle, and it is a remarkable fact, which we pursued in the discussion on the last day of the symposium, that this cherished doctrine of phonological correspondences conflicts directly with another cherished tenet in the belief system of comparativists: that Jones's proposal that Latin, Greek, Sanskrit, etc. must be "sprung from some common source" was a praiseworthy contribution to linguistics.

How is the clash between these two principles so easily over-looked? For those readers not trained in comparative linguistics, let it be pointed out that Sir William made his celebrated proposal not on the basis of regular phonological correspondences but on the basis of techniques that are condemned by modern conservative comparativists when employed by their contemporaries today. His conclusion (for which, by the way, he presented almost no evidence in the discourse) was based on "affinity . . . in the roots of verbs and in the forms of grammar" (see Cannon's paper in this volume for a more complete quotation and Greenberg's paper for further discussion of this point). Indeed it was not until almost 90 years after the Jones address that the concept of regular phonological correspondences was even formulated. Until the Danish linguist Karl Verner found an explanation for a set of exceptions to the usual developments of stop consonants in Germanic, which he formulated in a phonological "law" that bears his name, it was generally supposed that irregular phonological correspondences are quite normal (see also Lehmann's paper in this volume). Let it not be argued that what Jones did was acceptable because decades later other linguists did find phonological correspondences. Did his work suddenly become acceptable only after that of Karl Verner? But if *that* argument is adopted, let it also be applied to our contemporaries like Joseph Greenberg, and let us allow the same number of decades for linguists to discover the correspondences that will support his classifications, or at least those parts of his classifications that will turn out to be valid, before condemning him. And if some details of his proposals turn out to be invalid, as is surely likely, why should that justify blanket condemnation and indignation? In other fields, scientists who have labored hard to come up with bold hypotheses (take, for example, Darwin and evolution) find that the respect they have been held in has not eroded simply because further research has allowed later investigators to refine their hypotheses.

Another curious feature of the cautiousness that has characterized much genetic linguistics in recent years is the unscientific policy adopted by some of denying the hypothesis that is most likely to account for the data. The curious position has been taken, either consciously or unconsciously, that the possibility that any two given languages might be genetically related is so remote that any other possible hypothesis, no matter how outlandish, is to be given greater credence than genetic relationship. An extreme example of such thinking is described in Roy Miller's contribution in this volume.

Why is it so unlikely that two given languages might be genetically related, that they might have sprung from some common
source? The answer is that it is not unlikely at all. If we select, even
at random from a hat, without considering any linguistic evidence,
the names of any two European languages, the chances are overwhelming that the two languages are sprung from some common
source (as we now know, thanks to the last two centuries of research). What about other continents? They have not been studied as
intensively, but from what has so far been shown to be probable we
can say that although the chances that two such randomly chosen languages are related are not so overwhelming as in the case of Europe,
they are also far from remote. Of course those engaged in genetic
classification do not pull names of languages at random out of a hat.
They compare languages that exhibit resemblances to one another.
There are indeed other explanations besides genetic relationship for
resemblances among languages, but genetic relationship is far from
being unlikely. Why then should conservatives treat it as the most
unlikely hypothesis of all, the one to be reluctantly accepted only
after all others, no matter how contrived, have been abandoned? To
this question there appears to be no reasonable answer. If one exists, it is the conservatives' responsibility to come up with it.

Consider now a similar question: What is the likelihood that a
single language, taken at random from any location in the world, is
genetically related to some other language? If we consider only those
genetic relationships that are generally agreed upon, we will find
among the languages of the world less than 50 (some would say five)
genetically isolated languages—languages with no known relatives.
That is less than 1 percent of the world's roughly 5,000 languages. In
other words, the chances are better than 99 out of 100 that any randomly selected language has at least one genetic relative, by general
consensus. Does it make sense to assume that the situation in the
world at the time of Proto-Indo-European, perhaps the fifth millennium B.C., was so different from that observed in more recent times?
Is it not also probable that Proto-IE, at that time one language among
many in the world, had relatives? And is it not also likely that some
of them survived, to develop into what we now observe as linguistic
families in their own right? Is it realistic then to consider IE to be
unrelated to any other family simply because such a relationship has
not been proved beyond a reasonable doubt?

Sometimes the conservatives criticize new proposals because the
quality and quantity of correspondences adduced do not match
what we now have, after 200 years, for Indo-European. Perhaps it is

unnecessary to contest this position; merely bringing it to light may discredit it. But if it *is* necessary, two arguments may be mentioned: First, Sir William likewise did not present the evidence for IE that we now have; yet we honor him. Second, the various IE languages have now been diverging from one another for some 6,000 years or so (Latin, Greek, and Sanskrit had diverged for considerably less time). We have to expect that when languages have been diverging for 8,000 to 10,000 years they will not retain the same type and number of mutual similarities that we see among languages that have been diverging for only 6,000 years or less. And if languages have been diverging for 15,000 to 20,000 years, the types and number of resemblances will differ more greatly still. The job is therefore more difficult. But let us not therefore suppose that progress in this field is not possible. And let us not attack those who attempt it, even when they (like everyone else) commit occasional mistakes.

It is remarkable that there are still many linguists who, after 200 years of comparative linguistics, are unwilling to countenance efforts to move farther back than the "common source" of Sir William Jones in tracing the genealogy of the European languages. But at the same time it is encouraging that some linguists are undertaking the exploration despite the often bitter disapproval of many of their colleagues.

We would like finally to add a cautionary note against unrestrained "lumping," supporting that of Robert Austerlitz in this volume. We are not urging that everyone take to lumping. Rather, we urge simply that linguists retain a scientific and objective attitude toward their own work and that of their contemporaries. In brief, we favor more tolerance and less indignation.

Perhaps also, as Austerlitz seems to suggest, the time has come for more serious consideration of explanations that lie between genetic relationship and the usually recognized forms of diffusion. After all, the family-tree theory is in fact only a hypothesis, and it is commonly recognized to be imperfect. Yet it is used uncritically by lumpers and splitters alike.

Whatever course we take, let it not be a retreat into dogma. Likening the evolution of languages to that of organisms may be fraught with false analogy, but let it be seen that the early botanists and zoologists did not shrink from *their* great task, the power of dogma notwithstanding.

PART I

Sir William Jones and His Legacy

Sir William Jones, a very broadly educated man, was a jurist as well as a linguist. During his stay in India he also became a Sanskritist and Indologist. His celebrated discourse to the Asiatic Society in Calcutta in 1786, in which he declared that Latin, Greek, and Sanskrit must have "sprung from some common source," which was probably also the origin of Gothic, Celtic, and Persian, is generally considered a landmark in the history of linguistics, marking as it did the beginning of comparative Indo-European linguistics. The importance of his observation lies in two important ideas: first, the hypothesis of a genetic relationship among certain languages and, second (and presupposed by the first), the notion of a common origin different from any existing language as an explanation of similarities among languages, the hypothesis that the languages must have "sprung from some common source, which perhaps no longer exists."

But interest in the history of language and in relationships among languages did not suddenly appear with Jones's address. As Garland Cannon points out, Samuel Johnson had already written of the notion of related languages "descended from some common parent" in connection with the Germanic languages, in 1755. And the resemblance of Sanskrit to various European languages had already been noticed by certain European travelers and merchants—who had not, however, offered the cogent explanation for the resemblance that would be offered by Jones. At any rate, the time was right, in 1786, for his formulation to capture the imaginations of scholars, and as Puhvel suggests in Part II of this volume, its "packaging" too was ideal.

Jones made important contributions to other areas of knowledge as well, some indeed perhaps more important than the celebrated observation now so often referred to. As a pioneer in Indology and in Sanskrit studies, he made Sanskrit and its rich literature known to the West. It came as a great surprise (and it still comes as a surprise to many in the West even 200 years later) that there was in the East a great body of literature from ancient times comparable in extent and sophistication to the materials written in Greek and Latin. Indeed, the great epic known as the *Mahābhārata*, just one of the Sanskrit monuments, is eight times as long as the *Iliad* and the *Odyssey* combined. Another, the great grammar of Sanskrit attributed to one Pāṇini, who lived in about the fifth century B.C., is widely regarded as one of the best linguistic descriptions ever composed.

In this part, Cannon discusses Jones's life and work, with particular attention to the situation and events surrounding his discourse of 1786 and to his influence on subsequent research, and Winfred Lehmann provides a fitting introductory paper for the symposium, offering a very broad perspective on the Jones influence and legacy and some general lessons for the linguistic and semiotic sciences today. Jones's discourse is also discussed in Part II by Jaan Puhvel and in Part III by Joseph Greenberg.

As in all historical studies, an appreciation of Jones presents problems of interpretation. Although it is clear that Jones made a certain statement, which was evidently recorded word by word, and that his statement became influential in the history of linguistics and thus in the history of ideas, two points remain unclear: first, we do not know how much influence Jones's statement actually had on the next generation of pioneers in comparative Indo-European linguistics, particularly Rask, Bopp, and Grimm; second, we do not know how much and what kinds of scholarly effort, if any (beyond casual observation of data readily available to him), led Jones to his hypothesis. Concerning the latter point, Jones tells us nothing. In offering his conclusion, he says only that (1) it is based on comparison of the "roots of verbs" and the "forms of grammar" and that (2) "no philologer could examine [Latin, Greek, and Sanskrit] without believing them to have sprung from some common source." Taken at face value, his observation seems a rather casual one, based not on extensive research but on what he had learned of Sanskrit after his arrival in India, absorbed against a background of the Latin and Greek that he (like all educated Europeans of his time) had acquired anyway, and implies that any other philologer thus exposed to all three would have come to the same conclusion. Still, one can conjecture that the importance of his observation might be balanced on the scales of historical justice by some solid research effort that supported the hypothesis. Cannon's paper offers some educated guesses on this point and suggests that the influence of Jones's statement arose not just from the observation itself but also from the reputation he had already enjoyed from his previous work.

The Process of Linguistics

WINFRED P. LEHMANN

About 75 years ago Rice University, upon its opening, arranged inaugural lectures, one series of which dealt with the "theory of civilization." In three lectures Rafael Altamira y Crevea discussed this
topic, identifying as the "general problem of human history . . . the
problem of 'civilization'" (1912: 292). Altamira gives perspective to
his discussion by pointing out that "we have only to compare what
at the end of the eighteenth century was known of Greece, Egypt,
the oriental civilizations, and even of Rome itself, as regards the art,
industry, literature, science and jurisprudence of these countries,
with the information now at our disposal, to appreciate the immense
advantage which in many matters we possess over our predecessors"
(1912: 305).

The advantage recognized by Altamira we owe in large part to the
"great flowering of linguistics that occurred in the nineteenth century,
centered around comparative Indo-European," in the words of James
E. Copeland, Sydney M. Lamb, and E. Douglas Mitchell, the three organizers of this symposium. Their statement on the aims of the symposium presents questions similar to those posed by Altamira, the
first of which reads: "Is the process of human civilization something
continual and indefinite?" (1912: 292). The organizers pose such questions concerning the process of linguistics rather than that of human
civilization. In responding to their kind invitation I examine these
questions primarily with reference to the study of language, as the
symposium demands, but also with a view to the larger field of inquiry that occupied those predecessors who established this remarkable university.

The advances in our knowledge are obvious when we read the
lectures of Sir William Jones, the third of which this symposium especially celebrates. One of the most learned men of his day, a man
of letters and a specialist in law, Jones was concerned among other
matters to find in the newly discovered writings of the ancient Indi-

ans, of the ancient Chinese, and of other Oriental peoples evidence to support the account of the great flood reported in the seventh and eighth chapters of the Book of Genesis. Greater benefit came from his exploration of the ancient writings for the immediately practical need to know native Indian law, which was maintained in the classical language of India. That need led him to undertake the study of Sanskrit and thereupon to make the observation that we still quote with approval as we examine the extensive subsequent concern with the languages that have developed from a prehistoric language of about 3,000 B.C., now known as Proto-Indo-European.

Besides establishing the interrelationships of the Indo-European languages, an achievement ranked among the primary contributions to linguistics made during the nineteenth century, linguists developed methods to determine relationships within languages and between languages. Such methods were devised in accordance with the general principle that language is governed by rules. That principle has been stated variously. Karl Verner, who provided the most striking evidence in support of it, wrote in a letter of 1872 that the accepted proposition "no rule without exceptions" should be rephrased as "no exception without a rule." And in his greatly admired article three years later he put it: "There must be a rule for irregularity; the problem is to find it" (Pedersen 1931: 292). Verner's dramatic clarification of a problem that confronted linguists for 50 years virtually set the stage for subsequent work on language. Linguists considered language to be governed by rules, and in that faith they set out to discover those rules.

Jacob Grimm's contributions provide a standard by which we may appraise subsequent linguistic activities. His background in literary studies is well known, similar to that of Jones; with his brother Wilhelm, Jacob belongs to the group of German Romantic writers, of the same period as Brentano and Eichendorff among others. Also, like Jones, he concerned himself with the study of law. Moreover, both deal with language, Jacob Grimm far more extensively than Jones, though in the later years of a life longer than that of Jones. Grimm's *Geschichte der deutschen Sprache* was published in 1848, his sixty-third year, fifteen more than were granted Jones.

Since Grimm is one of the founders of the linguistic activities discussed at this symposium, the topics he treated in his history of the Germanic languages are not without interest. Of its 42 chapters, I cite the titles of the following chapters: 5, Agriculture, a topic in economics; 15, The Stops, a topic in phonology; 25, Lombards and Burgundians, a topic in ethnography; and 35, The Displaced Preterite, that is, modal auxiliaries, a topic in morphology and syntax. Clearly his history of the language is not limited to treatment of the rules of language, to formal linguistics. Indicating his approach to language, Grimm concludes his preface by stating that "his chapter [on modal auxiliaries] demonstrates clearly that one cannot dispense with things in dealing with words," that is, that linguistics cannot limit its attention to formal concerns.

But what was happening elsewhere in the meantime? The German steamroller in historical linguistics was well on its way. Grimm's rules setting forth the relationships between the Germanic consonants and those of Greek, Latin, and Sanskrit had received considerable attention. Published in 1822 with three sets of exceptions, as they came to be called, the rules were considerably bolstered by a solution to one set of exceptions presented fifteen years after Grimm's initial publication. A second set of exceptions was accounted for in 1862 by Hermann Grassmann, whose formulation is widely celebrated, even listed in desk dictionaries. The third and final set was accounted for in 1875 by Karl Verner, cited earlier, in his statement implying that language is totally rule governed. This course of events is well known. But what I would like to illustrate by reviewing it is the "process of linguistics" as it had developed in less than a century after Jones's address. By 1841 Robert G. Latham, in his book *The English Language*, could say that the set of rules Grimm presented for the Germanic consonants "is currently called Grimm's Law" (1841: 190). Some 50 years after Jones's observation and less than twenty after Grimm's publication of his rules, language had been elevated from a rule-governed to a law-governed phenomenon.

At the same time, linguistics was narrowing its concerns. The narrowed approach is solidified in August Schleicher's *Compendium of Comparative Grammar of the Indo-European Languages*, published in 1861. Its opening sentences leave no doubt about the approved treatment of language. The study of grammar is taken as part of linguistics, which is a part of the natural history of human beings. Linguistic method is essentially that of the natural sciences (1871: 1, ed. 3). That is, in Schleicher's words, "Like the sciences, linguistics requires exact observation, thereupon description, and conclusions [explanations] based on exact observations," a requirement subsequently restated, as by William Dwight Whitney and others who fail to give credit to predecessors who established these three requirements of linguistics. As Konrad Koerner, one of the most perceptive historiographers of

our field, has recently demonstrated, Schleicher is the dominant theoretician of linguistics in the second half of the nineteenth century.
His views directed those of the neogrammarians; his *Compendium*
provided a model that subsequent grammars followed.

I might comment that the topic of this symposium and the papers
prepared for presentation here would have delighted Schleicher. He
concludes the first paragraph of his *Compendium* with the statement:
"Relatively few linguistic families have been investigated extensively
so far, with the result that the solution of this principal task of linguistics can only be expected in the future" (1871: 1, my translation
with some omissions). Occasionally the future redeems the past.

In a more general sense it can be stated that the search for laws
and the identification of linguistic methods with those of the natural
sciences was leading the field. The *Compendium* provides an example.
Although we may recognize within the scope of grammar the study of
meaning and of syntax, the *Compendium* of 829 pages is limited to two
topics, phonology and morphology. Linguistics, as a search for rules
and laws, was concentrated on the forms of language, its system of
sounds, and its system of forms, chiefly inflectional forms; the social
situation, the speakers, and the ideas conveyed might have interested
Jacob Grimm and Jones but were no longer of interest because the
scope of linguistics had narrowed.

The rest of this sketch of linguistics away from a broad-based account of a language can be made quickly. A few years after Schleicher
came the neogrammarian manifesto of 1878 and the accompanying
handbooks that carried the day: Braune's for Gothic (1880) and Old
High German (1886), Sievers's for Old English (1882), and Noreen's
for Old Norse (1884). Like Schleicher's *Compendium*, each has a brief
introduction and thereupon two major sections, one for phonology,
one for morphology. The concentration on form has been maintained
through nineteen editions of Braune's model-setting Gothic handbook, the last edition published in 1981. Prokosch's *Comparative Germanic Grammar* of 1939 also observes the pattern, like many other subsequent handbooks.

An established tradition is often maintained most vigorously in
colonial areas. The recent history of linguistics supports this observation. Capping his training with study at Leipzig, the center of neogrammarians, Leonard Bloomfield sharpened the statements of
Schleicher in his "set of postulates for the science of language" of
1926. An exemplary publication of American linguistics, *Linguistic
Structures of Native America*, planned by Sapir, introduced by Bloom-

field with a note of appreciation to Boas, and edited by Hoijer (1946), concentrates on the phonology and morphology of thirteen languages in its 390 pages.

The concentration on form was maintained by Zellig Harris, the most highly regarded theoretician after Bloomfield; his proposed procedures, including also syntax, "go by formal distinctions" (1951: 3). While assuming a different stance toward psychology, a student of Harris, Noam Chomsky, continues the insistence on a "purely formal investigation of the structure of language" (1957: 12). Recent linguistics, whether in this country or elsewhere, maintains the approach of August Schleicher "writ large": treatment of language has become highly formalized. Topics investigated have become ever narrower. In its current activities, generative grammar is concentrating not on such subdivisions of grammar as phonology and morphology, but on specific features such as anaphora.

I will return to my discussion of the insistence from the time of Schleicher to the present on the formal study of language and the resultant narrowing of scope of concern, but, to be just, we cannot overlook other work. Although formal linguistics, often self-styled mainstream but more appropriately perhaps fashionable, was concentrating on sounds and forms, comprehensive grammars, which are greatly appreciated, were being produced and taken as basic for less exhaustive texts. One example is Raphael Kühner's Greek grammar, which in its third edition by Friedrich Blass consists of about 2,500 pages; some 300 pages deal with phonology, 400-plus with syntax. Kühner also states rules, as in deriving Greek adverbs from the genitive plural of adjectives by substituting -ōs for -ōn (II: 1.299), but the rules do not dominate his treatment. His work, to use a distinction made by Louis Hjelmslev, observes the procedures of classical linguistics rather than those of linguistic linguistics. It may be a strange feature about our field that its theoreticians have a limited impact; Schleicher may have admired Charles Darwin and may have modeled his procedures on Darwin's, but there has been no great outcry among the citizenry promoting time-honored views for the study of grammar, something like creationism. There has not been any occasion for it, since the impact of linguistic linguistics goes little farther outside linguistic departments than an occasional article in publications like *The New York Review of Books* or French intellectuals tired of the previous format for their rhetoric.

On the other hand, the widely used grammars follow classical, even traditional procedures. Such are the grammars of English by

Poutsma, by Visser, by Jespersen, even that by Quirk et al. 1972 and 1985; and the grammars of German by Curme 1922, or by the authoritative Duden group (Grebe, 1973). Linguistic linguistics provides no parallels, not to speak of improved handbooks. Occasionally there is comment on standard handbooks, even with quizzical approval. And these handbooks are mined for their data. But the successive proposals of rules for phonological, morphological, syntactic data find their acclaim in stacks of university libraries.

As early as the nineteenth century important work on language was neglected by the fashionable linguistic group, such as the work involving comparison for "universal laws," as Meillet put it. I cite only one such work, Henri Weil's essay of 1844 entitled "The Order of Words in the Ancient Languages Compared with that of the Modern Languages," which was used in the title of the translation prepared by Charles W. Super in 1887. Summing up his characterization of Latin word order, Weil prefaces illustrations from Latin agrarian law of 110 B.C. with the statement: "In fact nothing can more nearly resemble the general cast of the Turkish period than these sentences" (1978: 78). Stated in accordance with current expression, Weil's proposal of almost a century and a half ago (also in two subsequent French editions, followed by the English) that early Latin was a verb-final language was a conclusion that some Indo-Europeanists still resist. It is difficult to account for the neglect of Weil's and others' comparable contributions, though an explanation of that neglect may be indicated when one reads the quotation on the translator's title page; the quotation begins "Language is an art." By contrast, for fashionable linguistics language is a system, a structure, a rule-governed entity. Linguistic linguistics deals with language only to the extent that it can be represented in rules.

My discussion so far has dealt largely with analysis and presentation of language data and not with historical treatment or genetic classification. Regarding these topics I will be brief, since their generally observed scope and procedures came from August Schleicher and are in keeping with the views of Karl Verner, whose concern with the treatment of language as a natural science we have noted. That concern led Schleicher down a garden path, much as the rigorous concern with syntax in American linguistic study did some 80 years later, in both instances, to a tree. The family-tree theory of genetic classification may have lasted somewhat longer than "the theory of syntax" has, even in its revised standard form, or its extended revised standard form. Schleicher's successors continued his emphasis on rigor rather than undertaking a shift to a broader approach, to a concern with language as a means of communication intimately related to its users and their society. Szemerényi's Indo-European grammar of 1970, 1980, and 1989 is limited to phonology and morphology, as are the several volumes of the grammar inaugurated by Kuryłowicz.

The restrictiveness in historical method is as remarkable as the scope of its handbooks. The central scholars confined themselves to the comparative method. Schleicher extended the method by reconstructing forms, rather than simply comparing them or simply listing them side by side as Grimm did. But Schleicher's successors were chary of reconstructions. The great French Indo-Europeanist Antoine Meillet never pronounced a reconstructed form, nor did he propose many reconstructions. And the generally negative attitude to Schleicher's reconstructed, or better constructed, Indo-European fable, which of course involved cultural as well as syntactic considerations, did little to extend the concern of linguistics beyond sounds and forms.

Similar restraint among historical linguists was not evident in the formulation of laws. The term came to be used for proposed correlations in half a dozen or so instances. Collinge's 1985 book lists 39 laws, by no means exhausting formulations dubbed law and ascribed to a linguist.

While permitting such exuberance in proposing laws, historical linguists applied severe restraint in method. It is widely acknowledged that Saussure's use of internal reconstruction to propose unattested consonants for Proto-Indo-European was remarkably upheld by Hittite data discovered decades later. But serious reservations are maintained about internal reconstruction. The reconstructed laryngeals have been rejected by some on the grounds that they cannot be upheld by the comparative method; such publications might have been avoided inasmuch as everyone knows that with written evidence only in Anatolian there is no possibility of comparison. And the reaction to recent proposals to reconstruct a general framework for Indo-European syntax, which can make use of the comparative method, leaves no doubt that neogrammarian historical linguistics is still alive, kicking, and thoroughly indoctrinating the faithful, as at Harvard.

Recent advances have given historical linguistics a further method, which will be in evidence at this symposium, and accordingly I can deal briefly with it. I call it typological reconstruction, or typologically based reconstruction. Several centuries of attention to the patterns of language have given us considerable information on the possibilities

in phonology, syntax, and other areas. No language has been discovered, for example, in which contrasts in pitch, say, as many as 20,
provide the basic building blocks, and elements like consonants provide the signals for larger forms, words, phrases, and sentences. Instead, languages use consonants and vowels much as English does,
coupled with phenomena like pitch and stress. We know of course a
great deal about phonology. We also know some things about syntax,
and we can state them more concisely than did Weil and his predecessors, whose conclusions may be likened to Grimm's for phonology in
merely arranging correlations side by side. Although the method of
typological reconstruction is new, it has already led to remarkable
modifications of earlier views, as in the glottalic theory proposed for
Proto-Indo-European.

Typological reconstruction has done a good deal to "restore excitement to Indo-European linguistics," one of the concerns of the
organizers of this symposium, though the new energy is still found
only in restricted circles. The renewed relationship between linguistic
and prehistoric study is giving rise to more excitement and is invigo-
rated by new information and imaginative interpretation of that information (see, for example, Greppin 1986). Earlier efforts to relate
archeological findings to linguistic conclusions foundered around
the turn of this century because the cultural conclusions outstripped
the evidence. Thereupon for many years linguists within their university walls produced treatises on languages, languages as recent as
Old English and Latin or early, unattested languages like Proto-Indo-
European, with little attention to the societies maintaining the language or to the people speaking those languages. The situation has
changed dramatically, if again in restricted circles. It is still startling
to see a title like *The Politics of Early Old English Sound Change* (Toon
1983). Such a work makes use of the neogrammarian handbooks like
that of Sievers and successive editors, but the numerous variants of
a process like velar umlaut are identified not only by their area of
attestation, from Northumbrian through West Saxon and the like to
Kentish, but also by characteristics of the speakers and their social
and cultural relationships. The concern has broadened.

Returning to our concern with the process of linguistics, we note
that after a century and more of narrowing its purview, linguistics is
expanding its use of historical methods for gaining an understanding of the earlier periods and best of all is considering language in
relation to its speakers. In short, linguistics is taking a humanistic
approach.

Can we say the same for synchronic linguistics? The glimmerings
are still faint. Peter Matthews, invited to contribute the first Linguistic
Abstracts Survey to the new journal *Linguistic Abstracts* (1985), opens
his essay entitled "Whither Linguistic Theory?" with an answer pro-
claiming that theory is "at present in a state of transition." Dealing
largely and respectfully with Chomsky and generative grammar, he
quotes with approval a statement of Roger Lass concerning phonology that "the main preoccupation of the generative school will be seen
as an aberrant episode in the history of the discipline" (1985: 2). In regard to syntax and semantics, Matthews is less sure; "he wonders if
he [Chomsky] has not returned to a traditional, prestructural position" (1985: 5). Among structuralist assumptions noted by Matthews
are "firstly, that a language is a system governed by rules, and sec-
ondly, that languages as systems are distinct from the use of language"
(1985: 6). We ask whether Verner now is to be completely repudiated
for his theoretical approach? And will histories of languages once
again, like Jacob Grimm's, include chapters on agriculture, on social
groups, on grammatical constructions accounted for by relating words
to things?

Matthews' final evaluation of our field states that "much of the
interesting work is in pragmatics . . . a field in which, above all
others, we are not looking at languages as abstract systems. . . .
[Moreover] there is now a substantial body of work, by anthropologists and sociologists as well as linguists, which examines language
directly from a communicative standpoint" (1985: 6). Matthews even
suggests that it may be time to abandon our reification of language,
which he traces back to Plato, and produce "a linguistic theory which
is a theory of speakers" (1985: 7). The terminology reflects our own
time, but the ideas recall those of Jones and Grimm.

Looking more widely we may ask whether these queries about
fashionable practices and views are unique to linguistics. The growing fascination with Mikhail Mikhailovich Bakhtin indicates more widespread hesitancy about the structuralism that has been developing
for several centuries, extending its grasp over many intellectual fields.
Not that Bakhtin avoids consideration of language. One of his leading
interpreters, Michael Holquist, states that "a highly distinctive concept of language, . . . [is] at the heart of everything Bakhtin ever
did. . . . [That concept] stresses the fragility and ineluctably historical
nature of language, the coming and dying of meaning that it . . .
shares with . . . man." Further, Holquist quotes Bakhtin: "a language
is not stratified only into dialects . . . but also into languages that are

socio-ideological: languages belonging to professions, to genres, languages peculiar to [specific] generations" (Bakhtin 1981: xviii–xix). Like Matthews, but with assurance rather than speculation, Bakhtin associates language intimately with speakers and takes it as fluid, constantly changing, and highly complex.

Bakhtin is not a linguist but a philosopher of aesthetics especially concerned with literature. Yet Holquist says of him that he "is constantly working with what is emerging as the central preoccupation of our time—language" (1981: xvii). Many of us omit the prefix; when language as the central means of communication occupies more than half our work force, it is scarcely a preoccupation in the contemporary world.

To recall once again the process of linguistics, we may note substantial change in the 200 years since Jones's statement. Widely examined in the nineteenth century, language first seemed worthy of study to disclose early legal practices, early literature, early culture. That approach served well, opening up the past, as Altamira told his audience at Rice University in 1912.

Thereupon the study of language, language examined for its own sake, fashioned rigorous procedures to deal with language, procedures concentrating on its mechanisms, sounds, forms, and sentence patterns. Scrutinizing its intricacies and eventually divorcing language from its speakers, specialists became ever more specialized, the Saussurians by postulating language as a social abstraction and the generativists by postulating it as a mental abstraction, a state in a hypothetical language organ. The bankruptcy of this approach was slowly recognized by philosophers like Wittgenstein in his late years, by Austin, by Bakhtin, and by administrators who established at Rice a department charged to deal with language as our way of conveying meaning.

Language fills many functions for individuals and for social groups, every such function requiring thorough investigation comparable to that carried out on language as a system. The concern with it is indeed continuous, and the results of that concern may well be indefinite. To reject any of that concern, including highly analytic computational analysis, recalls the fear of the Luddites, who inhabit the academic as well as the industrial world. To limit one's attention to any facet, such as phonology or syntax, or to restricted patterns in either, viewed synchronically, or to semantics viewed formally, or to other selected segments, yields limited findings, with primary appeal to specialists with similarly limited concerns. Linguistic theory concerned primarily with an ideal language, however tempting to the academic mind, produces vapid results. Any investigation or theory of language will achieve and maintain valdity only when held by linguists who view language in its multiple uses by individuals and in its various roles by social groups. Language as the central concern of our time merits such concentrated attention by the leading intellects of this time, those who like the founders of Rice University are concerned with the general problem of civilization.

REFERENCES CITED

Altamira y Crevea, R. 1912. Three Inaugural Lectures. "The Theory of Civilization." In *The Book of the Opening of the Rice Institute*, vol. 2, pp. 288–320. Houston.

Bakhtin, M. M. 1981. *The Dialogic Imagination: Four Essays*. Ed. by M. Holquist. Trans. by C. Emerson and M. Holquist. Austin: University of Texas Press. (1st ed. 1880.)

Braune, W., and E. A. Ebbinghaus. 1981. *Gotische Grammatik*, ed. 19. Tübingen: Niemeyer. (Page vi lists the dates of the 18 previous editions and editors.)

Chomsky, N. 1957. *Syntactic Structures*. The Hague: Mouton.

Collinge, N. E. 1985. *The Laws of Indo-European*. Amsterdam: John Benjamins.

Curme, G. O. 1922. *A Grammar of the German Language*, rev. ed. New York: Macmillan.

Grebe, P., et al. 1973. *Duden Grammatik der deutschen Gegenwartssprache*. Mannheim: Bibliographisches Institut.

Greppin, J. A. C. 1986. "Language on the move." Review of T. V. Gamkrelidze and V. V. Ivanov: *Indoevropejskij jazyk i indoevropejcy*. *London Times Literary Supplement* (March 14): 278.

Grimm, J. 1868. *Geschichte der deutschen Sprache*, ed. 3. Leipzig: Hirzel.

Harris, Z. 1951. *Methods in Structural Linguistics*. Chicago: The University of Chicago Press.

Hoijer, H., ed. 1946. *Linguistic Structures of Native America*. New York: Viking.

Holquist, M. 1981. See Bakhtin.

Jones, Sir William. 1807. *The Works of Sir William Jones* (with the life of the author by Lord Teignmouth). 13 vols. London: Stockdale.

Koerner, K. 1981. "The Neogrammarian Doctrine: Breakthrough or Extension of the Schleicherian Paradigm." *Folia Linguistica Historica* 2: 157–178.

Kühner, R., and F. Blass. 1890–1904. *Ausführliche Grammatik der griechischen Sprache*, ed. 3. 2 vols. Reprinted 1966. Darmstadt: Wissenschaftliche Buchgesellschaft.

Kuryłowicz, J., ed. 1968. *Indogermanische Grammatik*. Heidelberg: Winter.
   I. 1.   Cowgill, W. "Einleitung." 1986.
       2.   Mayrhofer, M. "Lautlehre." 1986.

II.   Kuryłowicz, J. "Akzent. Ablaut." 1968.
III. Formenlehre. 1969.
      1.   Watkins, C. "Geschichte der Indogermanischen Verbalflexion."
Latham, R. G. 1841. *The English Language*. London: Taylor.
Matthews, P. 1985. "Whither Linguistic Theory?" *Linguistic Abstracts* 1: 1–7.
Pedersen, H. 1931. *Linguistic Science in the Nineteenth Century*. Trans. by J. W.
      Spargo. Cambridge: Harvard University Press.
Prokosch, E. 1939. *A Comparative Germanic Grammar*. Philadelphia: Linguistic
      Society of America.
Quirk, R., S. Greenbaum, G. Leech, and J. Svartvik. 1972. *A Grammar of Con-
      temporary English*. London: Longman. (Bibliography provides data on the
      grammars of Jespersen, Poutsma, and Visser.)
————. 1985. *A Comprehensive Grammar of the English Language*. London:
      Longman.
Scaglione, A. 1978. See Weil.
Schleicher, A. 1871. *Compendium der vergleichenden Grammatik der indoger-
      manischen Sprachen*, ed. 3. Weimar: Böhlau. (ed. 1, 1861; ed. 2, 1866.)
Szemerényi, O. 1970. *Vergleichende Sprachwissenschaft*. Darmstadt: Wissen-
      schaftliche Buchgesellschaft. (ed. 2, 1980; ed. 3, 1989.)
Teignmouth, Lord. 1807. See Jones.
Toon, T. E. 1983. *The Politics of Early Old English Sound Change*. New York:
      Academic.
Weil, H. 1978. *The Order of Words in the Ancient Languages Compared with That
      of the Modern Languages* (with an introduction by A. Scaglione, ed.). Trans.
      by C. W. Super, 1887. Amsterdam: John Benjamins. (ed. 1, 1844; ed. 2,
      1869; ed. 3, 1879.)

Jones's "Sprung from Some Common Source": 1786–1986

GARLAND CANNON

When Sir William Jones took his seat on the Bengal Supreme Court in September 1783, he had a reputation as the greatest language scholar of all time and one of the greatest translators. *A Grammar of the Per-sian Language* (1771) was already in the second of its nine editions and its two French ones. It was already influencing Asian grammars like George Hadley's *Grammatical Remarks on the Practical and Vulgar Dialect of the Indostan Language* (1772) and *Introductory Grammatical Remarks on the Persian Language* (1776), John Richardson's *Grammar of the Arabic Language* (1776), and Nathaniel Brassey Halhed's *Grammar of the Bengal Language* (1778), with others by Francis Gladwin, Robert Jones, John Gilchrist, Duncan Forbes, and so on yet to come. His translations from the Persian like *Histoire de Nader Chah* (1770), from the Greek like *The Speeches of Isæus* (1779), and from the Arabic like his *Mu'allaqāt* (1782) had received wide praise. His reputation was such that intellectuals were literally *expecting* major discoveries in colonial India. These advantages almost assured that his philologer's formulation in his Third Anniversary Discourse (1786) would eclipse the fragmentary generalizations that Filippo Sassetti, Père Cœur-doux, Père du Pons, Lord Monboddo, and Halhed had earlier made in generally little-known sources. These advantages also made it likely that posterity might credit Jones generally with the phonological and morphological breakthroughs that nineteenth-century scholars like Rasmus Rask, Franz Bopp, Jacob Grimm, and Friedrich von Schlegel were to make.

In this bicentennial time of celebrating Jones's founding of his innovative Asiatic Society, when the attention of prominent scholars has been focused on him, the purpose of this paper is to make a retrospective reassessment of (1) his 1786 formulation, (2) his various pronouncements on language families and the language that came

Portrait of Sir William Jones. Oil painting attributed to Arthur William Devis; painted in Calcutta *ca.* 1793. *F.840.*

to be known as Indo-European, and (3) his place in the history of the comparative method and linguistics. I will use some previously unknown or unpublished materials and particularly some of the many twentieth-century assessments.

THE 1786 FORMULATION

En route to Calcutta, Jones envisioned an Asiatic society composed of European intellectuals and Indian scholars for the purpose of systematic collaborative exploration of Asia because no one person could command the whole realm of knowledge. He thereupon founded a permanent research group and facility of international scope, as visualized in Bacon's academy in the *New Atlantis*. Results would be presented in his annual Anniversary Discourses, with a cumulative description of languages and letters, philosophy and religion, sculptural and architectural remains, and written memorials of arts and sciences. Such integration was revolutionary, especially in his according a formal place to language research.

He could not effectively overcome two constraints. First, his ethnocentric colleagues politely ignored his recommendations for membership of pundits and maulvis, who had to transmit to Europeans their few papers for reading or translation. Second, a prescientific matrix enveloped language study, where the trivial, speculative, and sensational sometimes led to wild conclusions. There was a continuing influence of the ideas of supposed immutability and of God's dispersion of languages after the destruction of the Tower of Babel. Some scholars were trying to locate the Garden of Eden and to verify Newton's dating of Jason's search for the Golden Fleece, despite the finding of disturbing fossils of primitive organisms unexplained by the catastrophe of the Flood. Monboddo, an influential theorist, had used a few secondhand data in 1774 (Burnett 1774–1792) to speculate that Greek and Sanskrit were similar in some "remote analogies and distant relations of things" and to conclude that the Indians and Greeks got their language and other arts from the same parent country, Egypt (2: 530–531).

Jones's omnivorousness included Jesuit missionary sources like the long reports in *Lettres édifiantes et curieuses* (Paris, 1717–1776; 34 vols.), where there was an occasional hint about similarities between Sanskrit and Latin and Greek. Amid his voluminous correspondence was his 1779 answer to questions from the Polish prince Adam Czartoryski: "How so many European words crept into the Persian language, I know not with certainty. Procopius, I think, mentions the great intercourse, both in war and peace, between the Persians and the nations in the north of Europe and Asia, whom the ancients knew by the general name of Scythians. Many learned investigators of antiquity are fully persuaded, that a very old and almost primæval language was in use among these northern nations, from which not only the Celtic dialects, but even the Greek and Latin are derived." Then he supplied Czartoryski with some pairs of Greek–Persian cognates and of a Latin–Persian pair (*Letters* 1: 285). So the germ of the idea of a protolanguage was already in his mind, more than four years before he went to India.

Sanskrit was notably omitted from this letter, which he wrote before receiving a copy of his friend Halhed's *Grammar of the Bengal Language* in which he later penned several marginal comments. There were generalizations about Sanskrit and its derivative relationship to some North Indic languages, with two sentences that hint at Sanskrit as the parent tongue of Greek and Latin, on the basis of a few isolated pairs of words. Because Jones's copy of the book is lost, we do not know whether he wrote comments on these two sentences (see Jones 1831, entry no. 352). He made no reference to Halhed in his Third Discourse. There is no evidence that the two talked about comparative language matters during Halhed's few weeks in Calcutta in 1784. Jones's letters during this time do not mention Halhed except for a brief derogatory reference in March 1785 (see Cannon 1981: 180). Moreover, Halhed was continuing to conjecture that Greek and Latin were derived from Sanskrit, which, he said, had a better claim to be their parent than Phoenician or Hebrew did (see his letter of 1779, in Rocher 1980b). Halhed's only possible direct influence on Jones's 1786 formulation was a list of Sanskrit roots and infinitives in Halhed's *Grammar* (pp. 130–136), which may have given Jones the idea of the part of his research dealing with affinity in verb roots. Because Sanskrit derivations come from verb roots, he was not excluding noun declensions from his evidence.

Another likely influence was the well-known *Dictionary of the English Language* (1755), by his friend Dr. Johnson, who had an abbreviated genealogical chart of Germanic languages on the first page of the prefatory "History of the English language." Johnson defined the three sets of descendants as Anglo-Saxon (i.e., Low German), Francick (High German), and Cimbrick (North Germanic). He stated that Saxon was the original form of English and was itself derived from

Gothic, or else Saxon and Gothic were "descended from some common parent." While disregarding Johnson's genealogical mistakes, we might note that this phrase was somewhat echoed in Jones's philologer's formulation. Indeed, several of the ideas in that formulation had been floating around in isolated form for centuries, including incisive observations made about the time of the birth of Christ as to similarities between Greek and Latin.

Two possible influences on Jones's formulation can be disregarded. First, until Charles Wilkins returned to England in 1786, the two were friends and correspondents, particularly after Jones began serious study of Sanskrit in September 1785 and needed help in translating obscure words in religious and legal texts. Although there was minor discussion of equivalent items in Old Persian, their correspondence included no comments about cognates, and Greek and Latin data were never included. Second, Monboddo's correspondence or famous book did not directly influence Jones's formulation, which Jones independently constructed from data that he did not print or even preserve. He viewed language materials as only a tool in constructing comparative explanations of cultural diffusion, rather than as actual learning. The study of languages was indispensable, as the writing of grammars and dictionaries was, but linguists should do much more to "enlighten the vast temple of learning, instead of spending their lives in adorning only its porticos" (*Works* 3: 7, 5: 167). In his Sixth Discourse (1789) he said that he would not abuse the society's patience "by repeating a dry list of detached words, and presenting you with a vocabulary instead of a dissertation," but stressed that he was including no unproved conclusions (*Works* 3: 111–112), in the spirit of scientific argument advanced by Descartes. Because he never listed Sanskrit words alongside Greek or Latin items that he believed were related, we cannot verify his comparisons. Two large parcels of his worksheets contain rich, often much-revised materials, some of which were later published, but contain no word lists. Several of his Sanskrit manuscripts have the interlinear Latin translations that he used to bridge the gap between Sanskrit and his ultimate English version.

These worksheets document the vital place of language, especially Sanskrit, in his Indian scholarship, even as the language orientation of the other 29 charter members of the Asiatic Society shows their interests. Persian figured prominently in their lives and the papers presented. They were so adept that John Rawlins communicated in Persian his "On the Manners, Religion, and Laws of the Mountaineers of

Tipri" in April 1787, which Jones had to translate to include in *Asiatick Researches*, the society's journal. Persian was Jones's first love, and he turned to Sanskrit only after Wilkins would not do the needed law translations from Sanskrit that Jones wanted done. Now let us set the scene for the night of February 2, 1786, when Jones read his Third Discourse to the largest attendance of any of the at least 99 meetings held during his decade-long presidency. Attendance at his Anniversary Discourses was always large, but this time his discourse was on India.

The governor-general, a Supreme Council member, Sir Robert Chambers (who collected 700 to 800 Sanskrit manuscripts costing more than £22,000), the other Supreme Court judge (John Hyde), and 31 others heard the discourse. The best-known Persian scholars there were Gladwin, Charles Hamilton, and John Herbert Harington. Wilkins was primarily working on Sanskrit, and the youthful Thomas Henry Colebrooke would later be influenced by Jones toward a career in Sanskrit studies. The society's *Manuscript Proceedings* show that the philologer's formulation was published exactly as Jones read it. Seldom do the *Proceedings* record any comments, and that night was no exception. The meeting ended with the secretary's traditional statement: "The thanks of the Society are voted to the President for the Discourse, with which he has favoured them."

This discourse was part of a series with a titanic scope, centering on the Indians, Chinese, Tatars, Arabs, and Persians. Jones's overall purpose was to determine "*who* they severally were, *whence* and *when* they came, *where* they now are settled, and *what advantage* a more perfect knowledge of them all may bring to our European world." The answers might determine whether these people had a common origin and whether the origin or origins agreed with the received view (*Works* 3: 28). At the beginning of the discourse, he rejected etymological speculation like his friend Jacob Bryant's, which, he said, would let one derive anything from anything, partly because it was synthetically rather than historically oriented. The mere resemblance of sounds or letters in two words of different languages rarely constituted derivational evidence. He used folk etymology as negative examples of the intuitive, impressionistic sort that Bryant enthusiastically employed. He noted that part of the problem was poor transliteration, which could make an Asiatic word seem phonologically closer to a European word than it actually was. Also, a linguist should avoid relying on "exotick names" of things or actions, since such items might have been borrowed from the language of a conquering people, and the two languages might have no genetic connection whatsoever. Presumably Jones followed his own advice and relied on basic vocabulary, rather than on exotic data in selecting comparative examples.

His problem was to attempt to find an analytical method that could separate actual cognates from similarities due to borrowing or accident. We cannot precisely characterize what he achieved, as opposed to what he only hoped for. In his Ninth Discourse (1792—*Works* 3: 198–200) he stressed certain conditions for reliable etymologies: the analyst must be "perfectly acquainted" with the languages in question, and the meaning of possible cognates must be identical or nearly identical. Vowels cannot be disregarded, and there can be no metathesis or consonantal insertions. Correspondence cannot be postulated solely on the basis of place of articulation, as in relating one palatal sound to another, or else it would be possible to "prove" that English *coot* and *goose* are cognates from some earlier word.

By contrast, etymology based on facts developed in an empirical manner could give reliable evidence, with grammatical structures also being compared to test the putative affinity. Etymological postulates proceed from provable facts, where an experimental hypothesis of affinity is successively refined (Aarsleff 1967). Jones's formulation was a postulating of the least that his facts could support, rather than a dramatic speculating on the most that untested data might permit, as is done even in modern times by otherwise good scholars (see Hockett's 1978 criticism of Swadesh's 1971 sweeping guesses about possible distant genetic affiliation in an effort to reach back to language origins). Jones's stress on evidence was partly motivated by his barrister's training and experience because he was an excellent trial lawyer and legal scholar. And he had the unique opportunity to be the first Westerner really to know Sanskrit and to be able to work with Sanskrit data firsthand, in comparing them with data from Greek and Latin, which, as we now know, had been diverging for only about 3,000 years, though his central purpose was to uncover antique Indian civilization and then use that knowledge.

To him, language findings were important primarily in proportion to their utility to humankind, in an early envisioning of applied linguistics that today has restored much of the ultimate focus that he wished for. Mainly, one studied a language to gain access to the philosophical, scientific, artistic, and moral treasures preserved in the writings within that language. In the First Discourse (1784) he said that Asian languages would open an immense mine that would delight scholars and benefit both Europeans and Asians through new information about nature, inventions, and literature. A major benefit was literary translations. In the preface to his *Poems, Consisting Chiefly of Translations from the Asiatick Languages* (1772), he had urged European scholars to study Arabic and Persian so that they could translate great Middle Eastern literature. The many new expressions, images, and themes acquired could rejuvenate jaded neoclassical European literature. Translations of Sanskrit and Arabic legal works would permit Europeans to rule India according to Indian laws and customs, and well-governed Indians would provide excellent industry that could add to the wealth of Europe and India. Study of a language could produce a pedagogical grammar, which was better than a linguistic grammar because it could teach Persian to Europeans and let them be better administrators in India. Thus Jones's best book was his pedagogical *A Grammar of the Persian Language*, a major influence on grammars of exotic languages for 80 years.

Intellectually, his jump from his 1779 generalization to a tested formulation in 1786 was fairly large, in moving somewhat naturally from Persian to Sanskrit, so that he could translate the *Mānava-Dharmaśāstra* into English for British judges in India. In learning Sanskrit in the classical manner, he was having considerable difficulty, which was eased by his knowledge of Old Persian because it was historically closer to Sanskrit than German and French were. It was the Sanskrit source that made his conclusion so provocative to European scholars, partly because it was so remote in distance and time from the traditionally studied European languages. At least as dramatic was his assertion that this language, once spoken by a supposedly savage people of a vastly different religion and culture, was linguistically related to these Western tongues. Moreover, the most famous scholar in the world judged it to be superior to them.

Bringing to bear his keen knowledge of Latin, Greek, and Persian, Jones often used his photographic memory to supply a similar feature from two or more of these languages when he encountered a precise formulation of Sanskrit grammar or sandhi. The school reworking of Pāṇini, which he evidently used, contained the most thorough analysis of phonology and morphology that he had ever seen. Within months he perceived "relationships between Pāṇini's explicitly stated basic morphemes and the similar, implicitly intuited basic morphemes which he already knew in the classical languages" (Emeneau 1955: 149). Seen in this light, the phrases "roots of verbs" and "forms of grammar" become clear: Pāṇini's minute analysis of derivations and inflections had led Jones to sketch comparable analyses of items in Persian and European languages that were similar to Sanskrit items. Apparently he explained similarities on the basis of probabilities. Common origin was a vastly better hypothesis than coincidence or borrowing, where each similar pair of items would require a separate hypothesis, rather than fitting all the similarities into one cosmopolitan explanation. As he constantly stressed that the Asiatic Society must *prove* their generalizations, we can speculate that he must have used phonetic similarity, morpheme by morpheme, and perceived the truly systematic nature of the resemblances. His few examples illustrated some of the sound shifts that Grimm, no doubt building on Rask, would later identify and group under a governing principle. Jones would have considered such pre-Grimm methodology as rather trivial points within his integrated historical goals. Clearly, he found so many similarities among Sanskrit, Greek, Latin, and Persian that the only tenable explanation was a genetic relationship; his breakthrough was in realizing that such a relationship was possible and that the source language might be previously unknown and no longer spoken because it had changed into other languages, which became Sanskrit etc.

I will now repeat his formulation:

The *Sanscrit* language, whatever be its antiquity, is of a wonderful structure; more perfect than the *Greek*, more copious than the *Latin*, and more exquisitely refined than either, yet bearing to both of them a stronger affinity, both in the roots of verbs and in the forms of grammar, than could possibly have been produced by accident; so strong indeed, that no philologer could examine them all three, without believing them to have sprung from some common source, which, perhaps, no longer exists: there is a similar reason, though not quite so forcible, for supposing that both the *Gothick* and the *Celtick*, though blended with a very different idiom, had the same origin with the *Sanscrit*; and the old *Persian* might be added to the same family, if this were the place for discussing any question concerning the antiquities of *Persia* [*Works* 3: 34–35].

Jones's comprehensiveness of vision is seen in his slightly earlier formulation in "On the Gods of Greece, Italy, and India," which also appeared in *Asiatick Researches* 1 and laid the groundwork for comparative mythology. It begins with an echo of the same general thesis: "when features of resemblance, too strong to have been accidental, are observable in different systems of polytheism, without fancy or prejudice to colour them and improve the likeness, we can scarce help believing, that some connection has immemorially subsisted between the several nations, who have adopted them" (*Works* 3: 319).

Although the notion of a family *tree* was not implied in his formulation, Jones's use of the word *family* was critical taxonomically, going far beyond Johnson's simple genealogical conception for part of the Germanic languages. Jones's intensive botanical study was being influenced by Linnaeus, and he wanted to apply to languages the then-visionary concept of a single comprehensive *flora* that would enable any scholar to identify and describe any specimen by using an agreed-upon binomial nomenclature that permitted grouping of the species within each order into genera (see Cannon 1975). Several other major linguists—August Schleicher, William Dwight Whitney, and Leonard Bloomfield—were later influenced by botany.

Jones was just starting a large-scale program to help his friend Sir Joseph Banks, the president of the Royal Society, secure Asian plants for the new Kew Gardens, a process that required Jones to correct the often erroneous descriptions of Indian plants and particularly to describe previously unknown ones, including plants named in Sanskrit literature. As a ruler of supposedly inferior peoples, Jones felt a responsibility to them and the world to acquaint Europeans with Indian cultural riches unknown in the West, and this goal led to his grouping several languages within an Indo-European family. In his letters of 1786–1787 he often referred to Sanskrit as the *sister* of Latin and Greek, and in the Eighth Discourse of 1791 he placed Ethiopic in the Semitic family as the *sister* of Arabic and Hebrew. He may have been the first to use the word *family* to describe groupings of languages derived from some earlier source in common. The fact that the tree diagram was used by some Linnaean botanists in the mid–eighteenth century does not diminish his accomplishment in applying this botanical concept to explain language similarities, a cross-disciplinary insight that was absent from eighteenth-century language theorists. Not until 1802 did Lamarck first fully describe phylogenetic trees, in *Recherches sur l'organisation des corps vivant*. These facts reduce the originality of August Schleicher's still-later development of the family-tree concept, with its inept attempts at Darwinism, in *Compendium of the Comparative Grammar of the Indo-European Languages* (English translation, 1874–1877), preceding the model of spreading, intersecting waves and the great neogrammarian debate on sound law (see Hoenigswald 1963).

Yet Jones's formulation did not wholly rise above its prescientific matrix. His value judgments about Sanskrit reflected contemporary thought about language superiority that nonlinguists echo today, and he implied that speech mixture can help to explain the differences between the stucture of what became Germanic sounds and morphemes and that of what became non-Germanic Indo-European ones. There was no insight into the necessary reconstruction of earlier languages that lack written records. He even cautiously left open the possibility that the Indo-European source might still be spoken (Pedersen 1931: 18; Cannon 1990), which, if true, would have seriously weakened his explanation.

REACTION TO THE FORMULATION

Jones's enormous correspondence, mainly with major intellectuals, sometimes required him to write as many as 100 letters during his annual vacation, a procedure characterizing scholarship in a time when there were few journals and no international congresses. His letters are so unevenly preserved that only Monboddo is known to have received a hand-written copy of the Third Discourse prior to its publication in *Asiatick Researches* 1 in late 1788. Dr. Johnson and Linnaeus had recently died, and Buffon was of an advanced age. Jones evidently had no correspondence with German intellectuals like Herder, Goethe, and Schiller, all of whom were greatly influenced by his 1789 translation of the *Śakuntalā*. Several of his acquaintances were quite old and evidently were not sent copies of the discourse: Benjamin Franklin, Johann David Michaelis, the Abbé Charles Michel de l'Épée, Francisco Pérez Bayer, and Bishop Robert Lowth. Jacob Bryant probably did not receive a copy because of his strong reaction to Jones's temperate criticism of his etymological speculating. Wilkins, who heard the discourse in person, still did not understand the importance of the formulation as late as 1808, when in the preface to his *A Grammar of the Sanskrǐta Language* he mentioned Halhed's 1778 comment on the similarity of certain Sanskrit, Greek, and Latin words and then quoted part of Jones's formulation as corroboration (pp. viii–ix). Jones was in frequent association with Gilchrist, whose *A Grammar of the Hindoostanee Language* (1796) showed little or no influence of the passage. By contrast, Monboddo promptly interpreted the formulation as verifying his assertion that Sanskrit was the original of many other languages and that Greek was a dialect of Sanskrit, or else they were both dialects of the same parent language, generalizations that he exuberantly sent to Jones in a wide-ranging correspondence (Cannon 1968). So, ironically, the formulation made Monboddo's speculations even more speculative and hardly otherwise improved the remaining volumes of his book.

The major dissemination was in *Asiatick Researches*, the influence of which was so stupendous that not even the French *Histoire de l'Académie Royale des Inscriptions et Belles-Lettres* and the Royal Society's *Philosophical Transactions* could seriously compete for a decade and a half. The Asiatic Society's lack of funds and of an official European distributor meant that only 700 copies were sent to London for possible sale, with none to Paris, Holland, Germany, Italy, or America. But there were many reviews and constant pirating of all of Jones's writings that editors could procure, and so Continental and American scholars had easy access, not to mention access through the numerous pirated editions of *Asiatick Researches* in England. There was a four-volume German translation in 1795–1797 and a 444-page French translation in 1803 (see Cannon's bibliography, 1979: 4–7). The major contemporary review was Thomas Ogle's five-part review in the influential *Monthly Review*, which quoted the formulation in a separate section without comment, thereby indicating that the formulation was perceived as being little more important than other passages that were massively quoted.

The most important general British assessment was the *Quarterly Review*'s retrospective article in 1866, where the formulation was quoted and acclaimed as the key to modern comparative philology (119: 211–212). This strong claim was echoed for a century by scholars of other disciplines and some linguists in a kind of publicizing of language study to the general educated reader that transcended the formulation's influence on the Continental linguists who followed his lead. The unnamed but perceptive reviewer reduced Schlegel and Friedrich Max Müller to being Jones's followers and chided Schlegel for falling victim to the potential pitfall that Jones was praised for having wisely avoided, that is, pronouncing Sanskrit to be the Indo-European ancestor. By this time the educated public considered philology to be a science, of which Jones was the pioneer. The view was best expressed in a state-of-the-art review in the widely respected *Quarterly Review* for October 1866, from which I will quote a singularly modern passage:

The mass of Sanscrit MSS. brought over to Europe furnished the missing key to the students of comparative philology. . . . [Sanskrit and Greek] were members of a great family of languages, stretching in a diagonal belt from India to Western Europe. It was then seen that comparative grammar was a true science, reposing upon sound foundations, and strictly conformed to the inductive method; that the elementary sounds may be classified according to the very organism of our speech, and their variations and interchanges explained by fixed laws; that thus a test is furnished to distinguish between the accidental resemblances of words and the real affinities which depend on fixed laws; and, above all, that the surest indication of a family connection between languages is furnished by the permanent structure of their grammar. Such were the leading principles of the new school of comparative philology, taught by A. von Schlegel, by Lassen, by the brothers Grimm, and by Pott, and embodied in the great "Comparative Grammar" of Bopp [120: 176].

How much credit does Jones deserve for the enormous progress in linguistics by the time of this general review? Not until 1963 did Hoenigswald discover that Jones's formulation perhaps had little or no admitted, direct influence on the major comparativists, though they all used his works. Lehmann went directly to the first German source, the translations and notes by Fick and Kleuker in 1795. Although the whole Third Discourse was translated, Kleuker did not comment on the formulation. While the pair performed a great service by making Jones quickly available, it clearly took some time for the full import of the formulation to be perceived in Germany (Lehmann 1984). Schlegel (1808: 28) gave an isolated quotation of Jones's "affinity" phrase but only indirectly utilized the hint in making the first reference to comparative grammar, in relation to comparative anatomy (see Aarsleff 1967: 154–159). Yet Schlegel's generalizations lack the sweep of Jones's formulation. Bopp 1816 did not directly utilize the formulation and, according to Greenberg, was the "pioneer application of the comparative method to genetically related languages" (1973: 167). Müller (1871 [1]: 172–184) quoted Jones's formulation alongside generalizations by Sassetti, Cœurdoux, Pons, and Halhed but did not evaluate it.

If in the history of ideas or specifically in the history of linguistics, the formulation must be evaluated on the basis of admitted direct cause-and-effect relationships, then modern comparative linguistics may be said to have begun with Bopp and Rask, with Grimm and Schlegel identifying the nature and role of sound shifts in language change and thus providing a guiding light. Grimm, for example, made no statement that he read the formulation and thereupon understood the relationship between, say, Latin *pastus* and Old Norse *fasta*. Nor should we expect to find such an admission of influence. Unlike Jones, most scholars of the day assembled ideas as they could and published in their own name. Only after the intellectual sequence was clear, after Verner had explained the troublesome exceptions in

Grimm's sets of shifts, did language scholars regularly give Jones large credit. Grierson (1903 [1]: 10) was among the first, quoting the formulation and concluding that "modern comparative philology dates from the introduction of Sanskrit as a serious object of study," following Jones's recognition of the existence of an Indo-European family.

Jespersen (1922: 33–34) remarked that the formulation was often quoted in linguistics books, and he quoted it. He concluded that Jones gave the *clue* to younger scholars, who carried out in detail the comparison that Jones had inaugurated. This assessment is valid today. Saussure is credited with saying that Jones, not Bopp, was the first to compare Sanskrit with German, Greek, Latin, etc., to record their similarities, and to state that they all belonged to a single family but that "Jones's few isolated statements do not prove that the significance and importance of comparison had been generally understood" before Bopp's great work (1966: 2). This assessment is only partly valid because Jones's comparative examples from a few Indo-European languages were scattered through numerous essays.

Pedersen was also hyperbolic, quoting Jones's "often quoted statement" and praising it as being extraordinarily clear and recalling few of the old ways of thinking (1931: 19). By now, his linguistic fame was accepted by all language scholars, though Bloomfield (1933: 12) hedged by saying that Jones *seems* to have been the first to explain that Sanskrit, Greek, Latin, etc. were divergent from a single prehistoric language. Partly exhilarated by the bicentennial observance of Jones's birth, Franklin Edgerton 1946 was the most hyperbolic of all: the formulation had been repeatedly hailed as the first clear printed statement of the fundamental assumption of the comparative method; no one had previously explained the resemblances in terms of common descent from an earlier language. We must reduce the first part of this assessment; that is, Bopp and Schlegel deserve the credit for developing the principles and details of the method, though again and again in Jones's Indian essays we find him insisting on a comprehensive, systematic comparison. He gave the *clue* to the scientific study of languages, on the basis of historical change.

By taking his formulation out of context, many scholars have overlooked the fact that in his total Indian writings he provided the West with a "germinal knowledge of . . . the native grammarians of Sanskrit" (Emeneau 1955: 148). It is highly unlikely that Bopp and Schlegel could have done their comparative work without having been introduced to the great Sanskrit grammars. Western descriptive linguistics might have languished in its impressionistic framework for additional decades. And the development of a competent linguistics still took decades, with Pānini's transparent sandhi descriptions an ever-useful model in the plotting of Germanic consonantal shifts. Bopp's comparisons could not have been as incisive if he had had to extract implicit theory and methodology from works like Erpenius's *Grammatica Arabica* (1613), Meninski's *Thesaurus Linguarum Orientalium Turcicæ, Arabicæ, Persicæ* (1680–1687), Parkhurst's *An Hebrew and English Lexicon* (1762), and Jones's *A Grammar of the Persian Language*.

In 1963 Hoenigswald considerably debunked the formulation, concluding that its influence had given it its importance and that scholars may have credited it with more originality than it had. Hoenigswald suggested that Jones's philosopher friends like Burke and Monboddo would have argued that the ancestor language mentioned by Jones was primitive, a point that is probably valid. Indeed, the philosopher William Robertson presented in his *History of America* (1777) a pioneering typological explanation of society as evolving from savagery to barbarism to civilization, that is, European-style culture. Jones was a cosmopolitan product of such colonial thought, but in India he quickly realized that an anthropologically ferocious, non-literate people could not have created the brooding Seven Pagodas at Mahabalipuram or the *Bhagavad-Gītā*. As he said in a letter in 1784, "I am in love with the *Gopia*, charmed with *Crishen*, an enthusiastick admirer of *Rām*, and a devout adorer of *Brihma-bishen-mehais*: not to mention that *Judishteīr, Arjen, Corno*, and the other warriours of the *M'hab'harat* appear greater in my eyes than Agamemnon, Ajax, and Achilles appeared, when I first read the Iliad" (*Letters* 2: 652).

For a classicist like Jones to make such a strong comparison with Homer, after only nine months in India, is additional evidence of the sort that permeates his essays. He was finding rich philosophy, the fascinating religion of Hinduism, beautiful literature, advanced astronomy and musicology, and so on recorded in the many thousands of preserved Sanskrit manuscripts. When he began intensively studying Sanskrit in September 1785, he had already rejected the notion of a barbaric India and was seeking to communicate the correct view (see Cannon 1986). In a passage in the Third Discourse preceding his famous formulation, he described the Sanskrit Golden Age, when the people were "splendid in arts and arms, happy in government, wise in legislation, and eminent in various knowledge" (*Works* 3: 32). His few comments on the Indo-European language indicate that he did not view it as a primitive, inadequate method of communication spoken by savages. Preceding the halcyon Sanskrit age, the Aryan forebears "cultivated no liberal arts, and had no use of letters, but formed a variety of dialects, as their tribes were variously ramified" (*Works* 3: 202). Even if Jones had known the modern premise that Indo-European may have had only one vowel (i.e., a single syllabic peak functioning in all environments—see Hockett 1978: 303), he did not view it as primitive. Moreover, his view of Indo-European— whether adequate or not—hardly affects the importance of his conceptualizing language families and the vital fact that a language can die or change into another language.

Hoenigswald's otherwise cogent paper was the low point in Jones's modern reputation. Rocher (1980b) recently echoed Hoenigswald, asserting that Jones was a precursor rather than the founder of comparative Indo-European linguistics. Hymes and Fought suggested that "a strong case can be made for the effective beginning of comparative-historical linguistics in Prussia and the other German states early in the nineteenth century, so far as an organized, concerted advocacy with continuous history is concerned" (1975: 1142). However, six years after Hoenigswald's paper and in the same series, Fairbanks (1969: 36) reassessed Grierson and gave Jones credit for founding comparative philology. Meanwhile, Hockett credited Jones with the first breakthrough in comparative method, by introducing a genetic hypothesis that "gave scholars something systematic to try, where before there had been no guide but whimsy" (1965: 185–186). This assessment stands as the modern evaluation of the traditional, sometimes exaggerated view. In fact, the paper in which this assessment occurs, along with Hockett's "Knowledge of the Past," are the only papers that connect the comparative method of linguistics with methods of historical inference and interpretation used in other disciplines, such as history. That was Jones's approach. The big difference in historical linguistic speculation between earlier attempts and the nineteenth-century method is that whereas earlier attempts tried to explain *similarities* among languages, a genetic hypothesis required the explaining of *differences*, or what Hockett called the "unexplained residue" (1965: 188–189). That is, forms similar enough in sound and meaning might be explained as cognates, but the unexplained residue should be steadily diminished as data are moved to the "explained" set. Jones contributed little or nothing to this important switch in methodology, although he recognized that some groups of languages are related and can be tested for genetic relationship.

Various scholars have seconded Hockett's assessment of Jones's breakthrough. Aarsleff's important book accorded Jones a complete chapter, crediting Herder, Bopp, Rask, and Grimm with large contributions but concluding that Jones "gave the impulse to the development of the new historical and comparative study on the Continent" (1967: 3). Robins agreed that Jones has been "accorded pride of place as having instituted scientific historical linguistics and the historical classification of languages" but stipulated that Jones was not the instant discoverer (1973: 19–20). Using a wide net, Lehmann credited Jones with stimulating "one of the major intellectual activities of the nineteenth century, the study of Indo-European linguistics, of historical linguistics, and of the philological topics involved in the elucidation of the associated texts" (1984). Thereupon Western scholars began making contributions to Sanskrit studies and helped to revive that long-dormant field in India. And, once the formulation had kindled the brilliance of a Schlegel, Jones's generalizations and tantalizing hints elsewhere in his essays of 1786–1794 were available in the many editions of *Asiatick Researches* and in fine German or French translations.

BICENTENNIAL REAPPRAISAL

As said, Jones's phrase "affinity, both in the roots of verbs and in the forms of grammar" reveals modern insights when considered in context. Thus the opening pages of his Third Discourse give two sets of triple cognates clearly selected because of their synonymy and similar form because he recognized that at least three languages should be compared in any cognate testing. Indeed, these and his other sets of cognates indicate that his formulation was the empirically tested conclusion from comparing many data. I have said that he did not view lexical data as being equal in comparative analysis. In his Sixth Discourse (*Works* 3: 119–120), he divided lexicons into two kinds of items. One kind consists of nonbasic vocabulary—the names of exotic animals, commodities, and arts, which are nonpredictive because they could have been borrowed through political or commercial intercourse with another people. Such intrusion, he said, has trivial or no effect on the grammar, even when a goodly number of exotic names for things and actions are borrowed, since the basic language is unchanged. He intuitively knew that borrowings could threaten the feasibility of the incipient comparative method (Hockett's "Knowledge of the Past"). Rather, the best predictive data are the names "of material elements, parts of the body, natural objects and relations, affections of the mind, and other ideas common to the whole race of man." In the Fourth Discourse (1787) he illustrated an incorrect analysis by using Sanskrit and Arabic morphology, particularly derivations, to show that the two languages belonged to different families.

So it all started with Jones, who pulled all the disparate threads together into a single theoretical formulation. The philologists who followed him had much of what they needed—the concepts of language families and change, use of basic vocabulary, much of the methodology, and warnings about etymological speculation. These painstaking scholars viewed an item and its analysis as valuable in its own right, even if they were not visionarily using their findings to advance a preconceived purpose like projecting migration routes and dates or explaining cultural diffusion. The fact that many linguists today hope to apply their findings to the ultimate betterment of society is an echo of Jones's far-sightedness. They draw ultimately on his Jonesian system, a pioneering transliterative system devised in "A Dissertation on the Orthography of Asiatick Words in Roman Letters" (the lead essay in *Asiatick Researches* 1), the first formal essay on transcription, which held the germ of ideas eventually culminating in the International Phonetic Alphabet.

Modern linguists have generally overlooked the fact that his later Anniversary Discourses refined and expanded his concept of families, introducing synonyms for the progenitor languages like *common stock* and *common parent*. He did not believe that a given parent monolithically gave forth languages equally and simultaneously; nor did he propose, uselessly, that all the world's languages could be grouped into a single family. Thus in his Fifth Discourse (1788) he postulated a family containing Turkish, Mongolian, and other tongues, all of which derived from a single earlier tongue. Moreover, Turkish was considerably different from the other members of its family, as different in kind as Swedish–German, Spanish–Portuguese, and Welsh–Irish were. In indicating such differences to people who knew comparatively little about Altaic, he was simultaneously suggesting separate Germanic, Romance, and Celtic branches of Indo-European. Here was another clue for later scholars, who might otherwise have wondered a bit longer as to why English, German, Swedish, and Gothic are mutually different within the Germanic branch. In the Third Discourse he noted that Hindustani inflections and verb regimen differ considerably from those of German, which in turn differs in the same respects from Greek. So Indic constituted another branch, though he nowhere suggested a kind of centum-satem differentiation. He placed Romany within the Indic branch but was understandably troubled by its differences from the Indic languages spoken in Bengal. In his Eighth Discourse he specified a Hellenic branch, which included Aeolic, Doric, and Attic, with Phrygian perhaps related. Tocharian and Hittite, which were discovered later, were naturally never mentioned.

In several essays he postulated a Semitic family, completing the conceptions that had been put forth by Scandinavian philologists. This included at least Ethiopic, Amharic, Chaldean, Arabic, and Hebrew. He gave political dominance to Arabic and Hebrew. Some of his Semitic comparisons were considerably based on similar verb inflections, with grammatical arrangement another measurement. In his Eighth Discourse he spoke of a Finno-Ugric family containing at least Finnish, Lappish, and Hungarian. Some of his data came from Old Persian and Sanskrit inscriptions, in the first serious use of inscriptions for analyzing earlier periods of a language. He urged his Asiatic Society to make reliable rubbings of all the inscriptions in India and to list and decipher them because they might contain primary texts, which could throw rich light on vanished cultures and languages (Cannon 1978). No doubt his not mentioning Dravidian languages weakened the political status of those languages vis-à-vis Indic-derived ones, though he seldom mentioned Indo-European Indian vernaculars either, stressing Sanskrit instead. He never attempted to link all families into one superfamily dating back to a first language or first languages (see Hockett 1978: 247), avoiding the problems that have plagued modern efforts to prove distant relationships between Indo-European and the Uralic and Afro-Asiatic families. He stressed that he could not find a single word in common among Arabic and the Tatar and Indian languages (*Works* 3: 199). Nor did he draw together into a single essay all of his language-family materials so as to present a genetic classification of some of the world's languages. His projections of the several Indo-European branches triggered dynamic activity in the following decades in defining the branches, together with consequent development of theories of language change and genetic classificatory methodology, in studying languages historically. At this time geologists were just starting to realize that rocks showed a succession of fossils through time and that this succession might be a record of the history of life. Jones's scientific predecessors had shown that at least some flora and fauna were not immutable. He completed the picture by conceiving and using the idea that languages also were not immutable. Indeed, their changes through time might be as revealingly studied as Buffon and Linnaeus had studied biota. It may be that linguistics required a model from the sciences in order to become modern.

Jones did not directly treat *how* a progenitor language might spawn derivatives and begin a family. In his Fifth Discourse he did state that "all the languages properly *Tartarian* arose from one common source; excepting always the jargons of such wanderers or mountaineers, as, having long been divided from the main body of the nation, must in a course of ages have framed separate idioms for themselves." These mountaineers formed language islands (*Works* 3: 84). His chief explanation for such change was time and isolation within new living conditions encountered as the result of the migration of small groups away from a parent body, evidently not recognizing that linguistic change may particularly come about as a result of social interaction (as opposed to a potential stasis and conservatism during isolation). Despite his realization that languages are not immutable, it is not clear that he anticipated the modern view that language change goes on constantly and that differentiation accompanies change just when there are weaknesses in lines of communication. He was aware of rapid change, like the abandoning of Norman French in England in the fourteenth century that nonetheless witnessed large additional borrowings into English at the same time, and he rejected the idea that the Flood or other catastrophes could explain the differentiation of languages into families with ramified branches. Still, in general, his view may have been almost as close to catastrophism as it was to uniformitarianism (Hockett 1965).

His fullest comment came in the Eighth Discourse: "any small family detached in an early age from their parent stock, without letters, with few ideas beyond objects of the first necessity, and consequently with few words, and fixing their abode on a range of mountains, in an island, or even in a wide region before uninhabited, might in four or five centuries people their new country, and would necessarily form a new language with no perceptible traces, perhaps, of that spoken by their ancestors" (*Works* 3: 163). He never described how conditions might change a migrating people from, say, Latin to Spanish, or change a nonmoving people from Latin to Italian. The process of diversification was clearly long and complicated, as illustrated by several pronouncements in his Ninth Discourse (*Works* 3: 185–204). Thus his tentative answer to the general question raised in his interlocking Anniversary Discourses was that three language families came out of the focal area of Iran—Semitic, Tartarian, and what became known as Indo-European—but that these eventual families were already being differentiated before the main outward migrations began. He concluded that the Indo-European family, principally excepting its large Indic branch and the Chinese and Japanese that he mistakenly thought probably came from the Indians, mainly migrated westward, into Greece, Italy, Scandinavia, and so on. His directional statement may have influenced the later devising of the term as *Indo-European* rather than as *Euro-Indian* or perhaps preferably *Kurgan* (see Gimbutas 1973, 1985).

Jones's pronouncements were not wholly unbiased by Christianity, which influenced his premise that all human beings came from one pair: "their numerous descendants must necessarily seek new countries, as inclination might prompt, or accident lead them; they would of course migrate in separate families and clans, which, forgetting by degrees the language of their common progenitor, would form new dialects to convey new ideas, both simple and complex." In any case, "the language of Noah" was irretrievably lost (*Works* 3: 188, 199). There was little deference to Hebrew and revealed religion, for Jones went out of his way several times to stress the extreme antiquity of Arabic. His language generalizations ultimately became the final, definitive rejection of the idea that God gave Hebrew to the first human being as a direct gift and that all languages came from Hebrew, an idea that Herder had earlier attacked in part (Cannon 1985a). Jones seldom mentioned the Garden of Eden and never attempted to associate it with the Indo-European homeland, which he nonetheless cautiously placed in greater Iran at a date after the Flood. No doubt his reputation, cogency, and Biblical knowledge played their part in keeping theological scholars from attacking him, as they attacked Darwin 70 years later, though he frequently expressed his belief in a Divine Being. In some ways he ultimately separated language from religion as clearly as Darwin later separated science from religion. He moved language study away from intuition and speculation, toward the sciences. In a few tantalizing phrases he even implied that mature language rose (evolved) from inept communicational beginnings (see modern scholars like Lieberman 1984).

His ultimate contribution was in discovering the Truth amid a welter of impressionistic generalizations. He introduced Sanskrit to Western scholars, who then handled all the detail and methodology to develop modern linguistics. His 1786 formulation was remarkably lucid and pithy, with a theoretical sweep, inclusiveness, and philosophical consistency that Sassetti, Cœurdoux, Pons, Monboddo, and

Halhed combined could not equal. Any linguist today who can envision and compose such an enduring explanation will have justified his or her scholarship. Jones was a gifted writer, with thirteen books (his own writings and translations) to his credit when he composed the formulation. Its style and word choice were urbane and polished, but there is no evidence that he especially refined it, any more than he always revised whatever he wrote. (His worksheets do not contain the draft of the Third Discourse.) It was in an original, dramatic context, a brick in a surging thesis that culminated in the rejecting of the West's philosophically negative image of India. He founded a society and a highly successful journal in which to disseminate the society's findings. By 1800, though still in a colonial time, Europeans were viewing Indians as having made rich intellectual and artistic contributions to world culture that had useful applications for European improvement. His transmission of Sanskrit knowledge to the West transcends his linguistic accomplishments and is comparable in its way to Marco Polo's opening the magical world of Cathay to a startled Europe, even as the resulting cooperation with India helped to lead to an Indian Renaissance. His materials on language families and migrations, with inevitable differentiation into dialects and subcultures, are still some of the most provocative ever written.

Jones's early life was a vain attempt to support himself by language scholarship. Like modern scholars, he learned the need for an assured income. He gained his lucrative Supreme Court judgeship because of linguistic accomplishments, thereby financially showing the advantage in studying languages. His Indian years, which were lavishly reported in the British press, popularized and stimulated the career study of language for 70 years, until the idea was permanent. His biography was included in numerous books with titles like *Portraits of Illustrious Personages* (London, 1849–1850, 8: 91–96), and always his language study was stipulated as the reason for his greatness. The list of 28 languages that he knew (*Works* 3: 264–265) was widely held up around the world as a predetermined model of how scholarship can provide a valuable career and of how a commoner can have a personally satisfying life that can serve humanity. His career gave language study an excitement and prestige that it never had before and in which linguists today still share. Two hundred years ago this modest genius composed a formulation that is unrivaled in the history of linguistics, though, ironically, he intended it as a small, substantiating part of a huge cross-disciplinary purpose.

Its total repetitions have made it one of the most quoted formulations among all scholarly formulations in all disciplines. In the history of ideas it stands as one of the great conceptions that attempt to explain human beings and their intellectual accomplishments and that discriminate Truth from mythology and speculation. In its ultimate implications it may be comparable to discoveries like Galileo's and Copernicus's breakthrough into scientific astronomy (from geocentric to heliocentric) and to Darwin's integrated explanation of change in organisms, where the expansive truth replaced the constricting false. It belongs in this elite set of conceptions of world knowledge.

ACKNOWLEDGMENT
Charles Hockett made many helpful suggestions in the revision of this paper.

REFERENCES CITED

Aarsleff, H. 1967. *The Study of Language in England, 1780–1860*. Princeton: Princeton University Press.
———. 1975. "The Eighteenth Century, Including Leibniz." *Current Trends in Linguistics* 13: 383–379.
Allen, W. S. 1953. "Relationship in Comparative Linguistics." *Transactions of the Philological Society*, pp. 52–108.
Arlotto, A. T. 1969. "Jones and Cœurdoux: Correction to a Footnote." *Journal of the American Oriental Society* 89: 416–417.
Asiatic Society, Calcutta. 1784–1794. *Manuscript Proceedings*.
Bingen, J., ed. 1980. *Recherches de linguistique: hommages à Maurice Leroy*. Brussels: Univ. Libre.
Bloomfield, L. 1933. *Language*. New York: Henry Holt.
Bonfante, G. 1954. "Ideas on the Kinship of the European Languages from 1200 to 1800." *Cahiers d'Histoire Mondiale* 1: 679–699.
Bopp, F. 1816. *Über das Conjugationssystem der Sanskritsprache*. Frankfurt: Andreas.
Burnett, J. [Lord Monboddo.] 1774–1792. *Of the Origin and Progress of Language*. 6 vols. Edinburgh: J. Balfour.
Cannon, G. 1968. "The Correspondence Between Lord Monboddo and Sir William Jones." *American Anthropologist* 70: 559–561.
———. 1975. "Sir William Jones, Sir Joseph Banks, and the Royal Society." *Notes and Records of the Royal Society of London* 29: 205–230.
———. 1978. "Sir William Jones and Sanskrit Epigraphy." *Journal of the Oriental Society of Australia* 13: 3–8.
———. 1979. *Sir William Jones: a Bibliography of Primary and Secondary Sources*. Amsterdam: John Benjamins.
———. 1981. "Letters of Sir William Jones and His Correspondents." *Comparative Criticism* 3: 179–196.

————. 1984. "Sir William Jones, Persian, Sanskrit and the Asiatic Society." *Histoire Épistémologie Langage* 6 (2): 83–94.

————. 1985a. "Sir William Jones's Founding and Directing of the Asiatic Society." (British Library) *India Office Library and Records Report 1984–1985:* 11–24.

————. 1985b. "Brief Edited Calendar of Asiatic Society Meetings, 14 Jan. 1784–1 May 1794." (British Library) *India Office Library and Records Report* 1984–1985: 25–28.

————. 1986. "The Construction of the European Image of the Orient: a Bicentennial Appraisal of Sir William Jones as Poet and Translator." *Comparative Criticism* 8: 166–188.

————. 1990. *The Life and Mind of Oriental Jones.* Cambridge: Cambridge University Press.

Chaudhuri, S., ed. 1980. *Proceedings of the Asiatic Society, 1784–1800.* Calcutta: Asiatic Society.

Edgerton, F. 1946. "Sir William Jones: 1746–1794." *Journal of the American Oriental Society* 66: 230–239.

Emeneau, M. B. 1955. "India and Linguistics." *Journal of the American Oriental Society* 75: 145–153.

Fairbanks, G. H. 1969. "Comparative Indo-Aryan." *Current Trends in Linguistics* 5: 36–45.

Fick, J. C., and J. F. Kleuker. 1795–1797. *Abhandlungen über die Geschichte und Alterthümer, Künste, Wissenschaften und Literatur Asiens von Sir William Jones und andern Mitgliedern der in Jahr 1784 zu Calcutta in Indien errichteten gelehrten Gesellschaft.* Riga: Hartknoch.

Gimbutas, M. 1973. "The Beginning of the Bronze Age in Europe and the Indo-Europeans: 3500–2500 B.C." *Journal of Indo-European Studies* 1: 163–214.

————. 1985. "Primary and Secondary Homeland of the Indo-Europeans." *Journal of Indo-European Studies* 13: 185–200.

Godfrey, J. J. 1967. "Sir William Jones and Père Cœurdoux: a Philological Footnote." *Journal of the American Oriental Society* 87: 57–59.

Greenberg, J. H. 1973. "The Typological Method." *Current Trends in Linguistics* 11: 149–193.

Grierson, Sir George A. 1903–1927. *Linguistic Survey of India.* Calcutta: Superintendent of Government Printing.

Halhed, N. B. 1778. *A Grammar of the Bengal Language.* Hooghly, India.

Hockett, C. F. 1965. "Sound Change." *Language* 41: 185–203.

————. 1978. "In Search of Jove's Brow." *American Speech* 53: 243–313.

————. Unpublished. "Knowledge of the Past."

Hoenigswald, H. M. 1963. "On the History of the Comparative Method." *Anthropological Linguistics* 5: 1–11.

————. 1984. "Etymology Against Grammar in the Early 19th Century." *Histoire Épistémologie Langage* 6 (2): 95–100.

Hymes, D., and J. Fought. 1975. "American Structuralism." *Current Trends in Linguistics* 13: 903–1176.

Jespersen, O. 1922. *Language: Its Nature, Development and Origin.* London: George Allen & Unwin.

Johnson, S. 1755. *Dictionary of the English Language.* London.

Jones, Sir William. 1784–1794. Parcel 698 of Jones's worksheets. (Owned by Cannon.)

———. 1784–1794. Parcel 699 of Jones's worksheets. (Owned by India Office Library and Records, London.)

———. 1807. *The Works of Sir William Jones.* 13 vols. London: J. Stockdale.

———. 1831. *Catalogue of the Library of the Late Sir William Jones.* Ed. by R. H. Evans. London: W. Nicol.

———. 1970. *The Letters of Sir William Jones.* Ed. by G. Cannon. 2 vols. Oxford: Clarendon Press.

Lehmann, W. P. 1984. "Fick and Kleuker on Jones: Riga 1795." Paper read at 1984 Modern Language Association.

Lieberman, P. 1984. *The Biology and Evolution of Language.* Cambridge: Harvard University Press.

Müller, F. M. 1871. *Lectures on the Science of Language.* Translation of 6th ed. 2 vols. London: Longmans, Green.

Pedersen, H. 1931. *The Discovery of Language.* Trans. by J. W. Spargo. Bloomington: Indiana University Press.

Robins, R. H. 1973. "The History of Language Classification." *Current Trends in Linguistics* 11: 3–41.

Rocher, R. 1980a. "Lord Monboddo, Sanskrit and Contemporary Linguistics." *Journal of the American Oriental Society* 100: 12–17.

———. 1980b. "Nathaniel Brassey Halhed. Sir William Jones, and Comparative Indo-European Linguistics." In Bingen 1980.

Saussure, F. de. 1966. Course in General Linguistics. New York: McGraw-Hill.

Schlegel, F. von. 1808. *Ueber die Sprache und Weisheit der Indier.* Heidelberg: Mohr and Zimmer.

Swadesh, M. 1971. *The Origin and Diversification of Language.* Ed. by J. Sherzer. Chicago: Aldine-Atherton.

Wilkins, C. 1808. *A Grammar of the Sanskrīta Language.* London: W. Bulmer.

PART II

Indo-European in Context

Part II focuses on Indo-European, with attention not just to the IE languages and their common source but also to the culture of the Indo-Europeans.

As Edgar Polomé demonstrates, the reconstruction of IE religious terminology is one way that comparative linguistics can help us to discover an ancient cultural pattern, for a common ancestral language presupposes a common religion of the people who spoke it. Polomé shows how the linguistic evidence reveals various properties of the religion of the Indo-Europeans, including its hierarchy of functional deities.

Jaan Puhvel also shows, in a study centered on Hittite, how closely language and culture are intertwined. The existence of ancient writings in Hittite and some languages closely related to it was unknown in Sir William's time. The ancient clay tablets, discovered in Asia Minor in the early years of the present century, turned out upon decipherment to have an Indo-European affinity, and they led to an enlarged view of the IE languages and culture. From the time of their decipherment, there has been disagreement on whether this newly discovered ancient family constituted a sister stock of IE or just another branch of the larger IE stock. In the former view, Proto-IE, the "common source" of the IE languages, is seen as separate from Proto-Anatolian, and these two closely related proto-languages are sprung from a still earlier common source called "Proto-Indo-Hittite." Unlike the Indic languages (the branch of IE to which Sanskrit belongs) the Anatolian languages became extinct many centuries ago, leaving no surviving daughter languages.

Marija Gimbutas, in offering an archeological perspective, shows that Europe underwent a drastic change when the female-oriented pre-IE culture of "Old Europe" was displaced by that of the male-dominated Indo-Europeans. The archeological evidence, when analyzed with the skill of an expert, provides a surprising amount of insight into the Old European culture. Like the other chapters of Part II, that of Gimbutas offers a broad view that helps us provide a cultural context for the IE language family.

Whence the Hittite, Whither the Jonesian Vision?

JAAN PUHVEL

Much has been made of Sir William Jones as the founder of Indo-European linguistics, too much perhaps, for it little matters in the end whether he was prefigured or understudied or even scooped by the likes of Nathaniel Halhed or James Burnett Lord Monboddo. In scholarship as in commerce, packaging is paramount, and Jones with his marvelous felicity for *callida iunctura* ended up stealing the show and running away with the credit for the past two centuries. Attendant vagaries have sunk into oblivion, but the revelatory dictum about the "common source, which, perhaps, no longer exists" stands out in bold relief.

If Jones really was the founder of Indo-European linguistics, he was an unwitting one. His Third Anniversary Discourse of February 2, 1786, has set off bicentennial fireworks, but he had barely taken the helm of his new Asiatick Society when in his First Discourse of 1784 he reiterated one of his guiding principles, which might send right-thinking linguists up the wall: "I have ever considered languages as the mere instruments of real learning, and think them improperly confounded with learning itself." Such downplaying of mere linguistics may nowadays sound extreme and misguided, but perhaps our own formalistic excesses could use a bit of Jonesian corrective. He reminds us that there is more to language than phoneme counting and structural analysis, that language is also a means to great ends, for conveying the culture that sustains it.

It may be worthwhile to recall that Jones was in equal measure the founding father of Indo-European comparative mythology, for in that same year of 1784, in his paper "On the Gods of Greece, Italy, and India," later published (like his 1786 discourse) in the first volume of *Asiatick Researches* (1788), he enunciated an equally compelling charter for the comparison of mythic traditions: "When features of resem-

blance, too strong to have been accidental, are observable in different systems of polytheism, without fancy or prejudice to colour them
and improve the likeness, we can scarce help believing, that some
connection has immemorially subsisted between the several nations,
who have adopted them."

The only segment of latter-day Indo-European researches where
prophetic resonance failed Jones is archeology. Here he could have
used a bit of cross-fertilization by a nearly coeval, equally seminal
mind in the New World, namely, Thomas Jefferson, who with his
excavations of Indian mounds in Virginia had laid the foundations
of archeological stratigraphy. Jones frequently saw Benjamin Franklin in England and France and was a great supporter of the American cause, sympathies that delayed his appointment to the judicial
vacancy in Bengal for five years and more than once tempted him to
emigrate westward. When Jones finally sailed from Portsmouth for
Calcutta in April 1783, Jefferson's arrival in Le Havre for his five-year
stint as Franklin's ambassadorial successor was as yet fifteen months
in the future. They might still have met down the years, for Sir
William and Lady Jones had planned a grand tour of the United States
on their way back from India, but illness and death intervened a decade later. Had Jones and Jefferson truly interacted, rather than
merely known of each other, Jones might in the end have made a first-
rate professor for the new University of Virginia. Instead he courted
early death in the pestilential swamplands of Bengal, most of the time
fighting off the administrative encroachments of Lord Cornwallis,
who had repaired from the debacle at Yorktown to the governor-
generalship of India. Small world indeed, even in the days when a
galleon took five months to sail from England to India.

So much for Jones' own *légende des siècles*. But his millennial vision
survived, persisted, and flourished. In a scientific revolution such
as the one that ensued, a crucial ingredient of any viable theory is
its power of prediction. It not only subsumes what is at hand but cogently anticipates as yet unrealized additions to its matrix. Jones had
drawn in Sanskrit, Greek, Latin, and Persian, and with reservations
about external intermixture also Germanic and Celtic. His conspicuous omission of Balto-Slavic was soon corrected from Franz Bopp
onward, and Jacob Grimm's law presently breached the Germanic
barrier to full membership. On the other hand, it took much of the
nineteenth century before Caspar Zeuss fully habilitated Celtic (although Jones related it to Sanskrit in his letters subsequent to the discourse), and a good many decades were needed before the sanskrito-

centrism started by Friedrich Schlegel was in full and final retreat. Even later, in 1875, Armenian was successfully detached by Heinrich Hübschmann from its misclassification as an Iranian dialect, and when at the end of the century Tocharian emerged from the caves of Kucha and Turfan in Chinese Turkestan, it readily found its niche as derived from that "common source, which no longer exists" (dispensing with Sir William's cautionary "perhaps").

Thus, up to our own century, the basic Jonesian hypothesis rendered unblemished service to the evolving discipline, no matter what family-tree or wave schemes were supposed to refine it further. Not so since the addition of Hittite and Anatolian generally. Neogrammarians with tidy minds, basking in the afterglow of Karl Brugmann's compendious *Grundriss*, were understandably not thrilled to have their circles upset by any further intruders, especially by Assyriological upstarts. Therefore Johan Knudtzon was hooted off the stage when in 1902 he first claimed Indo-European status for Hittite. After the material became plentiful from Boğazköy, another Assyriologist bearing Greek gifts, Bedřich Hrozný, could no longer be dismissed outright.

Since about 1915 the strange spectacle of Indo-Europeanist reaction to Hittite has played itself out, and much of it has not been a pretty picture. In the early days only one leading Indo-Europeanist, Ferdinand Sommer, had the fortitude to plunge into firsthand Hittite philology to help steer its comparative component away from well-meaning Assyriologists like Hrozný and past ingenious but sometimes misguided idea men such as Emil Forrer. Others were content to sit by, waiting for the Hittitological product to be served up in pre-processed gobs for easy consumption. In addition to the hagiology of the sainted Émile Benveniste, there exists other lore, not necessarily apocryphal, for example, that Benveniste never even learned to read cuneiform and hence was incapable of primary research in Hittite. Benveniste and Jerzy Kuryłowicz, the leading mid–twentieth century Indo-Europeanists, made up in dazzling cleverness what they may have lacked in firsthand grounding, but the Anatolian component of their great syntheses was nevertheless largely secondhand.

And herein lies the rub: secondhand refined matter may be all right, but hand-me-down raw material is risky stuff. The fact remains that Hittite has been and still is like unrefined ore that is as yet literally emerging from the ground. The bulk is large, it has doubled in the last 35 years, and Hittitology today is not the same as it was at midcentury. We have much more, we know much more, and we can benefit from the 70 years of availability and research, rather than behaving like bedazzled discoverers. Hittitology has not been and is not yet a mature subcomponent of Indo-European stud- ies, but we are on our way. I still vividly recall my revulsion to the second edition of Edgar Sturtevant's *Comparative Grammar of Hittite* in 1951. The first edition in 1933 had been a useful pioneering work. The theoretical Indo-Hittite aberration had not yet become oppres- sive, and the author clearly retained some interest in firsthand phi- lology. The new version was like some idiosyncratic ghostscape of Indo-Hittite wisps, littered with half-baked approximations and reconstruction gone haywire and laced with laryngeals and *shwa secunda*.

Slowly the realization dawned on me that the way out of such debacles would not come from further forced annexation of Hittite, or premature syntheses that misapplied Hittite, but must come from within Hittite itself. Indo-Europeanists simply had to start doing in earnest and in depth what Sommer tried; they had to become Hittit- ologists as well. Sanskrit had arrived on silver platters—predigested by Pāṇini and taught by pundits to Sirs Charles Wilkins and William Jones; a millennial tradition was there for the plucking. Hittite has proved a much pricklier fruit and not as attractively packaged.

Such has been my own toil for the past thirty-five years, during the second half of Hittitology up to now. Whatever these decades have taught me, one tenet stands out: Beware of all purveyors of alleged *Fernwirkungen*, or distant influences, be they "Indo-Hittit- ologists" from Forrer to Sturtevant to Cowgill, or "Nostraticists" of assorted stripes, most recently Henrich Wagner. Composed in Ire- land without benefit of specialized libraries, Wagner's *Das hethitische vom Standpunkte der typologischen Sprachgeographie* (Pisa, 1985) finds odds and ends to compare in Georgian, Sumerian, Akkadian, and elsewhere, ending up claiming for Hittite some kind of substratally bastardized or creolized status that he cannot in good conscience de- rive from archaic Indo-European. Quite the contrary, in my experi- ence, the more one delves into Hittite, the more profoundly Indo- European it reveals itself, in direct agreement with the basic Jones- ian vision. It may be that Wagner and I are at opposite poles of the innovation vs. retention game, but so be it: a straight-line Indo- Europeanist of the genetic persuasion cannot be otherwise.

The notion that Hittite is not pure Indo-European but somehow para-Indo-European is laid to rest merely by reciting some of the most basic root verbs. The paradigms of *es-* 'to be', *ey-* 'to go', and *ed-* 'to eat' in Hittite are perfect matches for the best-preserved specimens elsewhere: Hittite *ēsmi, ēssi, ēszi* cover Old Lithuanian *esmi, esi, esti*; Luwian and Hittite *iti, yanzi, idu, iyandu, iyant-* correspond to Vedic *éti, yánti, étu, yántu, yánt-*; and Hittite *edmi, ezsi, adanzi, ezdu, adandu, adant-* fit exactly over Vedic *ádmi, átsi, adanti, attu, adantu, adánt-*. I rest my case right there, for I know of no better definition for an Indo-European language. Those who lament that some other basic vocabulary sounds strange, that 'to do' is *iya-* and 'to give' is *piya-*, with little to compare elsewhere, might be reminded that French, for example, remains a Latin-based language, despite showing *il va* and *il mange* for Latin *it* and *ēst*. Old Iranian has lost practically all traces of Indo-European *ed-* 'eat', but that does not compromise its Indo-Iranian character.

But what about that notion dear to Indo-Hittitologists that Hittite with its early date of attestation is too simple in morphology to qualify as a certifiable Indo-European language, that it shows up unencumbered by the sine-qua-non paraphernalia of other members of the club, such as feminine gender, aorist and perfect tenses, future formations, and subjunctive and optative moods? Before faulting it on this issue, one should rather consider its dialectical position within Indo-European and keep in mind all that it has retained.

Hittite is a typical Indo-European fringe dialect, one of those that were spun off and isolated before the collapse of a terminal continuum. Others of the kind were Tocharian and Western Indo-European, although the latter formed its own subcontinuum with an extreme in Italic and gradually mitigated variants in Celtic and Germanic harking back toward the heartland via Baltic. The Center was the common cradle of Indo-Iranian and Slavic-Baltic, with the likely addition of Armenian, and an honorary membership in this *satem* club saved for Greek. It is fair to say that Greek is a *satem* language in everything but primary palatalizations, and it has plenty of combinatory ones in its makeup. The many similarities between Greek and Armenian are due precisely to their contiguity on the southern fringe of the Late Indo-European continuum. The image of Common Indo-European was shaped in the wake of Jones mainly by juxtaposing such members of Late Indo-European as Sanskrit and Greek with their elaborate verbal morphologies. Hittite simply forces a corrective and at the same time points the way to several criteria:

- A feature shared by Hittite with another fringe dialect or dialects (Western Indo-European or Tocharian) is Early Indo-European.

- A feature shared by Hittite with both fringe and central dialects is Common Indo-European and by definition also goes back to Early Indo-European.
- Early or Common Indo-European features missing in Hittite count as losses.
- Exclusive Central Indo-European features missing in Hittite are immaterial.
- Specific Hittite similarities with Greek, Armenian, Slavic, or Indo-Iranian are suspect of areal, diffusionary, culture-bound origin.

Armed with these tenets, let us take a brief tour d'horizon of Hittite language and culture.

The Hittite noun has an inventory of cases that can easily qualify as Common Indo-European; by distinguishing ablative and instrumental it is on a par with Indo-Iranian or Armenian, and by compromising or partly syncretizing only one case (the locative) it resembles the level of archaism in Slavic and Italic. Hittite retains such significant features as an alternative collective neuter plural in animate nouns, of the Greek *kúkloi* : *kúkla* or Latin *loci* : *loca* kind: *alpus* : *alpa* 'clouds', *aniyaddus* : *aniyatta* 'outfits, gear', *suppalēs* : *suppala* 'livestock', *warsulis* : *warsula* 'drops', *waspēs* : *waspa* 'garments'. Much has been made of the fact that the plural paradigm appears truncated and on the verge of collapse, with even the few discrete case endings (animate nominative *-es*, accusative *-us*, dative *-as*) subject to frequent confusion and with no credible dual forms in sight.

The disappearance of the dual is no surprise, for this Common Indo-European category, best retained in the Center (Indo-Iranian, Slavic, and Baltic), was generally on the run elsewhere, as in Classical Greek, surviving only in the noun in Old Irish, only in the second and third persons of Greek, and only in the first and second persons active in Gothic. It is gone in Italic and Armenian and nearly so in the Tocharian verb but is curiously hypertrophied in the Tocharian noun, even subdivided into a dual and a paral number. There is formal proof that Hittite, rather than intrinsically lacking the dual, actually lost it, because it has kept the ancient compositional device of the *devatā-dvandva*, the original double-dual pairing of divine names, mechanically transforming it into a double-plural compound: just as in Latin the *Dyāvā-Pṛthivī* 'Heaven-Earth' construction is matched by *Veneres Cupīdinesque* 'Aphrodite-Eros', even so in Hittite the paired demons of dread, 'Fear' and 'Fright', resembling the Greek *Deimos* and *Phobos*, appear as a plural sequence *Naḫsarattes Weritemes*.

Ancient matter survives in the genitive plural ending -*an* from *-*ōm* (as in *siunan antuḫsas* 'man of the gods, prophet'), but the so-called *pada* endings of the plural (of the Sanskrit -*bhis*, Latin -*bus* kind) have indeed been regressively suppressed in Hittite, as for that matter the corresponding Greek ending -*phi* disappears from Classical Greek.

Apart from the dative-locative ending, the Hittite plural paradigm is formally no more curtailed than the Greek, but syntactic decay is farther advanced. Several factors may have conspired here. Strictly speaking, full congruence in nouns and verbs is a luxury that can be dispensed with. This is notorious in the verb, where, for example, Lithuanian has no third person dual or plural, using the singular exclusively, or Scandinavian has made the third person plural obsolete. Hittite, like Greek, uses the singular verb exclusively with a neuter subject, whether singular or plural, and may have initiated a converse process of indicating animate number largely by the verb only.

The formal distinction of nominal neuter singular and plural is also a sometime thing in Hittite, tied in with the fate of the neuter plural marker A_2, the *a*-coloring laryngeal that disappeared in Hittite, unlike the A_1 that that shows up as the denominative verbal factitive morpheme in *newaḫḫ-* 'to make new' (Latin *novā-* from *novo-*). This laryngeal could either lengthen the vowel, as in Vedic *trī*, neuter plural of 'three', or vocalize as shwa, seen in Greek and Latin *tria*. Thus we have *āssū* 'goods' (like Vedic *vasū*) but *genuwa* 'knees' (like Latin *genua*). This A_2 is the same morphophoneme that underlies the creation of the Common Indo-European feminine morphemes, notably *-*ā* formed by its fusion with a preceding thematic vowel, or *y + A_2 with its various outcomes (as in Sanskrit *pátnī* vs. Greek *pótnia*). In Hittite the same would have yielded *-*ā* and either *-*ī* or *-*iya*. It is not impossible that such feminines once existed in Anatolian but failed to maintain themselves as distinctive noun classes, being absorbed into the standardized *a* and *i* stems by the time of our documents.

Perhaps the plene-spelling *isḫās* beside *isḫas* 'lord' really does mark an old distinction of grammatical gender, as in ᴰ*Isḫaras linkias isḫās* 'the goddess Isharas, mistress of the oath'. The creation of the marked feminine *isḫassaras* 'lady' is purely secondary, like our *mistress*. The profusion of *i* stems and -*iya*- stems in Hittite, both nominal and adjectival, may owe something to a prehistoric absorption of a large body of feminine forms. The grammatical suppression of the feminine gender recalls dislocations of the brittle three-gender system in later times, whether the disappearance of the neuter in the Romance languages or of the feminine in Scandinavian. The feminine was always marginal in the system, as shown by such phenomena as the two-ending adjectives in Greek, which lacked it altogether. Conversely the step from a neuter plural to a feminine singular remained an easy one, as when Latin *folia* ended up as Italian *una foglia* or Spanish *una hoja* or French *une feuille*.

If Hittite has folded up the fragments of a formal feminine, it has on the other hand remained alert to archaic functional nuances of the basic animate : neuter or acting : inert opposition, the type that in archaic Indo-European syntax precludes neuter nouns from serving as subjects of transitive verbs for lack of an agent case, an animate nominative. One need not delve into glottogony or adduce the loaded term "ergative" to appreciate how, for example, Old Latin and Russian express "the thunderbolts killed the man" or "the tree killed the man." The subjects *fulmina* in the *Leges Regiae* and *dérevo* in Tolstoy, respectively, are neuter and occur in the instrumental case, *hominem fulminibus occisit* and *čelovéka dérevom ubílo*, literally 'it killed the man by bolts (or by the tree)'.

Hittite, by the same token, has taken the instrumental ablative ending in -*anza* (as in *nepisanza* 'from heaven'), has reinterpreted it from paradigmatic to derivational status (as if it were an animate nominative -*nt*- stem), and uses it to form transitive-verb subjects of neuter nouns: *nu-wa-mu apāt wātar pesten . . . witenanza ēshar . . . parkunuzi* 'give me that water . . . water cleanses blood(shed)', going back to an impersonal 'by water it cleanses bloodshed' (i.e., 'by water there is a cleansing of bloodshed'). Similarly *ēshar* 'blood' itself, when subject, shows up in the construction *nu Hatti-ya apās ishananza arha namma zinnesta* 'this blood has furthermore finished off Hatti', literally 'by this blood it has put an end to Hatti' (i.e., 'by this blood it has come to an end for Hatti'). The very fact that these so-called animate derivatives in -*ant*- practically never occur outside their nominative subject position reinforces this interpretation and allows a glimpse into the functioning of early Indo-European syntax. It does incidentally strengthen the speculations of André Vaillant, A. N. Savčenko, and others, that the Indo-European nominative ending -*s*, both singular and plural, is identical in origin with the ablative (-genitive) -*s* as a primitive ergative agent case.

Hittite is also a bona fide marvel of Indo-European noun formation, not only in the usual inventory of vowel and consonant stems but also in the preservation and proliferation of the *r*/*n* heteroclites. These strange neuter nouns, with an *r* stem variant in the nominative-accusative and an oblique stem ending in -*n*-, are clearly Common Indo-European, for they persist in relics from Vedic *ásr̥g* 'blood' and *yákr̥t* 'liver' to Greek *éar* and *hêpar* to Latin *aser* and *iēcur*, and from Greek *pûr* and *húdōr* to English *fire* and *water*. Hittite not only has *ēshar*, *pah̬h̬ur*, and *watar* but also a whole system of verbal nouns using the suffixes -*tar*, -*sar*, and -*war* with such declension. That these are not isolated aberrations is clear from the fact that Indo-Iranian and Greek have derived quite a few of their infinitives from frozen oblique cases of the same types of nouns. Benveniste was the first to exploit these formations for the origins of Indo-European noun formation in 1935, and justly so; they are among the choicest gifts of Hittite to Indo-European linguistics.

In the pronominal declension we need only remind ourselves of the extraordinary similarities of the interrogative-relative-indefinite *kuis*, *kuiskuis*, *kuisa*, *kuiski*, *kuwat* /kʷat/, *kuwapi* /kʷabi/ to the Latin *quis*, *quisquis*, *quisque*, *quisquam*, *quod*, and *(c)ubi*; this set can only be common inheritance, in Anatolian and Italic respectively, from Early Indo-European. As is usual in pronominal systems, rank innovations tend to coexist with pieces of extreme archaism.

The verb is where the voice of the Indo-Hittitologist has been most often heard in the land. He simply cannot derive anything like that from standard Indo-European, and in a simplistic application of family-tree reasoning he jumps from a primary to a secondary degree of relationship. We already saw that basic root verbs are perfectly matched with Vedic or Lithuanian. Marked nonthematic present stems such as nasal-infixed ones are present in nonproductive fashion, as in Sanskrit (Hittite *sarnikzi* 'he repairs' beside Latin *sarcit*).

The main surprise has been the paucity of ordinary vowel-thematic stems of the trite Sanskrit *bhárati* type, which occur only in some derivative categories (presents with *-ye- and duratives with *-ske- suffix). Inordinate efforts have been expended on explaining the glottogonic sources of thematic conjugation, as in Calvert Watkins' *Geschichte der indogermanischen Verbalflexion*, largely on the basis of venturesome forays into the Hittite -*hi* conjugation and the mediopassive voice alike. Even a summary report on all that has been cogitated, assumed, argued, and advanced in this line, ever since Kuryłowicz and Christer Stang started comparing the origins of the perfect tense and the middle voice in the early 1930s, would require a sizable monograph. To my thinking a good deal of this has been misplaced ingenuity.

In understanding the Hittite verb, neither glottogony nor agonizing over discrepancies vis-à-vis the Greco-Indic type of verbal system is called for. The Indo-European perfect tense and mediopassive diathesis appear indeed to have their joint source in some kind of stative formation with its own set of markers, typologically comparable to the Semitic stative (earlier called "permansive"), but it is misguided to assume that Hittite somehow displays this primordiality in the raw. Rather the Hittite verbal system should be looked at with a cold eye in terms of individual innovation and orginality, the way we do with Italic, Germanic, or Tocharian.

The -*hi* conjugation is a stative perfect whose present-tense meaning is emphasized by the addition of the deictic -*i* by analogy of the normal present: just as IE **woyde* (Vedic *véda*, Greek *oîde*, or Gothic *wait*) means 'he is enjoying insight', Hittite *ārki* reflects **orĝhe*, 'he is engaged in coition'. In Luwian, without the re-marking by present deixis, the same formation has become preterital. The mediopassive, deponential or other, directly resembles the rest of Indo-European mediopassives, both marginal and central: *kitta* 'he lies' exactly matches Greek *keîto* or Sanskrit *śéta*, but an earlier level, without the *t* that smacks of active-ending analogy, is found in *arga* from **orĝho* 'he cohabits' or in *kisa* 'he becomes' from **geso* (cognate with Latin *geritur*). With the facultative addition of the increment -*ri*, thus *kisari*, Hittite joins those marginal dialects (Italic, Celtic, Tocharian) that have made a virtue of the *r*-increment in most forms of the mediopassive present, unlike Indo-Iranian, Greek, and Gothic, where its disuse prevailed. Here again Hittite is right at the crossroads of cross-Indo-European developments and not some strange cousin once or twice removed.

As regards the absence of formal moods in Hittite, let us be reminded that the Indo-European subjunctive was a brittle construct built on thematic-vowel oppositions only, one that crashed in Post-Vedic Sanskrit, survived only in broken-down uniformity in Greek, and yielded some future-tense elements in Latin. Its absence from Hittite is no more surprising than from Slavic or Germanic. The optative is more problematic, being otherwise attested from practically every other branch of Indo-European, from Celtic to Tocharian. But the injunctival use of the indicative (rather than imperative) in Hittite prohibition shows archaic syntactic patterning. The hypertrophy of third-person imperatives, on the one hand, and of modal particles in subordinate clauses, on the other (as in Greek), largely compensates for the formal suppression of both optative and subjunctive.

Much of the above is neither new nor original, but it needs to be stressed over and over. Sir William's basic postulate has well taken care of Hittite, with little modification.

Leaving linguistics and turning to Hittite culture, it is noteworthy that traits common to Indo-European peoples distinguish the Hittites from their Near Eastern neighbors. For example, although circumcision was known, it was not a standard custom. A medical text (*KUB* XLIV 61 Rs. 24–27) makes this explicit: "If a man is not circumcised, the physician forces back the foreskin, applies salve, and then draws the foreskin forward. Until the patient gets well, he keeps salving it." Thus this Egypt-centered religious and cultural practice, unknown among the original speakers of Indo-European and Uralic languages, had made at best limited inroads in second-millennium Anatolia.

As regards Hittite nonmaterial culture at large and religion in particular, the second Jonesian postulate comes into play. Indo-European comparative mythology, run into the ground during the nineteenth century, has enjoyed a measure of rehabilitation in the latter half of the twentieth. Here the subdivisions differ, for linguistic history and cultural evolution or archaism are not necessarily congruent. What can be reconstructed of Indo-European myth and religion is built largely on Indo-Iranian, Roman, and Germanic bases, thus on East-West polarities quite irrespective of any late dialectal Center. Here the nature of documents and traditions tends to outweigh the grammatical character of their linguistic vehicles, although the lexical element may indeed be of paramount importance.

At first glance the Hittite material may not look promising. In fact it is a commonplace that Hittite offers relatively little for comparative Indo-European mythology, that its exuberant, hypersyncretic polytheism reflects in the main the interaction of autochthonous Anatolian Hattic traditions with successive Hurrian and other Mesopotamian overlays. The storm god of Hatti and the sun goddess of Arinna assimilated to the Hurrian Teshub and Hebat, and the myths of Illuyankas and Telipinus, let alone such imported goods as the Ullikummi and Gilgamesh epics, are not data that endear Hittite to the Indo-European mythologist. As in the case of Greek tradition, one has to look beyond all the new syntheses and discover the underlay.

Even then it is wise to eschew genetic comparison with the adjacent branches of Indo-European, the Greek and the Armenian, both of which have themselves been feeding at the immemorial Anatolian trough. If the funeral rites for Patroklos and Hektor in the *Iliad* seem

to follow to the letter the mortuary texts of Hittite royalty, if almost
every event in Achilles' sports promotion at the same cremation can
be matched in the Hittite texts, and if Zeus's use of fate scales to
settle the doom of heroes replicates the ceremonial Hittite weighing
of the lives of royalty, all such matter belongs in an Anatolian, not
an Indo-European cultural sphere.

Nevertheless this is an aspect worthy of serious study, for to that
extent Hittite participates in the roots of Classical Greek culture. Hesiodic theogony derives from the same Hurrian sources as the Hittite
Kumarbi-Ullikummi literature. Homeric poetry, composed in Asia
Minor, reverberates uncannily to Hittite models. In Hittite law the
wronged party in a land deal sues the culprit before the sun god by
saying, "He has planted my scale in the earth." When Zeus's scales
tip against one party, that one's lot is said to sink to the earth. When
Agamemnon in his "Trojan oath" jointly invokes Zeus and Helios,
he echoes Hittite tandem worship of the storm god and the sun god
(you swore by the gods of the opposite party, in this case the Trojans of Asia Minor).

Poetic similes match: Hittite: "Even as the wind makes chaff fly and
carries it over the sea, let it sweep away blood-defilement"; Greek:
"As a gale wind scatters a heap of dry chaff and spreads it all over,
the monster-wave smashes Odysseus' raft." Here the attentive reader
might interject: "Wait a minute! What business do the Hittites have
with maritime similes, being centered on a high plateau in the inte-
rior of a subcontinent?" The answer is that there is other cogent evidence of a one-time Hittite homeland on a littoral. Whereas in Hurrian, Mesopotamian, and even Egyptian sources the sun is said to
rise from the mountains and even in later Iranian-based lore the sun
god Mithras was born from a rock, in the Hittite sun prayers the sun
god of heaven rises from the sea. The name of this god in Old Hittite is Sius, etymologically identical with Vedic Dyaus and Greek
Zeus, showing a fusion of day god and sun god, rather than sky god
and storm god as in Greek and Roman tradition. The Luwian name
of the sun god, Tiwaz, equals the Hittite word for 'day', *siwaz*. This
tradition points to an eastern littoral, which can hardly be other than
the Caucasian shore of the Caspian. The additional tradition of the
solar deity in water, *Sius weteni*, reminds one of the Iranian myth of
the solar nimbus, *xvarnah*, being guarded in the mythical Sea of Vou-
rukaša by the deity Apam Napāt 'Child of Waters'. This god, cognate with the Vedic Apā́m Nápāt, the Roman Neptūnus, and the Irish
Nechtan, is the archetypal "fire-in-water" deity with a solar tinge,

the Vedic *svâr* of Apắm Napāt. The Old Iranian form *Naptya* seems to survive in the Greek loanword *náphtha* as the quintessential fire-in-water substance, raising visions of oil seepage and oil flares on the shores of the Caspian during the early stages of Hittite and Indo-European migrations.

For all their syncretistic overlays of Akkadian Šamaš-motifs, the Hittite sun hymns have other features of Indo-European significance. Animals are implied to have divinely relevant souls and personalities, for the sun god is said to judge dog, pig, and beasts of the field along with mankind; we may compare the Iranian "Bovine's Lament," where the Soul of the Ox cries out to Zarathuštra against the cruelty of warriors who wish to butcher it. There was a comprehensive Hittite term for gods' creatures (*siunas ḫuidar*), *ḫuidar* being a neuter collective noun distinct from *antuḫsatar* 'mankind'. In addition to 'beasts of the field' (*gimras ḫuidar*) it denoted 'critters of the soil' (*tagnas ḫuidar*), 'creatures of the sea' (*arunas ḫuidar*), and specifically a wolfpack (*ḫuednas pankur = ulipnas pankur* 'wolf's family'). This heteroclitic noun has a clear Indo-European cognate in the Old Norse *vitnir*, which can be reconstructed as **Hwedniyos* and refers to the cosmic wolf Fenrir in Eddic poetry: *vitni at vega* 'to fight the *vitnir*'. It is also used in kennings such as *hróðvitnir* 'slaver-creature' for 'wolf' (the chained Fenrir's slaver formed the river Vón), and *grafvitnir* 'grave-creature' for 'snake'. Whatever the root meaning, the ancient noun type itself assures a very basic Early Indo-European term and concept, preserved only in Anatolia and Iceland.

The Hittite Law Code is a treasure trove for the searching Indo-Europeanist. Since we hit upon the topic of wolves and Anatolian-Norse isoglosses and isothemes, let these features also serve as cases in point. In paragraph 37 of the code, the abductor of a woman, by killing more than one member of a rescue posse, forfeits the right to wergeld. This means that he cannot offer *sarnikzel* 'reparations'; he cannot do what Roman law calls *damna sarcire* 'make good damages'; instead he is pronounced an outlaw by the words "Thou art become a wolf," *zik-wa ulipnas kistat*. There are, to be sure, various theriomorphic or bestiovestite functionaries in Hittite texts, called *pesnes ulipnes* 'wolf-men' or *pesnes ḫartagges* 'bear-men', as well as 'dog-men' and 'lion-men', but here the meaning is different. Both kinds of usage are uncannily paralleled in Old Norse tradition. Martial ecstatics went by the names *úlfheðnar* 'wolf-shapes' or *berserkir* 'bear-shirts', and a man outlawed for murder was a *morðvargr*, *vargr* being a synonym for *úlfr* 'wolf'. But *vargr* comes by this sense secondarily, as seen in the parallel term *vargr í véum* 'temple-robber' and in Old English *wearg*, Old German *warg*, which means 'robber' or 'criminal'. Similarly Gothic *launawargs*, which translates Greek *akháristos* 'ingrate', is literally 'reward-robber'. The Proto-Germanic **wargaz* can be reconstructed as either an Indo-European **Hworĝhós* 'strangler' or **Hwórĝhos* 'strangled one, gallowsbird, rascal'; ambivalent poetic (and legal) justice is implicit in the accentual opposition that Germanic has regrettably neutralized. The root is that of German *würgen* or Lithuanian *veřžti* 'constrict, throttle, strangle'. A nominative derivative with an *l*-suffix is present in Old Norse *virgill* and Old English *wurgil* meaning 'rope' and in Old German *würgel* 'strangler'. Hittite has also a cognate in the noun *ḫurkil*, which enables us to close the semantic circle and tighten the noose around meaningful Indo-European legal antiquities.

The term *ḫurkil* in the Law Code and elsewhere designates a man's illegal sexual relations with bovines and sheep and with a variety of relatives (mother, daughter, son, sister, stepmother, brother's wife, mother-in-law, wife's sister, female cousin, and so forth). It involves somewhat selective sanction against bestiality and incest. Equines are explicitly exempted from the ban, which recalls the fact that bestiality with horses occurred in ancient royal rituals from India to Ireland. The Hittite perpetrator "does not become priest," a statement that seems to place the practice squarely and restrictively in the warrior class. The potential victims of statutory rape are all female, except for the son sodomized by the father. Rape as such does not seem to be the target of this legislation; what matters is the degree of kinship and "status," thus factors of incest and perhaps miscegenation (unfree and "deportee" women are explicitly left to the mercies of the Hittite male). Everything is formulated from the vantage point of the man. Nothing is said from the standpoint of the passive partner in sodomy, and this silence is meaningful, for homosexual rape, statutory or other, is not dealt with from the bugger's perspective either. The whole subject, apart from its incestuous aspect, clearly did not interest Hittite legislation.

Yet it may matter in another context involving *ḫurkil*. Interspersed in one of the innumerable ritual texts we find a narrative (*KUB* XII 63 Vs. 21–34) that includes a dialogue between self-styled 'men of *ḫurkil*' (*ḫurkilas pesnes*) and the "house" of the storm god, whose bidding they are ready to perform. They are told to shorten long roads, lengthen short ones, lower high mountains and heighten low ones, catch a wolf by the hand and a lion with the knee, and bring a snake to the royal tribunal to be judged. Upon their return the men confess their failure on every point, and the story concludes that "the case was aggravated."

It sounds like a folk tale about overly confident ogre types, something like the Norse giants who come to grief in their dealings with gods. But nothing indicates supernatural status. Some of the tasks are absurd in the literal sense and may rather be figurative and proverbial ("lengthen short roads" = "go the extra mile"; "lower high mountains" = "leave no stone unturned"), in short, "do your darnedest" with the more feasible feats like catching wolves and lions. But the overearnest fellows take them literally, are fast demoralized when the impossibility sinks in, and report back as failures. They are clearly depicted as ineffectual and ludicrous.

In legal terms the wages of *hurkil* was normally death, subject to the king's discretion and sometimes local option in border areas. If we put together the legal meaning of "capital sex crime" and the etymological sense of "strangulation," the *hurkilas pesnes* seem to have been some kind of sex-related miscreants fit to be strung up but given a judicial chance to redeem themselves, to show their mettle by strangling animals as a form of substitute atonement. They were the opposite of macho men, thus effeminates, and most probably passive homosexuals. Although the Law Code is silent on the topic, it is possible that this old tale resonates with echoes of ancient customary law with respect to catamites.

Here again Old Germanic data support the conclusion. Those societies harbored murderous contempt for submissive partners in pederasty. Tacitus describes how cowardly, unwarlike, and bodily heinous persons were plunged into the mud of marshes and covered with hurdles as a form of suffocation. The hundreds of throttled Iron Age corpses found preserved in Danish and German peatbogs offer grisly confirmation. The key term for this kind of man in Old Norse was *argr* from IE *$\acute{o}r\hat{g}hos$ 'fuckee', vs. *$or\hat{g}h\acute{o}s$ 'fucker', with the same accent opposition as in *$Hw\acute{o}r\hat{g}hos$ vs. *$Hwor\hat{g}h\acute{o}s$, 'strangled one' vs. 'strangler'; *argr* and *vargr* are in fact attested rhyme pairs in Old Icelandic, choice terms of aggravated obloquy. But the real clincher to the Hittite tale is in the story that Ammianus Marcellinus (31.9.5) tells of the Germanic tribe of the Taifali:

"They are a shameful lot, so mired in depraved practices that among them young boys are coupled with the men in a bond of unspeakable cohabitation. . . . Yet if someone, upon growing up, alone catches a boar or kills a huge bear, he is freed from the stain of unchastity."

Catching a wolf and lion in Anatolia, a boar and bear in Germania, potentially vindicating *ḫurkilas pesnes* from penal retribution in one instance, rehabilitating a catamite *colluvione incesti* in the other— these are hardly trivial accordances. They are strong evidence of a common cultural, in this instance Indo-European, heritage.

This kind of close accordance between Hittite and a widely separated tradition, with "features of resemblance, too strong to have been accidental," truly shows the genuine Indo-European underpinnings of the oldest layers of Hittite tradition. No less than in language, Hittite myth and law are in their origins direct descendants of William Jones's "common source," which indeed "no longer exists" but which we are increasingly raising from oblivion.

Indo-European Religion and the · Indo-European Religious Vocabulary

EDGAR C. POLOMÉ

The study of Indo-European religion is as old as the study of the Indo-European languages. The nineteenth-century scholars who reconstructed the ancestral proto-language of the speakers of the languages whose close relationship to each other Sir William Jones had emphasized in his famous pronouncement at the Royal Asiatic Society in Calcutta on February 2, 1786, were also concerned with the culture and religion of the original users of this Indo-European mother tongue. The "discovery" of the Sanskrit texts by western Europe provided materials close to what was believed to be the conceptual world of the Indo-European *Urvolk*, and the renewal of the science of etymology made it possible to retrieve the very names of its deities.

On the model of Skt. *Dyauḥ*, Gk. Ζεύς, Lat. *Jup(p)iter*, and Gmc. **Tīwaz*, the most ingenious explanations were proposed for the original designation of a number of gods, whereas some scholars like Max Müller gave free play to their imagination to concoct corresponding myths. Whatever theory prevailed in ethnology served as a basis for the elucidation of Indo-European religion: because Vedic imagery resorted widely to nature, the ancient Indian gods were interpreted as mere nature gods, whose myths symbolized their functional activity, and so the release of the heavenly cows by Indra, for example, represented the thunder triggering the monsoon rains (de Vries 1977: 80–81). Adalbert Kuhn, presumably the founder of comparative mythology, focused in particular on this thunder mythology, whereas others considered the gods as personifications of the major heavenly bodies. The tradition of "nature mythology" maintained itself throughout the nineteenth century with scholars like Michel Bréal, Tito Vignoli, Albert Réville, and Hermann Oldenberg (de Vries 1961: 202–253, esp. 238–247).

Convinced that prehistoric man reasoned out his beliefs, some scholars, however, advanced speculative rationalistic explanations of the origin of religion: Edward Burnett Tylor postulated the survival of the individual soul after death and the existence of other spirits (including the deities) as the basic tenets of *animism*, and the British anthropologist Andrew Lang tried to apply Tylor's views to the explanation of the complex religious systems of tribal societies, pointing also to the irrationality of some mythical elements. Rejecting the conception of Herbert Spencer that the gods may have evolved from ghosts, Lang appears as a precursor of Father Wilhelm Schmidt with the idea of original monotheism because he believed monotheism preceded animism, which would be a "corruption and degeneration" of the original concept (de Vries 1977: 110–115).

In an article published in *Folk-Lore* in 1900, R. R. Marett, however, introduced a different preanimistic hypothesis: for him, the ever-present magical or mystical power that gods and spirits share alike and that the Melanesians call *mana* is the most ancient belief to inspire awe in man. Sir James George Frazer focused more on the way of thinking than on the emotions of early man: describing magic as a kind of primitive science, Frazer considered three stages in man's intellectual development: (1) the magical period, characterized by early attempts to manipulate nature; (2) religion, sprung from the realization that there are higher powers transcending nature with which man can directly interact; and (3) science. To illustrate his views he collected an impressive hoard of ethnographic material in his thirteen-volume *Golden Bough* (1890–1915), although he never managed to place his data within the proper cultural framework (de Waal Malefijt 1968: 53–55).

All these views had a considerable impact on the discussion of Indo-European myths and religion: the scope of the "nature myths" was broadened by Wilhelm Mannhardt, who stressed the importance of vegetation cults and agrarian rituals and emphasized the survival of myths in folklore, in his application of these views to his analysis of Germanic myths, which he traces back to an Indo-European source reflected by the Vedic tradition. In a typical Tylorian vein, Elard Hugo Meyer describes the Scandinavian pantheon in his *Mythologie der Germanen* (1903) as a reflex of "uralte religiöse Naturpoesie, die die Menschheit mit einer zaubervollen Märchenwelt umgab."[1] For the Swedish poet-scholar Viktor Rydberg, the creation and development of myths does not result from speculations on meteorological and

---

[1] [very] ancient religious nature poetry which surrounds mankind with a fairy-tale world full of magic.

other natural phenomena but from the conceptualization of the divinities as personal characters in the epical fight between chaos and order in the cosmos evidenced by the traditions of the Indo-Iranian and Germanic peoples (de Vries 1961: 248–253). But even when Indo-European myth is examined from the perspective of nineteenth-century ethnology, its interpretation remains fraught with romantic ideas: in an early work, Leo Frobenius combines symbolic thought, anthropomorphization, *mana*, apriorisms, and the like to account for the prevalence of sun myths: the daily sight of the glorious rebirth of the sun, drowned at nightfall in the ocean, fills man with awe and reminds him of the holiness and eventful career of the sun god! The persistence of such views accounts for the still dominant naturalistic interpretation in the two-volume *Arische Religion* of Leopold von Schroeder (1914–1916).

With an increasing awareness of the inadequacy of the too clear-cut theories of the previous era about magic, animism, and other elementary forms of belief, the twentieth century sorted out the views of pioneers with new approaches like W. Robertson Smith and Émile Durkheim, who had brought a sociological perspective into the study of religion; it scrutinized Lévy-Bruhl's concept of "prelogical mentality" in the light of new achievements in anthropology; it examined and criticized the assumptions of Freud and other promoters of a psychoanalytic interpretation of myth and the foundations of religion; with Rudolf Otto, it attempted to apply phenomenology to the study of religion; and with Max Weber, it tried to correlate religion with all the other aspects of culture.

That this increasing complexity of the field (of religion) has had a direct impact on the study of Indo-European religion is obvious from its development in the twentieth century: in France, where the influence of Durkheim and his school was prevailing, the linguist Antoine Meillet proclaimed in 1907 that the Vedic god *Mitra* is nothing but the divinized "contract," and in his conclusion to a lecture on Indo-European religion he stated that "les exemples qui ont été donnés suffisent pour révéler le caractère du dieu indo-européen: c'est un fait naturel ou social auquel on attache une importance particulière. Le dieu n'est pas une personne ayant un nom propre; c'est le fait lui-même, c'est son essence, sa force intime" (1948: 334).[2] The sociologist Marcel Mauss, in particular, exerts a lifelong influ-

[2] Enough examples have been provided to reveal the character of the Indo-European deity: it is a natural or social entity to which particular importance is given. The god is not a person with a proper name; it is the entity itself, its essence, its inmost power.

ence on French Indo-Europeanists with his essays on the nature and
function of the sacrifice (1899), the general theory of magic (1904),
the gift (1925), and other methodologically magistral writings. The
anthropologist Claude Lévi-Strauss provides a new structural framework for the analysis of myth (1955); and the linguist Émile Benveniste identifies the underlying tripartite structure of Indo-Iranian society (1932), strengthening the views that Georges Dumézil—like
himself, a student of Meillet—starts elaborating in the early 1930s
upon the trifunctional hierarchization of the Indo-European pantheon (Littleton 1982: 49–53).

In Germany, where the two syntheses by Herman Hirt and Sigmund Feist of the current knowledge about the Indo-Europeans had
appeared in the early twentieth century and where Alfons Nehring
had completed a second enlarged edition of Otto Schrader's *Reallexikon der indogermanischen Altertumskunde*, the study of Indo-European
religion was making a fresh start after discarding the obsolete views
of the nineteenth century, a renewal illustrated in particular by the
works of Hermann Güntert: *Kalypso* (1919) and *Der arische Weltkönig
und Heiland* (1923). Unfortunately, in the 1930s this progress was
stymied by the politically biased sidetracking of Indo-European and
Germanic studies to the service of an ideology. Thus, the only article
devoted to religion in the monumental *Hirt-Festschrift* in 1936 provides a typical example: "Familie, Sippe und Volk [sind] Urtatsachen
ewigen Willens,"[3] and the alleged "indogermanisches Gesetz von
der Reinhaltung des Blutes"[4] is described as "höchste Verantwor-
tung gegenüber einem von der Gottheit anvertrauten Gute" (Hauer
1936: 198).[5] A more traditional scholarly approach to the problem
is reflected, however, by the collective volume published the same
year in the Wiener Beiträge zur Kulturgeschichte und Linguistik:
Die Indogermanen und Germanenfrage: Neue Wege zu ihrer Lösung, which
opens with a 200-page monograph of Alfons Nehring on Indo-European culture and the problem of the original homeland.

Deriving from the nineteenth-century "discovery" of *mana*, the
concept of a world pervaded by a somatic magic power in which everything participates to a varying degree appears to have had a considerable impact on the views of the German-trained Indian scholar

---

[3] Family, lineage, and people are fundamental facts of an eternal will. (This literal
translation does not actually reflect the intent, which is to indicate that blood relationship is the *foundation* of society and reflects an *"eternal intent."*
[4] The Indo-European law of keeping the blood pure.
[5] Highest responsibility versus a divinely entrusted possession.

R. N. Dandekar, who considers "the all-penetrating magical potence" *asu* as most central in Vedic religious theology (1971: 253). The same idea of a cosmos filled with tremendous powers is elaborated by the Dutch Indologist Jan Gonda (1960: 26–47), whereas the Dutch classicist H. Wagenvoort devotes his study on Roman dynamism to the examination of the reflexes of the concept of *mana* in Roman language and behavior.

It is obvious that the twentieth century was searching for new solutions based on the seminal ideas of the previous period: While, in 1896, Usener still represents Max Müller's view that the development of personal gods was a linguistic process, Ernst Cassirer in 1923 associates the appearance of the individualized deities with the ability of the human mind to derive generally valid concepts from sets of separate single occurrences. To logical reasoning, which structures the world scientifically, Cassirer opposes mythical thinking, which correlates things and assumes their coincidence by participation in the same essence, which enables man to identify himself with his totemic animal. U. von Wilamowitz-Moellendorff 1931 insists on this contrast between λόγος and μῦθος and describes the gods as real entities, which are the object of a cult; myth is largely the product of poetic imagination, and it was originally nonexistent in Rome and in the Germanic world, as it presumably also was in Indo-European times! A deeper understanding of basic concepts is therefore promoted by the phenomenologists, such as G. van der Leeuw 1928, who stresses the contrast between our linear concept of time and the cyclical time of preliterate societies. Mircea Eliade has further developed this idea to explain why the concept of history is alien to early societies, where each ritualized process is merely a reenactment of an initial paradigm, the repetition of an archetype. Along these lines, Rudolf Otto breaks new ground with his detailed analysis of the idea of the holy (1917): his magisterial, though controversial, dichotomy of the sacred stimulated discussion and further probing of the problem, namely, in Germanic by Walter Baetke 1942 and in Indo-European by Émile Benveniste (1969: 179–207).

In the beginning of the twentieth century Wilhelm Wundt endeavored to establish the ethnopsychology of the previous century on solid foundations. Wundt described myth as the product of man's mythopoeic creativity based on actual experience. If myth tells how man sees reality through the prism of his imagination, religion derives from a mythical perception of the cosmos to help man cope with the facts of life. But more than Wundt's *Völkerpsychologie*, depth psychology influenced the thinking on Indo-European religion: Sigmund Freud's focus on the Oedipus complex became the starting point of the psychoanalytic examination of a number of myths, but his rather lopsided approach often led to implausible aberrant explanations. Carl G. Jung 1941 provided a better insight into the structure of the unconscious, and his definition of "archetypes" as constantly reoccurring patterns in myth as well as in the psyche of modern man proved quite productive in interpretation of myth and religious symbolism, as appears from his fruitful collaboration with the classicist Karl Kerényi and the work of his disciples, such as Erich Neumann, with his penetrating analysis of the archetype of the "Great Mother" (1955).

The study of Indo-European religion was hardly influenced by twentieth-century theories of religion developed by cultural and social anthropologists such as the British functionalists Alfred Reginald Radcliffe-Brown and Bronislaw Malinowski or by American fieldworkers studying American Indian cultures and religion such as Franz Boas and his students, for example, Leslie Spier and Paul Radin, and Robert Lowie and Ruth Fulton Benedict, who resorted to psychology as their major tool to explain human behavior. Although some American anthropologists focused on the study of religion in complex literate societies (like Clifford Geertz) or analyzed symbolism in religion and myth (like Victor W. Turner), their target culture was not Indo-European, and their approach had little impact on the thinking of Indo-Europeanists. Different was the case of the structuralists like Edmund R. Leach in Great Britain and Claude Lévi-Strauss in France, but the renewal of Indo-European comparative mythology and religion was nevertheless to come from another direction.

After trying his hand at the reconstruction of Indo-European myth along rather traditional lines, Georges Dumézil had formulated by the eve of World War II the essential principles of his functional tripartition of the Indo-European pantheon in (1) sovereign gods, (2) warrior gods, and (3) fertility deities presiding over wealth and health. These ideas matured in the late 1940s, when Paris was an intellectual center where Mircea Eliade was publishing his challenging *Traité d'histoire des religions* (1949) with a programmatic preface by Georges Dumézil and where Indo-European studies were experiencing a new blossoming under the leadership of Émile Benveniste. Discarding the Mannhardtian "naturalistic" explanations ascribing religious entities to the sacralization of natural phenomena, Dumézil rejected as decisively any recourse to *mana* to account for the holy and the numinous in the Indo-European world. Trained as a linguist, Dumézil had started his career with studies on onomastic correspondences: ἀμβροσία/*amṛtá-* in *Le festin d'immortalité* (1924), Κένταυροι/*Gandharvá-* in *Le problème des Centaures* (1929), Οὐρανός/ *Varuṇa* (1934), and *flāmen/brahman* (1935), but he soon recognized that purely etymological comparisons prove rather disappointing upon closer scrutiny. Therefore, in the late 1930s, Dumézil deliberately gave up these efforts to link Frazerian interpretations with linguistic data and embraced the sociological approach promoted by Marcel Mauss, the Sinologist Marcel Granet, and the Celticist H. Hubert (Rivière 1979: 12–19).

Georges Dumézil's method consists essentially in gathering all the available data about the religious concept under consideration and in systematically organizing this *complete* "dossier" into a structured complex, without eliminating any of the discrepant elements. The resulting documentation is then gauged against the prevailing ideology of the relevant society to determine the essential relationships that the data denote within the system, either through myths that dramatize them or through rites that actualize them (Rivière 1979: 21–22; Polomé 1984: 19–20). Over more than four decades this approach has enabled Dumézil to develop a body of comparative material that has put a refreshing new life in the study of Indo-European religion. Often attacked for his more sweeping interpretations, Dumézil has indefatigably defended his positions through the years with vigorous argument and sharp criticism of the flaws in the views of his adversaries, but those long polemical debates with Paul Thieme on the original meaning of the Old Indic root *ari-* have contributed considerably to clarifying difficult problems, as have Dumézil's controversies with Jan Gonda about dual deities and triads of gods in the Veda.

Although the assumption of a pervasive trifunctional pattern throughout all the aspects of Indo-European religion and mythology remains open to a number of serious objections, it cannot be denied that it has proved to be a most productive hypothesis: it has made it possible for Georges Dumézil and his disciples to open new avenues for the interpretations of the Vedic and Old Indic epic tradition, to bring Scandinavian and Celtic myths into a broader perspective, to demonstrate that the legendary early history of Rome was actually Indo-European myth in a euhemerized form, and to throw more light on the way of thinking and on the processes of conceptualization of the Indo-Europeans. Besides his own penetrating analysis of

numerous myths and divine figures, it will be to Dumézil's lasting
credit to have brought new depth and breadth to the study of Indo-
European religion and to have steered it away from the lopsided
naturalistic and primitivistic approaches inherited from the nineteenth century.

Even those who choose to stand aloof from Dumézil's views must
acknowledge that he has clarified considerably the problems relating
to sovereign deities and warrior gods, even if he has failed to cope
as thoroughly with the entities he assigned to the "third function"
of fertility, health and wealth. And when Bruce Lincoln 1981, for
example, took his distance from the Dumézilian system to deal with
the earliest Indo-European myths in the footsteps of Hermann Güntert on some new paths drawn by British anthropologists like E. E.
Evans-Pritchard, he actually based his argument on the socioeco-
nomic relations between the priestly class and the warrior class as
defined by Georges Dumézil and Stig Wikander 1938, in the perspective of a Maussian theory of the sacrifice!

A number of attempts have been made in recent years to summarize what we actually know about the religion of the Indo-Europeans
after decades of critical research and comparative study: in her synthesis of Zoroastrianism, Mary Boyce (1979: 3–16) sketches a picture
of the "old religion" of the Indo-Iranians, which had its roots in the
pastoral Stone Age culture of their Indo-European ancestors. She
points out that it was focused on rituals such as daily offerings to the
water and the fire and on prescriptions such as ritual purity, respect
for life, proper handling and consecration of the sacrificial animals,
and sharing of the sacrificial meat. She believes that they worshiped
several types of gods:

- Cult gods: Fire, the Waters, the divinized "Soul of the Bull" (Avestan gəuš urvan-), and the divinized juice of the "soma" plant
  (some kind of Ephedra?)
- Nature gods: personifying Sky and Earth, Sun and Moon, the rain-
  bringing wind (Avestan Vāta), and the breath of life (Avestan Vāyu)
- "Abstract" gods: such as those presiding over pledges, namely,
  *Varuṇa, literally 'binding promise, oath' (from the IE root *wer-
  'tie, bind'), and *Mitra, literally 'agreement between two parties,
  covenant' (from the IE root *mey- 'exchange').

The "abstract" gods received the title *asura- 'lord', and when the
Indo-Iranians became acquainted with the chariot, the Asuras be-

came charioteers and the zoomorphic god of victory, the wild boar *
Vr̥tragʰna- (Avestan *Vərəθrayna*), was replaced by the virile reckless heavy-drinking warrior Indra. Mary Boyce also considers that
the lofty concepts associated with **r̥ta* 'cosmic order' had already
evolved in the Stone Age and that some of the less moral elements
in the early aristocratic faith of priests and warriors, geared to obtaining prosperity in this world and bliss and salvation in the hereafter through generous offerings to the gods, were emphasized by
the developing cult of warlike deities like Indra, sponsoring the
ruthless acquisition of wealth and power.

Attractive as this presentation may be, it projects too many elements of later Indo-Iranian situations into the prehistoric society
from which they ultimately developed. It is obvious, indeed, that
there is no evidence outside Indo-Iranian to assume that the Indo-
European ritual practices included the crushing of the *soma* plant and
the consumption of its juice, although the use of intoxicating beverages of some kind may have been part of the cultic process. Nor is
there evidence that the *Gāthic* hymn on the "complaint of the soul
of the ox" attests to a cult rendered to the "Bull's Soul." More likely
it is indicative of the tensions resulting from bovines being carried
off by warriors in cattle raids to be consumed as meat instead of being surrendered to the priests for sacrificial purposes (Lincoln 1981:
140–162).

On the other hand, while it cannot be denied that a number of
celestial and atmospheric phenomena were interpreted by the Indo-
Europeans as manifestations of the divine or "hierophanies," as
Mircea Eliade would call them, it cannot be established that they ever
had a developed lunar cult. But clear traces of a solar cult are found
in the rock carvings of the Scandinavian Bronze Age, and Caesar
still reports that the sun, the moon, and *Vulcānus* (= the fire) were
the main deities of the Germanic people. Perhaps the solution is to
be sought in the direction indicated by Jean Haudry (1985: 74–75):
the Indo-Europeans venerated the luminous sky, its light and transcendence being associated with cosmogony and divine paternity (IE
*dyȇw-pətér-, reflected by Ved. *Dyauṣpitā́*, Grk. Ζεὺς πατήρ, Lat. *Jup-
(p)iter*, and so on). The deities of the diurnal sky (IE **deywós*) were
opposed to the demons of darkness, and Dawn was originally a demoniac being from whose grip the sun had to be released, but later
she became the daughter of the bright sky, driving away the shades
of night (Dumézil 1970: 50–55).

A better synthesis of Indo-European religion is given by Mircea

Eliade (1978: 189–195) when he endorses Dumézil's assumption of hierarchized functional deities besides the celestial and atmospheric hierophanies and when he apparently also defines gods on the basis of their domain rather than of their names: thus Gmc. *βunar[az], Celt. Taranis/Tanaros, Balt. Perkúnas, Slav. Perunъ presumably all represent the same Indo-European thunder god. But perhaps more important than the names of the gods were the activities pertaining to their worship: sacrifice played an important part in the cultic practices, and an extensive vocabulary covers the various aspects and forms of the sacrificial act: libation, ritual meal, fumigation, rite of light (Benveniste 1969: 2.209–231).

It can safely be assumed that the Indo-Europeans ascribed a magicoreligious power to the word, not only in solemn verbal engagements, but also in the chanting of religious formulas. They resorted to special rituals to consecrate space, not only consecrating the enclosure in which they celebrated the cult under the open sky but also "cosmicizing" the territories they occupied: they would consider their settlement as the center of the universe and would ritually renew the world periodically. Moreover, preserving their religious traditions by oral transmission, they must have had an elaborate mythology of which fragments have survived in the myths and beliefs of the various Indo-European peoples.

Reconstructing the mythological lore of the Indo-Europeans is the task of the comparativist, who takes into account all that related disciplines can tell us about the society and institutions of the Indo-Europeans, the varieties of their religious experience (shamanism, mystic experience, sacred awe, and so forth), their major material and spiritual concerns, the ecology of their habitat and its impact on their life and behavior, and so forth. Throughout the development of Indo-European studies, from Adalbert Kuhn and Adolphe Pictet to Émile Benveniste, through Victor Hehn, Otto Schrader, and many others, the work of linguists has shown that in such areas the study of the relevant lexicon is most informative.

In a comprehensive survey of Indo-European civilization published in 1962, Giacomo Devoto stresses that the core Indo-European vocabulary reflects a culture in which the observation of the majestic magnitude of the heavenly vault inspired the first religious feelings: the succession of night and day with the alternation of dark and light, the mysterious atmospheric phenomena of thunder, rain, and snow, the regular cycle of the seasons, and the movements of the two major heavenly bodies regulating time are genuine sources of wonder that early man has translated into magicoreligious speculations.

For the early Indo-European, according to Devoto, the world is dominated by a father figure, **dyeus*, linked essentially with the concept of "light" and not yet closely associated with a Mother Earth figure. The latter, whose vital force is also incarnated in chthonic demons, represents a "corrente di penetrazione sostanzialmente anti-indeuropea" (Devoto 1962: 221).

Examining the areal distribution of the Indo-European lexicon, Devoto then devotes a section to "religion" in which he deals with the concepts of the "pure" and the "holy," with the technicians coping with good and evil spirits, with divination, with the various aspects of the cult, and with the relation between body and soul. This provides him with an opportunity to probe the contrast between the cognates of Lat. *ignis* and Greek πῦρ, the animate gender of the former pointing to the divinized Fire (Ved. *Agniḥ*), whereas the latter, connected with IE **pewH₁-* 'pure' (Lat. *pūrus*), represents the fire as "instrument of purification"—a role that Devoto assigns to it in the incineration rites, which he explains as a means to free the soul totally from the prison of the body (Devoto 1961: 314).

Particularly significant is Devoto's analysis of the cult in which he examines successively (1) the magicoreligious role of speech as it is illustrated in curse, blessing, chanting, and prayer; (2) the elements intervening in the cultic process, mainly water and fire; and (3) the one to whom the cult is addressed—Greek θέος, providing a clue that the original object to which the ritual process was directed must have been a spirit (IE **dʰwes-*). This idea is further backed up by referring to the concept of "vital breath" (IE **anē-* > Lat. *animus* 'spirit, soul, mind') and "fate" as the share allotted to everyone (expressed by the IE roots **(s)mer-* and **ait-*, such as in Greek μοῖρα 'share, fate' and αἶσα 'allotted share, fate'). As a result, Devoto (1961: 312) concludes that Indo-European religion has evolved from a spirit cult into the worship of progressively personalized deities.

The major drawback of Devoto's presentation is that he fails to give sufficient evidence for the alleged religious connotations of a number of terms he discusses: thus he considers Lat. *vacca* 'cow' and Ved. *vaśā* 'heifer' as ritual terms associated with the priestly class simply on the strength of their occurring at the opposite ends of the Indo-European territory and is apparently not aware of the circularity of his reasoning when he assumes the high antiquity of the use of the heifer as a sacrificial animal on the basis of this correspon-

dence (Devoto 1961: 308). In other respects, however, his discussion
of the terms for "sacred" (Grk. ἱερός, G heilig, Lat. săcer, and so
forth), or "prayer" (IE *prek-) paves the way for the thorough analyses of Émile Benveniste.

In his penetrating study of Indo-European society and culture,
Benveniste has devoted the whole third part of the second volume
to religion (1969: 2.177–279), but vocabulary with religious connotations is also discussed in other parts of the work, such as Lat. daps
'sacrificial meal, banquet' (= Arm. tawn 'feast', ON tafn 'sacrificial
animal'; 1969: 1.75–76) and Skt. yoḥ 'welfare', Avest. yaoš 'purification', Lat. iūs 'law' (1969: 1.111–119). Referring to the corresponding
statement of Meillet (1948: 331), Benveniste stresses that comparative
linguistics can supply only little evidence about the religious life of
the Indo-Europeans. The only valid comparison concerning a divine
name leads to the reconstruction of *deywos 'luminous' and 'celestial' (as contrasted to man, the 'earthling' [Lat. homo ~ humus]), but
a number of archaic religious concepts can be clarified through etymological and semantic investigation.

Thus Benveniste illustrates the existence of an original dichotomy
of the "sacred" into "full of divine power" and "forbidden to human
contact" by analyzing the pairs: Avestan spənta- ~ yaoždāta-, Gothic
weihs ~ Runic hailag, Latin săcer ~ sanctus, and Greek ἱερός ~ ἅγιος.
While pointing out that there is no common Indo-European word
for "sacrifice," Benveniste shows the diversity of terms denoting the
sacrificial procedures: libation (Skt. juhoti, Grk. σπένδω), solemn
promise (Lat. uŏuĕō, Grk. εὔχομαι), festive meal (Lat. daps), fumigation (Grk. θύω), and rites of light (Lat. lustrō). These indicate
the specific differences in form and intent in the libations, for example, where "sprinkling" (Grk. λείβω) is contrasted with "pour-
ing" (Grk. χέω) and where Grk. λοιβή is apotropaic and Grk. σπονδή
is propitiatory!

Similarly, Benveniste tries to pinpoint the shades of meaning dif-
ferentiating the various words for "prayer" as they involve devotion
(Grk. [Homer] εὐχωλή), atonement (Grk. [Homer] λιτή), supplica-
tion, and so forth. His examination of omens and portents and his
analysis of the concepts of "religion" and "superstition" remain,
however, essentially confined to the relevant Latin vocabulary (except for a brief note on Greek θρησκεία). His tendency to restrict his
material to the classical languages, with a limited Indo–Iranian in-
put, is actually the major weakness of Benveniste's excellent collec-

tion of studies on religious terms: bringing Germanic and Hittite more into consideration, for example, definitely would have broadened the scope of Benveniste's inquiry and provided more interesting comparisons (cf. Polomé 1975).

In his recent introduction to the Indo–Europeans (1981; ed. 2, 1985), Jean Haudry tackles religion from a different angle: after specifying the major features of Indo–European religion—an ethnically oriented polytheism in which ritual prevails over faith and personalized divine beings control nature and social processes—Haudry (1985: 74–85) proceeds to examine the different types of deities:

- Cosmic gods (Sky and Earth, Sun and Dawn, and the "elements": Fire, Water, Air)
- Gods of the "four circles," that is, the concentric structure of the community described by Benveniste (1969: 1.293–319): family, clan, tribe, and "nation"
- Gods of the "three functions," that is, the Dumézilian three-tiered hierarchization of the social levels: sovereignty, war, and production.

In appendixes he further considers the epic traditions in which the gods live on as heroes and the "twilight of the gods"—for him, their survival in folklore and Christianized form!

Although Haudry's description of the gods of the three functions provides interesting insights into the earliest Hittite pantheon and a brief but challenging discussion of the Baltic and Slavic data, he has to confine himself to generalities as regards the gods of the four circles because no specific Indo-European divine entities can be identified with each of the circles of allegiance within the community. Moreover, when he deals with the "elements," Haudry merely refers to the Indo-Iranian wind god *Vāyu* in connection with the air, whereas he tries to resuscitate the abandoned etymological connection of Skt. *ulkā́* 'meteor' with Lat. *Vulcānus* while positing that IE *wḷkā-no-* designates the 'lord of the fire'. Except for the concept of "sacredness," Haudry does not deal in any detail with Indo-European religious terminology.

The ninth chapter in the second volume of the monumental *Indo-European and the Indo-Europeans* by Thomas V. Gamkrelidze and Vyacheslav V. Ivanov (1984: 800–831) is devoted to the reconstruction of Indo-European rituals and includes other activities of the Indo-European priestly class such as the practice of law and medicine. Its

assumptions are based on an extensive collection of terms relevant
to the "legal, religious, and ritual norms of ancient Indo-European
society."

A systematic review of this vocabulary is particularly instructive:
the basic religious concepts enumerated by Gamkrelidze and Ivanov
reflect long-established correspondences such as Skt. *śrad-dhá̄* 'faith',
Avest. *zrazdā-* 'believe', Lat. *crēdō* '[I] believe', OIr. *cretim* '[I] believe',
for which they uphold (against Benveniste 1969: 1.177–179) the
assumed etymological connection with IE *k̂erd-* 'heart' (in their
system, PIE *k̂ʰr-et'-* reflects the "active class" in the phrase *k̂ʰret'-
dʰeH-* [> *k̂red-dʰē-*], whereas the name of the organ, PIE *k̂ʰer-t'-*
represents the "inactive class"!). For the idea of the "holy," reference is made to Latin *sacer* (: Hitt. *šaklai-* 'rite, sacred custom'), to
Greek ἱερός (: Skt. *iṣiráḥ* 'powerful'), and to Avest. *spənta-*, Lith.
šveñtas, OPruss. *swent-* (in compounds) 'sacred', and OCS *svętъ*
'holy'. In reference to Benveniste, the concept of "eternity" in Indo-
European (as reflected by Skt. *ā́yu-* 'life force', Avest. *āyū* 'life span',
Grk. αἰών 'lifetime', Lat. *aeuum* 'age, century, eternity', Goth. *aiws*
'time, eternity, world') is presented as a "cyclical life force which
moved from one life to another." The same idea of "life force" is
recognized in IE *H̥ner-* 'manly power' (such as Hitt. *innarau̯atar*
'vigor', OIr. *nert* 'strength, vigor', and Grk. ἠνορέη 'manhood,
prowess'). Georges Dumézil has abundantly illustrated the association of IE *H̥ner-* with the second function (= physical strength)
in his study on *ner-* and *uiro-* in Italic (1953).

For religious rites, Gamkrelidze and Ivanov 1984 list a series of
terms that include the following:

- IE *arw-* 'pray, offer prayers' > Hitt. *aru̯aizzi* 'prays, bows', Grk.
  ἀράομαι '[I] pray, offer prayers'. However, Jaan Puhvel (1984:
  183–185) showed that the translation "pray" was erroneous for
  the Hittite word, which is rather to be connected with Lat. *ruō* '[I]
  fall down, collapse'.
- IE *or-* 'supplicate, entreat gods' > Hitt. *ari̯a-* 'determine by oracle'
  (Puhvel 1984: 136–138), Skt. *ā́ryati* 'praises', Lat. *ōrāre* (*deōs*) 'pray
  to the gods; request, say'.
- IE *Hewg ʷʰ-/Hweg ʷʰ-* 'praise solemnly while making sacrifice; offer
  prayer' > Skt. *vāghát-* 'who prays during sacrifice; organizer of sac-
  rifices', Avest. *aog-* 'announce solemnly, pronounce', Grk. εὔχομαι
  '[I] pray, solemnly promise, make a vow', Lat. *uŏuĕō* '[I] solemnly
  promise, make vow, sacrifice'; Gamkrelidze and Ivanov's reason

for positing the initial laryngeal is their assumption that Hitt. *huek-/huk-* 'conjure, pronounce invocation' is related, but the Anatolian term has also been connected with IE *[H]wek*ʷ*- 'word' (Tischler 1983: 255–256). The weakness of both assumptions is that there is no evidence in the other Indo-European dialects to back up the assumption of an initial $*H_2$ or $*H_3$ that would be reflected by *h-* in Hittite!

- IE *meld*ʰ*- 'address ritual words to the deity' (Pokorny 1959: 722) > Hitt. *maldai-* 'pray; solemnly promise to the gods to offer sacrifice', Arm. *malt'em*, Lith. *meldžiù* '[I] pray', OCS *moliti* 'pray' (also, without religious connotation, G *melden*; Benveniste 1969: 2.246–247).

Less convincing is the connection of Hitt. *mugai-* 'pray, entreat' with Lat. *mūgīre* 'moo' (cf. the gloss *commūgentō . conuocantō* '[they shall] call together' [fut. imperat.]), despite Umbrian *mugatu . muttītō*, because the idea of muttering, whispering, or making a loud deep noise (lowing, bellowing, rumbling, and so on) is presumably onomatopoeic in origin (cf. Grk. μύζω '[I] mutter, moan, growl', OHG *muckazzen* 'speak softly' [= G ⟨*sich nicht*⟩ *mucksen* 'not to make a peep, not to stir']; Pokorny 1969: 751–752). Unless the mantric syllable *mũ* had some mysterious magical potency in Indo-European, as the assumed derivation of Grk. μύστης 'initiate' from it might suggest, the religious connotation is therefore apparently an Anatolian development. Similarly, Hitt. *nahhan* 'respect, veneration', OIr. *nár* 'shy, bashful' (if from *nās-ro-*; cf. Vendryes 1960: N–3) can have developed its religious connotation in Anatolian.

The adduction of IE *k̑ens-* in the context of the Indo-European religious vocabulary (Skt. *śáṁsati* 'praises, proclaims', Avest. *saŋh-* 'solemnly pronounce', OPers. *θātiy* 'proclaims', Lat. *cēnseō* '[I] judge, evaluate, determine, maintain') requires further qualification: as Dumézil has shown (1969: 103–124), the verbal stem *k̑ens-* originally designated the weapon the priest or poet had at his disposal in the still unstable Indo-European society to set everyone in his right place: Praise would uplift leaders and heroes and glorify the gods; censure would bring down to size upstart swaggerers or ruin the reputation of usurpers.

As for the assumption that the use of IE *ĝen-* with a preverb to indicate the acknowledgment of guilt or sin (Hitt. *kaneš-*; cf. Ved. *prati-jñā́-* 'acknowledge, confess', OCS *sŭznati* (*sę*) 'confess', and so on) reflects an original Indo-European semantic development, it might be preferable, in view of the diversity of the formations (different prefixes; active or medial with suffix), to assume parallel specializations of the meaning "recognize, acknowledge" in the various dialects when *ǵen- is applied to mistakes, shortcomings, transgressions of divine or moral law, and the like.

Gamkrelidze and Ivanov also have a couple of entries referring to augural rites:

- IE *sāg- 'recognize by signs; ask (the gods' will)'> Hitt. šagai- 'omen, sign', Lat. sāgus 'prophetic, prescient', OIr. saigim '[I] try to find out, seek', Goth. sōkjan 'seek, judge', Grk. ἡγέομαι '[I] lead, guide'. However, these terms are usually considered, with Vendryes (1949, 1974: [S]12), as belonging originally to the language of hunters (applying to "tracking" by dogs).
- Hitt. ḫa- 'believe, consider true or reliable', Lat. ōmen 'sign, omen, augury', on the basis of which an IE root *Ho- is reconstructed, but it seems difficult to project these terms sharing only an initial laryngeal + /o/ into Indo-European when it is not even established that the Anatolian verb ever referred to augural rites (cf. Kronasser 1966: 461) and when there may have been an Old Latin form *osmen (Varro).

Next, Gamkrelidze and Ivanov proceed to examine the legal and ritual terminology, stressing that the "legal norms of society were part of the ritual system, controlled by priests who combined the functions of spiritual leaders and regulators of the social order." This situation is illustrated by comparisons such as Skt. yóḥ 'health, success' (in the phrase śáṁ yóḥ 'happiness and health'), Avest. yaoždā- 'make conformable to ritual prescriptions', OLat. ious (Lat. iūs 'law, system of rules'), OIr. huisse (< *yus-tyos) 'fair, legitimate'—a set of terms carefully analyzed by both Benveniste (1969: 2.111–122) and Dumézil (1953, 1969: 31–45). Their studies indicate that Latin and Indo-Iranian reflect two divergent developments of IE *yous: The Romans applied it to social relations as the definition of the maximal scope of an individual or group of persons' rights, whereas the Indo-Iranians apparently preserved its religious connotations while applying it either to the progress to an optimal ritual situation or to the removal of a blemish (= ritual purification).

Similar religious connotations can be assumed for IE *leyg-, which refers to binding obligations guaranteed by an oath (Hitt. lingai- 'oath, oath deity', Lat. ligāre 'bind, join'). Under reference to Cicero (de Legibus 2.16: uōtī sponsio quā obligāmur deō), it has often been assumed that the obligation versus the deity was originally marked materially by the wearing of some symbolic bond. On the basis of expressions like *religiō iūrisiūrandi* 'obligation under oath' (= bond created by the oath), *religiō* was similarly connected with the verb *religāre* as meaning essentially "binding oneself to the gods." Benveniste (1969: 2.267–272), however, has demonstrated that this was a late Christian reinterpretation of the Latin term, which is actually connected with *legere* 'gather, collect', *relegere* 'pick up again, go back over'; *religiō* is then a form of personal consciousness that causes one to reflect on the basis of some awe of the transcendental!

Less obvious are the religious connotations assumed for IE *deyk̑-* 'indicate', whose use in the language of law is well documented (Grk. δίκη 'custom, usage; order, right; justice, judgment', Lat. *dicis causā* 'for the sake of form' [applying to the authoritative formulation of law], and so on) (Benveniste 1969: 2.108–109). Adducing Gmc. **taikna-* (Goth. *taikns* 'sign, miracle', ON *teikn*, OE *tāc[e]n*, OHG *zeihhan* 'sign') to back up the antiquity of meanings like 'portent' for Grk. δίκη does not help, since the Germanic term presumably has an IE -g̑-; besides, Grk. δίκη is formally identical with Skt. *diśā-* 'direction, region of the sky', and its original meaning seems to have been "direction" as well (Chantraine 1968: 284).

The term *mH̥r/n-(t)-* 'hand, power; put at the disposal of, govern' (Hitt. *manii̯ahh̥-* 'hand over, turn power over, rule', Lat. *manus* 'hand, power', ON *mund* 'hand', *mundr* 'tutelage of husband over wife obtained by paying the bride price', Grk. μάρη 'hand' [used as synonym of χείρ in Homer]) undoubtedly associates the hand with power, but it does not at all show a religious connotation. On the contrary, Grk. ὅρκος 'oath' belongs definitely to the religious domain because it designates basically the destructive power of the deity that will strike the perjurer, as Benveniste (1969: 2.167–171) has demonstrated; but its etymological connection with Hitt. *šarnink-* and Lat. *sarciō* 'compensate for a loss (due to damage)', which Gamkrelidze and Ivanov fail to justify semantically, is questionable (cf. Chantraine 1974: 821), and so the association of these juridical terms with religion remains disputable!

Reviewing the legal terms they discussed, Gamkrelidze and Ivanov also examine their geographical distribution and point out that Anatolian-Italic correspondences prevail, which they explain either as retention of archaic lexical material in peripheral areas or common innovation within a dialectal area by specialization to the legal and ritual language—a case that they illustrate with examples like Hitt.

u̯erite 'fear, tremble', Lat. *verērī* 'revere, fear, worship', OIr. *có[a]ir* 'appropriate, correct' versus Grk. ὄρομαι '[I] look after [someone]', Goth. *war(s)* 'careful', OHG *biwarōn* 'guard', Latv. *véru* '[I] look, notice', and so on.

The main weakness of the presentation of Gamkrelidze and Ivanov is their failure to analyze the way the Indo-Europeans conceived "divine justice": with the all-pervasive dominance of the rules of cosmic order, of proper balance in the universe, one could expect that the gods would require adequate compensation and due atonement for any infringement. In this light the Hittite expression DINGIR^MEŠ *ešḫar* šanḫir 'the gods are thirsty for blood' may take a different meaning, such as the deities' requiring the proper price be paid for a criminal offense and the "undifferentiated legal and ritual concept of payment or compensation," illustrated by Avest. *kaēnā-* 'redemption; punishment, retribution', Grk. ποινή 'retribution, vengeance, blood feud, payment for murder', and Lith. *káina* 'price, payment' (such as the bride price), OCS *čena* 'price, payment', becomes easier to understand!

Referring to the terminology for ritual healing, Gamkrelidze and Ivanov merely quote the root **med-* (Avest. *vī-mad-* 'doctor, healer', Grk. Μήδεια 'Medea', interpreted as 'curer', Lat. *medeor* '[I] give treatment, cure'), which shows a characteristic areal specialization of its meaning. Although they neglect to go into the rich literature on shamanistic practices and recourse to magic for healing purposes, Gamkrelidze and Ivanov present an interesting synopsis of the relationship of the body parts with the Indo-European cosmogonic myth as illustrated by the *Puruṣasūkta* (*RV* 10.90), the Iranian tradition about *Gayōmart* in the *Bundahišn*, the myth of *Ymir* in Snorii Sturluson's *Gylfaginning*, and other mythological tales (Lincoln 1981: 69–95). They fail to exploit, however, the richness of the microcosm or macrocosm symbolism—now elaborated by Bruce Lincoln in his *Myth, Cosmos, and Society* (1986). This work also covers more extensively the Indo-European views on death and the Other World, the study of which is broached by the Soviet scholars in connection with such terms as IE **Henk̂-/Hnek̂-*, presenting death as an inevitable fate (Hitt. *henkan* 'plague, pestilence, death', Grk. ἀνάγκη 'compulsion, inevitability, fate', OIr. *écen* 'necessity, need'; Skt. *náśyati*, Avest. *nasyeiti* 'disappears, dies', Grk. νέκῡς 'corpse', Lat. *necō* '[I] kill', and so on), and the IE compound **Hnek̂-tr̥H-*, literally 'death-overcoming', designating the gods' drink of immortality (Grk. νέκταρ).

The fact that the Other World is conceived as a pasture is documented by Hittite, Indo-Iranian, and Greek evidence, which serves as a basis for Gamkrelidze and Ivanov's comparison of ON *val-* in *Valhǫll* (heavenly abode of the heroes fallen in combat) and *valkyria* (maiden picking up [choosing] the dead heroes for Óðinn from the battlefield) and Lith. *vëlìnes* 'remembrance of the dead' and *Veliuonà* 'god of the dead' with Hitt. *u̯ellu-* 'meadow, pasture of the dead', Toch. A *walu* 'dead', Gk. Ἠλύσιον πεδιόν 'Elysian field' < *ϝαλ-νύσι̯ο- (Puhvel 1969: 68), and so on. The transfer by boat over the waters of death is illustrated not only by the mythology of the boatman of the dead but also by the fact that the "very word *nāus* 'ship, boat' . . . could also acquire the secondary meaning 'death'," as in Goth. *naus* 'corpse' (*ganawistrōn* 'bury' would actually mean 'send off by boat'), ORuss. *navъ* 'corpse', OCzech *nav* 'grave, nether world', Latv. *nav* 'death', and so on.

Looking at cremation among the Indo-European peoples, Gamkrelidze and Ivanov surmise that the way the dead body was disposed of may have depended on the rank, sex, and age of the person, as well as the type of death he or she suffered, and they conclude that although cremation may have acquired a symbolic meaning through the process of purification by fire, it must have started as a mere prophylactic measure against the spread of the plague!

The analysis of Gamkrelidze and Ivanov is accordingly a quite useful and challenging survey of the IE religious terminology: despite its shortcomings, it reflects fairly well the present state of our linguistic knowledge, but it also indicates that further progress will be achieved in this field only if linguistic and, particularly, etymological studies are more closely integrated with the results of research in comparative religion, archeology, and the anthropology and ecology of paleocultures.

REFERENCES CITED

Baetke, W. 1942. *Das Heilige im Germanischen*. Tübingen: J.C.B. Mohr (Paul Siebeck).

Benveniste, É. 1932. "Les classes sociales dans la tradition avestique." *Journal Asiatique* 221: 117–134.

———. 1937. "L'expression indo-européenne de l'éternité." *Bulletin de la Société de Linguistique de Paris* 38: 103–112.

———. 1969. *Le vocabulaire des institutions indo-européennes. 1. Economie, parenté, société. 2. Pouvoir, droit, religion*. Paris: Editions de Minuit.

Boyce, M. 1979. *Zoroastrians: Their Religious Beliefs and Practices*. London: Routledge and Kegan Paul.

Cassirer, E. 1925. *Philosophie der symbolischen Formen*. II. *Das mythische Denken*. Berlin: Bruno Cassirer. (English translation by R. Manheim. 1946. *Philosophy of Symbolic Forms*. II. *Mythical Thought*. New York: Harper & Row.)

Chantraine, P. 1968–1980. *Dictionnaire étymologique de la langue grecque. Histoire des mots*. A–Δ (1968); E–K (1970); Λ–Π (1974); P–Y (1977); Φ–Ω and Index (1980). Completed by O. Masson, J.-I. Perpillou, and J. Taillardat. Paris: Klincksieck.

Dandekar, R. N. 1971. "Hinduism." In Bleeker, C. J., and G. Widengren, eds. *Historia Religionum: Handbook for the History of Religions. II. Religions of the Present*, pp. 346–371. Leiden: E. J. Brill.

Devoto, G. 1962. *Origini Indeuropee*. Florence: Sansoni.

de Vries, J. 1961. *Forschungsgeschichte der Mythologie*. Freiburg: Karl Alber.

———. 1977 (1967). *Perspectives in the History of Religions*. Trans. from the Dutch: *Godsdienstgeschiedenis in Vogelvlucht*, with an introduction by K. Bolle. Berkeley and Los Angeles: University of California Press. (First published by Harcourt, Brace & World under the title: *The Study of Religion: a Historical Approach*.)

de Waal Malefijt, A. 1968. *Religion and Culture: An Introduction to Anthropology of Religion*. London: Collier/Macmillan.

Dumézil, G. 1953. "*Ner-* et *uiro-* dans les langues italiques." *Revue des Etudes Latines* 31: 175–189.

———. 1969. *Idées romaines*, pp. 225–241. Paris: N.R.F./Gallimard.

———. 1970. *Archaic Roman Religion. With an Appendix on the Religion of the Etruscans*. 2 vols. Trans. by P. Krapp (from the French: *La Religion romaine archaïque*. Paris: Payot, 1966). Chicago: University of Chicago Press.

Eliade, M. 1978. *History of Religious Ideas*, vol. 1: *From the Stone Age to the Eleusinian Mysteries*. Translated from the French by W. Trask. Chicago: University of Chicago Press.

Feist, S. 1913. *Kultur, Ausbreitung und Herkunft der Indogermanen*. Berlin: Weidmann.

Gamkrelidze, T. V., and V. V. Ivanov. 1984. *Indoevropejskij jazyk i Indoevropejcy. Rekonstrukcija i istoriko-tipologičeskij analiz prajazyka i protokultury* (*Indo-European and the Indo-Europeans. A Reconstruction and Historical Typological Analysis of a Proto-language and a Proto-culture*). 2 vols. Tbilisi: Publishing House of the State University.

Gonda, J. 1960. *Die Religionen Indiens. I. Veda und älterer Hinduismus*. (Die Religionen der Menschheit, vol. 11.) Stuttgart: W. Kohlhammer.

Haudry, J. 1985. *Les Indo-Européens*. (*Que sais-je?* Vol. 1965; ed. 2). Paris: Presses Universitaires de France.

Hauer, J. W. 1936. "Die vergleichende Religionsgeschichte und das Indogermanenproblem." In Arntz, H., ed. *Germanen und Indogermanen: Volkstum, Sprache, Heimat, Kultur: Festschrift für Herman Hirt*. I. *Ergebnisse der Kulturhistorie und Anthropologie*, pp. 177–221. Heidelberg: Carl Winter.

Hirt, H. 1905–1907. *Die Indogermanen: Ihre Verbreitung, ihre Urheimat und ihre Kultur*. 2 vols. Strasbourg: Karl J. Trübner.

Jung, C. G., and K. Kerényi. 1941. *Einführung in das Wesen der Mythologie*. Amsterdam: Pantheon Akademische Verlagsanstalt. (English translation by R. F. C. Hull. 1949. *Essays on a Science of Mythology: The Myth of the Divine Child and Mysteries of Eleusis*. [Bollingen Series, vol. 22]. Princeton: University Press.)

Kronasser, H. 1966. *Etymologie der hethitischen Sprache*. I. 1. *Zur Schreibung und Lautung des Hethitischen*. 2. *Wortbildung des Hethitischen*. Wiesbaden: Otto Harrassowitz.

Lévi-Strauss, C. 1955 (1965). "The Structural Study of Myth." In Sebeok, T. A., ed. *Myth: A Symposium*, pp. 81–106. Bloomington: Indiana University Press. (First published by the American Folklore Society, Special Series, vol. 5; reprinted in the Midland Books.)

Lincoln, B. 1981. *Priests, Warriors, and Cattle: A Study in the Ecology of Religion*. Berkeley: University of California Press.

———. 1986. *Myth, Cosmos, and Society: Indo-European Themes of Creation and Destruction*. Cambridge: Harvard University Press.

Littleton, C. S. 1982. *The New Comparative Mythology: An Anthropological Assessment of the Theories of Georges Dumézil*, ed. 3. Berkeley: University of California Press.

Marett, R. R. 1900. "Pre-animistic Religion." *Folk-Lore* 11: 162–182. (Reprinted in *The Threshold of Religion*. New York: Macmillan, 1909; ed. 2. 1914, pp. 1–28.)

Mauss, M. 1925. "Essai sur le don, forme archaïque de l'échange." *L'Année sociologique* 1 [1923–1924]: 30–186. (English translation by I. Cunnison, with an introduction by E. E. Evans-Pritchard. 1967. *The Gift: Forms and Functions of Exchange in Archaic Societies*. New York: W. W. Norton.)

Meillet, A. 1948. "La religion indo-européenne." In *Linguistique historique et linguistique générale*, pp. 323–334. Paris: Honoré Champion. (Originally published in 1907 in *Revue des Idées* 4: 689.)

Meyer, E. H. 1903. *Mythologie der Germanen gemeinfaßlich dargestellt*. Strasbourg: Karl J. Trübner.

Nehring, A. 1936. "Studien zur indogermanischen Kultur und Urheimat." In Koppers, W., ed. *Die Indogermanen und Germanenfrage: Neue Wege zur ihrer Lösung*, pp. 7–229. Salzburg: Anton Pustet. (Wiener Beiträge zur Kulturgeschichte und Linguistik. Institut für Völkerkunde der Universität Wien, vol. 4.)

Nehring, A., and O. Schrader: 1917–1929. *Reallexikon der indogermanischen Altertumskunde*. 2 vols: ed. 1. Strasbourg: Karl J. Trübner; ed. 2. Berlin: Walter de Gruyter.

Neumann, E. 1955. *The Great Mother: An Analysis of the Archetype*. Translated from the German by R. Mannheim. New York: Pantheon Books. (Reprinted 1972: Bollingen Series, vol. 47. Princeton, N.J.: Princeton University Press.)

Otto, R. 1917. *Das Heilige*. Breslau: Trewendt and Granier.

Pokorny, J. 1959. *Indogermanisches etymologisches Wörterbuch*. Bern: Francke.

Polomé, E. C. 1975. "Old Norse Religious Terminology in Indo-European Perspective." In Dahlstedt, K.-H., ed. *The Nordic Languages and Modern Linguistics II*, pp. 654–655. Stockholm: Almqvist and Wiksell. (Umeå, Sweden: Kunglige Skytteanska Samfundets Handlingar, vol. 13). (Reprinted in Dil, A. S., ed. *Language, Society, and Paleoculture: Essays by Edgar C. Polomé*, pp. 285–295. Stanford, Calif.: Stanford University Press, 1982.)

————. 1984. "Some Thoughts on the Methodology of Comparative Religion, with Special Focus on Indo-European." In Polomé, E. C., ed. *Essays in the Memory of Karl Kerényi*, pp. 9–27. The *Journal of Indo-European Studies*. Monograph No. 4. Washington, D.C.: The Institute for the Study of Man.

Puhvel, J. 1969. "'Meadow of the Otherworld' in Indo-European tradition." *Zeitschrift für vergleichende Sprachforschung* 83: 64–69. (Reprinted in Puhvel, J. 1981. *Analecta Indoeuropaea*. [Innsbrucker Beiträge zur Sprachwissenschaft 35: 210–215.] Innsbruck: Sprachwissenschaftliches Institut der Universität.)

————. 1984. *Hittite Etymological Dictionary*. 1. *Words beginning with A*. 2. *Words beginning with E and I*. Berlin: Mouton.

Rivière, J.-C. 1979. "Georges Dumézil et les études indo-européennes." In Rivière, J.-C., ed. *Georges Dumézil à la découverte des Indo-Européens*, pp. 9–135. Paris: Copernic.

Tischler, J. 1983. *Hethitisches etymologisches Glossar*. I. *A–K*. (Innsbrucker Beiträge zur Sprachwissenschaft 20: 1). Innsbruck: Sprachwissenschaftliches Institut der Universität.

van der Leeuw, G. 1928. *La structure de la mentalité primitive*. Strasbourg: Imprimerie Alsacienne.

————. 1948. *La religion dans son essence et ses manifestations: Phénoménologie de la religion*. Paris: Payot. (English translation by J. E. Turner. 1963. *Religion in Essence and Manifestation*. New York: Harper & Row.)

Vendryes, J. 1949. "Sur quelques mots de la langue des chasseurs." *Archivum Linguisticum* 1: 23–29.

————. 1959–1981. *Lexique étymologique de l'irlandais ancien*. A (1959); B (1981); M, N, O, P (1960); R, S (1974); T, U (1978). Dublin: Institute for Advanced Studies. Also Paris: Centre National de la Recherche Scientifique.

von Wilamowitz-Moellendorff, U. 1931. *Der Glaube der Hellenen* I. Berlin: Weidmannsche Buchhandlung.

Wikander, S. 1938. *Der arische Männerbund*. Lund: C. W. K. Gleerup.

Wundt, W. 1905–1909. *Völkerpsychologie*. II. *Mythus und Religion*. 3 vols. Leipzig: Alfred Kröner.

Deities and Symbols of Old Europe and Their Survival in the Indo-European Era: A Synopsis

MARIJA GIMBUTAS

Old Europe is the name that has been given to the rich panoply of related cultures throughout all of Europe, as well as Asia Minor, before the infiltration of hordes of Indo-European-speaking nomadic pastoralist peoples from the southern Russian steppe in the period between 4500 and 2500 B.C. The worldview of the agricultural and matricentric Old Europeans was diametrically opposed to that of the patriarchal Indo-European ideology that more or less successfully destroyed it, transforming social structure and religion from matrilinear to patrilinear and from matrifocal to patrifocal, from matristic and gynandric (female/male balanced) to androcratic (male dominated). The Mediterranean region and especially its islands escaped the process of Indo-Europeanization the longest. There, Old European culture flourished in an enviably peaceful and creative civilization until 1500 B.C., whereas the central part of Europe had been thoroughly transformed by 3000 B.C.

Our synopsis focuses on the period beginning with early agriculture, some 9,000 years ago. Heirs of their paleolithic forebears, the Neolithic farmers evolved their own unique cultural patterns during the seventh, sixth, and fifth millennia B.C. and contemporaneously with similar developments in Anatolia, Mesopotamia, and Syrio-Palestine. Old Europeans shared a common central symbolic matrix, though different subcultures at different times emphasized some symbols more than others in outward expression.

The diverse cultures of the European Neolithic and the Copper Age were united by a rich symbolic system that has deeply influenced all later eras. Without an understanding of these symbols, any history of Indo-European religion, mythology, and art is necessarily far from complete.

The custom-bound life of the intimate matrilinear village is reflected in their Goddess-centered religion. It is obvious from the archeological record of statuary, pottery, and painted images that the Goddess, not a male God, dominates the Old European pantheon. There is no Creator *ex nihilō*—the Creatrix *ex ipsā* rules absolutely over human, animal, and plant life. She destroys and generates the life force and controls the lunar cycles and seasons. Reflecting this on the human plane, women are shown supervising the preparation and performance of rituals in temples.

Old European images and symbols are lunar and chthonic. They are linked with the earth, moist and mysterious, with her life-giving waters, plants, hills, stones, and animals, and with the female generative organs, uterine caves, and tombs. Old European images are cyclic as the moon and the female body. In no way could the philosophy that produces these images be mistaken for the pastoral, solar, sky-oriented Indo-European ideology, with its horse-riding warrior gods and heroes equipped with lethal weapons and its polar (day/night, shining/black, male/female, good/evil) structure of the world.

The main theme of Old European symbolism is the mystery of birth and death and the renewal of life, involving not only human life but also all life on earth and in the whole cosmos. Symbols and images cluster around a parthenogenetic lunar goddess who creates from herself—Virgin—without male participation. The symbols illustrate and celebrate her basic functions as Giver-of-life, Wielder-of-death, and Regeneratrix. This goddess is also the Earth Mother, the Fertility Goddess, maiden, woman, and hag—who rises and dies as plant life and the moon do.

IMAGES OF DEITIES AND THEIR SYMBOLS

The chief Old European divinities have their own identities as, perhaps, avatars of a Great Goddess. The Bird Goddess, the Serpent Goddess, the Birth-giver, and the Guardian of Young Life are each associated with water, moisture, and the creation and nurturing of life. Following is a discussion of the various stereotypes by which these goddesses are most often represented.

Bird Goddess

The Bird Goddess is the best-documented divinity from the Paleolithic, Neolithic, and later. She appears with a beak or a pinched nose, the long neck of a swan or goose, a hairdo or crown, human breasts, either wings or winglike projections, and protruding female buttocks outlining the shape of a bird's body. She wears a duck's or other bird's mask (Figure 1). From Paleolithic times she was a giver of life, wealth, and nourishment and, probably from as early as the Neolithic, was a weaver and spinner of human fate and giver of crafts. From the seventh millennium B.C. onward she was worshipped in shrines.

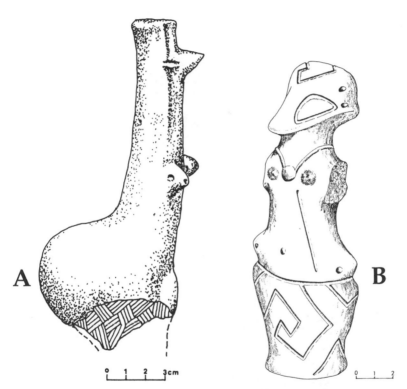

Figure 1. The Bird Goddess of the Neolithic and the Copper Age in central Europe. **A,** This terracotta figurine has slit eyes, a pinched nose (the beak), a round hole under the nose, breasts, and a cylindrical neck. The buttocks are outlined in the shape of a bird's body. (Neolithic, Starčevo/Körös culture [Szajol-Felsőföld, SE Hungary; *ca.* 5500 B.C.]) **B,** Duck-masked deity from the Vinča culture. (Yugoslavia; 4500–4000 B.C.) (**A** from Raczky, P. 1980. "A Körös kultúra újabb figurális ábrázolásai a Közép-tiszavidékről és történet összefüggéseik." *A Szólnok Múzeumok Évkönyve 1979–1980* (Szólnok), pp. 5–33. Budapest: National Museum. **B** from Vasić, M. 1936. *Prehistoric Vinča*, vols. 2–4. Belgrade: Belgrade National Museum.)

Her body parts are life creating:

- *Breasts* are *pars pro tōtō* of the Bird Goddess in her life-, nourish-ment-, and wealth-giving functions. In tombs, breasts may represent regenerative powers of the same Bird Goddess but in the guise of a bird of prey (Figure 2).
- Her *mouth* or *open beak*, either round-depressed or wide-open, stresses this Goddess's function of giving and increasing (Figure 3).
- *Vessels* or *water containers* are a metaphor of the Goddess's life-creating body (Figure 4).

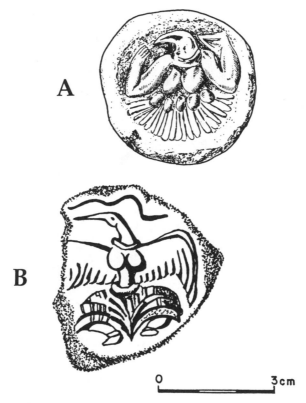

Figure 2. Breasts were prominently portrayed on images of the Bird Goddess or her priestesses. These bird-headed and winged figures with large breasts appear on Minoan seals. (Zakro, E. Crete; 1500–1450 B.C.) (**A** from Alexiou, S. 1958. *I Minoiki Thea meth' Upsomenon Kheiron.* Heraklion, Crete: Heraklion Museum. **B** from Alexiou, S. 1902. *Journal of Hellenic Studies XXII.* Heraklion, Crete: Heraklion Museum.)

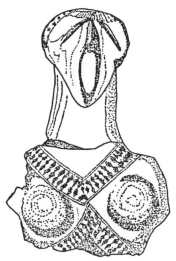

Figure 3. Bird Goddess figurine with a wide-open beak. The V motif is between her large breasts. Butmir culture (Butmir, at Sarajevo; early fifth millennium B.C.). (From Radimsky, V., and M. Hoernes. 1895. *Die neolithische Station von Butmir*. Sarajevo Zemaljskij Museum.)

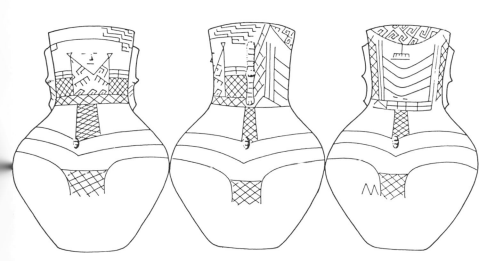

Figure 4. Life-giving or Regenerating Goddess as a vessel (water container). Her face is above the M sign and is associated with "brush" (energy) signs, nets, and meanders. Early Tisza culture (Battonya, SE Hungary; *ca.* 5000–4500 B.C.). (From Goldman, G. 1979. "Gesichtsgefässe und andere Menschendarstellungen aus Battonya." *A Békés Megyei Múzeumok Közleményei* (Békés) 5: 13–60. Budapest: National Museum.)

Symbols or insignia of the Bird Goddess (Figure 5):

- V's or *chevrons* are the emblem of the Bird Goddess and were probably derived from the vulva. V as a sign appears in the Upper Paleolithic; the chevron is a doubled or tripled V.
- *Streams* represent spring and rain water, healing, and thermal waters. They are found in the Upper Paleolithic.
- *Zigzag, serpentiform, striated*, and *checkerboard bands* indicate nets, streams, or grids of life energy.
- M is a sign for water and is associated with the life-giving or regenerating divinity in the shape of a vessel.
- *Meanders* represent life-creating water expanses and also water snakes.
- The number *three*, as three lines or three dots, indicates totality, abundance, a triple source. "Three" is documented from the Upper Paleolithic and refers also to three aspects of the Goddess (life/death/regeneration, maid/mother/crone, and so on).

Her epiphanies and sacred animals and birds:

- *Water birds*, including *ducks, geese, swans, cranes*, and others, are epiphanies of the Bird Goddess in the function of apportioner, or bringer of luck, wealth, and nourishment.
- *Cuckoos* are prophetic birds of spring and are the main epiphany of the Goddess as Fate.
- *Swallows, larks*, and *doves* are birds of spring. They are also recorded in mythology as being departed human souls, or being signs of immanent death.
- The *ram* is a magic, wealth-bringing animal. Ram horns interchange with snake-coil motifs. The ram appears in early Neolithic symbolism at about the seventh millennium B.C.
- *Fleece* or *sheepskin* indicates wealth and appears associated with loom weights and Bird Goddess figurines in the fifth millennium B.C.

Serpent Goddess

The Serpent Goddess, double of the Bird Goddess, is half-woman, half-snake. She has serpentine hands and feet, a long mouth, and usually round eyes; she wears a crown, symbol of wisdom. The snake as her epiphany is an incarnation of spontaneous life energy, which renews itself each spring. As house-shrine Goddess, docu-

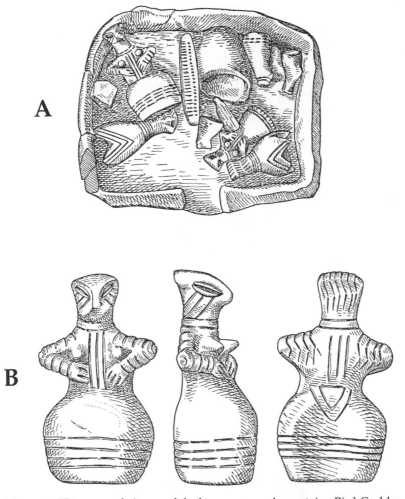

Figure 5. This open shrine model of two rooms, **A,** contains Bird Goddess type of figurines marked with tri-lines and chevrons. The largest figurine, **B,** occupied the left room together with a smaller and schematized figurine. Six were placed in the second room around the oven. The sizes and placement of figurines are suggestive of a hierarchical order. The model probably was an offering to the Goddess on the occasion of the laying of the foundation of the house. Dimini culture, Tsangli phase (Zarkou at Larisa, Thessaly; early fifth millennium B.C.). (From Gallis, K. J. 1985. "A Late Neolithic Foundation Offering From Thessaly." *Antiquity* 59: 20–23. Larisa Archaeological Museum.)

mented from the early Neolithic, she was a guardian of a family's
fertility and increase (Figure 6).

Birth-giver

The Birth-giver, anthropomorphic, is portrayed in a birth-giving
pose and is documented from the Upper Paleolithic (Figure 7).

Symbols of the Birth-giver:

* The *vulva* is *pars pro tōtō* of the Goddess in her birth-giving aspect. It is lens or seed shaped.
* The *seed* is a symbol interchangeable with the vulva (Figure 8, *A*).
* *Plants* or branches appear occasionally instead of vulvas on figurines representing this Goddess (Figure 8, *B*).
* *Wells* are considered a source of life, owned by the life-giving goddess and sacred to her. They are usually associated with standing
  stones (menhirs).

Epiphanies of the Birth-giver:

* *Deer, elk-doe*, and *bear*, primeval pregnant mothers, are shown
  giving birth to humans and animals.

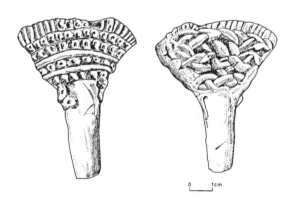

Figure 6. The crown of the Serpent Goddess. The back reveals a mass of
writhing snakes. Middle Minoan I (Kophina; *ca.* 2000 B.C.). (From Alexiou,
S. 1958. *I Minoiki Thea meth' Upsomenon Kheiron*. Heraklion, Crete: Heraklion
Museum.)

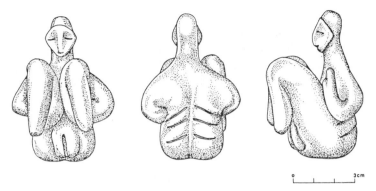

Figure 7. Birth-giver, portrayed in a naturalistic birth-giving pose. In the Neolithic, the birth-giving posture is a seated one. This terracotta figurine is from the Early Sesklo culture (Achilleion II, Thessaly, Greece; 6300–6200 B.C.). (From Gimbutas, M., S. Winn, and D. Shimabuku. 1989. *Achilleion. A Neolithic Settlement in Thessaly, Greece, 6400–5600 B.C.* Monumenta Archaeologica 14, Institute of Archaeology, University of California, Los Angeles. Larisa Archaeological Museum.)

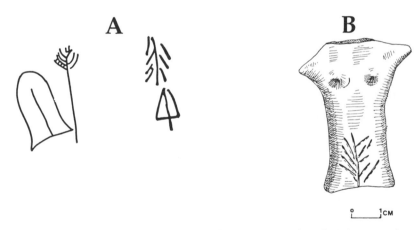

Figure 8. Sprouting seeds and young plants are paired with vulvas or take the place of vulvas on figurines. **A,** Vulvas paired with branches from the Upper Paleolithic (El Castillo and La Mouthe caves). **B,** Early Vinča terracotta figurine (Jela, N. Yugoslavia; *ca.* 5200 B.C.). (**A** from Graziosi, P. 1973. "Nuove manifestazioni d'arte mesolitica e neolitica nel riparo Gaban presso Trento." *Rivista de Scienze Preistoriche* 30.1–2: 237–278. **B** from Winn, S. M. M. 1981. *Pre-writing in Southeastern Europe: the Sign System of the Vinča Culture ca. 4000.* Calgary: Western Publishers. Jela City Museum.)

Guardian of Young Life

The Guardian of Young Life, shown as a Nurse and Mother holding a child, is variously anthropomorphic, ornithomorphic, or zoomorphic. She is portrayed as a bear holding a bear cub or as a bear-masked woman carrying a pouch for a baby (recorded from the early Neolithic and later) (Figure 9). Mother or nurse images also appear in the shape of the Bird or Serpent Goddess, holding a little bird-masked baby or snake, as well as in an anthropomorphic shape.

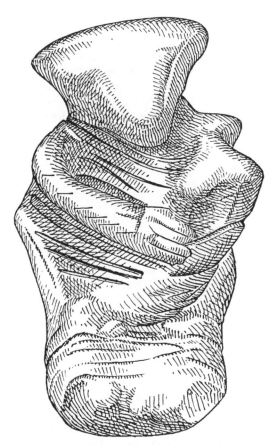

Figure 9. Bear Mother, Guardian of Young Life. (Height 5.7 cm.) Vinča culture (Fafos, Kosovska Mitrovica, S. Yugoslavia, *ca.* 5000 B.C.). (From 1968. National Museum of Belgrade, Catalogue, p. 96. Kosvska Mitrovica Archaeological Museum, Yugoslavia.)

DEATH AND REGENERATION

Death and Omens of Death

- As an *owl* (Figure 10), *vulture* (Figure 11), *crow, raven,* or other bird of prey, or by their *wings* or *claws,* the Goddess is represented as foreboder or bringer of death.
- The *cuckoo* in its winter aspect is a foreboder of death; in recorded mythology the cuckoo often becomes a hawk at the end of summer.
- The *boar* and the *white* or *gray dog* are sacred animals of the Goddess in this aspect.

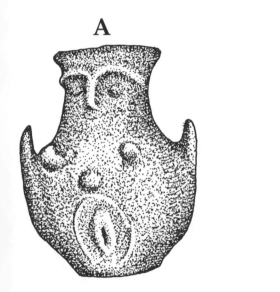 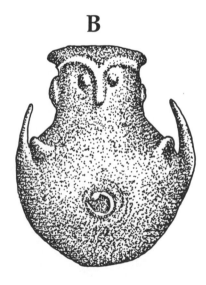

Figure 10. Striking owl-shaped burial urns are a tradition throughout Europe and Anatolia. They have the universal Owl Goddess face and breasts; regeneration is emphasized by large vulvas, **A,** or serpentine umbilical cords, **B. A,** Poliochni, town on Lemnos; *ca.* 3000–2500 B.C. **B,** Troy II–III, N. Aegean–W. Anatolian Early Bronze Age, 3000–2500 B.C. (From Schliemann, H. 1976. *Ilios, the City and Country of the Trojans.* New York: Arno Press; **A,** Poliochni Archaeological Museum; **B,** Athens Natural Museum.)

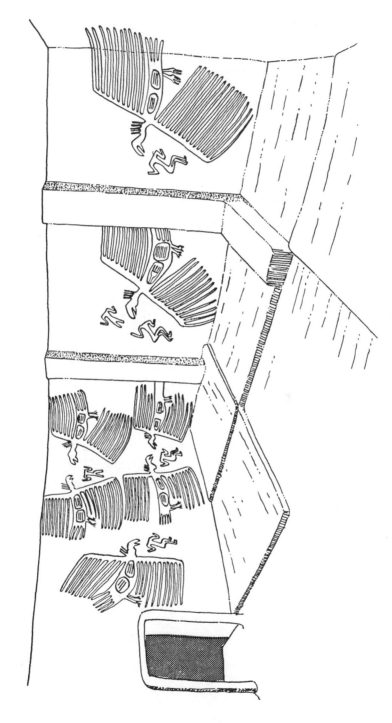

Figure 11. Vultures with tremendous wings like brooms swooping down on headless humans. Wall painting of Shrine in Level VII, 8 at Çatal Hüyük, Central Anatolia. (From Mellaart, J. S. 1967. *Çatal Hüyük: a Neolithic Town in Anatolia.* New York: McGraw-Hill. Ankara Archaeological Museum.)

- The *White Lady*, an anthropomorphic stiff nude, is portrayed with folded arms that are tightly pressed to her bosom and with closed or tapering legs. She is masked and sometimes has a *polos* on her head. Her large, supernatural pubic triangle is the center of attention. She is evidenced from the Upper Paleolithic through the Old European period, with an extension into the mid–second millennium B.C. in the Aegean area and in the Danube valley. She is usually found in graves (Figure 12).

Figure 12. The White Lady— Death—carved of bone. She is nude, stiff, has folded arms. The head on a long cylindrical neck is masked. (Height *ca.* 8 cm.) Sardinian Neolithic (Monte Miana Cave, Santadi, 4500–4000 B.C.). This type of stiff nude continued into the Aegean Bronze Age. The most well-known are the Cycladic marble sculptures of the mid–third millennium B.C. (From Gimbutas, M. 1989. *The Language of the Goddess.* San Francisco: Harper & Row, Figure 316. Cagliari Archaeological Museum, Sardinia.)

Regeneration

Symbols of death are also symbols of regeneration. The Owl Goddess is marked with labyrinths, an umbilical cord, and a snake coil. Her eyes are large and have magical regenerative powers. She is associated with energy symbols—the brush, ax, hook, and spiral. There are other shapes of the Goddess of Regeneration.

- The *regenerative triangle* (the pubic triangle) is a reduced image of the Goddess as regenerating womb. It is traced back (as triangular stones) to as early as the Mousterian period. The triangle is the earliest motif to appear on painted pottery and is also prominent in engravings in megalithic tomb-shrines, where it often appears in threes.
- The *hourglass* (two triangles joined together at the tip) forms the body of the Goddess and appears in caves and megalithic graves as well as painted on vases. *Bird's claws* attached to the hourglass shape identify it as a manifestation of a Bird-of-Prey Goddess in the regenerative aspect. This image also appears in ritual-death or winter-dance scenes painted on vases and on cave walls (Figure 13).
- *Frogs, toads*, and *other amphibians* also symbolize the Goddess. Symbolically a "regenerative uterus" (the "wandering uterus" of Egyptian, Greek, and Roman sources and folklore), the Frog Goddess appears in the Upper Paleolithic and is prominent throughout

Figure 13. The Goddess of Regeneration in dual-triangle form with V-shaped arms and bird's claws. Three vertical lines in place of head and lower triangle. Y signs and dots flank the figure, incised on a panel of the rectangular vessel. (Szelevény, SE Hungary; *ca.* 5000 B.C.) (From Gimbutas, M. 1989. *The Language of the Goddess.* San Francisco: Harper & Row. Budapest National Archaeological Museum.)

Old Europe (carved of semiprecious stone), as well as Anatolia. She survives to this day (Figure 14).
*   The *Hedgehog* Goddess, also a regenerative uterus, had particular importance as protectress of animals and probably originated from the similarity of a cow's uterus to a hedgehog (bovine uteri have warts; cf. the German *Igel* 'hedgehog' and 'cow's uterus'). In Old Europe, this goddess is a hedgehog with a human face; she survived to the twentieth century as a spiky ball given in offering to the Virgin Mary (Figure 15).
*   *Hares,* as epiphanies of the Goddess or as zoomorphic goddesses, survived associated with Artemis into classical times.

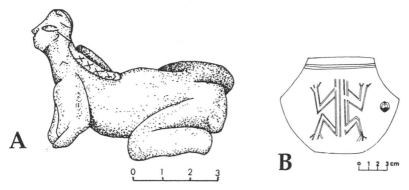

Figure 14. The Frog Goddess of Regeneration as a terracotta figurine and engraved on a vase. **A,** This ceramic example has a human head and a froglike body. Central Anatolian Neolithic (Level VI, House Q.VI.5, Hacilar; end of the sixth millennium B.C.). **B,** Stylized Frog Goddess's effigy incised on a Linear pottery vase, central Europe (Nová Ves, Bohemia; early fifth millennium B.C.). (**A** from Mellaart, J. S. 1970. *Excavations at Hacilar, I* and *II.* Edinburgh: Edinburgh University Press. Ankara Archaeological Museum. **B** from Müller-Karpe, H. 1968. *Handbuch der Vorgeschichte,* 2, Jungsteinzeit. Prague: National Museum.)

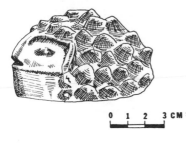

Figure 15. Hedgehog Goddess: Pottery lid in the form of a hedgehog with a human face. Karanovo (Gumelniţa) culture (Vidra at Bucharest; *ca.* 4500 B.C.). (From Dumitrescu, V. 1974. *Arta Preistorică în România.* Bucharest: Meridiane. Bucharest City Museum.)

SYMBOLS OF REGENERATION

- *Eggs* and *wombs* are universal symbols of regeneration. The Goddess's womb and caves and graves are one.
- The *womb* is often symbolized by the pubic triangle, as labyrinthine internal organs, and as a pregnant belly. The tomb as pregnant belly symbolizes the Goddess's regenerative womb.
- *Blood*, or the color *red*, represents the Color of Life, essential for regeneration.
- The *bucranium*, or *bull's skull*, was chosen originally as a symbol of regeneration because of the accidental similarity of the woman's uterus and ovaries to the bull's head and skull. This is documented from the earliest Neolithic but may possibly originate in the Upper Paleolithic (Figure 16).
- *Bulls* are associated with waters of regeneration and are associated with lakes and rivers. Their strength and roundness are symbolic of the full moon.
- *Tombs* in Old Europe are universally representative of the Goddess's womb. They are egg shaped (pit graves, rock-cut tombs, hypogeae) and vagina and uterus shaped (passage graves) (Figures 17 and 18). They are anthropomorphic, with the Goddess lying on her back with spread-out legs (Irish court-tombs), pubic-triangle shaped (cairns above court-tombs, Lepenski Vir shrines and graves), and bone shaped (English long barrows).

Figure 16. The bull head as uterus is placed below the abdomen on this anthropomorphic marble vase from the Cyclades. (Height 10.5 cm.) Early Cycladic I (Provenance unknown; *ca.* 3000 B.C.). (From Thimme, J. 1977. *Art and Culture of the Cyclades: Handbook of an Ancient Civilization*, trans. and English ed., P. Getz-Preziosi. Karlsruhe: C. F. Müller Private xollection.)

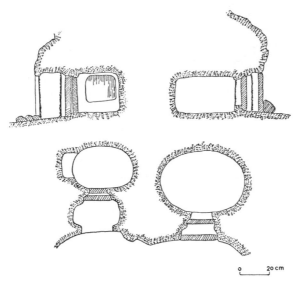

Figure 17. Egg- or womb-shaped rock-cut tombs. Early Bronze Age Sicily (Castellucio, Noto, SE Sicily; early third millennium B.C.). (From Bernabó Brea, L. 1957. *Sicily before the Greeks*. Ancient People and Places, vol. 3. London: Thames & Hudson.)

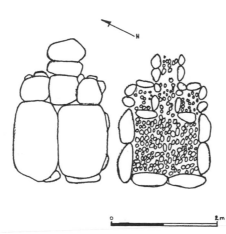

Figure 18. A grave built of large stones in the shape of a seated corpulent goddess. Havel group of Funnel-necked Beaker culture (Mierzyń, W. Poland; 3500–3000 B.C.). (From Hensel, W., and T. Wiślański, eds. 1979. *Prahistoria ziem polskich*, vol. 2 [Neolit]. Wrocław: Polska Akademia Nauk.)

- *Labyrinths* represent the regenerative womb in the form of the female internal organs surrounding a life-producing vulva. They may also represent, as they have in historical times, our journey through life, from birth to death to rebirth (Figure 19).
- *Nets* represent uterine moisture, the "water of life," pubic hair, and wool. They are associated with fish, lozenges, and regenerative functions and epiphanies of the Goddess and are interchangeable with checkerboard and honeycomb designs, of Upper Paleolithic origin (Figure 20).
- *Eyes* are an energy source with regenerative powers. In the Neolithic and the Copper Age they are associated with the image of the Owl Goddess and with aquatic symbolism. Eyes are interchangeable with sun, snake coil, ram horn, and cupmark symbols (Figure 21).
- The *sun* is a generative source interchangeable with snake coils and eyes. The Sun is an epiphany of the Goddess at Winter Solstice as Cosmic Regeneratrix and is occasionally portrayed with eyes in caves and tombs.

Figure 19. The body of this owl-faced figurine from an Irish passage grave dissolves into a labyrinthine design suggestive of life-giving waters; at the center is a large vulva. It was found in the corridor just to the right of the chamber. (Knowth West, County Meath, Ireland; mid–fourth millennium B.C.) (From Herity, M. 1974. *Irish Passage Graves: Neolithic Tomb-Builders in Ireland and Britain 2500 B.C.* New York: Barnes & Noble; Dublin: Irish University Press. National Museum of Antiquities, Dublin.)

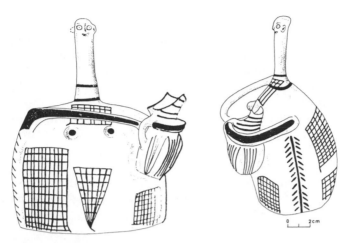

Figure 20. The net is associated with the pubic triangle on this anthropo-morphic vessel with serpentine neck and arms; perforated breast spouts indicate its ritual use. The net-patterned rectangles that cover the body may represent reservoirs of life-giving water. Early Minoan II (Myrtos, S. Crete; early third millennium B.C.). (From Warren, P. 1972. *Myrtos: an Early Bronze Age Settlement in Crete*. London: Thames & Hudson. Agios Nikolaios Museum, Crete.)

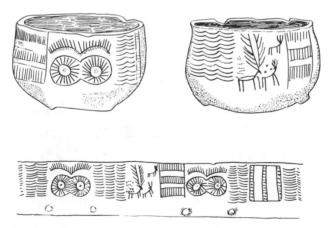

Figure 21. Radiant divine eyes like suns on Los Millares vase (Almeria, Spain; *ca.* 3000 B.C.). The association with antlered deer and aquatic symbols suggests a relationship to spring-summer growth rites. (From Almagro, M., and A. Arribas. 1963. *El poblado y la necrópolis megalíticos de Los Millares*. Madrid: Madrid National Archaeological Museum.)

Symbols of "Becoming" and Energy

- The *crescent*, or *crescent moon*, denotes the beginning phase of the lunar cycle and is a potent energy symbol (Figure 22).
- *Horns* are prominent symbols in this category and are related to crescents, hooks, and spirals. They are first found in the Upper Paleolithic.
- *Whirls* and *four-corner designs* are catalysts of motion, stimulators of natural cycles and forces of regeneration. They are associated with the rising Goddess, life columns, and trees of life (Figure 23).
- *Centaurs*, or more properly *bull-men*, represent stimulators of rising life power. They are found from the Copper Age, fifth millennium B.C. (Figure 24).

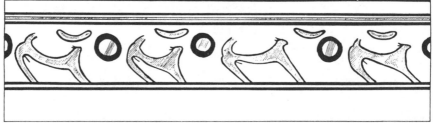

Figure 22. The dog (epiphany of the goddess?) in association with the crescent and full moons. Painted black on red on a Cucuteni vase. (Truşeşti, NE Romania; 3800–3600 B.C.) (From Dumitrescu, V. 1974. *L'art préhistorique en Roumanie*. Bucharest: Iaşi Archaeological Museum.)

Figure 23. Fourfold designs that promote the turning of the great cycles of life are often composed of four circles or eggs around a common center, as on this Late Cucuteni bowl. Chicks in each egg stress the regenerative energy. Cucuteni B$_2$ (Buznea near Peatra Neamţ, Moldavia; 3700–3500 B.C.). (From Mihai, C. 1972–1973. "Aşezările Cucuteniene de la Giurgeşti şi Buznea în Zona Tîrgului Frumos." *Danubius* VI–VII, Muzeul Judeţean de Istorie, Gelaţi.)

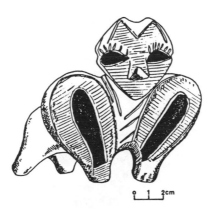

○ 1 2cm

Figure 24. Centaur (bull-man) with a human mask. This terracotta Vinča centaur is incised with an **M** at the forehead, a tri-line on the chest, and uteri over the forelegs. Painted red and black. (Valać, near Kosovska Mitrovica, S. Yugoslavia; 5000–4500 B.C.) (From 1968, National Museum of Belgrade, Catalogue, and Gimbutas, M. 1974. *The Gods and Goddesses of Old Europe: 7000 to 3500 B.C. Myths, Legends and Cult Images.* London: Thames & Hudson, and Berkeley: University of California Press. National Museum of Kosovska Mitrovica, S. Yugoslavia.)

Symbols of Rising Life

- *Life column* or *Tree of Life*: Rising life energy is often portrayed rising as a watery mass, multiple arcs, a vertical snake, a snake and tree combined, a phallus, or a plant. This energy is usually portrayed in vertical panels starting with early Neolithic wall and vase painting.
- *Vertically winding snake, lightning,* or *zigzags* (in panels) represent the life column. They are associated with water sources, the moisture of amniotic fluid, and thereby the Goddess's womb.
- The *phallus* as life column is related to plants, especially mushrooms, and to vertically winding snakes. As a potent symbol of life regeneration and stimulation, the phallus appears combined with the Goddess's body (as a phallus head and neck) in the Upper Paleolithic and Neolithic (Figure 25).
- The *bee* and the *butterfly* are epiphanies of the Goddess of Regeneration, symbolizing transformation from death to new life. They are often portrayed emerging from bucrania (uteri), from the

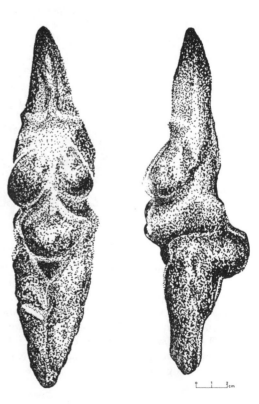

Figure 25. The phallus is often fused with the female body, whose inherent power is enhanced by the life force manifested in the column. On this Upper Paleolithic figurine of steatite the head is replaced by a featureless phallus. Gravettian/Grimaldian culture (Savignano, N. Italy). (From Graziosi, P. 1973. "Nuove manifestazioni d'arte mesolitica e neolitica nel riparo Gaban presso Trento." *Rivista de Scienze Preistoriche* 30.1–2: 237–278, and Delporte, H. 1979. *L'image de la femme dans l'art préhistorique*. Paris: Picard. Pigorini Museum, Rome.)

Neolithic and continuous in the Minoan Bronze Age (Figure 26).

- The *double ax*, interchangeable with the butterfly, is a horizontal hourglass shape, which is also an epiphany of the transforming Goddess of Regeneration (the Vulture Goddess), and appears from the Neolithic and is continuous in the Minoan Bronze Age (Figure 27).
- *Lozenges* (two triangles joined at their bases) and *a triangle with a dot* indicate pregnancy and earth fertility (Neolithic) (Figure 28).

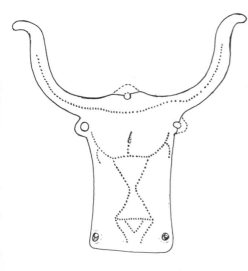

Figure 26. The new life arising from a bucranium is often portrayed as the Goddess in her epiphany as a bee. Here a punctate silhouette of the Bee Goddess is rendered on a bull's head carved of bone plate. Late Cucuteni culture (Bilcze Zlote, upper Seret valley, W. Ukraine; 3700–3500 B.C.). (From Gimbutas, M. 1974. *The Gods and Goddesses of Old Europe: 7000 to 3500 B.C.: Myths, Legends, and Cult Images.* London: Thames & Hudson, and Berkeley: University of California Press.)

Figure 27. The association of bull, bee, and butterfly is clear on this onyx gem; the Goddess as bee has over her head two sets of bull horns and a double ax or butterfly. The winged dogs that flank her reinforce the theme of becoming. Late Minoan II (Knossos, Crete; fifteenth century B.C.). (From Evans, A. 1921–1935. *The Palace of Minos: a Comparative Account of the Successive Stages of the Early Cretan Civilization as Illustrated by the Discoveries at Knossos.* Vol. 1 [1921], vol. 2 [1928], vol. 3 [1930], vol. 4 [1935]. London: Macmillan. Heraklion Museum, Crete.)

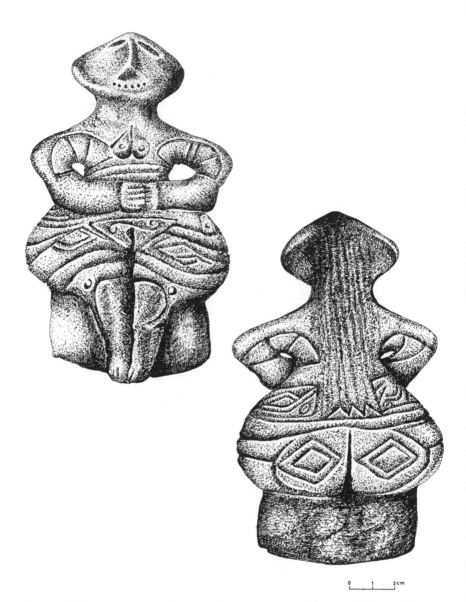

0   1   2cm

Figure 28. Lozenges mark the weighty buttocks and thighs of this goddess seated on a stool. Karanovo culture (Pazardžik, at Plovdiv, Bulgaria; *ca.* 4500 B.C.). (From Gimbutas, M. 1974. *The Gods and Goddess of Old Europe: 7000 to 3500 B.C.: Myths, Legends, and Cult Images*. London: Thames & Hudson; Berkeley: University of California Press. Naturhistorisches Museum, Vienna.)

PREGNANCY, GROWTH, MULTIPLICATION

The Pregnant Goddess

The Pregnant Goddess, from the Upper Paleolithic through the Neolithic, was portrayed naturalistically as a nude with hands placed on her enlarged belly. The abdominal part of her body is always emphasized. In the infancy of agriculture, her pregnant belly was apparently likened to field fertility; earlier she may have been a goddess of human fertility (Figure 29).

Double images of two goddesses, sometimes one slightly larger than the other, may represent a mother and daughter aspect of the Earth Mother.

Figure 29. Pregnant Earth Fertility Goddess in an open shrine model. A round hole for libations is in front of her. Slim and schematic male figurines flank her, possibly representing kouretes. Cucuteni culture (Ghelaești-Nedeia, county of Piatra Neamț, NE Romania; 3900–3800 B.C.). (From *Romania Today* 1984, no. 6 (June). Peatra Neamț Archaeological Museum.)

Symbols of the Pregnant Goddess

* The *pregnant belly* is a symbol of the Earth Fertility Goddess, the Grain Mother, Earth Mother, and Mother of the Dead. These probably developed from the Pregnant Goddess of the Upper Paleolithic (Figure 30).
* *Hills, mounds,* and *ovens* represent the pregnant belly of the Earth Fertility Goddess from Neolithic times (Figure 31).

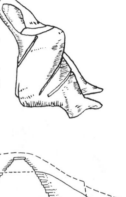

Figure 30. A Neolithic miniature figurine of the Pregnant Goddess with hands on her bulging abdomen. Sesklo culture (Achilleion, Thessaly, Greece; *ca.* 5800 B.C.). (From Author's excavation 1973. Larisa Archaeological Museum.)

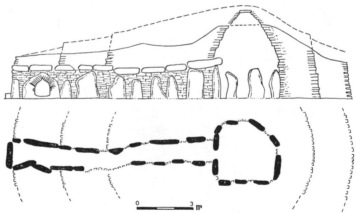

Figure 31. In this passage grave the beehive-shaped chamber (belly of the Earth Mother) is topped by a flat stone (omphalos). A slab at the passage's entrance is engraved with the same mound-and-knob configuration. The lines emanating from the mound may represent resurgent plant life. Armorican Neolithic (Île Longue, Larmor Baden, Brittany; *ca.* early fourth millennium B.C.). (From Twohig, E. S. 1981. *The Megalithic Art of Western Europe.* Oxford: Clarendon Press.)

- *Buttocks, two seeds or fruits grown together,* and *double figures* (caterpillars, snakes, goddesses, phalluses) are symbols of the strength of two, deriving from the Upper Paleolithic and continuing throughout the Old European period (Figure 32).

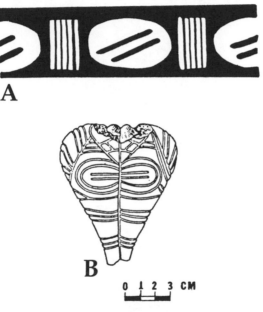

Figure 32. **A,** The bi-line within an egg is a favorite ceramic motif. Dimini culture (Thessaly, N. Greece; early fifth millennium B.C.). **B,** Abundant fertility is symbolized by twin embryos in the womb and a double egg on the buttocks. The double eggs often contain two straight lines across both halves. Classical Cucuteni culture (Novye Rusešty I, Soviet Moldavia; 4500–4000 B.C.). (From Theocharis, D. R., ed. 1973. *Neolithic Greece.* Athens: National Bank of Greece, and Markevich, V. I.1970. "Mnogoslojnoe poselenie Novye Rusešty I." *Kratkie soobščeniya Instituta Arxeologii.* Moscow: Nauka 123: 56–68. Kišenev Archaeological Museum.)

MALE DIVINITIES

There are two stereotypes of male divinities that can be distinguished.

The Young and the Sorrowful Ancient

Sculptures of young males in ithyphallic posture most likely express the potency of springtime fertilizing powers. This strong young God could have been the consort of the Goddess.

The Sorrowful Ancient is portrayed as a peaceful man sitting on a stool, hands either resting on his knees or supporting his chin. Since these figurines appear together with Pregnant Goddess figurines, probably representing Harvest Goddesses (old hags), it can be assumed that the image portrays a dying vegetation god (Figure 33).

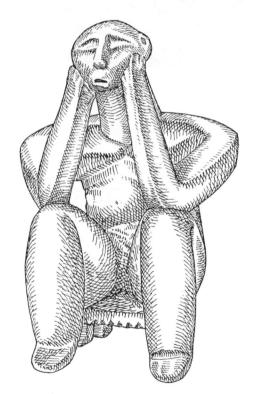

Figure 33. The "Sorrowful Ancient" terracotta figurine found together with a female figurine (probably harvest goddess, "Old Hag") in a grave. (Height 11.5 cm.) Hamangia culture (Cernavoda, E. Romania; 5000–4500 B.C.). (From Berciu, D. 1966. *Cultura Hamangia*. Bucharest: Bucharest National Museum.)

The Master of Animals

The Master of Animals, a god holding a hook or crosier, may be, on the one hand, related to the historically known Silvanus, Faunus, and Pan, forest spirits and protectors of forest animals and hunters. On the other hand, he may derive from the animal-robed and animal-masked figures of the Upper Paleolithic (Figure 34).

Other images of the masculine principle, such as nude men with animal masks, were probably portrayals of participants in rituals.

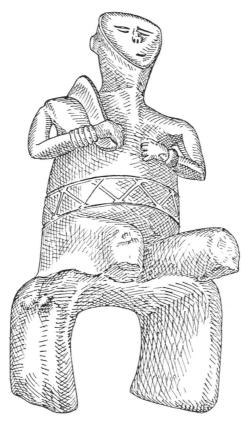

Figure 34. Male god holding a hook. (Height 25.6 cm.) Tisza culture (Szegvár-Tüzköves, SE Hungary; *ca.* 5000 B.C.). (From Gimbutas, M. 1974. *The Gods and Goddesses of Old Europe: 7000 to 3500 B.C.: Myths, Legends, and Cult Images.* London: Thames & Hudson; Berkeley: University of California Press. Budapest National Museum.)

CONTINUITY IN THE INDO-EUROPEAN
AND CHRISTIAN ERAS

The outcome of the clash of Old European religious symbols with alien Indo-European religious forms, particularly after the second infiltration of pastoral and patriarchal "Kurgan" peoples in the middle of the fourth millennium B.C. is visible in the dethronement of Old European goddesses, the disappearance of temples, cult paraphernalia, and sacred symbols and signs, as well as in the drastic reduction of religious images in the visual arts. This impoverishment began in east central Europe and gradually came to affect all of central Europe. The Aegean islands, Crete, and the central and western Mediterranean regions continued Old European traditions for several millennia more, but the core of Old European civilization was by then lost.

The process of the Indo-Europeanization of Europe was not, however, a replacement of one culture with another but a gradual hybridization of two different cultures and symbolic systems. Because the androcentric ideology of the Indo-Europeans was that of the new ruling class, it has come down to us as the "official" belief system of ancient Europe. But there was never a total uprooting of Old European sacred images and symbols; these most persistent motifs were too deeply implanted in the psyche of the European population. They could have disappeared only with a total extermination of the female population, who, most intimately concerned with the folkways of pregnancy and birth, preserved them from grandmother to granddaughter and midwife to mother.

The Goddess's religion went underground. Some of the old traditions, particularly those connected with birth, death, and earth-fertility rituals, have continued to this day without much change in some regions; in others they were assimilated to Indo-European ideology.

In ancient Greece, assimilation into the Indo-European pantheon of gods resulted in the creation of strange and even absurd images. Such a process is most strikingly visible in the conversion of Athena, the Old European Bird Goddess, into a militarized figure carrying a shield and wearing an owl helmet. The belief in her birth from the forehead of Zeus, the ruling god of the Indo-Europeans in Greece, shows how far the transformation went—from a parthenogenetic goddess to her birth from a male god! And yet this is not entirely surprising: Zeus was a bull—in Indo-European symbolism the Thunder

God is a bull—and Athena's birth from the head of a bull could well have been influenced by the memory of birth from a bucranium, which, as we have seen, was a simulacrum of the uterus in Old European symbolism.

The Death-Wielder, the Goddess as a bird of prey, was also militarized. Portrayals of the Owl Goddess on stone stelae acquired a sword or dagger during the Bronze Age in Sardinia, Corsica, Liguria, southern France, Brittany, and Spain. The Greek Athena and Irish Morrígan and Badb are known to appear in battle scenes as vultures, crows, or ravens. The transformation of this Goddess into a mare probably took place during the Bronze Age.

Parthenogenetic goddesses creating from themselves without the help of male insemination gradually changed into brides, wives, and daughters; they were "eroticized," linked with the principle of sexual love, in response to a patriarchal and patrilinear system. For example, Greek Hera, probably a reflex of the Old European Snake Goddess, became the wife of Zeus. Furthermore, Zeus had to "seduce" (with a nod toward historical accuracy we might prefer the term "rape") hundreds of other goddesses and nymphs to establish himself. Everywhere in Europe the Earth Mother lost her ability to give birth to plant life without intercourse with the Thunder God; in Indo-European belief, only after the first thunder does grass begin to grow and water become purified.

In contrast, the Birth- and Life-giver, the Fate or Three Fates, remained remarkably independent in the beliefs of many areas of Europe. Greek Artemis, Irish Brigit, and Baltic Laima, for example, did not acquire any of the features of an Indo-European god, nor were they married to gods. Baltic Laima appears in mythological songs together with Dievas, the Indo-European god of the light of the sky, to bless the fields and human life—not as his wife but as an equally powerful goddess. Thus we see that the process of the assimilation of goddesses into Indo-European ideology took place at various times and to varying degrees. The Life-giver escaped assimilation.

A remnant in the historical era of the ruling power of goddesses is indicated by the use of the term "queen" for the goddesses who were not married to Indo-European gods but who continued to be powerful in their own right. Herodotus wrote of "Queen Artemis," and Hesychius called Aphrodite "the queen." The Roman counterpart of the virgin Artemis, Diana, was invoked as *rēgīna*.

In Christian times, the Birth-giver and Earth Mother partially fused with the Virgin Mary. It is not surprising that in many Catholic countries the worship of the Virgin surpasses that of Jesus. She is still connected with life-water and miraculous healing springs, with trees, blossoms, and flowers, and with fruits and harvests. She is pure, strong, and just. She is still the Great Earth Mother. In folk sculptures of the Mother of God, she is huge and powerful, holding a tiny Christ on her lap.

Old European goddesses appear in European folktales, beliefs, and mythological songs in a variety of epiphanies. The Bird Goddess and anthropomorphic Life-giving Goddess continue as a Fate or Fairy and also as a luck- and wealth-bringing duck, swan, or ram. As a prophesier, she is a cuckoo. As a primeval mother, she is known as a supernatural deer (in Irish mythology) or bear (in Greek, Baltic, and Slavic mythology). In her death-bringing aspect, she is still a vulture, owl, pelican, or other large bird or bird of prey. As personified Death, she is a frightening White Lady who is able to walk through fences and doors, preceded or accompanied by a white dog.

The Snake Goddess has largely vanished from European beliefs except as a crowned snake, the symbol of wisdom and omniscience. Worship of the grass snake as a symbol of fertility, immortality, and happiness continued until the twentieth century in the Baltic and Slavic countries. Part of the proscription of the snake as a benevolent force is doubtless due to its portrayal in Genesis 3.

The lunar Goddess of Death and Regeneration was transformed into a witch of night and magic who causes destruction and nightmares but who at the same time has regenerative healing powers. She is an overseer of cyclic life energy. She prevents plants from thriving and takes milk from cows; she destroys so that humans, plants, and milk may be born anew. As the Greek *Hekatē*, Celtic *Morrígan*, Slavic *Baba Jaga*, and Lithuanian *Ragana*, she can be a beautiful woman or a nightmarish creature. Her main epiphanies are the toad or frog, hedgehog, mouse, fish, and the butterfly, moth, or cicada. She has the ability to fly; her cottage in Slavic mythology stands on a chicken leg.

There is no question that Old European sacred images and symbols remain a vital, if transformed, part of the cultural heritage of Europe. Many of us even in this day were surrounded in childhood by the fairy world, which contained many images transmitted from Old Europe. In some nooks of Europe, as in my own motherland, Lithuania, there still flow sacred and miraculous rivers and springs; there flourish holy forests and groves, reservoirs of blossoming life; there grow gnarled trees bursting with vitality and holding the power to heal; and beside the holy waters there still stand menhirs, called "goddesses," full of mysterious power.

Old European culture was the matrix of much later beliefs and practices. Memories of a long-lasting gynocentric past—the Golden Age of balance and harmony, the *Satyá-yuga* (the 'Age of Truth')—could not be erased. To an archeologist it is an extensively documented historical reality. To a mythologist or historian of religion it is the palimpsest upon which later myth and belief were written, the framework that built our own culture. To a linguist it is the unrecorded substratum that caused, in part, the transformation of Indo-European phonology and grammar.

To us all, it can be a world of dreams and teaching, a heritage which can bind us together again as children of and partners with one another and the Earth that bore us.[1]

[1] For a detailed analysis of Old European symbols, see Gimbutas, M. 1989. *The Language of the Goddess*. San Francisco: Harper & Row. (With about 2000 illustrations.)

PART III

The Search for Relatives of Indo-European

This part of the volume takes up some recent work on possible relationships of Indo-European to other families.

Both Greenberg and the joint authors Shevoroshkin and Manaster-Ramer propose higher-order genetic units having IE as one among several branches. Although the two proposals agree in large part, they do not on all points. The group of Russian linguists represented at the symposium by Shevoroshkin has worked mainly with a Nostratic phylum having western and eastern branches, the western branch including Afro-Asiatic, Kartvelian, and IE and the eastern branch including Uralic, Altaic, and Dravidian. Greenberg agrees that all these probably fall together at a very distant level but maintains that the major division of the overall group should be into northern and southern branches. Greenberg's northern tier includes IE, Uralic-Yukaghir, Altaic, Japanese-Korean-Ainu, Gilyak, Chukotian, and Eskimo-Aleut, whereas his southern tier (not treated in his paper here except for brief mention in footnote 4) includes Afro-Asiatic and Dravidian as well as Nilo-Saharan. In recent years the Russian comparativists have revised and augmented their Nostratic classification as the result of several studies mentioned in the paper by Shevoroshkin and Manaster-Ramer, and their Nostratic is now closer to Greenberg's independently derived Eurasiatic in two important respects. First, they now see Afro-Asiatic as likely to be more distantly related, perhaps a sister superstock to Nostratic rather than part of it, and second, they have added further stocks to the northeast, extending as far as Eskimo-Aleut. An important disagreement still to be resolved concerns the position of Dravidian.

Adding further to the diversity of findings, Carleton Hodge, who concentrates on the Afro-Asiatic connection alone, comes up with, among other things, certain sets of phonological correspondences different from those postulated by the Russian group.

Although the work of present-day long-range comparativists like Greenberg and Shevoroshkin is often criticized as too radical, an earlier, quite similar version of Nostratic was proposed by the greatly respected Danish linguist Holger Pedersen over half a century ago. His Nostratic included Semitic, IE, Uralic, Yukaghir (uncertain), Altaic, and Eskimo-Aleut. That is, except for the inclusion of Semitic at this level, his proposal is quite similar to Greenberg's.

Saul Levin's scope is narrower in one trivial sense because he concentrates just on certain resemblances of IE to Semitic, one of the branches of the diverse Afro-Asiatic group. But in another sense it goes beyond much comparative linguistics in challenging the family-tree theory usually followed in genetic linguistics. As Levin has written previously, it is of great importance but commonly overlooked that most of the correspondences that scholars have brought forth linking IE to Afro-Asiatic, including some involving basic vocabulary, are not demonstrably correspondences to Afro-Asiatic as a whole, since the Afro-Asiatic side is represented only by Semitic and not by its other branches. The implication is that IE is closer to Semitic than it is to other branches of Afro-Asiatic. It is thus not coincidental that Levin does not follow the family-tree model of linguistic genealogy but is content just to lay out the facts and the analysis and to let the explanation follow when it will, after sufficient analysis will have made a proper theory supportable. The explanation of Gamkrelidze and Ivanov is that the early Indo-Europeans were in close contact with early Semitic peoples for a long time. If this is correct, this hypothesis must lead to a reassessment of the degree to which diffusion can involve basic vocabulary with phonological correspondences. But perhaps diffusion is not even the proper term. Perhaps we need a new theory that more clearly distinguishes different kinds of diffusion-like processes. Austerlitz suggests one possibility in his paper in Part V; and as Egerod mentions in Part IV, another possible case in point is Japanese, if indeed it does turn out to have basic connections with both Altaic and Austric.

Finally, the paper of Shevoroshkin and Manaster-Ramer also reviews some of the recent work of the Russian group involving long-range groups other than Nostratic, particularly Sino-Caucasian, a phylum linking the languages of the Northern Caucasus with Sino-Tibetan. This paper thus forms a bridge to the next part of the volume.

Some Problems of Indo-European in Historical Perspective

JOSEPH H. GREENBERG

This chapter has two related purposes. My first is to put into historical perspective my own methodology of linguistic genetic classification with particular reference to the subject of this symposium, the celebrated pronouncement of 1786 by Sir William Jones regarding the family of languages now generally known as Indo-European. My second purpose is to consider some grammatical problems of Indo-European in the broader context of a family I will call Eurasiatic, of which Indo-European is a member. The composition of this family is outlined later.

Of the considerable lexical and grammatical evidence I have assembled, it will be possible within the scope of this chapter to consider only two grammatical problems. Such a discussion is particularly appropriate in relation to the bicentennial we are commemorating; we are, as it were, extending Jones's original brilliant conjecture one step further by citing but a small part of the evidence for a larger stock of which Indo-European is itself a member. This broader Eurasiatic will have sprung from a common source, just as, in Jones's original formulation, Sanskrit, Greek, and Latin along with several other languages were declared to have a common source in which we now call "Proto-Indo-European."

Regarding the first of the two major topics to be discussed here, namely, the methodology of genetic linguistic classification, it will be possible to include only a few basic considerations. Beginning with Greenberg (1949) in the introductory section of the initial version of my classification of African languages and reprinted in later versions of the classification (Greenberg 1955, 1963) and successively restated in expanded and more detailed form (Greenberg 1957, 1987), I have set forth what I conceive to be the main considerations involved in genetic linguistic classification. In particular *Language in the Americas*

(Greenberg 1987), a publication devoted to the classification of the indigenous languages of the Americas, contains as its initial chapter a quite detailed treatment of the subject, and anyone interested in a more complete discussion than I can attempt here is referred to this source.

In starting with Jones and his statement, while also taking into consideration the work of two of the chief pioneers who first worked out in detail the implications of Jones's hypothesis, namely, Rask and Bopp, I will in effect be simply reformulating and analyzing the bases of the "old-time religion." How did these pioneers discover and accurately delimit the membership of Indo-European?

For this purpose let us cite Jones's statement of 1786.[1]

The Sanskrit language, whatever may be its antiquity, is of a wonderful structure; more perfect than Greek, more copious than Latin, and more exquisitely refined than either; yet bearing to both of them, both in the roots of verbs and the forms of grammar, a stronger affinity than could have been produced by accident; so strong that no philologer could examine the Sanskrit, Greek, and Latin without believing them to have sprung from a common source, which, perhaps, no longer exists. There is a similar reason though not quite so forcible, for supposing that both the Gothic and Celtic had the same origin as Sanskrit.

One can make several observations regarding Jones's statement. The most obvious, and the one that is almost exclusively emphasized, is indeed central; it is that Jones did not derive Greek, Latin, and the other languages from Sanskrit but rather posited for all of them a common source, which "perhaps no longer exists."

A second point, though less explicit, is also truly fundamental: In his statement Jones mentions "the roots of verbs and the forms of grammar." It is clear from the rest of Jones's work that when he talked of the "forms of grammar," just as when he adduced verb roots, he meant resemblances involving simultaneously sound and meaning of specific related forms. For example, when he compared Latin and Sanskrit, what impressed him were such resemblances as -*m* 'first person singular', -*s* 'second person singular', and -*t* 'third person singular' in the verbal inflections of both languages. He seems to have been quite clear in his understanding of the distinction between what we today would call genetic and typological criteria. In fact in my first statement of the methodology of genetic classifica-

[1]The statement is quoted here in slightly modified form as cited in Robins (1968: 134). Compare the quotation in Chapter 2 by Garland Cannon, page 31.

tion (Greenberg 1949) I cited these precise words in my introductory article.

A third point is less obvious and in fact is only implied in Jones's statement and in his other work. This is, that with Jones's background knowledge of Arabic and, no doubt, Hebrew, on the one hand, and Latin, Greek, Germanic, and so forth, on the other, the addition of Sanskrit to his repertoire enabled him to see a valid grouping based on differential resemblances. In later work he accurately outlined the Semitic and Finno-Ugric families (see Cannon's chapter, this volume). In other words, even though he did not state it explicitly, he was in effect applying what I called earlier the method of mass comparison and more recently multilateral comparison (Greenberg 1987), a term that I find is being used by Nostraticists writing in English.

Rask is the linguist of the pioneer period of comparative linguistics that followed Jones who seems to have most clearly articulated this point. Diderichsen (1974: 297) paraphrases Rask as follows: "The more languages and dialects you take into the comparison, the more gaps you are able to fill by intermediate forms." Diderichsen then goes on to quote from one of Rask's letters, probably written in 1809 (*Sammlede Afhandlinger* 1: 15), in which he states, "that I discovered such a fundamental coherence between so distant languages (Greek, Latin, Gothic, Icelandic, German) led me to investigate so many tongues as time would allow."

We may note that Bopp, generally considered the true founder of comparative Indo-European studies, in his first major work (1816) compared the conjugation systems of Sanskrit, Greek, Latin, and Germanic. It was against the background of the common traits of these languages that he successively added Lithuanian (1833), Celtic and Slavic (1839), Albanian (1855), and Armenian (1857).[2] In these later studies he continued to include all the previously distinguished Indo-European languages in his comparisons. He thus eventually embraced in his comparisons all those languages known at the time that are now generally agreed to be Indo-European.

All this occurred, of course, before linguists recognized the principles of regular sound change and of phonetic correspondences. If, as is commonly stated, this is the only scientific method by which

---

[2]In regard to Armenian, however, Bopp, though recognizing its Indo-European affiliation, considered it to be an Iranian dialect. Its status as a separate branch of Indo-European was established by Hübschmann (1877).

genetic relationship can be proved (the answer to the wrong question anyway, since classification is primary), Bopp's achievement becomes a miracle, since the number of ways of classifying even twenty
languages is on the order of 10^{47}.

Further, contrary to widely accepted assumptions, it is not true
that the Neogrammarians believed that relationship can be proved
by recourse to sound laws. In Wilbur's entire volume (1977) devoted
to the literature on the controversy regarding the regularity of sound
changes, one will not perceive the slightest hint that the validity of
Indo-European as a genetic family is at stake.

Delbrück, a major figure among the Neogrammarians and the collaborator of Brugmann in the famous *Grundriss*, states (1904: 121) the
following:

My starting point is that specific result of comparative linguistics which is
not in doubt and cannot be in doubt. It was proven (*erwiesen*) by Bopp and
others that the so-called Indo-European languages are related. The proof
(*Beweis*) was produced by juxtaposition (*Nebeneinanderstellung*) of words and
forms of similar meaning. When one considers that in these languages the
formation of the inflectional forms of the verbs, nouns, and pronouns agrees
in essentials and likewise that an extraordinary number of inflected and un-
inflected words agree in their lexical parts, the assumption of chance agreement must appear absurd.

In an earlier mention of the same work (1884), Delbrück stated
concerning sound laws that "Such laws have only a tentative value.
Since, of course, obvious (*einleuchtende*) etymologies are the material
from which sound laws are drawn and since this material can always
be increased and changed, therefore new sound laws can be established and old ones transformed."

Uralic, at least in regard to its main branch, Finno-Ugric, was proposed in the eighteenth century by Sajnovics and Gyarmathy, and
not even the most conservative will dispute it. Yet as late as Szinnyéi
(1910), a standard handbook, only back and front vowel harmony is
reconstructed for the vowels, and even this is based on a rather arbitrary "majority rule" among certain key languages. Among the consonants, the sibilants, in particular, present numerous problems.

Collinder (1960: 405) reconstructs Proto-Uralic forms but notes
that "It is a matter of course that in many instances the reconstruction of a PU (Proto-Uralic) or PFU (Proto-Finno-Ugric) word is more
uncertain than the etymology on which it is based."

To claim that Sanskrit *bhar*- 'to carry' is etymologically related to

Greek *pher-* with the same basic meaning is clearly less of a claim than that the Proto-Indo-European original is *bher-*. In fact, Schleicher had earlier reconstructed *bhar-*, but the assumption that the first consonant is *bh* is now challenged by Gamkrelidze and others on typological grounds. Throughout all this, and even going back to Bopp, the etymological connection of these forms has never been questioned.

Hrozný, who first convinced the learned world of the Indo-European affiliation of Hittite, describes his reason for accepting this hypothesis in the following terms (1917: vii).

Everyone who wishes to interpret the Boghazköi texts, from the moment of their publication, will, like the author, come to the same conclusion on the basis of instances like the fact that *wadar* means 'water', that its genitive is not *wadaras* but, remarkably enough, *wedenas*, that the Hittites have a participle in *-nt*, that 'what' (masc.) is *kuis* and in the neuter *kuid*, that 'I' is *ug* (cf. Latin *ego*), 'to me' *ammug* (cf. Greek *emoige*), 'thou' *zig* (cf. Greek *suge*), 'to thee' *tug* (Gothic *thuk* etc.), that the Hittite present is inflected *jami, jasi, jazi, jaweni, jatteni, janzi,* etc. etc.

Hrozný does not present a table of correspondences of the kind that have become *de rigueur* in the pages of *IJAL*, nor has anyone since. The reason is simple: the new Hittite data themselves revolutionized our ideas about the Proto-Indo-European sound system. Moreover, as a result of this the considerable consensus of Indo-Europeanists concerning the phonological structure of Proto-Indo-European that existed before the discovery of Hittite and the other Anatolian languages was shattered, and at present there are few points on which all Indo-Europeanists are agreed.

Note also that the resemblances adduced by Hrozný as decisive are with various Indo-European languages or with none in particular as with the verb paradigm he cites. It is, in other words, against a broad background of knowledge of Indo-European languages, particularly in their earlier forms, and not by hypotheses of relationship with one language that Hrozný presented the thesis now accepted by all Indo-Europeanists.

I will consider the particular problems of Indo-European with which we are concerned here against the background of its membership in a larger family, which I will call "Eurasiatic." It is posited to have the following membership: (1) Indo-European, (2) Uralic, Yukaghir, (3) Altaic (Turkic, Mongolian, Tungus), (4) Ainu, Japanese, Korean, (5) Gilyak, (6) Chukotian, and (7) Eskimo-Aleut.

Although the definition of Eurasiatic is new, it should not be wholly surprising. There have been numerous, mostly pairwise, comparisons among these languages. Many Altaicists accept Korean or Japanese, or both, as Altaic, but it seems clear to me that Mongolian and Tungus within traditional Altaic are much closer to each other than either is to Korean or Japanese, whereas the work especially of Samuel Martin (1966) has served to document the closer relationship of Korean to Japanese.

And I do not believe that there is a specially close relationship between Uralic and Altaic as was widely accepted in the nineteenth century on typological grounds. In regard to the absence of a special relationship I agree with what I believe to be the general consensus at the present time. There is enough, however, in the way of concrete resemblances to support the membership of both in the larger Eurasiatic family as I have outlined it here.

What then of Indo-European and Semitic? A hypothesis regarding their special relationship is clearly motivated by nonlinguistic factors but does not, of itself, invalidate the hypothesis. It is clear, on the one hand, that Semitic is closer to Afroasiatic than it is to Indo-European, since it shares whole paradigms and common lexical items with the other branches of Afroasiatic (Egyptian, Berber, Cushitic, and Chadic). On the other hand, Indo-European shares a whole series of grammatical and lexical traits with other language groups in Euroasiatic not found in Afroasiatic. It is to Uralic within this grouping that most attention has been paid. Thus Anttila in his well-known textbook of historical linguistics, after mentioning Indo-Semitic, Indo-Uralic, and Ural-Altaic, states (1972, 320) that "the Indo-Uralic hypothesis is particularly strong because the agreement is very good in pronouns and verbal elements as well as in basic vocabulary."[3]

I am not denying a relationship between Indo-European and Afroasiatic or between Uralic and Altaic with Dravidian. These are the most common hypotheses that cut across the grouping proposed here.[4] It is progress that in more recent work the notion of an Indo-European connection with Semitic has largely been replaced with that of a connection with Afroasiatic as a whole rather than with Semitic in particular.

[3]The Indo-Uralic hypothesis has, of course, been supported by several other scholars. Pedersen, who introduced the term "Nostratic" for a family that would include Indo-European, Semitic, Uralic, and possibly others, stated on several occasions that Indo-European was more closely related to Uralic than to Semitic (Pedersen 1933, 1935).

[4]Concerning Afro-Asiatic, see footnote 3. In regard to Dravidian, I have noted a fair number of vocabulary resemblances, including the first and second person pro-

I believe, however, that these other connections are more distant. It is the purpose of genetic linguistic classification to delineate valid genetic groups, that is, sets of languages that are more closely related to each other than to any languages outside the stock. Thus the Germanic languages constitute, at a relatively low level, a valid genetic unit, whereas a group of languages consisting of Swedish, Hindi, and Czech is not one, although these languages are related, since they are all Indo-European.

In a book still in preparation, to be called *Indo-European and Its Closest Relatives: the Eurasiatic Language Family*, I will present data regarding approximately 70 grammatical elements, of which about 50 are found in Indo-European. In the present context I can discuss just two of them.

The first of these is the nominative of the first person singular pronoun in Indo-European, now commonly reconstructed as $*e\hat{g}(h)om$. It is in suppletive alternation with $*m$- in other cases. The reason for the parentheses around the h is that Sanskrit irregularly has an aspirated consonant not reflected in the other languages. There are forms without -m, such as Greek *egṓ*, in this case alongside a form in final -n that derives from $*$-m. The forms without the final -m were early explained as analogical with the -$ō$ of the first person present indicative active of the verb (Schmidt 1899: 405) and fairly generally accepted (as in Brugmann 1904: 71, and the etymological dictionary of Pokorny 1959: I. 291). However, $*e\hat{g}(h)om$ itself was generally analyzed as consisting of an initial deictic element, whereas the final -om was interpreted by Brugmann as probably a neuter with abstract meaning. Brugmann translates the entire form as *"meine Hierheit"* (literally 'my hereness') but also talks of the problem of its interpretation in a striking metaphor as leading into the distant abysses of Proto-Indo-European in which we can find our way about only by groping. He also says that the identification of the initial e- with the deictic element found, for example, in Greek *ekeînos* 'that', alongside *keînos* is well worth considering (*"sehr erwägenswert"*).

More recently, the suggestion of Savchenko (1960) that the final -m of $*e\hat{g}(h)om$ is to be identified with the common first person singu-

---

nouns, and agreement in grammatical irregularities as well as bound markers with Nilo-Saharan. Moreover, Nilo-Saharan shares important grammatical features with Eurasiatic. All this requires more study, but my tentative conclusion is that Nilo-Saharan, Dravidian, and, no doubt, Elamite belong to a different grouping related to Eurasiatic at a deeper level. An example of a feature common to Eurasiatic, on the one hand, and Nilo-Saharan and Dravidian on the other, is probably the personal plural in -r discussed later in this chapter.

lar *m*, which we have already found in the oblique cases of the pronoun but which is also found in verb-subject affixes, has received support from Myrkin (1964) and is accepted in the standard comparative work of Szemerényi (1978: 275). However, these more recent interpretations, though identifying -*m* with the first-person marker of Indo-European, consider that *$e\hat{g}(h)om$ is a late formation within Indo-European. It is supposed that the real marker of the first person is the initial part and that -*m* has been redundantly added.

The most important Eurasiatic evidence on this problem comes from the Chukotian group. In Chukchi itself the first person singular predicative form is *igəm* ~ *egəm*, in which *i* ~ *e* is a vowel-harmony alternation.[5] The corresponding second person singular is *igət* ~ *egət*. This pattern is found only in the first and second person singulars.

The existence of these Chukotian forms obviously strengthens the case for -*m* in Indo-European being the indicator of the first person singular. They also, however, suggest that, contrary to Savchenko and others who have supported his hypothesis, the form itself is very old, since it has correspondence in Chukchi and, as we shall see, elsewhere in Eurasiatic.

Thus far I have cited only the Chukchi predicative forms. These contain an initial *i* ~ *e* and have several uses. The main one is predication as in *ənpənačg-egəm* 'I am an old man'. The same form also occurs, as would be expected, in stative forms of the verb as in *ge-čejv-igəm* 'I am gone'. In this usage we have a prefix *ge-* ~ *ga*, not discussed here. Its resemblance to German *ge-* is striking and can be shown not to be accidental. Thus we might paraphrase the form just cited as *ge-gangen-bin ich* in German. This topic is not pursued here. The second major use of these "predicative" forms is as object suffixes on the verb. In addition, however, to *igəm* ~ *egəm* there is a shorter form *gəm* 'I', which corresponds to the second person singular *gət* 'thou'. These are used much as independent pronouns as in languages like Latin or Greek. The contrast in Chukotian of forms with and without the initial vowel obviously supports Brugmann's conjecture that the initial vowel is a separate element, and its function in predication in Chukotian is a plausible one for a deictic.

A further use of the short form in all the languages of the Chukchi-Koryak languages, the major subgroup of Chukotian, from which Kamchadal stands somewhat apart genetically, is as object in the set

[5] In accordance with the practice of specialists in Chukchi, Eskimo, and Aleut, I symbolize the voiced velar fricative as *g*. These languages have no voiced velar stop.

of bipersonal subject-object markers of the transitive verb. We find -*gət* suffixed to indicate the second person singular object with both first and third person subjects, whether singular or plural. Examples from Chukchi are *tə-l'u-gət* 'I saw thee' and *ne-l'u-gət* 'they saw thee'. The first person as object occurs only with third person plural subject, as in *ne-l'u-gəm* 'they see me'. In Kamchadal -*gən* is used to indicate second person singular object as in Chukchi-Koryak, such as *an'chi-gən*, 'he teaches thee'. Whether the final -*n* of Kamchadal corresponds to the -*t* of Chukchi is uncertain.

The employment of -*gət* as suffixed second singular object is also found in Eskimo. It is found in the bipersonal suffix for first singular subject acting on second singular object, a form that can probably be reconstructed as **mkət*. This form, whose reflexes can be found everywhere in Eskimo from the deviant, probably Yuit dialect of Sirenik in Siberia to the Inuit dialects of Greenland, is termed "irregular" by Uhlenbeck (1906: 61) in what is still the only general survey of Eskimo morphology. Practically all dialects have extended this form analogically to designate first person dual and first person plural subject with second person singular object but in different ways. What is irregular about **mkət* and is not explainable within Eskimo is the *k*. It is clear that *m* indicates first person singular and *t* second person. The *k* of *kət* corresponds exactly to Chukchi *g*. There is only a single series of basic stops in Eskimo, and the unvoiced is the fundamental form. There is a system of internal consonant gradation that is typologically similar to that of Finnish (Ulving 1953), and only *k* can appear as the second member of a consonant cluster.

Turning to Aleut of the Eskimo-Aleut branch of Eurasiatic, I find one striking agreement with the forms being discussed. Aleut is divided into western, central, and eastern dialects. In Menovshchikov (1968: 389), a description of a Siberian Aleut language as spoken on Bering Island and derived from a central dialect by a migration within the last century, I find an anomalous suppletive form of the first person plural possessive independent pronoun, that is, *ga-mas*. In this formation the latter part is -*mas*, the usual affix of the first person plural in this dialect. The rest of the independent possessive pronominal paradigm is based on a singular base *ti-* and a plural base *txi-* followed by bound possessives, such as *tiŋ* 'I'. Elsewhere in Aleut I find analogical replacements for the first person plural with the same base found in the remainder of the paradigm. An example is *ti-man* in Unalaska (eastern dialect) as reported by Veniaminov in the nineteenth century. The irregularity of the first person plural reported by Menovshchikov indicates that it must be an old formation.

The remaining evidence is from Uralic. In Hungarian there is an independent accusative pronoun that in the first person singular has the variants *engem* and *engemet*. Correspondingly in the second person singular we find *teged* and *tegedet*. The remainder of the paradigm is of quite different formation and need not be cited here. The analysis of the first and second person singular is clear. The facultative *-et* is simply the nominal accusative singular ending that has been added analogically and is not yet established. The initials *en-* and *te-* are the independent first and second person independent pronouns *én* and *te*. This leaves us with *-gem-* and *-get-*, which are obviously similar to the Chukchi *gəm* and *gət*. As in Chukchi, we see the forms without initial vowel used independently. The Hungarian pronouns I have been discussing are related to the emphatic pronouns of Vogul (Mansi), also a member of the Ugric branch of Finno-Ugric. From Vogul I cite the form *am-kke-m* 'I alone' from the Middle Sosvin dialect. The analysis once more is clear. The initial element is *am*, identical with the independent first person singular pronoun, and the remainder *-kkem* is cognate with Hungarian *gem*. The gemination of *k* is historically secondary. Vertés (1967: 214) connects the Vogul forms with the Hungarian independent accusative pronouns previously discussed.

Unlike Hungarian, however, the entire pattern has been extended analogically through the entire paradigm so that it occurs in all three persons and in the singular, dual, and plural.

The final bit of evidence comes from the Kamas (Southern Samoyed) suppletive stem of the verb 'to be', which is found only in the present. 'I am' is *ig-äm*. The stem *ig-* is conjugated for all persons and numbers. If the Kamas form belongs here, we could find a further confirmation of the use of the variant with the initial vowel as a predicative.

On the basis of the foregoing evidence the most probable conclusion is that the forms I have been discussing were original in the first person singular and probably in the second person singular also because of the agreement of Hungarian, Chukotian, and Eskimo. Sometimes it has spread analogically through the entire pronominal paradigm as in Vogul and possibly Kamas.

The other Indo-European grammatical element I should like to treat in a comparative perspective is the *-r* passive and deponent.

This was early considered to be a Celtic-Italic isogloss that strengthened the case for a special relationship between these two branches of Indo-European. However, it was later discovered in Tocharian as well as in Hittite and the other Anatolian languages.

It was early equated (Zimmer 1888) with the -*r* third person plural verb ending of Italic and Indo-Aryan, later also discovered in Tocharian and Hittite. To demonstrate the connection between the third person plural and the passive, Zimmer pointed especially to the impersonal -*r* of Italic, as in Umbrian *i-er* 'they go, one goes', and the Brythonic Celtic, as in Breton *am gweler* 'one sees me, I am seen'.

Zimmer's view has been widely accepted (Kammenhuber 1969: 317; Georgiev 1985: 226). Rosén (1978: 144) interprets the -*t*- of Latin *amā-t-ur* 'he is loved' as the third person *t* functioning as object so that he paraphrases the Latin form as '*liebt-ihn-man*'.

Diachronic parallels for the development of a passive from the reinterpretation of a third person plural subject are easily found. Masai, a language of the Eastern Sudanic subgroup of Nilo-Saharan, has a verb form that is usually treated as a passive in descriptive grammars. Both internal reconstruction and comparative evidence indicate that it involves a suffixed -*i* that is identical with a third person plural pronoun in other languages of the group (Greenberg 1959). Another instance is the Chamorro language of Guam, noted by Shibatani (1985: 829), who cites approvingly the interpretation by Topping (1973: 257) in his grammar according to which the third person plural *ma* is related to the passive prefix *ma* in the same language.

In the case of Indo-European there are complications because of the existence of a middle voice, which has sometimes affected the passive forms in -*r*. These matters are complex and have often been discussed. They are not treated here.

The tentative conclusion at which I have arrived up to this point is that the Indo-European *r* passive has its source in the third person plural subject suffix -*r* of the verb. The existence of similar typological developments elsewhere, the fact that the passive usually develops in those branches of Indo-European in which the *r* third person plural exists, and the fact that the details of the development differ in each specific subfamily all indicate that these may be parallel independent developments in different branches.

Before proceeding to a discussion of other branches of Eurasiatic, however, I should say something about the specific phonological form it takes in Indo-European. García-Ramón (1985) interprets the

Hittite present middle passive -ri as a reduced grade of *-rei, which he posits for Proto-Anatolian.[6] There is widespread Eurasiatic evidence for r(i) as a third person or general person plural and also as an indicator of the passive, middle, or intransitive.

It is a common typological development for a nominal plural to be attached to a verb to express a third person plural subject. A well-known example is Turkish lar ~ ler (vowel-harmony variants), which also secondarily expresses third person subject plural when affixed to the verb, as in Turkish el-ler 'the hands' and gel-di-ler 'they came'. Note also what may be called the "floating plural" of Moru, a language of the Central Sudanic branch of Nilo-Saharan, which may be attached either to the subject noun or the verb to express plurality of action but not to both. In some non-Chuvash Turkic languages the originally nominal lar plural has spread even further and been added redundantly to the first and second person plural pronouns biz and siz, which are no longer transparent when compared to the singulars ben and sen. We have thus an authenticated route of typological change by which an originally personal nominal plural can become an indicator of third person plurality and then spread to the first and second persons.

If we turn once more to Chukchi, we find the independent first and second person plural pronouns mu-ri and tu-ri. These are easily analyzable as containing the very widespread first and second person pronominal forms m and t followed by the personal plural ri, which we deduced from Indo-European and Altaic evidence. These forms, in fact, are the plural members of the same paradigm discussed earlier in which the singular is first person (i)gəm and second person (i)gət. However, in the plural there is no distinction between the independent and the predicative form, except that the latter, which is always bound, shows the vowel harmony variants muri ~ more and turi ~ tore. In Chukchi the third person plural independent pronoun is in the nominative ət-ri, in which ət represents t, the most common Eurasiatic demonstrative and third person exponent, well known, of course, from Indo-European. In addition, -r- functions in Chukchi as a plural marker in the oblique cases of certain

---

[6]There is much evidence, besides the variation igəm ~ egəm discussed earlier, for a vowel alternation i ~ e in Eurasiatic (compare Greenberg, to appear). If it is valid, however, it becomes relevant to note the third person plural perfects in -re of Latin and West Tocharian, which have often been equated. In fact, Latin -re could originate from the other proposed variant ri, since e in word-final position in Latin has as one of its sources i (compare mare 'sea' [nom. acc. sg.] < *mar-i).

plural nouns (proper names and kin terms), the only ones that have a number distinction in these cases. The sequence here is noun stem + *r* + oblique-case markers. In Altaic also there is evidence for the personal plural *r* in Tungus and the Turkic languages. In Tungus, Manchu forms a plural *-ri*, which is confined to certain kin terms, as in *mufa-ri* 'grandfathers'. Benzing (1955) reconstructs *-ri* for the plural of reflexive pronouns. He also posits for the Proto-Tungus aorist tense an *-r-* in the aorist plural subject suffixes *-r-bün* (1 pl. excl.), *-r-pu* (1 pl. incl.), and *-r-sün* (2 pl.).

The Turkic languages fall into two branches, one constituted by Chuvash and another by the remainder. Sometimes Chuvash *r* corresponds to non-Chuvash *r*. This is reconstructed as Proto-Turkic $*r_1$ and is presumed to be *r* phonetically. Sometimes, however, we find non-Chuvash *z* corresponding to *r* in Chuvash, and here the reconstruction is symbolized as $*r_2$, and this sound is considered by many to be a palatalized *r*, for which $*ri$ would be a natural source.

In the first and second plural pronouns of Turkic the generally accepted reconstructions are $*mi-r_2$ and $*ti-r_2$. These are based on non-Chuvash Turkic *biz*, *siz* and Chuvash *ĕpir*, *ĕsir*. The initial *ĕ-* of Chuvash may be identified with the *e* of Indo-European *eǵ(h)om*, as discussed by Menges (1968: 19), but the topic is not pursued here.

In Korean the first person pronoun is *u-li*. Korean has a single liquid phoneme, which is transcribed here as *l*. It has been proposed that *u-li* derives from *wu-li* with initial *w-* corresponding to Turkic *b* (Ramstedt 1939: 46). Whether this is accepted or not, it is clear that the pronominal plural *-li* of Korean is exactly what we would expect as the correspondent of the Turkic pronominal plural markers.[7]

A further example of this formation is Amur Gilyak *me-r* 'we (inclusive)'; compare *me-gi* 'we two' in the same dialect. The first part, of course, contains the first person *m*, which is found in every branch of Eurasiatic except Ainu.

Japanese has a personal plural *-ra*, seen, for example, in *kodomo-ra* 'children', which probably is related to the forms we have already cited. Finally it survives in a single Yukaghir form *uo-r-pe* 'children', a hypercharacterized formation in which the general and productive Yukaghir nominal plural *-pe* has been added to the older plural in *-r*.

A development parallel to that of Indo-European by which a personal plural has given rise to a passive or passivelike construction

---

[7] I formerly included here also Korean *-il-*, an exponent of the intransitive and middle, but as pointed out by Ramstedt (1939), this is historically secondary. I am indebted to Samuel Martin for bringing this to my attention.

(middle, intransitive, stative) has taken place in Altaic and Japanese. This is a productive method of verb derivation in Mongolian. Examples from Classical Mongolian are *asqa-* 'to spill' (tr.) with *asqara* 'to be spilled' and *ebede-* 'to break' (tr.) with *ebedere-* 'to go to pieces'. In Turkic it is found only in the most archaic form of non-Chuvash Turkish, that is, the language of the Orkhon Inscriptions in which there is an *-r-* middle-verb derivational morpheme.

Finally in Japanese, I cite first the language of the Ryukyus in which there is a verbal suffix *-ri* characterized by Chamberlain as passive potential. This same formation is productive in standard Japanese where it has developed several variants. These may be illustrated by some examples: *kaka-ru* 'hang' (tr.) with *kak-ar-u* (intr.); *ok-u* 'put' with *ok-are-ru* 'be put'; and *i-ru* 'shoot' with *i-rar-eru* 'be shot'.

The examples considered here are, of course, but a small sample of instances in which the consideration of the languages most closely related to Indo-European helps to confirm, disprove, or in a few cases present new solutions to problems of Indo-European reconstruction. Of course, such deep comparative work always involves evidence considered in the light of internal factors within each of the branches. There is clearly no contradiction here. Thus, in the famous instance of Verner's law, internal Germanic reconstruction led to the positing of consonant alternations that received a satisfactory solution only when accentual data that were in Indo-Aryan and Greek but no longer even in the earliest Germanic were taken into consideration.

REFERENCES CITED

Anttila, R. 1972. *An Introduction to Historical and Comparative Linguistics*. New York: Macmillan.

Benzing, J. 1955. "Die tungusischen Sprachen, Versuch einer vergleichenden Grammatik." *Abhandlungen der Geistes- und Sozialwissenschaftlichen Klasse* 11: 947–1099.

Bopp, F. 1816. *Über das Conjugationssystem der Sanskritsprache in Vergleichung mit jenem der griechischen, lateinischen, germanischen, persischen und germanischen Sprachen*. Frankfurt: Andraische Buchhandlung.

———. 1833. *Vergleichende Grammatik des Sanskrit, Zend, griechieschen, lateinischen, gotischen und deutschen Sprachen*, vol. 1. Berlin: Dümmler.

———. 1839. *Die celtischen Sprachen in ihren Verhältnissen zum Sanskrit, Zend, Griechischen, Lateinischen, Germanischen, Litauischen und Slavischen*. Berlin: Dümmler.

———. 1855. *Über das Albanische in seinen verwandschaftlichen Beziehungen*. Berlin: Stargardt.

————. 1857. *Vergleichende Grammatik des Sanskrit, Zend, Armenischen, Griechischen, Lateinischen, Litauischen, Altslavischen, Gotischen und Deutschen,* vol. 1. Berlin: Dümmler.

Brugmann, K. 1904. "Die Demonstrativpronomina der indogermanischen Sprachen." Leipzig: Königliche Sächsiche Gesellschaft der Wissenschaften. *Abhandlungen der philologischen-historischen Klasse* 22: 6.

Collinder, B. 1960. *Comparative Grammar of the Uralic Languages.* Stockholm: Almqvist and Wicksell.

Delbrück, A. 1884. *Einleitung in das Sprachstudium,* ed. 2. Leipzig: Breitkopf and Hartel.

————. 1904. *Einleitung in das Sprachstudium,* ed. 4. Leipzig: Breitkopf and Hartel.

Diderichsen, P. 1974. "The Foundations of Comparative Grammar: Revolution or Continuation?" In Hymes, D., ed. *Studies in the History of Linguistics,* pp. 277–306. Bloomington: Indiana University Press.

García-Ramón, J. L. 1985. "Die Sekundärendungen des 1 sg. Medii im Indogermanischen." In Schlerat 1985: 207–217.

Georgiev, V. I. 1985. "Das Medium: Funktion und Herkunft." In Schlerat 1985: 218–228.

Greenberg, J. H. 1949. "Studies in African Linguistic Classification, vol. 1. Introduction, Niger-Congo." *Southwestern Journal of Anthropology* 5: 79–100.

————. 1955. *Studies in African Linguistic Classification.* Branford, Conn.: Compass Press.

————. 1957. *Essays in Linguistics.* Chicago: The University of Chicago Press.

————. 1959. "The Origin of the Masai Passive." *Africa* 29: 171–176.

————. 1963. *The Languages of Africa.* Bloomington: Indiana University Press.

————. 1987. *Language in the Americas.* Stanford: Stanford University Press.

————. 1990. "The prehistory of the Indo-European vowel system." In Shevoroshkin, V., ed. Proto-languages and Proto-cultures, pp. 77–136. Bochum, Germany: Brockmeyer.

Hrozný, F. 1917. *Die Sprache der Hethiter.* Leipzig: Hinrichs.

Hübschmann, H. 1877. "Über die Stellung des Armenischen im Kreise der indogermanischen Sprachen." *Zeitschrift für vergleichende Sprachforschung* 23: 5–49.

Jones, Sir William. 1788. *Asiatick Researches* 1. Calcutta.

Kammenhuber, A. 1969. "Hethitisch, Paläisch, Luwisch und Hieroglyphenluwisch." In Spuhler 1969: 119–357.

Martin, S. 1966. "Lexical evidence relating Korean to Japanese." *Language* 42: 185–251.

Menges, K. 1968. *The Turkic Languages and Peoples.* Wiesbaden: Harrassowitz.

Menovshchikov, G. A. 1968. "Aleutskij jazyk." In *Jazyki narodov SSR* 5: 386–406. Moskow: Nauka.

Myrkin, V. Ja. 1964. "Tipologija lichnogo mestoimenija i voprosy rekonstruktsii jego v indoevropejskom aspekte." *Voprosy Jazykoznanija* 13 (5): 78–86.

Pedersen, H. 1933. "Zur Frage nach der Urverwandschaft des Indoeuropäischen mit dem Ugrofinnischen." *Mémoires de la société finno-ougrienne* 67: 308–325.

——. 1935. "Il problema delle parentele tra grandi gruppi linguistici." In *Atti del III Congresso internazionale dei linguisti*, pp. 328–333. Florence: Felice de Monier.

Pokorny, J. 1959. *Indogermanisches etymologisches Wörterbuch*. I. Bern: Francke.

Ramstedt, G. J. 1939. "A Korean Grammar." *Mémoires de la société finno-ougrienne*, vol. 82.

Robins, R. H. 1968. *A Short History of Linguistics*. Bloomington: Indiana University Press.

Rosén, H. B. 1978. "*amamini* und die indogermanischen Diathesen- und Valenzkategorien." *Zeitschrift für vergleichende Sprachforschung* 92: 143–178.

Savchenko, A. N. 1960. "Problema isxodenija lychnyx okanchanii glagola v indoevropejskom jazyke." *Lingua Posnaniensis* 8: 44–56.

Schlerat, B. ed. 1985. *Grammatische Kategorien, Funktion und Geschichte*. Wiesbaden: Richert.

Schmidt, J. 1899. "Die kretischen Pluralnominative auf -*en* und Verwandtes." *Zeitschrift für vergleichende Sprachforschung* 36: 400.

Shibatani, M. 1985. "Passives and related constructions: a prototype analysis." *Language* 61: 821–848.

Spuhler, B., ed. 1969. *Handbuch der Orientalistik*, erste Abteilung. Leiden: Brill.

Szemerényi, O. 1978. *Introducción a la lingüística comparativa*. Madrid: Gredos.

Szinnyéi, J. 1910. *Finnisch-ugrische Sprachwissenschaft*. Leipzig: Goschen.

Topping, D. M. 1973. *Chamorro Reference Grammar*. Honolulu: Hawaii University Press.

Uhlenbeck, C. C. 1906. "Ontwerp van eene vergelijkende vormleer der Eskimotalen." *Verhandelingen der Koninklijke Akademie van Wetenschappen te Amsterdam. Afdeeling Letterkunde*, nieuwe reeks, deel 8, no. 3.

Ulving, T. 1953. "Consonant gradation in Eskimo." *International Journal of American Linguistics* 19: 45–52.

Vertés, E. 1967. *Die ostjakischen Pronomina*. The Hague: Mouton.

Wilbur, T. H., ed. 1977. *The Lautgesetz Controversy: a Documentation (1885–1886)*. Amsterdam: John Benjamin.

Zimmer, H. 1888. "Über das italo-keltische passivum und deponens." *Zeitschrift für vergleichende Sprachforschung* 10: 224–292.

Indo-European and Afroasiatic

CARLETON T. HODGE

The concept of the genetic relationship of languages, expressed so neatly by Sir William Jones, has stimulated a great deal of discussion since the early nineteenth century about the connections between Indo-European (IE) and what has been known of Afroasiatic (AAs = Lisramic). The number of etymologies presented, say, from Lepsius 1836 to the present, is enormous. How does one judge which is correct among many competing ones? The solution I have chosen has been to examine the data (relatively) independently of previous efforts. By using a core vocabulary and beginning with the two earliest attested branches, Egyptian and Semitic, a partial set of sound correspondences was established, and this in turn was compared to sets from other branches of AAs (Hodge 1981a) and IE (Hodge 1981b). By using these correspondences as a base and generally continuing to use core vocabulary, further etymological sets were developed and a system of presentation adopted designed to facilitate verification, correction, or amplification.

Archeological evidence indicates that the time depth of the proto-language involved is over 16,000 years, possibly 20,000 (Munson 1977, Hodge 1978). The proportion of items attested as having survived over 4,000 years within Egyptian (Hodge 1975) gives us confidence in the relatability of languages at the greater time depth (Swadesh 1959: 27).

Two aspects of phonology have shown themselves to be of special significance: (1) prothetic alif (ʔV- before CCV-) and (2) consonant ablaut. The first of these provides evidence that both patterns CVC(C) and CCV(C) may occur with the same root in all branches, including IE (examples below). This finding indicates that the root-and-pattern system familiar from Semitic was probably a feature of the proto-language (Hodge 1987a). Consonant ablaut refers to the kind of alter-

nation found in the roots reconstructed by Jungraithmayr and Shimizu for proto-Chadic (pCh), such as the following:

1.

C	Cʔ	NC	Meaning
d	dʔ	ⁿd-r	'to do'
k-d	k-dʔ-r	k-ⁿd-r	'fat' (1981: 173, 99)

Such alternations are found throughout AAs and IE and involve what
Puhvel has termed "occlusive-variation" in IE (1984: 474). They need
to be considered in terms of the stop inventories of the branches involved. Compare the following:

2.1 pSem	2.2 Eg	2.3 pBer	2.4 pCh	2.5 pEC	2.6 pIE
p t k	p t k	t k	p t k	t k	p t k
b d g	b d g	b d g	b d g	b d g	b d g
ṭ q	f ǧ q	ḍ	bʔ dʔ kʔ	dʔ dʔ₁ kʔ	bh dh gh
			ᵐb ⁿd ⁿg		

NOTE: 2.1 [proto-Semitic] Bergsträsser-Daniels 1983.3; 2.2 [Egyptian] Gardiner 1957.27; 2.3 [proto-
Berber] Prasse 1972.1.105; 2.4 [proto-Chadic] Jungraithmayr-Shimizu 1981.19–20; 2.5 [proto-
Eastern Cushitic] Sasse 1975.5; 2.6 [proto-Indo-European] Szemerényi 1970.48. Egyptian *f* is here
treated as derived from *p* or *b* by the addition of ʔ or *H*. Illič-Svityč interpreted it as *ph* (1966: 34).

All these systems show what may be called a plain voiceless or
voiced set plus one or more series that have an additional factor,
such as glottalization, velarization, aspiration, prenasalization. Although these are written with symbols that imply the presence (*bʔ*)
or absence (*kʔ*) of voice, they do not occur in contrasting voiceless-
voiced pairs at this prehistoric time. IE illustrates this by the correspondence of Skt. *bh dh gh* to Gk. *ph th kh*. One must, however, distinguish between earlier and later NC combinations in IE to account
for such contrasts as Lat. *vincō* 'I conquer' and *fingō* 'I shape'. The
understanding of consonant ablaut is crucial to the setting up of
sound correspondences (Hodge 1986).

Set Conventions

The following conventions have been used in presenting the numbered illustrative etymological sets:

The protophoneme illustrated follows the article number (**3** on),
and then comes the numbered core item (after the 310 list of Hodge

1987b) and a consonantal root reconstruction. Hyphens separate the consonants of roots given without vowels.

The presentation is in language branch columns in the order Egyptian (Eg), Semitic (Sem), Berber (Ber), Chadic (Ch), Omotic (Om), Cushitic (Cu), and Indo-European (IE). The comparison is of these seven branches, not of AAs as a group vs. IE as a group. The whole represents what has been termed "Lislakh" (Hodge 1978).

Except for Egyptian, the primary comparison is between reconstructed forms in the various branches. When a protoform is unavailable or when it is otherwise useful to cite an actual language form, this is given on a separate line, with l ('language') in the left margin.

Where the meaning is unambiguously the same as that of the core item, it is not repeated as a gloss. The meaning is given as a gloss if it is different or if any doubt could arise.

Where a form has been selected because of its semantic relationship to the core item, it is put on a separate line, with s ('semantic similarity') in the left margin.

Where formal similarity is the main reason for citing a form, f is used. In some cases where both are clearly involved, fs is used.

There are many stem formative affixes involved. A stem with an affix that is identifiable as such and relevant to our intrabranch comparison is given on a separate line, with − in the margin. Consonant ablaut variation is considered affixal, with ʔ given for glottalization, H for aspiration, N for nasalization, C_2 for gemination. -C indicates an unspecified consonant suffix, C-C reduplication, s- the 'causative', etc. Forms of the stems so extended may continue for several lines.

The letter *l* is used in the base reconstruction where there is variation between *l*, *r*, and *n*. L plus pharyngealization (ʔ, H) yields *r*, while N plus *l* yields *n*. The examples do not cue the ʔ, H, and N as affixes to *l*.

A reference is given for most of the items cited. *CTH* indicates a form I have furnished. For abbreviations of other references, see References Cited.

3. *p 51. 'fly' (vb) *p-l

	Eg	Sem	Ber	Ch	Om	Cu	IE
	p-ꜣ (Fa 87)		*f-r-(w) (D 46)	*parə (N 26) *p-r (J/S 153)	Dauro fal (Fl 74.89)	pSC *pur- (E 321)	*per- (P 816) *pleu- (W 52; P 835)
1							
+C₂		*prur- (F 5.66)					
+ʔ						*pʔAr- (D 45)	
+N				*mb-r (J/S 153)			

NOTE: The IE forms illustrate the patterns CVC- and CCV(C)-, the latter with -w.

4. *t 269. 'thou' *t-ʔ

	Eg	Sem	Ber	Ch	Om	Cu	IE
Verb suffix							
	-t-ʔ (Ed 271)	*-tā (m) *-ti (f) (B/D 13)	*-ta *-ti (Pr 3.16)			pSam *-t-a *-t-ay (H 34)	*-(s)tA-e (?) (EL 173) Anat. -ti
1				Piðimdi -tu (Kr 84)	Dizi -to (Fl 76. 313)		
Independent		*antā (B/D 7)				*ʔAntA (D 133) pEC *ʔat- (S 10) pSC *ʔaata (E 282)	Skt/Gr -tha (Sz 228f)
1				Tera to (Kr 94)			

NOTE: t for second person singular occurs sporadically in Chadic; k is the more common (see Kraft 1974). PSOM (proto-South Omotic) is reconstructed as *ya:, but North Omotic has some t forms (Fleming 1976: 313–315; 1974: 85–86).

5. *k 32. 'burn' / 82. 'fire' / 126. 'hot' *k-w

	Eg	Sem	Ber	Ch	Om	Cu	IE
32		*-kwiŋ- (F 7.58)	*khh (Pr 3.139)	*kaw- 'fry' (N 26) *k-w 'fry' (J/S 114)			*kēu- (W 31) *kēu- (P 595)
+ s-	s-č-t 'kindle' (Fa 256)						
1			Tou uku (intr) (Fo 2.720)		Oyda mičəne 'it burns me' (Fl p.c.)		
82				*akʷa (N 26) *-k-w (J/S 114)		*wAk- (D 262) pSC *ʔeekʲʷ- (E 318)	126 *kāi- (P 519)

NOTE: Touareg *uku*, pCh *akʷa, and perhaps the Cushitic forms derive from a CCV- (*kwV-) pattern, plus prothetic alif ʾV-. Semitic *-khub- 'burn' (Fronzaroli 7.67) indicates that the earliest traceable root is *k-b and that the phylum-wide *k-w forms are secondary (cf. Newman 1977: 10 re b/v alternations in Chadic). Palatalization, attested here in Egyptian, Omotic, and IE, may go back to the protolanguage. One may note the parallel development of *kʸ in Egyptian and Greek: Eg. k-b-w-ʾ 'soles (dual), sandals' > čᵡ-b-w-ʾ > Co. *tooue* /tówe/ (Vycichl 1983: 224), pre-Greek *ki 'what' (with loss of the labial) > ti.

6. *b 39. 'clothe' *b-s

	Eg	Sem	Ber	Ch	Om	Cu	IE
f				*b-s 'sew' (J/S 223) Ha bisà 'on' (N/N 13)			*wes- (W 78; P 1172)
1 f							
						pEC *huwo- (S 38)	
+ ḥ-	ḥ-b-s (Fa 167)	*ḥ-b-s restrain (cf. Ai 99)					
f		*l-b-s (cf. Ai 168)	*l-s-ḥ (Pr 2.72)				
+ ɛ	ʔ-ȝ-b-s 'headdress' (Fa 16)						
N	n-m-s 'wig cover' (Fa 133)						

NOTE: Eg. ʔ-ȝ-b-s reflects ʔV-CCVC. Cohen's choice of an Egyptian cognate for Semitic l-b-s, n-m-s, is an N form of this root (1947: 183). Egyptian n is a recognized correspondent of Semitic l.

7. *d 112. 'hand' / 98. 'give, place, put' *d-

	Eg	Sem	Ber	Ch	Om	Cu	IE
112	d HAND D46 (G 455)	*yad- (F 2.80)					
fs			*əd/*yid 'with' (Pr 1.225); *dey 'in' (Pr 1.225)				*ad- 'to, at' (W 1; P 3)
+ -s							*dous- 'arm' (P 226)
+						/H	*me-dhi 'with' (P 702)
98	m d-ʔ 'with' ('at hand of') (V 145); d-(w) (Fa 308)						*dō- (W 15; P 223)
+	w-d-ʔ (Fa 72)	*w-d-y 'throw' (cf. K/B 372)					
+ -n l		Akk -din (vS 138); *-ndin- (vS 25*)					
N				Sha "di (J 284)			
(+) ʔ/H	(r)-g̃-ʔ (Ed 205)						
l				Ngizim dʔàáwú 'put' (Sc 214)			
f				*dʔ- 'do' (J/S 173)			*dhē- (W 13; P 235)

NOTE: The ordinary OEg/MEg word for 'hand' is g̃-r-t (an extended ʔ form of this root). The base form d is reflected in the hieroglyph d (D46) and in the LEg phase m d-ʔ 'in the hand of' (= 'with' etc.), which alternates with m g̃-r-t n 'in the hand of' (Vycichl 1983: 145). Both Coptic nte /ʔəntế/ and IE *medhi are fossilized forms of the phrase. See also set **15**.

8. *g 167. 'mountain' *g-b-l

Eg	Sem	Ber	Ch	Om	Cu	IE
	*g-b-l 'hilly country' (cf. Bi 65)				*gAr- (D 61) pEC *gub- (S 15)	*gwer- (W 25; P 477)
					Oromo gooroo (S 82.84)	SC gora (CTH)
	Ar jabal (W/C 111)				Dasenech gum (S 15)	

1

1 N

9. *g 251. 'strong' *g-b-l

Eg	Sem	Ber	Ch	Om	Cu	IE
	*g-b-r (cf. K/B 168)					*gwer- 'heavy' Celtic: 'strength' (W 25; P 476) *gwiyā- 'might' (P 469)

f

g-b-3 'arm' (Fa 288)

g-m-ȝ
'temple'
(Fa 289)

(J/S 129)

give
(W 20; P 407)

NOTE: See Buck (1949: 125) for the idea that 'mountain' and 'heavy' may be connected. Of the above correspondences, that of AAs *b* with IE *w* is of great significance (see Hodge 1981b: 375–377). There is evidence on the AAs side of a protodialect that had this change (see set 5). The pIE of this period must have been such a dialect. Proto-*b* survived in IE under certain circumstances (and also sporadically, that is, dialectically). but the general shift of *b* to *w* accounts for the rarity of *b*'s in IE as it is traditionally reconstructed. Another example is set 10.

10. *b* 86. 'flow' / 'cause to flow' = 'pour' / 287. 'water' *k-b*

	Eg	Sem	Ber	Ch	Om	Cu	IE
287							*akwā- (W 1; P 23)
86							*seiku- pour out' (W 56; P 893)
+ s-		*s-k-b 'pour, throw down, lie' (cf. Ai 304) Ar sakaba 'pour out' (W/C 416)					
1							
+ ʔH	q-b 'pour libation' (Fa 277)					⌐EC *ɣuʔ- 'rainy season' (S 53)	*gheu- 'pour libation' (W 22; P 447)
+ s-	s-q-b-b 'make cool' (Fa 249)						

11. *p 168. 'mouth' (cf. Skinner 1977, deleting Coptic) / 24. 'blow' *p-w. The examples here are of somewhat greater complexity.

	Eg	Sem	Ber	Ch	Om	Cu	IE
11.1		*p- (F 2.50)		*pwə (IS 29)	pSOM *af/*ap (Fl 74.90)	*ʔAp(p)- (D 135) pSC *afo (E 281)	
1		Chaha ʔafʷ (Ap 11)		Ha ʔafàà 'throw in mouth' (N/N 2)			*epi 'near' (P 323)
f	p MAT Q3 (G 500)						
f1		Akk apu 'hole' (CAD 1.2.197)					
s = 24				*fi (N 23)		pEC *ʔuff- (S 19) pSC *ʔuuf- (E 294) *ʔ,ʔUpp- (D 44)	*pu- (W 53; P 847)
+ ʔ							*peis- (W 48; P 796)
+ -s							*pī- 'drink' (W 52; P 839)

N? 1

					Lat
168					*bihere*
+ N	*b-, *m-*	*bihik* *ê-mihiw*			(W 52)
	(J/S 187)	'put in mouth'			
		(Pr 2.126)		*pl(e)u-*	
				'lung'	
C-C 1		Ar *famu*		(P 837)	
		pl *ʔafwâtu*			
		(W/C 728)			

11.2 With suffix -*l* *p-*l* 24. 'blow'

f s		*ê-faranfrah*			*bhlē-*
		'snorting'			'blow'
		(Pr 2.72)			(W 9; P 120)
f s C-C	*b-r*			pR	
	'blow'			*bara?-*	
	(J/S 47)			'blow'	
+ ʔ H		*w-f-ꜣ*		(E 338)	
		'lungs'			
		(Fa 60)			

12. The basic patterns of phonological development are

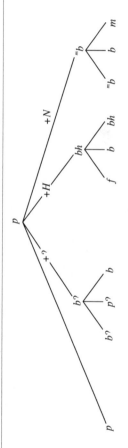

Not all of these postulated changes are illustrated in **11**, but all may be expected to occur.

13. The Semitic evidence shows the root in **11.1** to be *p-w (see the Chaha and Arabic forms). The w may remain, be assimilated to a following vowel, or be lost:

Assimilation	*ʾɘpɑṷ́ > *ʾɘpuṷ > Akk. $p\bar{u}$-, Ar. $f\bar{u}$	
Loss	*ʾɘpɑṷí > *ɘpí > Greek epí	

The assumption that IE *epi is 'at the mouth of' is based on semantic parallels as well as the form. Cf. Heb. *peh ʾel peh* 'mouth to mouth' = 'face to face', Gk. *epí* 'in the presence of', Akk. *ana pî* 'according to (the tablet)', Gk. *epí* 'according to (the rule)'. Note also Skt. *api-gam-* (Ved.) and *api-pad-* 'to go into, enter' (Monier-Williams 1964: 55).

The meaning 'opening', reflected in Akk. *apu* 'hole', *aptu* 'window' helps us understand why the hieroglyph p MAT reflects this morpheme. When an Egyptian door was open, a mat was lowered from the lintel to block the entrance. 'Opening' became 'mat' (Hodge 1987a: 99–100).

The voiced labials of 'drink' in IE have been a problem: Skt. *pibati*, OIr. *ibid*, Lat. *bibit*. Some scholars have posited a laryngeal to account for it, pH > b (such as Lindeman 1970: 83). This is a possibility in our scheme, as the chart in **12** shows. I have taken this IE b to be from *$^m b$, but the matter is not settled. The b forms in pCh and pR are taken to be from *$^m b$ or *b? Note the b/m alternations in Berber and Chadic. The change of bh to b is presumably attested in Germanic and Slavic, *inter aliā*.

14. *b 124. 'bee, honey' / 89. 'fly' (n) 14.1 *b- 14.2 *b-l

	Eg	Sem	Ber	Ch	Om	Cu	IE
14.1 *b-							
124 **+ H**		*nūb-(at-) (F 5.84)		*b-w- (CTH)			*bhei- (W 6; P 116)
+ N				*ami (N 28)		pER *yam 'honey' (E 337); Dahalo *tan-ame (E 225); pSC *naʔaam- 'honeycomb' (E 185)	*embhi- 'bee' (?) (P 311); *me-dhu 'honey' (W 39; P 707)
89 + ð-				*d-b (J/S 111); *diua (N 26)			
+ C₂ **l**		*ðubb- (Di 55)	Izn izebb 'horsefly' (R 321)				
+ N				*z-m 'bird' (J/S 41)			*mū- 'fly' (W 43; P 752)
f + ð-		*dibš- 'honey' (F 5.85)					
124 **+ ð-**							

14.2 *b-l

1				*d-m 'bee' (J/S 37)	pSC *ⁿtsoom- 'kind of bee' (E 201)
+ʔ		Akk zumbu 'fly' (F 5.82)	Ha zumàà 'bee, honey' (N/N 141)		pSC *dʔa-aba- 'honeycomb' (E 188)
124	*ꜥbꜣꜥt (CTH) Co ebiō				
+ H				*b-l (J/S 141)	*bher- 'pierce' (W 7; P 133)
1+					Pol barḗ 'bees' nest' (St 27)
1 + C-C					Skt bhra-mara ba-mbhara (B 192)
+ N				*m-n 'honey' (J/S 141)	*mel-it-'honey' (W 41; P 723)

NOTE: Chadic *b-w is based on forms in Schuh 1981 (Ngizim za-buw-à) and Kraft 1981 (Bade cà-vùw-án). The reading of the Egyptian with ꜣ is new, the older one being b-ꜣ-t (that is, b-ʔ-t; Sign List L2, Gardiner 1957: 477; see Hodge 1987a, 95–96). The root is *b-l, with *b resulting from loss of l. The prefix *ꜣ- is the same root as Ar. ðū 'possessor of'.

15. *b 8. 'at'. Base: *b-w 'place'. With affixes: '(to, at, from) a place'

15.1 *b-w 'place'

	Eg	Sem	Ber	Ch	Om	Cu	IE
I	b-w (Fa 81)	*bi- 'in' (B/D 19) ESA b-n 'from' (Bi 45)		*ba (N 30)		*bAj- (D 38) Beja -'b 'in' (Hu 110)	*wi- 'apart' (W 78; P1175) GAv aibī LAv aiwi 'to' (K 168) Lat ab 'from' (E/M 2) *obhi 'to' (P 287) *-bhyos/*-bhis 'DA/I' (Sz 146) *ambhi 'around' (W 2; P 34)
+ N?							
??							
+ H							
+							
+ H N							
+ N	Co ma (cf. V 103) m- ('place prefix') (Ed 109) m 'in, from' (Fa 99)	*min 'from' (cf. B/D 20) m- ('place prefix') (Mo 80)	*min 'without' (Pr. 1.232)	*m-bə (IS 19) m- ('place prefix') (J 422)			*me- 'in middle' (W 39; P 702) *mēi-t-to 'place' (P 709) *-mos/*-mis 'DA/I' (Sz 146) *me-dhi 'with' (P 702)

15.2 *b-l 'place'

1	*(ē-)barin 'toward' (Pr 1.233)	Ha uurii (N/N 134)	SOm Hamer -bar 'at, from' (Fl 76.411)
+ N	*ᵐb-(r) (J/S 204)	*ᵐb-t 'near' (J/S 204)	pSam *meel (H 69)

NOTE: It is assumed that specializations such as 'in the place of' = 'in' and 'from the place of' = 'from' were originally different morphologic complexes having affixes such as case endings or other deictic elements that carried the various meanings. IE *-bhi, which is clearly the 'place' part of several of the above forms and which yields Gk. -phi 'among (et sim.)' has locative -i.

It is not possible to differentiate clearly between a b that goes back to *b and one that derives from *b or *ᵐb (see set 13), OP abiy, Av (Gathas) aibī, and LAv aiuui are usually linked to Skt. abhí (as in Kent 1950: 168), but the w of aiuui goes back to *b, not *bh, raising the question whether the b of abiy and aibī (MPers. be-) is a survival of *b, not a development from *bh. Lat. ab 'from' is from *b-w 'mouth,' and so belongs here, not with Gk. apó (contrā handbooks). Note the Latin variants au- (*b), ab- (*ᵐb/*b?), af- (*bh) (Ernout-Meillet 1959: 2). Gk. apó is from *p-w 'mouth,' as is epí (see set 11, and for apó and epí, Pokorny 1959: 53). To relate Lat. ab and Gk. apó, as is usually done, it would be necessary to assume that the roots of 11 and 15 were the same, basically *p-w 'mouth'. All the b forms would then be from *b? or *ᵐb (or *-bb- ?). This is possible, but it seems unlikely.

The IE dative-ablative and instrumental plural endings are seen to be based on the root for 'place'. The familiar m/bh alternation is part of the consonant ablaut of this root (cf. Hodge 1981b: 377–378).

16. *ḅ 117. 'heart, abdomen' *l-b

	Eg	Sem	Ber	Ch	Om	Cu	IE
	ʾ-n-b/*ʾ-ӡ-b (Ho 81a.408)		*wilih (Pr 2.128)	*l-b 'belly' (J/S 39) *-n-v (J/S 134)		pSC *lib- (E 205)	*arwā 'intestines' (?) (P 68) *reu-to- 'intestines' (P 873) Eng liver
1			Tou ul, pl. ulawön (Pr 2.128)	Kanakuru rúwò (N 74.132)	Kullo ulwə 'belly' (Fl 76.328)		
+ 1							Lith pi-lva-s 'belly' ski-lvi-s 'stomach' Latv ški-lva 'maw of birds' (B 254) Gk koi-lia 'belly' (B 253)
+ C₂		*libb- (F 2.73)				*1Abb- (D 163)	
1					Basketo lippe 'belly' (Fl 74.89)		

				Germanic *rebh- 'covering of chest cavity' (W 53; P 853)
+ H					
+ ʔ1		Oromo lapʔe 'lower chest' (CTH)			
+ δ- H1			Gk de-lphú-s 'uterus'		
+ N1				Angas erém 'liver' (Nt 9)	
+ C-C1					Lat volba, volva, bulba 'vulva' (Wa 856)

NOTE: Baltic shows -lv- with some unidentified prior elements, *ski-* and *pi-*. The *-ki-* of *ski-* fits with the *koi-* of Gk. *kollia* and may tentatively be considered as from *(s)keu-* 'cover' (Pokorny 1959: 951). The *pi-* is in all likelihood the *p-w* 'mouth' morpheme (11). This identification is suggested by the fact that 'stomach' in Egyptian is *r-ʔ-ʔ-n-b* 'the mouth of the heart.' Latvian *pazirds* 'stomach' is also likely to be 'mouth (*pa*) of the heart,' rather than 'under (*pa*) the heart' (as Buck 1949: 254). The Latin pronunciations with *b* (*volba* and the popular *bulba*) are survivals of *b.

17. *k_s 25. 'bone' *k-s

	Eg	Sem	Ber	Ch	Om	Cu	IE
+ʔ	q-s Co. kas (Fa 281)		*ē-γasah (Pr 2.72)	*k'ʔ-s₃ (J/S 49)	*k'ʔus (Fi 74.87)	*kAς- (D 266)	*kos-t- (W 32; P 616)
f	q-s (T2O) BONE HARPOON POINT (G 514)					pSC *k'ʔoos- 'bow and arrow' (E 253)	*ǵhaiso- 'spear' (W 20; P 410) *ǵhas-to- 'rod' (W 21; P 412)
f1		Ar. qassa 'remove marrow' (Hv 604)					

NOTE: The crucial association here is the Eg. q-s written with a bone harpoon point and the use of the word as 'harpoon'. This makes its relationship to IE *ǵhaiso- and *ǵhas-to-, which fit the sound correspondences (k'–ǵh, s–s), certain. The other IE word for bone, *ost(h)- (Pokorny 1959: 783), is related to Sem. *ςaẓm- 'bone' (Fronzaroli 2.33). Anatolian shows a laryngeal here (Hitt. xastai-, Luw. xastai-; Luw. xassa [Lindeman 1970: 35]), which the Semitic indicates was ςayin.

18. *x 176. 'nose' *x-n-(t-)

	Eg	Sem	Ber	Ch	Om	Cu	IE
	x-n-t 'face, brow' (Fa 194)		*himmitw (?) 'forehead' (Pr 2.171)	*həN-tir (Ro n505)		pSC *ⁿtse 'in front' (E 197)	*xant- 'front' (IHL 62) Lat ante 'before'
1		Ar. xanna 'speak nasally' (W/C 263)		Ha. hancii pl. hantunàà (N/N 50)			

NOTE: The Egyptian hieroglyph NOSE EYE & CHEEK (D19) is used in writing 'face, nose, smell, in front of', etc. (Gardiner 1957: 452).
The comparison of AAs and IE has always held the promise of allowing us to reconstruct roots with the velar, laryngeal, and glottal sounds known commonly as "laryngeals." Egyptian and Semitic each have several such consonants, the other branches of AAs fewer.

Egyptian x x̂ ḥ ḫ   Semitic x ḥ h
                            γ   ς   ʔ

As ς and γ merge in Egyptian, we look for Semitic evidence (as in Arabic, South Arabic, and Ugaritic) to decide between these two. The examples in sets **18** to **20** provide evidence for some Hittite spellings with x.

19. *ḥ 149. 'live' * ḥ-w / * ḥ-y (* ḥ-w-y?)

	Eg	Sem	Ber	Ch	Om	Cu	IE
+		*ḥ-w-y/*ḥ-y-y cf. Ai 101 *ḥayiy- (F 2.08)				*ḥA/Aw- (D 156)	*$h_x$wi- (CTH) *aiw- (W 1; P 17)
						pSC *niḥ- (E 186)	
s l	h-w-w 'cattle' (Fa 165)	Ar. ḥayyu 'living being' (W/C 200)					Hitt x^ui-tar 'animals' (Fd 72)
+ -s l							Hitt $x^u$is- (Fd 71)
+ C-C							*$h_x$wi-ḥw-os (CTH)
l							Lat vivus

NOTE: This is clearly a far superior etymology for the Latin than derivation from *ǵʷei- (Pokorny 1959: 467).

20. *ḥ affix *ḥ- / *-ḥ (noncore)

	Eg	Sem	Ber	Ch	Om	Cu	IE
l	(-)ḥ(-)	*(-)ḥ(-)					*ḥ Hitt. -ax

NOTE: This is a widely used affix in the three branches in which it is attested. Leslau called attention to its use in AAs, and his Semitic examples are particularly important (1962). There are excellent examples in Egyptian, such as q-b 'pour a libation' with q-b-ḥ 'purify' (see Edel 1955: 110, 189). It occurs in Hittite as -ax and is connected with the -ā- of Lat. novāre 'renew' (Sturtevant-Hahn 1951: 124–126). Its function appears similar in AAs and IE, but the entire material has yet to be collected.

21. *ʕ 'small cattle' *ʕ-w (noncore, but cf. 26. 'bovine')

	Eg	Sem	Ber	Ch	Om	Cu	IE
	ʕ-w-t 'small cattle' (Fa 39)			*ʔa(w)ku 'goat' (N 27)			*$H_o$owi-s > B-S *owi-no(s) f. *owi-kā (Hp 84)

NOTE: This is based on Hamp (1984), whose reconstruction for IE fits the Egyptian and Chadic evidence very well. The laryngeal is to be reconstructed as ʕ, unless Semitic evidence turns up that it was ɣ. (There is no more appropriate laryngeal than ʕayin for o-coloring in IE, though it has e-coloring in Akkadian and a-coloring in Hebrew.)

Following is a brief summary of some of the results of this inquiry:

- Sufficient sound correspondences have been presented (here and in other papers) to establish the genetic relationship of IE and the six branches of AAs.
- Recognition of consonant ablaut has enabled us to clarify many relationships, while emphasizing regular sound correspondences.
- The traditional reconstruction of IE stops has been shown to be basically sound.
- The *m*/*bh* alternation of IE is seen to be part of the consonant ablaut pattern.
- The paucity of *b*'s in reconstructed pIE is seen to be due to the general change of **b* to *w*.
- The occurrence of both CVC(C) and CCV(C) patterns with the same root is shown to be of considerable help in understanding forms in all branches.
- The laryngeals in selected IE words have been identified with sounds in AAs.
- Several etymologies have been revised or clarified, and some words are given reliable etymologies for the first time. The latter may be reclassified from poor cousins to happy legomena.

REFERENCES CITED

Ai   Aistleitner, J. 1963. *Wörterbuch der ugaritischen Sprache*. (BUSAWL 106, 3) Berlin: Akademie-Verlag.

Ap   Appleyard, D. L. 1977. "A Comparative Approach to the Amharic Lexicon." *Afroasiatic Linguistics* 5.2.

Bender, M. L., ed. 1976. *The Non-Semitic Languages of Ethiopia*. East Lansing: Michigan State University.

B/D   Bergsträsser, G., and P. T. Daniels. 1983. *Introduction to the Semitic Languages*. Winona Lake: Eisenbrauns.

Bi   Biella, J. C. 1982. *Dictionary of Old South Arabic: Sabaean Dialect*. (HSS, 25) Chicago: Scholars Press.

B   Buck, C. D. 1949. *A Dictionary of Selected Synonyms in the Principal Indo-European Languages*. Chicago: University of Chicago Press.

Burrow, T. 1959. *The Sanscrit Language*. (The Great Languages) London: Faber & Faber.

CAD   *The Assyrian Dictionary of the Oriental Institute of the University of Chicago*. 1956–. Locust Valley: J. J. Augustin.

Cohen, M. 1947. *Essai comparatif sur le vocabulaire et la phonétique du chamito-sémitique*. (Bibliothèque de l'École des Hautes Études, 291) Paris: Honoré Champion.

EL   Cowgill, W. 1965. "Evidence in Greek." In Winter W., ed. *Evidence for Laryngeals*, pp. 142–180. (Janua Linguarum, SM, 11) The Hague: Mouton.

Di   Diakonoff, I. M. 1965. *Semito-Hamitic Languages*. (Languages of Asia and Africa) Moscow: Nauka.

D   Dolgopolsky, A. B. 1973. *Sravnitel' no-istoričeskaja Fonetika Kušitskix Jazykov*. Moscow: Nauka.

Ed   Edel, E. 1955. *Altägyptische Grammatik*, I. (AnOr, 34) Rome: Pontifical Biblical Institute.

E   Ehret, C. 1980. *The Historical Reconstruction of Southern Cushitic Phonology and Vocabulary*. (Kölner Beiträge zur Afrikanistik, 5) Berlin: Dietrich Reimer.

E/M   Ernout, A., and A. Meillet. 1959. *Dictionnaire étymologique de la langue latine*, 4th ed. Paris: C. Klincksieck.

Fa   Faulkner, R. O. 1962. *A Concise Dictionary of Middle Egyptian*. Oxford: Griffith Institute.

Fl 74   Fleming, H. C. 1974. "Omotic as a Branch of Afroasiatic." *Studies in African Linguistics*, Suppl. 5.81–94.

Fl 76   ———. 1976. "Omotic Overview." In Bender 1976: 299–323.

Fo   Foucauld, C. de. 1951–1952. *Dictionnaire Touareg-Français: Dialecte de l'Ahaggar*. 4 vols. Paris: Imprimerie Nationale de France.

Fd   Friedrich, J. 1952. *Hethitisches Wörterbuch*. Heidelberg: Carl Winter.

F   Fronzaroli, P. 1964–1971. "Studi sul lessico comune semitico, I–VII," *Rendiconti dell'Accademia Nazionale dei Lincei, Classe di Scienze morali, storiche e folologiche*, Series VIII, 19: 155–172, 243–280; 20: 135–150, 246–269; 23: 267–303; 24: 285–320; 26: 603–642. (References are to list and number.)

G   Gardiner, A. H. 1957. *Egyptian Grammar*, ed. 3. London: Oxford University Press.

Hp   Hamp, E. P. 1984. "Indo-European and Balto-Slavic 'Sheep'." *Journal of Indo-European Studies* 12.192.

Hv   Hava, J. G. 1915. *Arabic-English Dictionary*. Beirut: Catholic Press.

H   Heine, B. 1978. "The Sam Languages: a History of Rendille, Boni and Somali," *Afroasiatic Linguistics* 6(2): 23–115.

    Hodge, C. T. 1975. "Egyptian and Survival." In Bynon, J., and T. Bynon, eds. *Hamito-Semitica*, pp. 171–191. (Janua Linguarum, SP, 200) The Hague: Mouton.

Ho 76   ———. 1976. "An Egypto-Semitic Comparison." *Folia Orientalia* 17: 5–28.

    ———. 1978. "Lislakh." In Paradis, M., ed. *The Fourth LACUS Forum 1977*, pp. 414–422. Columbia: Hornbeam Press.

Ho 81a   ———. 1981a. "Comparative Evidence for Egyptian Phonology." In Young, D. W., ed. *Studies Presented to Hans Jakob Polotsky*, pp. 401–413. East Gloucester: Pirtle & Polson.

    ———. 1981b. "Lislakh Labials." *Anthropological Linguistics* 23: 368–382.

    ———. 1986. "Indo-European Consonant Ablaut." *Diachronica* 3: 143–162.

    ———. 1987a. "Lislakh Cluster Resolution." *Anthropological Linguistics* 29: 91–104.

————. 1987b. "The Status of Lisramic (Hamito-Semitic) Sound Correspondences." In Jungraithmayr H., and W. W. Müller, eds. *Proceedings of the Fourth International Hamito-Semitic Congress*, pp. 11–24. Amsterdam: John Benjamins.

Hu   Hudson, R. A. 1976. "Beja." In Bender 1976, pp. 97–132.

IS   Illič-Svityč, V. M. 1966. "Iz istorii čadskogo konsonantizma: labijal'nye myčnye." *Jazyki Afriki*, pp. 9–34. Moscow: Nauka.

J   Jungraithmayr, H. 1970. *Die Ron-Sprachen*. Glückstadt: J. J. Augustin.

J/S   Jungraithmayr, H., and K. Shimizu. 1981. *Chadic Lexical Roots*. II. (Marburger Studien, Serie A, Afrika, 26) Berlin: Dietrich Reimer.

K   Kent, R. G. 1950. *Old Persian*. (AOS, 33) New Haven: American Oriental Society.

K/B   Koehler, L., and W. Baumgartner. 1967, 1974. *Hebräisches und Aramäisches Lexikon zum Alten Testament*, ed. 3. Parts 1 and 2. Leiden: E. J. Brill.

Kr   Kraft, C. H. 1974. "Reconstruction of Chadic Pronouns, I." In Voeltz, E., ed. *Third Annual Conference on African Linguistics*, pp. 69–94. (IUP, African Series, 7) Bloomington: Indiana University Press.

————. 1981. *Chadic Wordlists*. 3 vols. (Marburger Studien, Serie A, Afrika, 23) Berlin: Dietrich Reimer.

Lepsius, R. 1836. *Zwei sprachvergleichende Abhandlungen*. Berlin: Ferdinand Dümmler.

Leslau, W. 1962. "A Prefix ḥ in Egyptian, Modern South Arabian and Hausa." *Africa* 32: 65–68.

Lindeman, F. O. 1970. *Einführung in die Laryngaltheorie*. (Sammlung Göschen, 1247[a]) Berlin: Walter de Gruyter.

Monier-Williams, M. 1964 [1899]. *A Sanskrit-English Dictionary*. Oxford: Clarendon Press.

Mo   Moscati, S., A. Spitaler, E. Ullendorff, and W. von Soden. 1964. *An Introduction to the Comparative Grammar of the Semitic Languages*. (PLO, N.S., 6) Wiesbaden: Harrassowitz.

Munson, P. 1977. "Africa's Prehistoric Past." In Martin, P., and P. O'Meara, eds. *Africa*, pp. 62–82. Bloomington: Indiana University Press.

Nt   Netting, R. 1967. "A Word List of Kofyar." *Research Notes* 2. Ibadan: University of Ibadan.

N 74   Newman, P. 1974. *The Kanakuru Language*. (WALM, 9) Leeds: Institute of Modern English Language Studies.

N   ————. 1977. "Chadic Classification and Reconstruction." *Afroasiatic Linguistics* 5.1: 1–42.

N/N   Newman, P., and R. Ma Newman. 1979 [1977]. *Modern Hausa-English Dictionary*. Ibadan: Oxford University Press.

P   Pokorny, J. 1959. *Indogermanisches etymologisches Wörterbuch*, vol. 1. Bern: Francke.

Pr   Prasse, K.-G. 1972, 1974, 1973. *Manuel de grammaire touarègue*. 3 vols. Copenhagen: Akademisk Forlag.

Puhvel, J. 1984. *Hittite Etymological Dictionary*, vol. 1–2. (Trends in Linguistics, Documentation, 1) Berlin: Mouton.

R Renisio, A. 1932. *Étude sur les dialectes berbères*. (Publ. of the Institut des Hautes-Études Marocaines, 22) Paris: Ernest Leroux.

Ro Rossing, M. O. 1978. *Mafa-Mada: a Comparative Study of Chadic Languages in North Camaroun*. University of Wisconsin Dissertation. Ann Arbor: University Microfilms.

S Sasse, H.-J. 1979. "The Consonant Phonemes of Proto-East-Cushitic (PEC): a First Approximation." *Afroasiatic Linguistics* 7.1: 1–67.

S 82 ———. 1982. *An Etymological Dictionary of Burji*. (Cushitic Language Studies, 1) Hamburg: Helmut Buske.

Sc Schuh, R. G. 1981. *A Dictionary of Ngizim*. (UCPL, 99) Berkeley: University of California Press.

Skinner, N. 1977. "'Fly' (Noun) and 'Mouth' in Afroasiatic." *Afroasiatic Linguistics* 4.1: 51–62.

Sł Sławski, F. 1952–1956. *Słownik etymologiczny języka polskiego*. Kraków: Towarzystwo Miłośników Języka Polskiego.

vS Soden, W. von. 1952. *Grundriss der akkadischen Grammatik*. (AnOr, 33) Rome: Pontifical Biblical Institute.

IHL Sturtevant, E. H. 1942. *The Indo-Hittite Laryngeals*. (WDWLS) Baltimore: Linguistic Society of America.

Sturtevant, E. H., and E. A. Hahn. 1951. *A Comparative Grammar of the Hittite Language*, vol. 1, rev. ed. New Haven: Yale University Press.

Swadesh, M. 1959. "Linguistics as an Instrument of Prehistory." *Southwestern Journal of Anthropology* 15: 20–35.

Sz Szemerényi, O. 1970. *Einführung in die vergleichende Sprachwissenschaft*. (Die Altertumswissenschaft) Darmstadt: Wissenschaftliche Buchgesellschaft.

V Vycichl, W. 1983. *Dictionnaire étymologique de la langue copte*. Leuven: Peeters.

Wa Walde, A. 1910. *Lateinisches etymologisches Wörterbuch*, ed. 2. Heidelberg: Carl Winter.

W Watkins, C. 1985. *The American Heritage Dictionary of Indo-European Roots*, rev. ed. Boston: Houghton Mifflin.

W/C Wehr, H. 1976. *A Dictionary of Modern Written Arabic*, ed. 3. Ed. by J. M. Cowan. Ithaca: Spoken Language Services.

Full and Other Key Words Shared by Indo-European and Semitic

SAUL LEVIN

It devolves on me to point out the necessity of comparing Indo-European phenomena directly with Semitic, instead of treating Semitic as just a subdivision of Afro-Asiatic. The preoccupation with Afro-Asiatic, no matter how intense, cannot really give to this loose constellation of language families a coherence on the order of Indo-European (IE), but it can and does keep many linguists from noticing the phenomena within Semitic and within IE that are clearly linked *across* family lines.[1]

I

Over 150 years ago Pott (1836: 189) noted this etymology: "[Breton] tarv, tarô (taureau; vgl. Altkelt. Adelung, Mithr. II. p. 72); Gael. tarbh, a bull; Böhm. [= Czech] tur, Auerochs; Chald. [= Aramaic] תּוֹר bos; Dän. tyr (Stier, Ochs, Rind), Lat. tauro[-]." His inconspicuous remark did not pass unnoticed; but the *morphological* importance of this word for 'bull' remained hidden, not only from him, but also from those successors who, besides the Aramaic {to^{w}r},[2] brought in the Arabic {þawr} (alas, without the endings). Now, so much later, thanks to the help of my dear old friend and recent collaborator, John Pairman Brown, I can show the true extent of the correspondence (Brown 1979: 170; Levin 1985: 101; Brown and Levin 1986: 81, 90, 95).

---

[1] This is not a criticism of Prof. Carleton Hodge, who at the symposium in Houston represented Afro-Asiatic studies. On the contrary, he is noteworthy for his deep interest in Semitic as well as IE.

Accusative singular: Greek ταῦρον [taûron],[2] Latin *taurum*, Lithuanian *taũrą*;

acc. sing. absolute: Arabic ثَوْرًا {þawran},

Akkadian {-am}.[3]

Genitive singular: La. *taurī*, Gaulish -*I*,[3] Arabic [þawri:] at the end of a verse instead of

ثَوْرٍ {þawrin}.

Nominative dual: Gk. ταύρω [taúrɔ:], Li. -*ù*;[3]

nom. dual construct: Arabic ثَوْرَا {þawrā},

Ak. {šūrā}, Hebrew {-ʷ}[3] (rare).

Genitive dual: Gk. -οιν[3] [-oin] (Homeric -οιϊν[3]);

Arabic ثَوْرَيْنِ {þawrayn} (terminal absolute),

Ak. {šūrīn} (Assyrian {-ēn}[3]), cf. Hb. {-ɔ́yim}[3] (terminal), Aramaic {-áyin}.[3]

Nominative plural: Gk. ταῦροι [taûroi], La. *taurī* (-ei in early inscriptions),[3] Li. *tauraī*;

construct pl.: Hb. שׁוֹרֵי {šoʷreʸ} (post-Biblical), Aramaic תוֹרֵי {toʷreʸ}.

Genitive plural: Gk. ταύρων [taúrɔ:n], La. -*um*[3] (-ом[3]), Li. *taurū̃*;

cf. Arabic ثِيرَانْ {þīrān} 'many bulls' (terminal).

Feminine singular nominative (and acc.): Gk. Ταυρώ [taurɔ́:] (epithet of the goddess Artemis);

Old Aramaic שׁוּרה {s/š wrh} 'cow',

which would have come out *{toʷrɔ́ʰ} [tʰ-] in Biblical Aram. (cf. Θουρώ [tʰourɔ́:], the Phoenician cow-heroine in Boeotia).

The most surprising upshot is that within the great system of noun inflection the dual is the subsystem with the most correspondence between Greek and the Semitic languages. In the dual, unlike the singular and plural, Greek is actually closer to Arabic than to Sanskrit and other IE languages. That is the fact, regardless of what theory we may entertain as to the cause of it.

If these endings had been noticed four generations ago, how much more might have been achieved in comparative linguistics!

[2]Transliterations of languages not ordinarily written in the Latin alphabet are shown by curved braces { }. Square brackets [ ] are meant, at least ideally, to indicate the actual sound; of course, in languages of the past that is not always ascertainable.

[3]My hyphen indicates that the ending is quotable with some other words in the corpus but not this one.

II

Prof. Marija Gimbutas has delineated the pre-IE culture surviving in parts of Europe and identified the earth goddess at the core of that culture. I suggest that the *gender* of this term is a weighty detail in the Indo-Europeanization of Europe. And since one noun of feminine gender in the Germanic languages is found either with the distinctly feminine marker, as in Old English *eorþe*, or without it, as in Old Norse *iorð*,[4] it becomes highly relevant that the Semitic languages have a similar feminine noun, though without a feminine marker except for the Akkadian {arṣatu(m), erṣetu(m)}.

The geographical gap between the Germanic and Semitic peoples argues that in most of Europe this word succumbed to the progress of Indo-Europeanization. For there are a few traces of it in Greek, although they do not show gender: a gloss in the lexicon of Hesychius, ἐρεσιμήτρην [eresimέ:trɛ:n]• τὴν γεωμετρίαν, that is, 'earth-measurement', and moreover, an inflected form in the Homeric ἔραζε {éraze} 'to the ground', found only at the end of verses; the Hebrew that means the same thing is

אַרְצָה {ʔɔ́rəcɔʰ} in a terminal position, אֶרֶץ {ʔárəcɔʰ} elsewhere

(Levin 1971: 339, 343–346).

The sound of both the letter ζ in Homer and the Hebrew צ is problematical (Steiner 1982), but the structure of the entire word is strikingly parallel in the two languages. Other phonetic details loom large. The glottal stop at the beginning is shared by Semitic and Germanic languages. In standard High German *Erde* ['ʔɛrdə], it remains to this day, and the rules of alliteration in Old English poetry and in the kindred languages reveal the effect of this consonant.[5] Indo-Europeanists must not play it down as though it were an odd development within Germanic and somehow irrelevant to the debate over the IE laryngeals. Given the Semitic parallel in this word and a few

---

[4] I have not been able to confirm Prof. Polomé's oral remark that in Norse runic inscriptions a vowel is written after the fricative consonant—proof that until relatively late there was a feminine marker in Norse too.

[5] Levin 1984b, for example, *Beowulf* 801–802:

  sawle secan   Þone synscaðan 'to seek the soul, that sin-scathed one',
  ænig ofer eorÞan   irenna cyst 'any choice one of the irons on earth [would not touch]'.

The unwritten consonant ['] before *æ-*, *eo-*, *i-* has the same alliterative power as the *s-* in the previous line.

others, the Germanic glottal stop is, for the connoisseur of primeval sounds, a priceless relic (see Décsy 1977: 43–54).

Besides that, the wobbly vowel *eo* in the nucleus of the stressed syllable of OE [ʔ]*eorþe* takes on a vastly different significance when we compare it to the varying vowel of Hebrew:

אֶ֫רֶץ {ʔέrɛc} when nonterminal,
אָ֫רֶץ {ʔɔ́rec} when terminal,
but with the definite article always הָאָ֫רֶץ {hɔʔɔ́rec}

—nearly the same two vowel qualities. Within Germanics the Old English *eo* and the Norse *io* have been treated as cases of "vowel breaking," as though from an originally firm, simple vowel (as in Campbell 1959: 54–60, Noreen 1970: 87). But the phenomenon, rather, constitutes an indispensable clue for tracing how the *fluctuating articulation* of vowel sounds was gradually but not fully *stabilized*. Where the Old English vowels resemble the Hebrew and wherein they differ is the most salient evidence that fortunately remains.

Because the Hebrew scriptures were texts chanted meticulously and because in time they were equipped with an extremely accurate written notation, we can use the data from them to clarify some very fine points in the cognate languages too, just as the precision of the Brahman custodians of Sanskrit redounded to the benefit of IE studies in general. But now the cognate languages include not only the Semitic, closely related to Hebrew, but also the distant IE, as well as the Afro-Asiatic (as in Levin 1980).

III

The IE and Semitic cognates of the English adjective *full* are of the greatest morphological import. Outside of the obvious Germanic forms such as Gothic *full* (neuter; masc. *fulls*), also closely akin are Lithuanian *pilna*, Church Slavonic {plŭno}, and Avestan {pərənəm}, to cite the neuter forms; these can be derived from an IE +*pl̥nom*. To account for the long vowel in Sanskrit {pūrṇám} and Irish *lán*, Pokorny (1959: 798–800) posited *$pl̥no$-. More recent Indo-Europeanists attribute the length to a laryngeal consonant *$ə_1$ or *H_1, which would also have caused the long vowel in Latin *plēnum*. The same laryngeal may well be reflected in Greek πλῆρες [plê:res], which on the other hand has no trace of *n (Chantraine 1968: 902). Many verb forms, too, in Greek, Latin, and Sanskrit have no *n* but a reflex of a laryngeal.

The irreducible root consists of a labial consonant and the sonant *l* or a modification of it. A laryngeal besides that is more problematical. For in a related word that means 'much'—Skt. {purú}, Gk. πολύ [polú][6]—the sonant is followed by the vowel [u] with no hint of anything else. Greek has, besides, compound adjectives such as πολύ-καρπος [polúkarpos] 'fruitful, full of harvest'. The Greek and Sanskrit vowels in the first syllable show no usual correspondence; for Skt. {u} is normally represented by the same vowel in Greek, and Gk. [o] by either {a} (that is, [ʌ]) or {ā} in Sanskrit (cf. Strunk 1969: 3).

A far greater complication enters with *multum*, the Latin word for 'much', beginning with the labial nasal consonant instead of a labial plosive. Within Latin the syllable *mul-* alternates with the consonant group *pl-* in *plūs* 'more', *plēnum* 'full', and so forth. The conservative etymologists have posited two separate IE roots that came to be associated in their meaning (Ernout and Meillet 1979: 517; Walde 1965: 328; Pokorny 1959: 720). I believe rather that these are all from one root and that the anomalies are due to partial preservation of archaic features.

Throughout the Semitic group the consonantal root {m-l-ʔ} is found, or its reflexes; forms also occur with the first and second consonants but no trace of the glottal stop.[7] If a correspondence extends to three consonants or includes vowels, it is less liable to be coincidental than if limited to two consonants. Two consonants of the Semitic root recur in Latin *multum*; there may be a vestige of the third, the glottal stop, in the vowel at the end of Gk. μάλα [mála], which means 'very' or 'quite' and is similar in use to [polú] before adjectives, except that [polú] is followed by adjectives in the comparative or superlative degree, [mála] by simple (or "positive") adjectives:

μάλα κᾱλόν 'very handsome' (*Iliad* 21.447)

πολὺ κάλλιον 'much handsomer' (*Odyssey* 3.358, etc.)

πολὺ κάλλιστος 'much the handsomest' (11.239)

All the other correspondences involve a Semitic {m-} but a different labial in IE:

[6] [polú] in Attic, but in most other dialects [-ú].

[7] No cognates reported in Berber, Egyptian, or Cushitic; but *fal* in Hausa. Also vaguer resemblances in Tagálog *punô*, Malay *pĕnoh*; Turkish *dolu*; Zulu *-gewele*, *-zele*. Bargery 1934, Panganiban 1969, Wilkinson 1959, Redhouse 1969, Doke 1958.

1. The first and most exact, segment for segment including the accent, is

Gk. [polú] : Hb. וְמָלֵ֖י {mɔlúʷ} (occurring only in Ezekiel 28:16).[8]

The Arabic cognate is مَلَوُ; the letters {mlw} are identical with the Hebrew מלו, but the superscript marks call for the pronunciation [maluʔa], not *[maluwa], in the standard dialect of the Qurʔān, which differed somewhat from the one for which the consonantal spelling had been set.

2. The usual form in Hebrew is

מָלֵא {mɔléʔ},

which is most like Arabic مَلِئَ. Here, however, the consonantal spelling {mly} resembles the Hebrew less than the Qurʔānic pronunciation [maliʔa] does. The Hb. א at the end was, to be sure, no longer a pronounced glottal stop when the vowel notation was added to the text (a century or more after the Muslim conquest of the Holy Land); the word then was actually [mɔlé].

These Arabic forms are stative verbs, 'he [or a grammatically masculine 'it'] is full'. The Hebrew forms can be just as well stative verbs, like the Arabic, or masculine singular adjectives. {mɔléʔ} does not closely correspond to anything IE, but adding the feminine suffix, accented as an adjective, entails a momentous change:

מְלֵאָה {məleʔɔ́ʰ}

is much more like the Greek feminine adjective πλείη [plé:ɛ:] in Homer, πλέα [pléa:] in Attic. The two letters ει should not be taken for a diphthong [e + i], since in the spelling standardized after 400 B.C. the digraph often represents what had been a plain long vowel [e:]. So the structural match between the Greek and the Hebrew, segment by segment, is close, except that the Greek word has recessive accent. In Hebrew it is precisely the fixed accent on

---

[8] מָלְ֣וּ תוֹכְךָ֖ חָמָ֑ס {mɔlúʷ toʷkəkɔ́ xɔmɔ́sɔ} means 'your midst is full of violence'. Translators from ancient to modern times have had trouble with the *hápax legómenon*, although the Targum and especially the Latin Vulgate ('repleta sunt interiora tua iniquitatis') construed it nearly as I do. The {-uʷ} looks offhand like a plural suffix, but it can hardly be that here. For the noun is singular; and modern attempts to make it the object, 'they have filled your midst with violence,' are not supported by the context, which supplies no antecedent, whether specific or loose, for "they."

the feminine suffix that entails the reduction of the vowel [ɔ] in [mɔlé] to šəwɔ (as the Hebrew grammarians called it) in [məleʔɔ́]. Somewhat like the umlaut or epenthetic [i] in the early Germanic languages (except Gothic) and in Avestan, that preaccentual back vowel [ɔ] peculiar to Hebrew is an anticipation of the accent upon the next syllable. Only a single consonant can separate [ɔ] from the accented vowel.

The accentually conditioned reduction of the vowel [ɔ] to [ə] in Hebrew gives us an idea of what happened prehistorically in IE to bring about an alternation such as the Latin *mul-* : *pl-*. Whereas in Hebrew a bare remmant of the vowel is still pronounced and thus [m + l] does not constitute a consonant group, the vowel quite vanished in IE and would have left an unwieldy consonant group **ml-*. That is what we find actualized as *pl-*. Why not **bl-*, since the nasal [m] is more like a voiced plosive than an unvoiced? Greek indeed has μέλι [méli] 'honey' but βλίττειν [blítte:n] 'to take honey'. Many Indo-Europeanists have theorized, however, that the voiced labial plosive *b* was lacking at an important early stage. Whatever may have been the phonetic features of the labial consonants in existence then, there is no difficulty in envisaging that the one closest to [m] came out [p] in Latin, Greek, and certain other historical languages.

But we do face a difficulty in Gk. [polú] and other forms in which the labial and *l* are separated by a vowel. None of these, to be sure, are in Latin. In other IE languages it would seem that the forms with *pl-* were prominent enough to draw the ones with **mVl-* into the less divergent pattern *pVl-*. For an anomalous alternation to be eliminated in most of the IE domain calls for no surprise; that happens generally in the diachronic changes of any language. Rather it is any anomalous alternation preserved that demands an explanation of its origin.

3. Another form of the Hebrew feminine singular adjective is recorded only once:

מִשְׁפָּט מְלֵאֲתִי . . . קִרְיָה {qiryɔ́ʰ . . . məleʔắtíʸ mišpɔ́ṭ}

'a city . . . full of justice' (Isaiah 1:21). The Greek parallel is πλησι-φαὴς σελήνη [plɛ:sipʰaɛ̀:s selɛ́:nɛ:] 'the moon full of light' (Philo, *De congressu eruditionis gratia* 106 = 3.93.20–21 Cohn-Wendland etc.). Although not datably attested before the Christian era, πλησιφαής is archaic in its formation and has turned up also in a papyrus fragment of an epic poem in the Homeric or Hesiodic style (Kroll 1901: 3–4). The [-si-] morpheme, corresponding to Hb. [-tí], is not just accidentally associated here with a feminine noun; it distinguishes the feminine [helkesi-] from the masculine [helke-] in

Τρωάδας ἑλκεσιπέπλους 'the daughters of Tros, trailing the robe' (*Iliad* 6.442 etc.)
'Ιάονες ἑλκεχίτωνες 'the Ionians, trailing the tunic' (13.685)

Most other compound adjectives with [-si-] (or [-ti-]) in Homer, though not all, have a feminine reference.[9]

4. The masculine plural πλεῖοι [plê:ɔi] (nominative, *Odyssey* 12.92) finds a cognate in post-Biblical Hebrew:

מְלֵאֵי עָוֹן {məleʔeᵞ ʕowon}

'full of sin, sinful' (Brown and Levin 1986: 91).

5. An obsolete Latin verb is attested in the third person plural passive *plentur* 'they are filled' by the lexicographer Festus (pp. 258–259, Lindsay). Compounded with prefixes—*implē, complē, replē,* and so on—it is commonly used in the active sense 'fill.' With passive endings it has virtually the same meaning as the Hebrew stative, and one of those endings, the second person singular *-re* (< *-se*), could be cognate to the Hebrew {-tɔ}; thus *-plēre* :

מָלֵאתָ {mɔléʔtɔ}

'you are full' (Job 36:17).[10]

6. Finally, besides the adjective {məleʔɔ́ʰ}, accented constantly on the feminine suffix {-ɔʰ}, there is the stative verb {mɔləʔɔ́ʰ} 'she is

---

[9] οὖρον . . . πλησίστιον [ô:ron . . . plɛ:sístion], however, means 'a breeze filling the sails', not 'full of sails' (*Odyssey* 11.7, 12.149; the noun is masc.). While the sole occurrence of Hb. {məleʔātíᵞ} is stative 'full', not active, the masculine {mɔléʔ} sometimes admits of either syntactical interpretation, as in

מָלֵא כְבוֹד־יְהוָה הַבָּיִת: {mɔléʔ k̄əb̄oʷd̄-(ʔăd̄onɔ́y) habbɔ́yit̄}

'full of the LORD's glory is the house' or 'the LORD's glory fills the house' (Ezekiel 43:5). In the masculine plural we find unquestionable instances of active meaning:

מָלְאוּ אֶת־הָאָרֶץ חָמָס {mɔləʔúʷ ʔɛt̄-hɔʔɔ́rɛc xɔmɔ́s}

'they have filled the land with violence' (Ezek. 8:17; cf. 30:11, Jeremiah 19:4).
[10] Likewise *ʋerēre* :

יָרֵאתָ {yɔréʔtɔ}

'you are afraid' (II Samuel 1:14). Levin 1971: 672–680; 1984a: 102. The horizontal superscript over [ʔ] and [ʰ] indicates that the Hebrew letter was no longer pronounced by the punctators of Tiberias.

full' with variable accent: if the next word is accented on the first syllable, we find

מָלְאָ֣ה גַּ֔ת {mɔ́ləʔɔʰ ggát}

'[the] wine-press is full' (Joel 4:13); but if the next word is accented otherwise,

מָלְאָה הָאָ֖רֶץ {mɔ́ləʔɔ́ʰ hɔʔɔ́rɛc}

'the earth is full' (Jeremiah 23:10 etc.; Levin 1984a: 87, 98–100). The alternation between {-ɔ́ʰ} accented on the suffix and {-ɔ́-} on the root is partly reminiscent of Lithuanian, which is recorded only since the sixteenth century but maintains many archaisms. One feature pertinent to this comparison is an accentual alternation in many adjectives, exemplified by the feminine *pilnà* and the neuter *pìlna* (Senn 1966: 142, 359). Lithuanian, like the related Baltic languages, has no neuter nouns—only masculine and feminine, as in Semitic—but it has a neuter form of predicate adjectives, distinguished by accent from the feminine form. The accentual alternation between feminine and neuter is not peculiar to Lithuanian, although it has no parallel in Greek or Sanskrit. The "short form" of the feminine adjective in Russian, notably, is {polná}, the neuter usually {pólno}.[11]

So far we see nothing *semantically* akin to the Lithuanian and Russian in the Hebrew alternation between {mɔ́ləʔɔʰ} and {mɔləʔɔ́ʰ}. But the initial consonant of the word after {mɔ́ləʔɔʰ} is doubled (or strengthened), and that is characteristically, in Hebrew, the outcome of a nasal consonant completely assimilated: [mɔ́ləʔɔggát], structurally *[mɔ́ləʔɔᴺ gát]. The unaccented *[-ɔᴺ], with a nasal of unspecified quality, reminds us of the ending -ον [-on] in Greek and {-am} in Sanskrit (where this nasal undergoes assimilation to the ensuing consonant).

Phonetically [mɔləʔɔ́] is closest to the Greek feminine adjective πολλή [pollέ:], and *[mɔ́ləʔɔᴺ] to the neuter πολλόν [pollón] except for the accent. The origin of the double [-ll-] has been debated long but inconclusively (Chantraine 1968: 902; Frisk 1970: 577–578). I suggest it may be due to the absorption or assimilation of a glottal stop.[12] There is no great semantic gap between Hb. {mɔləʔɔʰ} 'is full' and Gk. [pollέ:, pollón] 'much' (the neuter form being synonymous and

[11] Some dictionaries also list полнó.
[12] In the Germanic *full* (and so on) the geminate is derived from *ln. The Indo-Europeanists, however, do not favor the same explanation of Gk. [poll-] (Schwyzer 1939: 284).

interchangeable with [polú]). But syntactically they will very seldom mesh; here is an approximation:

יָמַי מָלְאוּ {mɔləʔúʷ yɔmɔ́y}

'my days are full' (= completed; Genesis 29:21)
περὶ δ' ἤματα πολλὰ τελέσθη [perì d' é:mata pollà telésthɛ:]
'many days were ended' (*Odyssey* 19.153, 24.143; cf. 19.443).

What is there in common between the *unaccented feminine* verb ending {-ɔʰ}, that is, *[-ɔⁿ], in Hebrew and *neuter* gender in IE? The only kind of Hebrew noun that can follow the unaccented {-ɔʰ} is one that *lacks the feminine marker* {-ɔ́ʰ}. Otherwise the feminine stative verb will also end in the accented {-ɔ́ʰ}, comparable to the accented -*a* of feminine adjectives in Lithuanian, Russian, and so on. Some Hebrew nouns that have no feminine marker but are feminine in their agreements are represented in IE by neuter nouns. Conspicuous among them are certain parts of the body; the paired ones in particular are nearly all feminine in Semitic (see Table 1). None of these Hebrew words happens to be found right after a feminine verb form—for example, *{mɔ́ləʔɔʰ qqɔ́rɛn} 'a (the) horn is full'—such that we could point to the syntagma as morphologically equivalent to an IE neuter noun preceded by an agreeing adjective in *-*on* or *-*om*.[13] But

אֶרֶץ רָגְזָה {rɔ́gəzɔʰ ʔɔ́rɛc}

'the earth is a-tremble' (Pr. 30:21) gives us a hint of how it must have been. To be sure, the glottal stop, like other guttural consonants, is not subject to strengthening in Hebrew (as the gutturals are in Arabic); besides, the word for 'earth' is feminine in IE—more precisely, in Germanic—as well as Semitic (see discussion II). The earth, because of its reproductiveness, could hardly have fallen into neuter gender, whereas the neuter gender of those other IE counterparts to Semitic feminines is quite understandable.

We have here not just a verb root *ᵐ/ₚ-l(-ʔ) but substantial remains of an extensive grammatical system that developed and lasted over thousands of years in the forerunners of the known Semitic and IE languages. The perplexing discrepancies in accent between Balto-

---

[13] Whereas the Semitic {ʔ} in {m-l-ʔ} does not correspond to the Baltic and Slavic *n* in *p-ln-*, we can cite Hb. *{ʔɔ́rək̄ɔʰ qqɔ́rɛn} 'a (the) horn is long' and the Lithuanian neuter cognate *ilga* (fem. *ilgà*), Russian neuter {dólgo} (fem. {dolgá}) (Levin 1984a: 95–97).

TABLE 1

	Hebrew		Gothic		Russian	English
Terminal	קֶרֶן קֹרֶן	{qérɛn} {qɔ́rɛn} }	:	*haurn*		'horn'
	אֹזֶן	{ʾózɛn}	:	*auso*[a]	:	{úxo}	'ear'
Terminal	עַיִן עָיִן	{ʕáyin} {ʕɔ́yin} }	:	*augo*[a]	:	{óko}	'eye'
	קֶרֶב	{qérɛb}[b]	:	*hairto*[a]	:	{sérdce}[c]	'heart'

[a] Outside of the nominative and accusative singular, these nouns show a stem in *-n* in the Old Germanic languages (as in Gothic *ausona* 'ears') and to some extent in the modern ones (Levin 1971: 343).
[b] Gender not determined from any Biblical occurrence.
[c] With a diminutive suffix.

Slavic and the more anciently recorded Sanskrit and Greek have been much studied by Indo-Europeanists and explained by "Hirt's law" and "Saussure's (or Fortunatov's) law" (Illich-Svitych 1979: 9–15, 58–59, 61–64, 79–81, 136–139, 145–147). It becomes essential from now on to "factor in" the evidence from Hebrew, supplemented by other Semitic languages. For this contributes something quite new, by showing *what sort of sentence environment* set the specific processes in motion.

REFERENCES CITED

Bargery, G. P. 1934. *A Hausa-English Dictionary and English-Hausa Vocabulary.* London: Oxford University Press.

Brown, J. P. 1979. "The Sacrificial Cult and Its Critique in Greek and Hebrew (I)." *Journal of Semitic Studies* 24: 159–173.

Brown, J. P., and S. Levin. 1986. "The Ethnic Paradigm as a Pattern for Nominal Forms in Greek and Hebrew." *General Linguistics* 26: 71–105.

Campbell, A. 1959. *Old English Grammar.* Oxford: Clarendon Press.

Chantraine, P. 1968. *Dictionnaire étymologique de la langue grecque.* Paris: Klincksieck.

Décsy, G. 1977. *Sprachherkunftsforschung*, vol. 1. Wiesbaden: Otto Harrassowitz.

Doke, C. M., et al. 1958. *English and Zulu Dictionary.* Johannesburg: Witwatersrand University Press.

Ernout, A., and A. Meillet. 1979. *Dictionnaire étymologique de la langue latine*, ed. 4 by J. André. Paris: Klincksieck.

Frisk, H. 1970. *Griechisches etymologisches Wörterbuch*, vol. 2. Heidelberg: Carl Winter.

Illich-Svitych, V. M. 1979. *Nominal Accentuation in Baltic and in Slavic.* Trans. by R. L. Leed and R. F. Feldstein. Cambridge, Mass.: MIT Press.

Kroll, Guilelmus [= Wilhelm]. 1901. *Analecta Graeca*. Greifswald: J. Abel.
Levin, S. 1971. *The Indo-European and Semitic Languages*. Albany: State University of New York Press.
———. 1980. "An Accentual Correspondence between Hebrew and Hausa." *Forum Linguisticum* 4: 232–240.
———. 1984a. "Indo-European Descriptive Adjectives with 'Oxytone' Accent and Semitic Stative Verbs." *General Linguistics* 24: 83–110.
———. 1984b. The Glottal Stop in the Germanic Languages and Its Indo-European Source." *General Linguistics* 24: 233–235.
———. 1985. "Review of Allan R. Bomhard, *Toward Proto-Nostratic*." *Diachronica* 2: 97–104.
Noreen, A. 1970. *Altnordische Grammatik*, vol. 1. Tübingen: Max Niemeyer.
Panganiban, J. V. 1969. *Concise English-Tagalog Dictionary*. Rutland, Vt.: Charles E. Tuttle.
Pokorny, J. 1959. *Indogermanisches etymologisches Wörterbuch*. Bern: Francke.
Pott, A. F. 1836. *Etymologische Forschungen auf dem Gebiete der indo-germanischen Sprachen*, vol. 2. Lemgo: Meyer.
Redhouse, J. W. 1969. *Revised Redhouse Dictionary, English-Turkish*, ed. 7. Istanbul: Redhouse Press.
Schwyzer, E. 1939. *Griechische Grammatik*, vol. 1. (Handbuch der Altertumswissenschaft, 2. Abteilung, 1. Teil). Munich: Beck.
Senn, A. 1966. *Handbuch der litauischen Sprache*, vol. 1. Heidelberg: Carl Winter.
Steiner, R. C. 1982. *Affricated Ṣade in the Semitic Languages*. (American Academy for Jewish Research, Monograph No. 3.) New York.
Strunk, K. 1969. "Verkannte Spuren eines weiteren Tiefstufentyps im Griechischen." *Glotta* 47: 1–8.
Walde, A. 1965. *Lateinisches etymologisches Wörterbuch*, ed. 4 by J. B. Hofmann. Heidelberg: Carl Winter.
Wilkinson, R. J. 1959. *A Malay-English Dictionary*. London: Macmillan.

Some Recent Work on the
Remote Relations of Languages

VITALY SHEVOROSHKIN
ALEXIS MANASTER RAMER

In this chapter, we offer a brief survey of work on three proposed macrofamilies of languages: Nostratic, Sino-Caucasian, and (superordinate to Sino-Caucasian) Dene-Caucasian. Obviously, this covers only some of the recent studies on remote relations of languages, for we have chosen to concentrate on work that has for the most part been done by Soviet linguists and that is neither well known nor widely accepted in the West. It is not our purpose here to argue for these hypotheses or to debate the critical literature. It is rather to present the basic proposals that have been made, to sketch some of the reasons why the linguists working in this area find these hypotheses both plausible and fruitful, and to suggest some possible resemblances between the proposed macrofamilies and between them and the hypothetical Amerind macrofamily suggested by the American linguists Greenberg and Ruhlen. It is our hope that you will be encouraged thereby to use the primary literature, much of which is being made more accessible by publication in English translation (e.g., Shevoroshkin and Markey 1986), in making your own judgments on the validity of the proposed classifications and reconstructions.

Some 200 years ago in a speech in Calcutta, William Jones suggested that Latin, Greek, and Sanskrit must have "sprung from some common source," one that was also the probable origin of Persian, the Germanic, the Celtic, and other languages. Half a century later Franz Bopp began the process of reconstructing the Indo-European proto-language, and since that time a number of other proto-languages of Eurasia have been established. At a 1963 conference the late Björn Collinder expressed the hope that someone would soon prove that these were ultimately related. Collinder's suggestion did not have to wait as long as Jones's for direct confirmation in the form of a reconstruction. Even as he spoke, two linguists working independently of each other in Moscow were figuring out the relationships of several of the language families of Eurasia and establishing a common proto-language. These were Vladislav M. Illič-Svityč, who died in 1966 at the age of 31, and Aaron B. Dolgopolsky, who moved to Israel in 1976 (see Illič-Svityč 1964; Dolgopolsky 1964 and 1964a). Illič-Svityč's work linked Proto-Indo-European (PIE), Proto-Afro-Asiatic (PAA), Proto-Kartvelian (PK), Proto-Uralic (PU), Proto-Dravidian (PD), and Proto-Altaic (PA). His results were in the main corroborated by Dolgopolsky, who did not consider Dravidian and who treated Proto-Turkic (PT), Proto-Mongolian (Proto-Mong), and Proto-Tungusic (Proto-Tung) as separate though related branches of the new family rather than reconstructing Proto-Altaic (PA).[1] The new proto-language was called "Nostratic" (N), following a suggestion made at the beginning of the century by Holger Pedersen, who guessed at the genetic relationship of the major linguistic families of Eurasia but did not attempt to prove it.

In recent years, data have been presented that point to the Nostratic origin of Chukchi-Kamchatkan (Golovastikov and Dolgopolsky 1972) and Eskimo-Aleutian (Mudrak 1984). On the other hand, it is beginning to be accepted that, unlike in the original proposals, Afro-Asiatic may have been coordinate with Nostratic rather than descended from it, in other words, a "sister" and not a "daughter."

More recently Starostin (1984) proposed another macrofamily of languages comprising Northeast Caucasian, Northwest Caucasian, Sino-Tibetan, and Yeniseian. These comparisons became possible as a result of the reconstruction of North Caucasian (uniting Northeast and Northwest Caucasian), Sino-Tibetan, and Yeniseian. Starostin's reconstruction of North Caucasian was based on earlier comparative work by A. Kuipers, T. E. Gudava, S. Nikolaev, and his own (for references see Starostin 1985: 75). The Proto-Yeniseian reconstruction was from Starostin (1982), and the Sino-Tibetan from Peyros and Starostin (1984). Work on the reconstruction of Proto-Sino-Caucasian is continuing. Several ancient languages of the Middle East (Hurrian, Urartean, and Hattic) and Etruscan have also been suggested as members of the Sino-Caucasian family, and it is possible that Basque belongs here as well. Furthermore, Nikolaev (1988)

---

[1] Illič-Svityč's Proto-Altaic is extremely close to his Proto-Nostratic, which suggests that he had actually arrived at something like Proto-East Nostratic. See Ivanov (1986: 20) and Shevoroshkin and Markey (1986: xix) for discussion of this issue.

argues for a relationship between Sino-Caucasian and the Na-Dene languages of North America, a connection that had been anticipated by Edward Sapir, and he has proposed the term "Dene-Caucasian" for this macrofamily.

Apart from the Nostratic Eskimo-Aleutian and the Dene-Caucasian Na-Dene, the remaining indigenous languages of North America as well as South America are believed by some linguists to belong to a single family called "Amerind." The most extensive work on this family has been done by Greenberg (1987) and Ruhlen (this volume), but before any reconstruction of Proto-Amerind can be possible, it will be necessary to have reconstructions of the individual subfamilies.

These recent proposals substantially reduce the number of families that need to be postulated for the languages of the world. At this point, it looks as though we have four very large macrofamilies—Nostratic, Dene-Caucasian, perhaps Amerind, and probably Austric (that is, Austronesian and Austro-Tai)—and a few smaller families—Khoisan (see Ivanov 1983; 153 ff.), Indo-Pacific, and Australian (see Shevoroshkin et al. 1988). Several of what once seemed to be language isolates (Basque, Etruscan, Hattic, and Hurro-Urartean) have been classified as belonging to one or another of the macrofamilies.

NOSTRATIC

Dybo and Terentjev (1984: 3–20) published a review of Nostratic studies, from which we cite the following sets of proposed reconstructions of some Nostratic roots as well as affixes and particles[2,3]:

Pronouns and Pronominal Affixes

[1] N **mi 'I' > PU *mi, PIE *me, PK *me/*mi (cf. PA *bi with *b- < *m-).

[2] **t'i and **Si 'thou' > PA *ti-, *si-, PU *ti, PD *-ti, PIE *te, *-s, PK *se-/*si-, PAA *[ʔan-]tV, *t-.

[3] **mä 'we (inclusive)' > PA *bä- (for *b-, see [1]), PU *mä-/*me-, PIE *me-s, PK *m-, PAA : PChadic *m(n).

[4] **nV 'we (exclusive)' > PD *nā-m, PIE *ne-/*no-, PK *naj, PAA *n-.

[2] Note that a consonant symbol followed by a prime denotes a glottalized consonant, whereas a consonant symbol with a superscripted prime denotes a palatalized consonant.

[3] Abbreviations used in these reconstructions are listed at the end of the chapter before the References Cited.

Nominal Affixes

[5] **na (originally a locative particle) > PA *-na, PU *-na/*-nä, PD *n(V), PIE *en/*n, PK (?) *nu, *-n, PAA *-n.

[6] **-NA (plural animate) > PA *-na/*-nä, PU (?) *-NV, PK *-(e)n, PAA *-ān.

[7] **-tV (plural marker, inanimate) > PA, PU *-t, PK *-t-, PAA *-āt, etc.

Verbal Affixes

[8] **s(V) (causative-desiderative) > PA *-su/*-sü and *-sa/*-sä, PD *-ic- (PD *c < N **s), PIE *-se-, PAA *šV-, *-š-.

[9] **t'V- (causative-reflexive) > PA: Proto-Turkic *-t-, PU *-t(t)-, PD *-tt-, PAA *tV-, **-t- (PAA *t usually from N **t, PAA *t' < **t'; but in grammatical morphemes *t < **t').

Affixes Used in Word-formation

[10] **-k'a (diminutive suffix) > PA *-ka/*-kä, PU *-kka/*-kkä (PU intervocalic *-kk- < N *k'; cf. PU *-tt- < **t'; PU *-pp- < **p'), PD: Kuruh -kan, PIE *-k-, PK *-k'- (*-ak'- and *-ik'-).

[11] **-l[a] (suffix of collective nouns) > PA *-l(a), PU (?) *-la, PD *-ḷ, PK: Svan (?) *äl, etc.

Particles

[12] **mä (prohibitive particle) > PA *mä-/*bä-, PD *ma-, PIE *mē, *PK *mā/*mō, PAA *m(j).

[13] **k'[o] (intensifying and copulative particle) > PA *-ka, PU *-ka/*-kä, IE *kʷe, PK *kwe, PAA *k(w), etc.

Body Parts

[14] **q'iwlV 'ear, hear' > PA *kʕul-, PU *kūle-, PD *kēḷ, PIE *ḱleu-, PK *q'ur-, PAA *q(w)l (q = k').

[15] (Only in East N) **k'/q'awinga 'armpit' > PA *kʕawiɲi, PU *kajŋa(-lV), PD *kavuṅka, etc.

Man, Kinship

[16] **kälU 'female in-law' > PA *käli(n), PU *kälü, PD: North Dravidian *kal-, PIE *ǵlōu, PK (?) *kal- (cf. Georgian kal- 'woman'), PAA: Proto-Semitic *kl(l).

[17] **k'/q'ülä 'kin' > PA: Proto-Turkic *külä, PD: South Drav. (?) *kūḷ, PIE *kʷel-, PAA *q(w)l, etc.

Animals

[18]   **k'/q'üjnA 'wolf, dog' > PA (?) *kʕina-, cf. Tung. *xina-da
'dog', PU *küjnä 'wolf', PIE *kʷōn-/*kun- 'dog', PAA (?) *k(j)n
etc. 'dog, wolf'.

[19]   **gurHa 'antelope' > PA: Proto-Mong. gūra, PD *kūr-, PAA
*g(w)rH, etc.

Nature

[20]   **wete 'water' > PA: Proto-Tung. *ödV 'rain', PU *wete, PD
*ōtV-/*wetV 'wet', PIE *wed-.

[21]   **kiwE 'stone' > PU *kiwe, PD *kw-a, PAA: Chad. *kw-.

[22]   **burV 'storm' > PA *bu/orV, PU purV-, *pur-kV, PIE *bher-,
PAA (?) *bwr-, etc.

Spatial Terms

[23]   **qant'V 'front side' > PA antV, PU (?) *[e]Nte- 'first', 'face',
PIE *Xant-, PAA *xnt (*nt < **nt').

Actions and States (Verbs)

[24]   **ʒegU 'eat' > PA *ǯē-, PU *s[ē]γE (< *s[e]γü ?), PIE *seX(w)-
'sat(iat)ed', PK *ʒeγ- 'become sated', PAA (?) *zγ- (< *zuγ- ?)
'be fed/abundant'.

[25]   **ńamo 'grasp' < PU *ńomV/(?)*ńamV-, PD *ñamV-, PIE *i̯em-
(*i̯ can originate both from **j and **ń) etc.

Qualities

[26]   **k'ut'V 'little' > PD *kuḍḍ-, PK *k'u/ot'-, PAA *q(w)t'/*k(w)t'/kt.

[27]   **gi[ɬ]hu 'smooth' > PA *gilu/a- 'smooth, shiny', PU *kī[ɬ]V
'smooth, shiny', PIE *ǵhelH-/*ǵhleH-/*ǵhloH- 'shiny', *ghleH-dh-
'smooth, shiny', PK: Georgian (?) glu-, PAA *glḥ (?) (= 'bold'
in Proto-Semitic).

[28]   **berg[i] 'high, tall' > PU: Samod. p[e]r[kV], (?) PD *pēr̲, PIE
*bherǵh-/-bhreǵh-, PK (?) *brg-e, PAA *brg; etc.

Illič-Svityč reconstructed some 600 Nostratic etyma. Since these
include no words for cultivated plants, we may suppose that the
speakers of Proto-Nostratic had not developed agriculture. There are
also no Nostratic words for domestic animals, with the possible exception of the dog, but the root in question (no. [18]) also applied to
the wolf, and so we cannot conclude that Canis familiaris was already
known. Thus the Nostratic speakers must have gathered and hunted

their food, which puts them at around 10,000 B.C. This is also the approximate time of the other proto-language that has recently been proposed, Proto-Sino-Caucasian (Starostin 1984). The geographical location of Nostratic has been placed by some scholars (Illič-Svityč, Dolgopolsky) in the Near East, the later home of the Indo-Europeans, but there is no comparable result for Sino-Caucasian.

As we have already mentioned, the Eskimo-Aleutian family was not originally considered a part of Nostratic, but recent work by Mudrak (1984) places it well within Nostratic. Some examples of the Proto-Eskimo/Nostratic correspondences follow:

[29]   P(roto-)E(skimo) *alku-/*aluk- 'lap' : N **lak'V 'lick' (PU *lakkV-, PD *nakk-, PIE *lak-, PK *lak'-, PAA *lk'-).
[30]   PE *aŋ-lu '(ice-)hole' : N **Hanga 'open, hole'.
[31]   PE *ciku 'snow, ice' : N **šiŋgV 'snow'.
[32]   PE *ciku 'needle(point)' : N **CinKV 'insert, sharp point'.
[33]   PE *c[u]- 'see' : N **ćuHV 'see'.
[34]   PE *ima 'sea' : N **jamV 'sea, body of water'.
[35]   PE *im(m)u 'milk' : N **H[E]mi 'suck(le)'.
[36]   PE *irə 'eye' : N: PAA *irʕ 'sce, look'.
[37]   PE *kuja 'joint, elbow' etc. : N **küjñA 'joint'.
[38]   PE *qa- 'mouth' : N **qowa 'mouth, opening'.
[39]   PE *kuma 'louse' or *quma 'flea' : N **KVmV 'biting insect'.
[40]   PE *λi- 'to lie' : N **LVgV id. (PIE *legh- etc.).
[41]   PE *ma 'region, place' : N **magi 'earth'.
[42]   PE *mac(j)a 'sun' : N **mV[ź]V id.
[43]   PE *məlu 'breast (woman)' : N **mälgi id.
[44]   PE *ñarə- 'forehead' : N **ñe[rH]i 'front of the head'.
[45]   PE *pali 'tan' : N **paĺ(H)V 'to burn'.
[46]   PE *putu 'hole' : N **p'ut'V 'hole, vagina'.
[47]   PE *t[u] 'deep' : N **t'uba id.
[48]   PE *utu- 'old' : N **w[e]tV 'year; old'.

Examples of grammatical morphemes follow:

[49]   PE *wi 'I' (for *w < **m, cf. PA *b < **m) : N **mi id.
[50]   PE *wa 'we (incl.)' : N **mä id.
[51]   PE *ci 'thou' : N **t'i/*Si id.
[52]   PE *ta 'you' : N **t'ä id.
[53]   PE *ta 'this' : N **t'ä id.
[54]   PE *ki- 'who', *qa- (interrog. pron.) : N **Ke, **Ko id.
[55]   PE *-t (plural marker) : N **tV id.

[56]   PE *-tV- (causative affix) : N **-tV- id.
[57]   PE *-l- (verbal negation) : N **ʔVlV (negative particle).
[58]   PE *na- 'no' : N **nV (negation), etc.

Especially interesting are correspondences between PE and PA or individual Altaic languages; we shall quote only a few examples from Mudrak's long list:

[59]   P(roto-)B(ering-)E(skimo) *alV 'tear (in eye)' : P(roto-)T(urkic) *āl id.
[60]   PBE *alə- 'variegated' : PA *ala- id.
[61]   PE *ama 'yes, and' : PA *amV id.
[62]   PBE *aŋwa-n- 'clavicular hollow' : PT *äŋ[i]n 'shoulder'.
[63]   PE *atə 'name' : PT *āt id.
[64]   PE *caki 'breast' : Old Japanese (an Altaic lang.) *caki 'front part, breast'.
[65]   PE *im[u] 'now, today' : PA *em-dE 'now'.
[66]   PE *inə- 'to lie' : Old Jap. in- 'go to bed'.
[67]   PE *maki 'bone with meat' : Mong. məka 'meat'.
[68]   PE *kə-təŋi 'heel' (*kə- = body parts) : PA *tuŋi 'heel'.
[69]   PE *ulu 'tongue' : PA *dUli id. (For the anlaut, cf. PE *unu 'night' : PT *dün; PE *aja- 'lean, support' : PT *daja- id.)

SINO-CAUCASIAN

We now present some of Starostin's (1984) cognate sets linking North Caucasian, Yeniseian, and Sino-Tibetan and leading to the reconstruction of Proto-Sino-Caucasian:

[70]   P(roto-)N(orth-)C(aucasian) *cV- 'all' : P(roto-)S(ino-)T(ibetan) *chia (no cognates from PYen. [= Proto-Yeniseian]).
[71]   PNC *jĕr(ĕ)k'wi 'heart' : PST *ʔrăk/ŋ : PYen. *r/təga (for the correspondence 'heart' : 'breast', cf. PIE *kerd- 'heart' : PK *m-k'erd- 'breast' < N *k'erdV).
[72]   PNC *purV 'to fly' : PST *phur (also *bhur).
[73]   PNC * 2ŏc'V 'full' (2 = voiced [ʔ]) : PYen. *ʔute.
[74]   PNC *śīnV/*śǟnV 'green' : PST *r-siaŋ) (> *sriaŋ) : PYen. *son-.
[75]   PNC *zo 'I' : PYen. *ʔaʒ.
[76]   PNC *huq(ʕ)V(n)- 'long' : PYen. *ʔux-.
[77]   PNC *Hi-[ś]winə 'night' : PST *sen : PYen. *sin-g (> *sig).

Starostin also cites numerous cognates designating people, kinship terms, plant and animal species, artifacts, and so on. The phonetic correspondences between the three branches of Sino-Caucasian are not fully worked out: Starostin mentions difficulties in establishing the phonetic laws relating North Caucasian to the other two branches (apparently because of the typologically unusually high number of distinct consonants in North Caucasian, which finds no analog in the other two branches). However, the limited results on detailed sound correspondences need not be taken to negate the conclusion that these languages are indeed related or that the cognate sets are genuine. After all, Indo-European was established long before linguists learned to look for exact sound correspondences.

As already noted, Čirikba (1985) has argued that Basque, the otherwise isolated language of the Pyrenees, belongs to the North Caucasian language family. As in the case of the proposed membership of Eskimo-Aleutian within Nostratic, we cite some of the proposed evidence here.

[78]   B(asque) *ar-* (causative prefix) : NWC: Abkhaz *ar-*.
[79]   B *-z* (instrumental suff., pronounced [s]) : Abkh. *-(a)s*.
[80]   B *-ar* (plural suff.) : Abkh. *-ar*, NEC: Lezgian *-ar* etc.
[81]   B *d-* (3rd sg. marker) : Abkh. *d-* (same, animate).
[82]   B *-n* (past tense marker) : Abkh. *-n*.
[83]   B *-n* (locative suff.) : Abkh., Ubykh *-n*.
[84]   B *no-* (particle in interrog. adverbs) : Abkh. *-n* (particle in interrog. auxiliaries).
[85]   B *ni* 'I' : PNEC *$nɨ$.
[86]   B *gu* 'we' : PNEC *$\check{y}ü$ 'we (inclusive)'.
[87]   B *zu* 'you' : NWC: Adygei *śwă*, PNEC *$źwV$ (Lak *zu* etc.).
[88]   B *au* 'this' : NWC: Abaza *a-u-j* 'that', Abkh. *wa* 'there', Adygei *au(ă)* 'there', PNEC *$wĕ$ 'this', 'that' (Lak *wa* 'this' etc.).
[89]   B *an* 'there' : Proto-Abkhaz-Tapantan *ana 'there'.
[90]   B *ara* 'there (direction)', *ori* 'this', etc. : Abkh. *ara-x́* 'here (direction)', *ar-i* 'this', *ur-t* 'those, they', etc.
[91]   B *beri* 'this same' : Abkh. *a-bri* 'this' (= *a-bari*).
[92]   B *ika 'one' (in *ama(r)-ika* 'eleven', i.e. '10 + 1') : Abkh. *ak'ə*, *za-k'ə* 'one' (< *$k'ə$ 'one').
[93]   B *tzi 'ten' : Proto-Abkh.-Adygan *$(b-)ć'wV$.
[94]   B *la(i)ster* 'quick' : Abkh. *lassə* (metath. in NEC *$\check{s}ɨlä$).
[95]   B *mara-mara* 'abundant' : Abkh. *i-marə-maža*.
[96]   B *atso* 'yesterday' : Abkh. *jacə*, Adygei *dəR-asă*.
[97]   B *bizi* 'alive, living' : Abkh. *a-bza*.
[98]   B *eze* 'damp' : Abkh. *aʒa* (cf. *a-ʒə* 'water, river').
[99]   B *zar-tzu* 'sharp' : Abkh. (Abzhui dialect) *-c'ar*.

[100] B *beso* 'hand' : PNEC *bač'i* 'paw'.
[101] B *be-larri* 'ear' (*be-* = body part pref.) : P-Abkh.-Adyg. *í̆V,
       PNEC *lĕrħʕV.
[102] B *bi-zkar* 'back (body)' : Abkh. *a-zkwa*.
[103] B (*be-*)*atz* 'finger' : Abkh., Ubykh -*cwa*.
[104] B *uxuri* 'urine' (*x* = [š]) : Abkh. -*c̆xwa-ra*, PNEC *c̆V̆xwV*.
[105] B *al* 'be able' : Abkh. *al*, *al-ša-ra*.
[106] B *itz* 'word' : Abkh. *cwa*.
[107] B *izu* 'fear' : Abkh. -*šwa-ra*.
[108] B (dial.) *xor* 'dog' : P-Abkh.-Adyg. *xwa* (with regular loss of
       -r), PNEC *xwar*.
[109] B *une* 'place' : Abkh. -*nə* 'place, country'; cf. Bzyb *Apś-nə*
       'Abkhazia' (cf. also B, Abkh. -*n* locative suff.).
[110] B *otz* 'cold' : P-Abkh.-Tapant. *c'a-ʕa* (cf. PNEC *Vc'c'Vr-* 'to
       freeze').
[111] B *izar* 'star' : Abkh. -*jac'wa*, Adygei *źwaRwă*, PNEC *Hă-ʒʒwărʕi*,
       etc.

Čirikba's proposals have not won general acceptance, but there is
some plausibility to many of his comparisons. The main difficulty, of
course, is the relatively recent date of attestation for Basque and the
lack of significant diversity within Basque (which makes the reconstruction of a "Proto-Basque" difficult).

It appears that it is much easier to demonstrate the Sino-Caucasian
affinities of several extinct languages of the ancient Near East, Hurrian and Urartian (Diakonoff and Starostin 1986), as well as Hattic
(Ivanov 1985).

The complicated problem of Etruscan has recently been attacked
by Ivanov (1983a: 36ff.), who suggests that it is a Sino-Caucasian
language, specifically North Caucasian. Although he admits that not
many Etruscan words have clearly established meanings, Ivanov
puts forward a small number of plausible cognate sets linking Etruscan with Hattic and Hurrian and with modern North Caucasian lan-
guages. (Note: probable Etr. values: c = [k], θ = [tʰ], v = [w], χ = [kʰ],
and z = [ts]; *ś* is uncertain.)

[112] Etr. *ci* 'three' : Hurri. *ki-g*, P-Nakh. *qo-*, PNWC *k̕-*.
[113] Etr. *ma𝜒* 'five' : NEC: Batsbi *pxi*, Khinalug *pxu* < *pku*.
[114] Etr. *huθ* 'six' : NEC: Batsbi *i̯eth*.
[115] Etr. *s/śa* 'four' : NWC: P-Abkh.-Abaz. *-š̕-*, Ubykh -*í̆ə*.
[116] Etr. -*𝜒va* (plural; things) : NWC: Abkh. -*k'wa*, Abaz. -*kwa*,
       Ub. -*xwa*.

[117]   Etr. *-r* (pl.; animate) : Abkh. *-r(a)*, Abaz. *-ra*.
[118]   Etr. *mi* 'this' (not 'I') : PNC **m-*.
[119]   Etr. *al-* 'give' : Hurri.-Urart. **ar-*.
[120]   Etr. *hus-* 'son, boy' : PNEC **hwVswV-* 'man' (cf. Urart. *ʔaše*
        'men').
[121]   Etr. *lupu(-ce)* 'to die' : NWC: Adygei *lʕapʕə* 'death bed/hour'.
[122]   Etr. *ziχ* 'book', *zic/χ-* 'write' : PNWC **tx-* 'write'.
[123]   Etr. *zilat/θ* 'praetor/dictator/princeps' : Hatti. *zilat*.

One item of special interest in this connection is set [118], since the Etruscan pronoun *mi* is often analyzed as a first person form. However, Ivanov argues that this was actually a third person form, which appears to make good sense in a number of inscriptions. A more detailed study of the connection between Etruscan and North Caucasian has been published by Orël and Starostin (1990).

DENE-CAUCASIAN

Quite recently, Nikolaev (1989; ms) has proposed a number of correspondences linking Proto-North Caucasian with the Na-Dene languages of North America. If these are correct and if Yeniseian and Sino-Tibetan data are found to agree with these results, then we have a case for a Dene-Caucasian language family, whose living descendants are spoken on both sides of the Bering Strait. However, this work is preliminary, and no reconstruction of a hypothetical Proto-Dene-Caucasian language has been offered.

[124]   PEAth. **k'Vm* 'fog' : PNC **k'k'wōmV* 'cloud, fog'.
[125]   PEAth. **k'ʷùs* 'neck, back of the head, throat' : PNEC
        *k'(w)V̄s/s̄V 'back of the head, throat'.
[126]   PEAth. **č'ĭd* 'soil, dirt' : PNEC **čVʕd(w)V/*č'VʕɨwV*.
[127]   PEAth. **c'ék'* 'navel' : PNC **c'onk'V*.
[128]   PEAth. **Lū?ɬ* 'rope' : PNEC **HV-ć'wolV* 'leather strap, rope'.
[129]   PEAth. **ɬV(M)d* 'firewood' : PNEC **ɬwimɨ̄V*.
[130]   PEAth. **t'àh/x* 'foot' : PNEC **t'wēhwV*.
[131]   PEAth. **gàn* 'arm' : PNEC **ɢɢwiʕnV*.
[132]   PEAth. **k'ám* 'to burn' : PNEC **k'w[i]mV*.
[133]   PEAth. **ǯéx(w)* 'ear' : PNEC **lĕh̄lV*.
[134]   PEAth. **šwĭ* 'I' : PNEC **zwo*, but cf. PNC **zo* 'I' (Starostin).
[135]   PEAth. **lV-* 'we' : PNEC **L[ä]*, etc.

SOME METHODS AND CONSEQUENCES
OF THE WORK ON REMOTE RELATIONS

There has been considerable discussion of the merits of various proposals mentioned. Some of the relevant Russian literature is now available in English translation (Shevoroshkin and Markey 1986). There are some methodological points that have arisen in the course of the work on Nostratic and other macrofamilies (and their proto-languages) that may be worthwhile to discuss in some detail.

One concern is the importance of stable vocabulary. The first and most important step in comparing language families is the decision about what items to compare. To solve this problem, Dolgopolsky (1986) surveyed 140 languages of Europe and Asia in an attempt to make a list of the meanings that typically were reflected by words that had almost never been replaced either by borrowing or by neologism but rather appeared to represent the original etyma of their proto-languages. Since in many cases the proto-language was not fully known, Dolgopolsky followed the simple procedure of assuming that if a given meaning is expressed by several unrelated words in related languages, this is, necessarily, a case of replacement, whereas if a given meaning is represented by cognate forms in all or nearly all members of a family, this may be presumed to represent the original etymon. The latter would then be words that could be studied for evidence of common ancestry for any languages or language families, since it would be highly probable (Dolgopolsky provided some statistical estimates) that languages sharing words on this list would have to be related. To avoid comparisons based on superficial similarities, Dolgopolsky eliminated all words involving onomatopoeia, interjections, and baby talk.

Dolgopolsky then produced a list of meanings that are expressed by words that are seldom or never replaced. The stablest fifteen were the words with the following semantics, given in the order of decreasing stability:

1. I/me [first person sg. pronoun]
2. two/pair
3. thou/thee [second person sg. pronoun]
4. who/what
5. tongue
6. name
7. eye
8. heart
9. tooth
10. no/not [negative and prohibitive particles]
11. fingernail/toenail
12. louse/nit
13. tear(drop)
14. water
15. dead

These meanings were represented by words that ranged from those that had not been replaced in any of the 140 Old World languages studied to those where replacement had taken place in no more than a fourth of the languages studied. In a second list, the words were subject to replacement only slightly more frequently:

16.	hand	20.	full
17.	night	21.	sun
18.	blood	22.	ear
19.	horn	23.	salt

These lists can be of considerable use in evaluating competing hypotheses about the relationships among languages and language families. Similarly, the lists of cognate sets proposed for each of the proto-languages cover the stablest lexemes (as well as grammatical morphemes), including but not restricted to those on the Dolgopolsky list.

Of considerable importance in all of the work surveyed here has been the assumption that multiple comparison is better than binary. The validity of this assumption is borne out when we consider the sets of correspondences within any language family. The crucial point is that certain contrasts are preserved better in one branch than in another. For example, in Nostratic the vowels are best preserved in the eastern languages (PD, PA, and especially PU), the stops in PK and PAA, the sonorants in PU, laryngeals in PAA, the $**\hat{k}'$: $**q'$ distinction in PK, and so on. Binary comparisons would either miss entirely or discover only belatedly many of the archaic distinctions that must be the building blocks of a Nostratic reconstruction.

An important criterion for the success of any hypothesis about the relatedness of languages or language families is whether a proposed relationship—and the proto-language reconstructed on the basis of it—throws light on problems in the history of each member of the proposed family or phylum that could not be solved internally. For example, Nostratic data provide a new understanding of the origins of some hitherto troublesome subsystems of PIE phonology. One involves the three-way contrast, in PIE, of velars (k, g, gh), palatovelars ($\hat{k}$, $\hat{g}$, $\hat{g}h$), and labiovelars (k^w, g^w, h^w). The validity of such a ternary system has sometimes been questioned. However, we now

---

[4]Several other Kartvelian-Indo-European items are not on the Dolgopolsky list but seem to be quite stable as well and are thus likely to be genuine cognates (e.g., PK *diqa* 'clay' : PIE *dhĝh-em-* 'earth', PK *tep-* 'warm' : PIE *tep-* [ditto], and so on).

see that it faithfully reflects a three-way conditioned split of Nostratic velars depending on the quality of the following vowel. Although Nostratic **a, **e, and **o all give PIE *e, preceding velars yield (true) velars (as in [10]), palatovelars (as in [27]), and labiovelars (as in [13]) respectively.

Another traditional crux of Indo-European linguistics that may be solved with the help of Nostratic data involves the so-called laryngeal consonants originally postulated for PIE by Kuryłowicz on the basis of Saussure's reconstruction of abstract phonological units and Hittite data indicating the occurrence of Hittite or Luwian ḫ and ḫḫ in some of the same places. Although there has been considerable controversy over the exact system of these consonants to be reconstructed for PIE, Nostratic data clearly indicate the existence of Proto-Nostratic **h, **$ḥ$, **$ʕ$, **x, **γ, **q, and **g (back, or uvular, g). Hittite data show that PIE had at least two laryngeals, a stable *X, preserved in Hittite or Luwian as ḫ or ḫḫ, and an unstable *H, which was lost in Hittite. Comparison with Nostratic now demonstrates that the stable laryngeal comes from Nostratic uvulars **x, **g, **q, **g, and perhaps **h, whereas the unstable one derives from the Nostratic pharyngeals **$ḥ$ and **$ʕ$ as well as from **$ʔ$. Interestingly, it seems that we can now show that the original qualities of Nostratic vowels (which, in general, all went to *e in PIE) were preserved next to a laryngeal (cf. set [23]; for details, see Kaiser and Shevoroshkin 1986).

Nostratic data may also throw light on the previously unresolved issue of the phonetic nature of the three series of PIE stops traditionally reconstructed as voiceless (we will use T as a cover symbol), voiced (D), and "voiced aspirated" (Dh). According to a recent theory advanced by Gamkrelidze and Ivanov (1986) the D series was actually glottalized (T'), with the traditional Dh being $D(h)$, and the traditional T being $T(h)$. Now, Nostratic data show an original system of glottalized (T'), voiceless (T), and voiced (D). The correspondence with PIE (in its traditional reconstruction) are as follows:

Nostratic	PIE
T'	T
T	D
D	Dh

In view of the Nostratic facts, it makes sense to revise the traditional PIE values, but in a different way from that proposed by Gamkrelidze and Ivanov. We would assume that the PIE values were tense voiceless, lax voiceless, and voiced. This system is similar to what we find in Germanic and Armenian.

We need only assume that PIE shifted Nostratic glottalized consonants to voiceless tense (denoted by $\underline{T}$).

Nostratic	PIE
T'	$\underline{T}$
T	T
D	D

Certain other IE languages shifted $\underline{T}$ to T and T to D. In these languages, the original D either merges with the new D ($< T$) or else gives an aspirate. Except in Indo-Iranian, this aspirate is voiceless, and indeed it is only in Indo-Iranian that we find the values that were traditionally taken to represent the PIE state of affairs.

PIE	Indo-Iranian
$\underline{T}$	T
T	D
D	Dh

However, it is noteworthy that Indo-Iranian had developed a fourth series of consonants in addition to the three PIE ones. These were phonetically voiceless aspirated (*Th*), and they were etymologically unrelated to the PIE tense stops. Since it has been suggested that languages avoid having two distinctive series of voiced (including breathy) consonants and only one of voiceless ones, it may be that the rise of this fourth series was a necessary condition for the Indo-Iranian developments, thus explaining why this is the only branch of IE to have voiced values for two of the PIE series.

Finally, the proto-languages that have been proposed should, in all likelihood, be more similar to each other than any two (or more) languages of different macrofamilies, at least on the assumption that all or most of mankind's languages must ultimately be related. As a matter of fact, it has been suggested that Nostratic and Dene-Caucasian are related. We discuss these suggestions in the next section. And in the following one we point out that there are striking similarities between the Nostratic and Dene-Caucasian reconstructions, on the one hand, and the Amerind proposals of Greenberg and Ruhlen. If these comparisons are valid, they would provide strong support for the individual reconstructions, in addition to their own self-evident significance for the understanding of our linguistic prehistory.

WIDER CONNECTIONS: NOSTRATIC AND
SINO-CAUCASIAN

We now proceed to review some evidence suggesting even deeper connections, linking two or more of the proto-languages discussed so far. We begin with the possibility that Nostratic and Dene-Caucasian are themselves related. First of all, Starostin (1989) cited some Nostratic roots (as reconstructed at that time by Illič-Svityč) that appear to resemble Sino-Caucasian roots. Some of his 225 examples (all obeying essentially regular sound correspondences) are as follows:

[136] N *lajp'V 'leaf' : SC *λ'ApE 'leaf' (ST *λēp, PYen *jep, PNC *λ'api).

[137] N k'ap'V 'vessel, pot, scull' : SC *qAp'V 'vessel' (OC *khāp, PYen *qä(ʔ)p 'boat', PNC *qāp'ā 'vessel; boat').

[138] N *Homsa 'meat' : SC *jVmcV 'ox; meat' (PST *chu 'a kind of ox', PYen *ʔise 'meat', PNC *jəmco 'ox').

[139] N *śVnV 'year; old' : *SC swEnV 'year; old' (PST *s-niŋ, PYen *sin 'old', *si(n)-ga 'year', PNC *swän(H)i 'year').

[140] N *küni 'wife, woman' : SC *qwEnV 'woman' (PYen *qVm, PNC *q(w)änV).

[141] N *mi 'I' : SC *ŋV (PST *ŋV, PYen *b-, PNC *nV/*mV).

[142] N *mu 'this' : SC *mV 'this' (PYen *wV, PNC *mV).

[143] N *k'a/*k'o 'who' : SC *xV 'who, what' (PST *qhā, PNC *xV̱).

[144] N *mi 'what' : SC *mI 'what' (PYen *wi/we, PNC *mV).

While Starostin insists on the preliminary nature of this comparison (and on the many limitations of the existing Nostratic and Sino-Caucasian reconstructions), he concludes that there may have been "a distant genetic relationship between the two macrofamilies of the Old World."

Likewise, Verner (1977) compared some Proto-Yeniseian roots with Nostratic, apparently in the conviction that the Yeniseian languages were Nostratic. If we accept Starostin's view that they are Sino-Caucasian, Verner's comparisons—if valid—would imply a relation between Nostratic and Sino-Caucasian *as a whole*. As a matter of fact, after we eliminate likely loanwords and some rather loose comparisons, Verner's work does seem to yield some exact correspondences between Proto-Yeniseian (which we may take to represent Sino-Caucasian) and Nostratic:

[145] PYen. *pʰal 'hot' : N *p'alV- 'burn'.

[146] PYen. *as-pVl 'cloud' (*es- 'sky' + *bVl) : N *bilwi 'cloud' (ac-

cording to Illič-Svityč 1971: 179, PU *pilwe, PA *buli-t, PAA *bjl; Verner cites N *bil(w)V after Illič-Svityč 1967).

[147] PYen. *qʰoRV 'kill, die' : N *qʼo(H)lV 'kill'.

[148] PYen. *kiʔaj 'story' : N *kiXV 'sing' (in Uralic languages also 'pronounce incantations by shaman', etc.); a borrowing in Yeniseian?

[149] PYen. *tʰum 'black' : N *tʼumV 'dark'.

[150] PYen. *tʰVq 'clay' : N *diqa 'earth, clay'.

[151] PYen. *u: 'strength' : N *woj[H]V id.

[152] PYen. *si 'be born' : N *š[e]wV 'give birth'.

[153] PYen. *(k)olV 'worm' : N *kutV id. (*-o- in PU).

[154] PYen. *sej in *pʰVl-sej 'to sew' : N *sigjU 'tie together'.

[155] PYen. *g/kit 'to smear, soil, dab' : N *kʼadV.

In this last set the Nostratic etymon is the main Nostratic building term, which includes the meanings proposed for the Proto-Yeniseian one.

CONNECTIONS WITH AMERIND

Recent work by Greenberg (1987) and Ruhlen (this volume) argues for a genetic relation among most of the languages of the Americas, excluding Eskimo-Aleutian and Na-Dene, and points to some tentative reconstructions of an *Amerind* language family. Ruhlen (1989) has further sought to connect Amerind with various other language families, including Indo-European. If the proposals for remote relations sketched in this article are at all valid, a relation with Nostratic should be even clearer, and so we present a list of possible Amerind-Nostratic comparisons, derived from Ruhlen's Amerind–Indo-European ones. It should be noted, however, that Proto-Amerind has not been reconstructed—and indeed there is still much doubt about the validity of the proposed Amerind language family. The Amerind forms cited here are taken from Ruhlen's very preliminary work (with some emendations and additions made by Shevoroshkin).

[156] N *kʼ/qʼüjnA 'wolf, dog' : Am. *(a)kuan 'dog', rather *(a)kʼuan.

[157] N *m[a]H- 'hand, take' : Am. *ma 'hand'.

[158] N *pʼatV 'foot' : Am. *pe(t) id.

[159] N *buHi 'grow, become' ('be' in PIE and PA) : Am. *buhi (not *ipu); cf. Penutian *bUh- 'live, exist' (Wintun bOh- 'live', Patwin bo:, Klam. pᵛ 'be').

[160] N *m[a]nV 'man' : Am. *mano 'husband, man'.

[161]   N *m[o]nV or *m[o]n[g]V 'many' (Illič-Svityč 1967: 348) : Am.
          moni 'many'.
[162]   N *magV* 'big' : Am. *mek* 'large'.
[163]   N *d[i][w[H]V* 'die' (PIE *dheu-/*dhweiH-, PSem. *dwj/*dwʔ) :
          Am. *ti* 'die'.
[164]   N *kʼ/qʼo* 'who' : Am. *kV* (interrog.).
[165]   N *tʼogV or *tʼägV 'burn' : Am. *tʼVk-* 'burn', with vocalism
          *a-*i-*u.
[166]   N *je(HV)* 'come' : Am. *ja(ʔ) 'go'.
[167]   N: PA *tālu* 'shoulder (blade)', PD *tōḷ* 'shoulder, upper arm' :
          S Am. *tala* or rather *tāla* (< *taHla) 'shoulder'.
[168]   N: PU *tōye-* 'give, bring' : Am. *tuk* 'bring'.
[169]   N *ńan[g]V* 'tongue' (PU *ńaŋk-će-m*, PK *nina/*ina, etc.) :
          Am. *nene*, *nik*.
[170]   N *küni* 'woman, wife' : SE Am. *kuna* 'woman'.
[171]   N *kälV* 'female in-law' : SE Am. *kila* 'woman'.
[172]   N *m[a]nV* 'think' : Am. *mana* 'wish'.
[173]   N: PK *laɣw-* 'meat' : Am. *lau* id. (South America).
[174]   N *mV[ź]V or *mV[ʒ́]V 'bright, sun' : Am. *me[c]a* 'star'.

There are many other, quite plausible, parallels, but the comparison is severely hampered by the lack of exact reconstructions of Proto-Amerind.

There also appears to be a significant sound correspondence involved. Ruhlen (personal communication) pointed out that there was a large number of glottalized stops in the Nostratic forms. Shevoroshkin's provisional work suggests that these are also reflected as glottalized stops in Northern Amerind (specifically in the Penutian, Hokan, and Almosan-Keresiouan languages). These correspondences are involved in eight roots:

[1]   N *tʼogV* 'burn' : Am. *tʼVk-*.
[2]   N *kʼutʼV/*kʼotʼV* 'small, little' : North. Am. *kʼutʼi* 'thin' and
       SE Am. *kuta* 'young'.
[3]   N *pʼatʼV* 'broad' : N Am. *pʼatʼla* 'broad'.
[4]   N *kʼ/qʼajwV* 'dig' : Am. *kʼua/okʼua* 'dig'.
[5]   N *HotʼV* 'fire' : Am. ?*otʼi.
[6]   N *kʼüjnA* 'wolf, dog' : Am. (a)kʼuan.
[7]   N *kʼi* 'this' : Am. *kʼi/kʼo.
[8]   N *kʼV/*qʼV* 'allative' : Am. *kʼ.

On the other hand, there are two Nostratic roots with nonglottalized stops corresponding to nonglottalized stops in Northern Amerind. These numbers are not impressive, but regular correspondences may be involved.

[175]   N *te[h]V 'say' (Illič-Svityč 1967: 365) : Am. *ti.

[176]   N *käjwV 'chew' : Am. *kua 'bite'.

We have listed some possible correspondences between Nostratic and Sino-Caucasian and between Nostratic and Amerind. We conclude now by citing a few possible cognates linking Sino-Caucasian with Amerind.

[177]   Am. *pok 'arm' : PNEC *p'weʕk'V/*q'weʕk'V 'hand/wrist, palm', PST *b/bh/piak 'hand', PYen. *boq 'hand, palm'.

[178]   Am. *po/*pe 'foot' : PNEC *bVmɬV 'leg/foot, hoof', PST *phŏl 'ankle, calf', PYen. bul 'leg/foot'.

[179]   Am.: Hokan *ɬVlV 'foot' (after Leščiner [p.c.]), Penutian: Nisenan lu:l 'leg', etc. (ɬ in Tsimshian) : PNC *šēɬHV 'foot/leg' (š = [λ]); N ʒ = *λ?

[180]   Am. *kua 'bite' (or rather *qwa, cf. Penutian: Klamath qwᵛ etc.) : PNC *ʔV-ggV, PST *k(h)aj.

[181]   Am. *[c]ar(i) 'cold' : PNC *čwĕrHV, PYen. *ʒVr̩- id.

[182]   Am. *s[i]n- or *s[ü]n- (cf. Klamath p-sin, Wintun son-, Salishan: Sechelt məq-sə́n, etc.) : Sino-Cauc.: PST *(s)na, PYen. *(h)aŋ.

[183]   Am. *teq- 'earth, mud': Wakashan *tq- 'mud', Penutian: Takelma tʰga 'earth, land', Wintun teq- 'to daub' etc. : NC: PYen. *tʰVq 'clay'.

[184]   Am. *paq' 'bone, gristle' (as in Penutian: Wintun paq 'bone', Maidu pâk' 'gristle' etc.) : NC: P-Abkh.-Adyg. *Pʠə 'bone'.

[185]   Am. *toki 'sun' : NC: Proto-Abkh.-Adyg. *təγa 'sun'.

Obviously, anything at all we say about the external relations of Amerind will ultimately depend on a precise reconstruction of Proto-Amerind. In this and in many other areas, everything remains to be done.

The remote relations of languages are being studied as never before, and for the first time a significant number of scholars accept the monogenesis of all languages both as a plausible working hypothesis and as one that should be subject to verification—or refutation—in the near future. With linguists looking so far into the past, a new relationship is being forged with human genetics, physical and cultural anthropology, and archeology. Whatever the ultimate status of the hypotheses discussed here, a new and exciting chapter in the history of linguistics is being written.

ABBREVIATIONS

AA	= Afro-Asiatic
Abkh.	= Abkhaz
Adyg.	= Adygan (not Adygei)
Am.	= Amerind (not Amerindian)
B	= Basque
Chuk.-Kamch.	= Chukchi-Kamchatkan
Etr.	= Etruscan
IE	= Indo-European
Kartv.	= Kartvelian
Mong.	= Mongolian
N	= Nostratic
N Am.	= Northern Amerind
NC	= North Caucasian
NEC	= Northeast Caucasian
NWC	= Northwest Caucasian
OC	= Old Chinese
P(-)	= Proto-
PA	= Proto-Altaic
PAA	= Proto-Afro-Asiatic
PBE	= Proto-Bering-Eskimo
PD	= Proto-Dravidian
PE	= Proto-Eskimo
PEAth.	= Proto-Eyak-Athapascan
PIE	= Proto-Indo-European
PK	= Proto-Kartvelian
PNC	= Proto-North Caucasian
PNEC	= Proto-Northeast Caucasian
PNWC	= Proto-Northwest Caucasian
Proto-Abkh.-Adyg.	= Proto-Abkhaz-Adygan
Proto-Mong.	= Proto-Mongolian
Proto-Tung.	= Proto-Tungusic
PSem.	= Proto-Semitic
PST	= Proto-Sino-Tibetan
PT	= Proto-Turkic
PU	= Proto-Uralic
PYen.	= Proto-Yeniseian
S Am.	= Southern Amerind
SE Am.	= Southeast Amerind
Samod.	= Samoedian
SC	= Sino-Caucasian
Tung.	= Tungusic
Yen.	= Yeniseian

REFERENCES CITED

Bengtson, J., and M. Ruhlen. ms. "Selected Global Etymologies."
Bomhard, A. R. 1984. *Toward Proto-Nostratic: a New Approach. Current Issues in Linguistic Theory*, vol. 27. Amsterdam: John Benjamins.
Čirikba, V. A. 1985. "Baskskij i severokavkazskie jazyki," pp. 95–105. In *Drevnjaja Anatolija*. Moscow: Nauka.
Diakonoff, I. M., and S. A. Starostin. 1986. *Hurro-Urartian as an Eastern Caucasian Language*. (Münchener Studien zur Sprachwissenschaft, Beiheft 12, Neue Folge.) Munich: R. Kitzinger.
Dolgopolsky, A. B. 1964. "Metody rekonstrukcii obščeindoevropejskogo jazyka i vneindoevropejskie sopostavlenija." In *PSG*.
———. 1964a. "Gipoteza drevnejšego rodstva jazykov Severnoj Evrazii (problemy fonetičeskix sootvetstvij)." *VII Meždunarodnyj kongress antropologičeskix i ètnografičeskix nauk*. Moscow: Nauka.
———. 1985. "On Personal Pronouns in the Nostratic Languages." *Gedenkschrift Björn Collinder*. Vienna: W. Braumüller.
———. 1986. "A Probabilistic Hypothesis Concerning the Oldest Relationships among the Language Families in Northern Eurasia." In Shevoroshkin and Markey, eds. 1986.
Drevnjaja Anatolija. 1985. Moscow: Nauka.
Dybo, V. A., and V. A. Terentjev. 1984. "Nostratičeskaja makrosemja i problema eë vremennoj lokalizacii," part 5, pp. 3–20. In *Konf. 1984*.
Gamkrelidze, T. V., and V. V. Ivanov. 1984. *Indoevropejskij jazyk i indoevropejcy*. 2 vols. Tbilisi: Izdatel'stvo Tbilisskogo Universiteta.
Golovastikov, A. N., and A. B. Dolgopolsky. 1972. "Rekonstrukcija čukotsko-korjackix kornej i nostratičeskie ètimologii," pp. 27–30. *Konferencija po sravnitel'no-istoričeskoj grammatike indoevropejskix jazykov*. Moscow: Nauka.
Greenberg, J. H. 1987. *Language in the Americas*. Stanford, Calif.: Stanford University Press.
Illič-Svityč, V. M. 1964. "Genezis indoevropejskix rjadov guttural'nyx v svete dannyx vnešnego sravnenija." In *PSG*.
———. 1967. "Materialy k sravnitel'nomu slovar'u nostratičeskix jazykov," pp. 321–373. In *Ètimologija 1965*. Moscow: Nauka.
———. 1971. *Opyt sravnenija nostratičeskix jazykov (semitoxamitskij, kartvel'skij, indoevropejskij, ural'skij, dravidijskij, altajskij)*. Vvedenie. Sravnitel'nyj slovar' (b - K). Moscow: Nauka.
———. 1976. [As above] Sravnitel'nyj slovar' (l - ӡ). Ukazateli. Moscow: Nauka.
———. 1984. [As above] Sravnitel'nyj slovar' (p - q). (Po kartotekam avtora). Moscow: Nauka.
Ivanov, V. V. 1983. *Istorija slavjanskix i balkanskix nazvanij metallov*. Moscow: Nauka.
———. 1983a. "K istolkovaniju ètrusskix tekstov na osnove sravnitel'nogo jazykoznanija," pp. 36–45. In *Tekst: Semantika i struktura*. Moscow: Nauka.
———. 1985. "Ob otnošenii xattskogo jazyka k severozapadnokavkazskim," pp. 26–59. In *Drevn'aja Anatolija*. Moscow: Nauka.

————. 1986. "Proto-languages as Objects of Scientific Description," pp. 1–26. In Shevoroshkin and Markey, eds. 1986.

Kaiser, M., and V. Shevoroshkin. 1986. "On Indo-European Laryngeals and Vowels. I. Laryngeals before Vowels." *Journal of Indo-European Studies*.

————. "On Recent Comparisons between Language Families: the Case of Indo-European and Afro-Asiatic. *General Linguistics*. In press.

Klimov, G. A. 1964. *Ètimologičeskij slovar' kartvel'skix jazykov*. Moscow: Akademija Nauk.

————. 1965. *Kavkazskie jazyki*. Moscow: Nauka.

Konf. 1977 = *Konferencija: Nostratičeskie jazyki i nostratičeskoe jazykoznanie*. Tezisy dokladov. Moscow: Institut slavjanovedenija i balkanistiki AN SSSR.

Konf. 1984 = *Lingvističeskaja rekonstrukcija i drevnejšaja istorija Vostoka*. Tezisy i doklady konferencii. Parts 1–5. Moscow: Nauka.

Kuipers, A. H. *A Dictionary of Proto-Circassian Roots*. Lisse: Peter de Ridder Press.

Mudrak, O. A. 1984. "K voprosu o vnešnix svjazjax èskimosskix jazykov," part 1, pp. 64–68. In *Konf. 1984*.

Nikolaev, S. 1989. "Eyak-Athapascan—North Caucasian Sound Correspondences," pp. 63–65. In V. Shevoroshkin, ed. *Reconstructing Languages and Cultures*. Bochum: Universitätsverlag Brockmeyer.

Nikolaev, S. L. ms. *Sino-kavkazskie jazyki v Amerike*.

Orël, V., and S. Starostin. 1990. "Etruscan as an East Caucasian Language," pp. 60–66. In V. Shevoroshkin, ed. *Proto-Languages and Proto-Cultures*. Bochum: Universitätsverlag Brockmeyer.

Peyros, I. A., and S. A. Starostin. 1984. "Sino-Tibetan and Austro-Tai." *Computational Analyses of Asian and African Languages* 22: 123–127.

PSG = *Problemy sravnitel'noj grammatiki indoevropejskix jazykov*. Tezisy dokladov. Moscow: Universitet. 1964.

Ruhlen, M. 1987. *A Guide to the World's Languages*. Stanford, Calif.: Stanford University Press.

Ruhlen, M. 1989. "Nostratic-Amerind Cognates," pp. 75–83. In V. Shevoroshkin, ed. *Reconstructing Languages and Cultures*. Bochum: Universitätsverlag Brockmeyer.

Shevoroshkin, V. 1982. "Penutian Labial Stops (Initial Position)." *California and Oregon Languages Newsletter*.

Shevoroshkin, V. V., and T. L. Markey, eds. 1986. *Typology, Relationship and Time: a Collection of Papers on Language Change and Relationship by Soviet Linguists*. Ann Arbor, Mich.: Karoma.

Starostin, S. A. 1982. *Praenisejskaja rekonstrukcija i vnešnie svjazi enisejskix jazykov. Ketskij sbornik. Antropologija, ètnografija, mifologija, lingvistika*, pp. 144–237. Leningrad: Nauka.

————. 1984. "Gipoteza o genetičeskix svjazjax sinotibetskix jazykov s enisejskimi i severnokavkazskimi jazykami," part 4, pp. 19–38. In *Konf. 1984*.

————. 1985. "Kul'turnaja leksika v obščeseverokavkazskom slovarnom fonde," pp. 74–94. *Drevnjaja Anatolija*. Moscow: Nauka.

————. 1989. "Nostratic and Sino-Caucasian," pp. 42–66. In V. Shevorosh-

kin, ed. *Explorations in Language Macrofamilies*. Bochum: Universitätsverlag Brockmeyer.
Starostin, S., and S. Nikolaev. (ms in preparation). *North Caucasian Etymological Dictionary*.
Verner, G. K. "Voprosy èvoljucii obščeenisejskogo jazyka v svete nostratičeskix rekonstrukcij." In *Konf. 1977*, pp. 7–10.

PART IV

Linguistic Genealogy in Europe, Asia, and America

The studies on possible relatives of Indo-European inevitably focus attention on those various potential cousins such as Uralic, Altaic, and Kartvelian, and our attention thus turns to Asia and the Caucasus. And so this section surveys the comparative linguistics of these areas, which border on IE to the northeast and east. In this section we include also Merritt Ruhlen's study of certain implications of Joseph Greenberg's new classification of the Amerindian languages.

Søren Egerod, who for many years headed the Asiatic Institute of the University of Copenhagen, opens this section with a comprehensive overview and discussion of the languages of East Asia, combining considerations of both typological and genetic factors, both grammar and lexicon, both genetic relationship and diffusion in the consideration of lexical resemblances. His Table 10-1 is noteworthy as a non-family-tree way of registering proposals of genetic relationship, while also, and separately of course, summarizing typological features. All the dotted lines in the network are historically significant, since each represents either genetic relationship or extensive intimate borrowing. Findings of the latter kind can be just as important for our understanding of prehistory as those of the former kind.

Ian Catford, a long-time investigator of the amazingly diverse languages of the Caucasus area, provides here a survey of these languages. The area borders on the generally presumed homeland of Indo-European, and its languages exhibit some of the world's most interesting phonological systems. Although the region is relatively small, it has three distinct genetic stocks, the two northern ones of which are probably related. The third, Kartvelian, whose best-known representative is Georgian (the native language of Josef Stalin), is now increasingly seen as a relative of Indo-European.

Both of these skillful surveys are based on extensive knowledge of the languages treated and the methods of analysis and comparison employed, and Egerod and Catford also exhibit a refreshing willingness, sometimes not seen in establishment comparativists, to entertain objectively and dispassionately even the most far-reaching proposals for long-range genetic relationships.

Thanks largely to work done during the past couple of decades by two of our authors, Samuel Martin and Roy Miller, it is now widely accepted that Japanese and Korean, once considered to be genetically isolated languages, are related to each other. Less clear is their connection to Altaic, which Miller accepts with little reservation whereas Martin remains somewhat skeptical. As seen in the preceding part, Greenberg connects Japanese and Korean to Altaic but not more closely than to other branches of his sweeping Eurasiatic phylum. Japanese has also been linked with Austronesian, however, as mentioned in Egerod's paper, and some have considered it to be a mixed language, with affinities in both directions and thus a contradiction of the family-tree model. Another proposal, linking Japanese with Dravidian, is compatible with a version of the Nostratic hypothesis that would include both Dravidian (as Shevoroshkin does) and Japanese (as Greenberg does).

Martin provides here a carefully detailed comparison of Japanese and Korean, whereas Miller describes the current rather bizarre state of Altaic studies, a field that has been overtaken by an extreme resistance to the recognition of genetic relationship, as if the phenomenon of languages being sprung from some common source were so unlikely that any other explanation for correspondences, no matter how improbable, should nevertheless be preferred.

Since the native languages of America have long been of great interest to American linguists (in part because of their great diversity, which has provided a rich collection of puzzles for comparative linguists) and since Greenberg's Eurasiatic and Shevoroshkin's Dené-Caucasian extend to North America, we have also included in this volume one paper on the Amerindian languages, by Merritt Ruhlen. It represents a type of exploration that will be found too innovative for more conservative comparativists. First, he is so bold as to accept the methods and findings of Greenberg. This offense alone is sufficient to bring forth the indignation of some conservatives. Second, undeterred by his critics, he even has the audacity to make use of Greenberg's findings and to base further work on them! The method he uses here is simply to study the distribution of Greenberg's proposed etymologies among the eleven subgroups of his vast Amerind phylum. Although some of Greenberg's etymologies will doubtless have to be revised or thrown out when more detailed comparative work is done and new ones not uncovered by Greenberg will surely be forthcoming, the numbers of tentative etymologies may be large enough to provide a statistical basis for rough preliminary measures of degrees of relatedness. Although the results cannot claim to be as definitive as those that will emerge from the detailed comparative work that is yet to be done, they are helpful as a first approximation in the shaping of future work.

Far Eastern Languages

SØREN EGEROD

A great variety of languages is spoken in East Asia and Oceania (see map, p. 206). Describing and grouping them has for a long time constituted one of the most difficult tasks of comparative linguistics. As the collection and the analyzing of data progressed, the methodology of linguistic work changed. The procedure that had worked so well for Indo-European languages could not easily be transferred to languages and language families of which few had a written tradition to reveal earlier stages and whose place in history is little known. In grouping Indo-European languages, grammatical resemblance has played a role as well as word comparisons because Indo-European grammar happens to be of a very special, easily recognizable kind (an inflectional type with complicated conjugations and declensions). The East Asian languages are predominantly isolating (non-inflectional) or agglutinating (with regular accumulation of inflectional elements), each type spread over a large area consisting of languages that would often not be thought of as genetically related on the basis of these structural similarities alone. The methods of comparison must be adapted and refined with due consideration of the nature of the material and the tenability of the results. All resemblances among languages that are not based on regular phonological correspondences must be considered instances of typological relationship, which can have causes other than original genetic relations (such as borrowing, mutual influence, spontaneous development). But even in the case of regular phonetic correspondence in different languages among words with the same meaning, the possibility of their being loanwords has to be taken into account (massive borrowings from one language into another have their own regular sound

This is an updated and revised translation of a talk given in 1977 and published in Danish by the Royal Danish Academy of Sciences and Letters, Copenhagen. Pamphlet 3.1977.

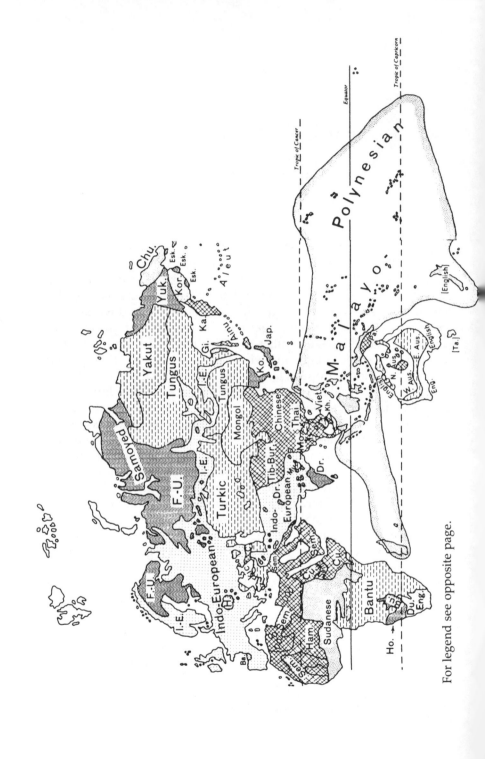

For legend see opposite page.

laws). Only correspondences within basic vocabulary point to genetic relationship with some degree of likelihood. The number and
kinds of words and morphemes covered by sound laws give some
hints as to when two languages began to diversify or to approach
each other.

The fact that typological agreement does not indicate or prove genetic relationship in no way renders the results of the typological
approach less important or less promising. On the contrary, typology contributes in a fundamental way to our understanding of linguistic structure and linguistic change. It becomes apparent how unrelated languages can deeply influence each other and how far the
waves of structural patterns can spread. The languages of East Asia
in the midst of apparent chaos yield the grandest example of such
fascinating processes that break down sets of similarities and surprisingly establish others in ever-changing manifestations.

I shall deal here with those language families generally known as
Altaic, Sino-Tibetan, and Austric as well as the practically extinct language of Ainu (Sakhalin and Hokkaidō). We shall not treat the somewhat enigmatic minor language groups sometimes joined under the
designation Paleo-Siberian (Gilyak, Luoravetlan, Yukaghir, and Ket).

Altaic languages may include Turkish, Mongolian, Tungusic with
Manchu, and, according to some, also Korean and Japanese (Egerod
1980). If Korean and Japanese were not originally Altaic, they may or
may not together form a separate group (East Altaic). Sino-Tibetan
(formerly Indo-Chinese, Egerod 1974) divides into Sinitic (= Chinese), consisting of many languages ("Chinese dialects"), and Tibeto-Karenic, consisting of Tibeto-Burman and Karenic (which may
however have sprung from the Sinitic side). Tibeto-Burman consists
of Tibetic, Baric, and Burmic. See Figure 1. Austric (Figure 2) is supposed to consist of Austro-Viet (Austro-Asiatic) and Austro-Tai (Aus-

---

Map: Eastern hemisphere language groups. ABBREVIATIONS: Aus. = Aus-
tralian, Ba. = Basque, Bu. = Bushman, C. = Caucasian, Chu. = Chukchi,
Cu. = Cushitic, Dr. = Dravidian, Du. = Dutch, Eng. = English, Esk. =
Eskimo, F.-U. = Finno-Ugrian, Gi. = Gilyak, H. = Hungarian, Ham. =
Hamitic, Ho. = Hottentot, I.-E. = Indo-European, Jap. = Japanese, Ka. =
Kamchadal, Kh. = Khmer, Ko. = Korean, Kor. = Koryak, Mo. = Mon, Mu.
= Munda, Pa. = Papuan, Sem. = Semitic, Ta. = Tasmanian, Tib.-Bur. =
Tibeto-Burman, Viet. = Vietnamese, Yuk. = Yukagir. (From Hjelmslev,
1963.)

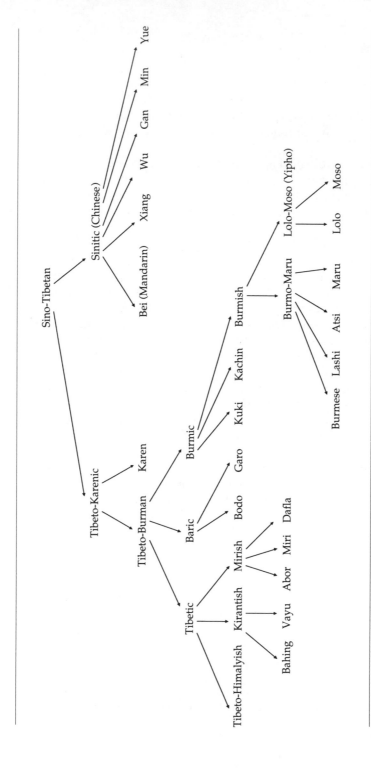

Figure 1. Sino-Tibetan language tree.

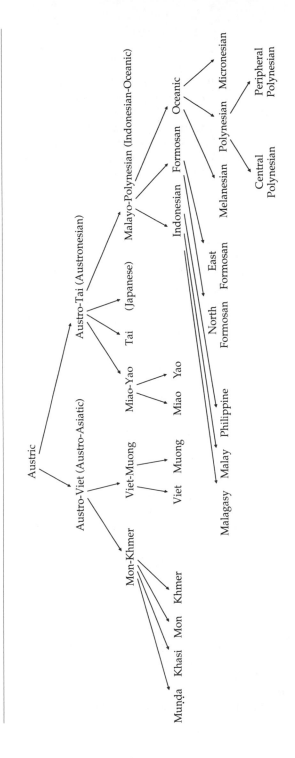

Figure 2. Austric language tree.

tronesian), but the two may be genetically unrelated (Benedict 1975). Austro-Tai is divided into Malayo-Polynesian and Tai with probably Miao-Yao as an early branching out and possibly Japanese, if the Japanese-Austro-Tai connection is considered more basic than the Japanese-Altaic one (Egerod 1980; Benedict 1990). Malayo-Polynesian consists of Indonesian, Formosan, and Oceanic. See Figure 2.

TYPOLOGICAL CLASSIFICATION ACCORDING TO WORD STRUCTURE

A linguistic zone consisting of China and some contiguous areas is characterized by the fact that words or morphemes are very short, usually monosyllabic, whereas the languages north and south of this zone have words of several syllables. We can thus distinguish between monosyllabic languages on the one hand and northern or southern polysyllabic languages on the other. It is further characteristic of the monosyllabic languages that all or most syllables possess tones, which create minimum contrasts the same way consonants and vowels do. Tones are distinguished by relative pitch (high, mid, low) and contours (falling, rising, even, circumflex) (Egerod 1970), and they may be pure or laryngealized. Meaningful sets of distinctions, manifested through laryngealization, are known as phonation types (Catford 1964; Egerod 1971). Concomitant laryngealization is common in the monosyllabic, tonal languages; phonation types as here defined are found in a number of southern polysyllabic languages.

A genetic classification, established on the basis of related vocabulary, and a typological classification according to word structure (monosyllabic vs. polysyllabic, tonal vs. nontonal, laryngealized vs. nonlaryngealized) are summarized in Figure 3.

The northern polysyllabic languages, group 1, are characterized

---

Figure 3. Chain of relationships of languages of the Far East and Oceania. **A**, Typological classification according to word structure. **1** = Northern polysyllabic languages. **2** = Tonal monosyllabic languages. **3** = Southern polysyllabic languages. *Stippled lines* indicate posited genetic relationship. *Solid lines* indicate typological relationship (only when it is not evident from the arrangement of the illustration). **B**, Genetic classification according to word correspondences. NOTE: Japanese is considered a branch of Austro-Tai by Benedict (1990).

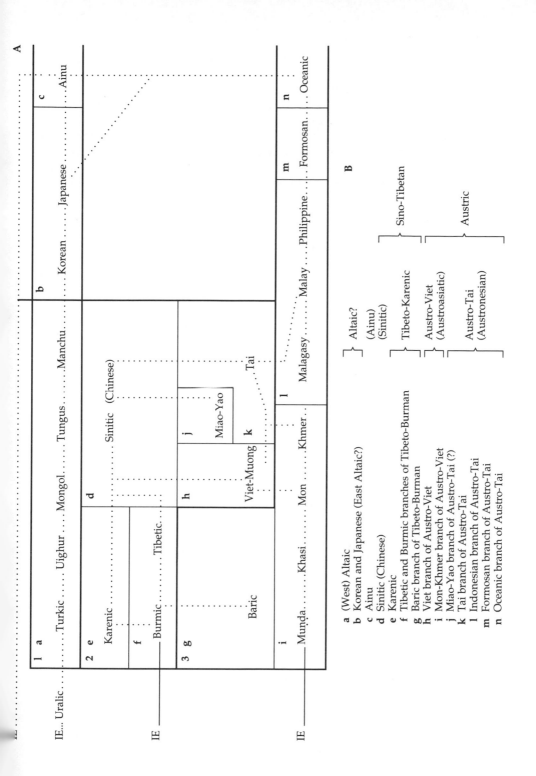

by clear, easily analyzable consonants and vowels. There is not more than one consonant at the beginning of a word. The first vowel of a word determines which vowels can occur in the remaining syllables (vowel harmony, a type of progressive umlaut), a phenomenon formerly but no longer present in Japanese, which has developed another type of suprasegmental government (Egerod and Hashimoto 1982):[1] an accent or register system in which some syllables are pronounced high, others low.

Among the tonal monosyllabic languages, group 2, the Sinitic languages (Chinese "dialects") are most important and best known. Sinitic possesses a written tradition going back almost 4,000 years. It can be divided into North Sinitic and South Sinitic. Bernhard Karlgren's (1915–1926, 1956) reconstructed "Archaic Chinese" (also known as "Old Chinese") from the first millennium B.C. exhibits typical North Sinitic features, whereas his "Ancient Chinese" ("Middle Chinese"), which spread all over China during the Tang dynasty (618–906), is rather of the South Sinitic type. The older reconstructions are made on the basis of structure of the Chinese writing system combined with the rhyming system of the oldest poetry, whereas the younger reconstructions use dictionaries from A.D. 600 as well as loans to and from Chinese. The modern Sinitic languages are the result of old migratory patterns, influence from non-Sinitic local languages, and gradual standardization in connection with the introduction of the writing system.

Modern Standard Chinese (pǔtōnghuà, 'common speech'), which is based on the language of Beijing (Peking) is North Sinitic with a considerable layer of loanwords and loan expressions from Written Chinese. It has four word tones, of which one (the so-called third tone, or low falling/rising tone) goes back to Old Chinese syllables with some kind of closed phonation type, and of which another one (the fourth tone, or falling tone) goes back to a more open phonation type. A similar connection is known, for example, from Scandinavian, where Danish glottalization corresponds to a certain register or tone in Swedish and Norwegian. Standard Chinese first and second tones (that is, high level and high rising tones) go back to syllables with pure (nonlaryngealized) phonation—the first tone with voiceless and the second tone with voiced initial (the connection between degree of voicing and tonal height is also a well-known phenome-

---

[1] Stress accent, musical accent, vowel harmony, and sandhi are all examples of suprasegmental government of content or expression.

non). Many words consist of more than one meaningful syllable (some of colloquial origin, cf. English *eardrum, toothache*; others learned, cf. English *tele-phone, bi-cycle*). In some such words the last syllable is stressed (has word tone and stress accent); in others it is unstressed (has neither word tone nor stress accent). Standard Chinese is well on its way to becoming a polysyllabic language.

Some Northwest Sinitic languages have fewer tones than the Beijing language and are even more similar to the northern polysyllabic languages in structure. In other words an intermediary zone has developed between the two big typological groups: group 1, northern polysyllabic languages, and group 2, monosyllabic tonal languages. This zone is no doubt the result of bilingualism, in areas where people speak several languages of different typology (such as Manchu and Chinese, Uighur and Chinese). Actually the replacement of vowel harmony with register in Korean and Japanese can hardly be considered independent of Sinitic influence. Such unilateral or bilateral influence of course plays a great role where linguistic areas meet and can be shown to be the driving force in the interaction of unrelated contiguous languages.

In the very south of China the Sinitic Yuè languages are spoken, of which Cantonese (Canton = Guǎngzhōu) is best known (it is also the standard language of Hong Kong and Macau). In Cantonese the closed phonation type has resulted in two rising tones and the open phonation type in two even tones (split according to originally voiced or voiceless initial). What corresponds to Beijing first and second tones are both falling in Cantonese, and three extra tones arise in words ending in a stop. Cantonese has therefore nine tonal manifestations corresponding to four in Beijing. Whereas in Beijing tones three and four still have a trace of laryngealization (Egerod 1970), in Cantonese they are purely tonal.

A consequence of the survival of traces of laryngealization in modern North Sinitic tones is the phenomenon called "tonal sandhi." When a syllable with third tone (falling/rising, glottal friction) precedes another syllable with the same tone, the tone is changed into a pure second (high rising) tone, and when a syllable with fourth tone (breathy falling/diminuendo) precedes another syllable with this tone, the tone is changed into a shortened pure (and falling) tone (Egerod 1971). Both of these sandhi changes are examples of progressive dissimilation, caused by the inconvenience of pronouncing two alike phonations in a row. The Yue languages, which have no traces of laryngealization, also have little or no sandhi. Another phenomenon that is connected with laryngealization is vowel alternation dependent on tone (some Standard Chinese vowels are more open with the laryngealized third and fourth tones than with the non-laryngealized first and second tones). Such vowel alternation is found precisely in those Sinitic languages that also possess tonal sandhi.

I have mentioned vowel harmony as found in northern poly-syllabic languages—an influence by one syllable upon others. The North Sinitic languages are on their way to becoming polysyllabic and display just such phenomena as are typical of polysyllabic lan-guages (contrasts of accent, which in some languages play the same structural role as vocalic harmony in others, and sandhi, also an interaction between syllables, but interestingly enough vowel har-mony is a type of assimilation, whereas sandhi is dissimilation; in this way languages obtain parallel results by different or opposite means). South Sinitic is still predominantly monosyllabic and thus possesses a structure much like that of surrounding Tai languages, which were originally spoken in most of the area that is now Yue speaking. They have in general the same consonants and vowels as Yue, and the tonal development has been quite parallel. The North Sinitic languages have a strong structural affinity to the northern polysyllabic languages, and the South Sinitic similarly to the south-ernmost tonal monosyllabic languages, that is, besides Tai, also Miao-Yao and Viet-Muong. These languages are, however, not originally Sino-Tibetan, but Austric (Miao-Yao probably Austro-Tai and Viet-Muong, of course, Austro-Viet). Just as mutual interaction can be demonstrated between Altaic and North Sinitic, so too it can be demonstrated between Austric and South Sinitic, with the conse-quence that North Sinitic is on its way from group **2**, tonal mono-syllabic, into group **1**, northern polysyllabic, whereas some Austric languages (Miao-Yao, Tai, Viet-Muong) have already moved from group **3**, southern polysyllabic, into group **2**, tonal monosyllabic. During these moves from one type to another, pronunciation and word structure have been totally altered, and even grammar, es-pecially syntax, has been profoundly influenced, as I shall discuss further (Egerod 1983).

Within group **2** we find most Sino-Tibetan languages (spoken in China, Tibet, Burma, and the Himalaya region), that is, all Tibeto-Karenic languages, except for one subgroup under Tibeto-Burman: the Baric languages of Assam, group **3**, subgroup **g**, in Figure 3. Baric languages have no word tones but have words of more than one syllable. They therefore fall under group 3, southern polysyllabic, even though genetically they are Sino-Tibetan. The Baric languages are not the only Tibeto-Burman languages that possess polysyllabic words. Just as we found a tendency toward polysyllabicity among the North Sinitic languages, so too we find the same tendency among the southwest Tibeto-Burman languages of the Himalaya region (as in Kiranti within Tibetic and Kuki and Kachin within Burmic). These languages form an intermediary type between groups 2 and 3, being tonal but polysyllabic. Among the western Tibeto-Himalayan languages some are tonal only in nouns of more than one syllable (which is perhaps also true of Lepcha, spoken in Sikkim but hard to place systematically), another intermediary type.

The remaining languages within group 3 fall into two subgroups, i, Mon-Khmer (part of Austro-Viet), and l-m-n Malayo-Polynesian (Indonesian-Oceanic, part of Austro-Tai). The Mon-Khmer languages have polysyllabic words, but consisting of only one minor plus one major syllable (minor syllables have a reduced phoneme inventory). Laryngeal phonation types with rudimental tonality (high register vs. low register) have developed in both Mon and Khmer based on degree of voicing of initial consonants (the same way as high and low tones in Sinitic and Tai languages). But in contradistinction to Sinitic and Tai no tones have developed from syllable-final laryngealization.[2]

Malayo-Polynesian is geographically widespread, represented from Madagascar (Malagasy) to Malaysia and Indonesia, the Philippines, Taiwan (Formosa), (and Japan?) and all the way through Oceania to Hawaii, or almost halfway round the globe. Formosan, **m**, is geographically placed between Indonesian, **l**, and Oceanic, **n** (as is Japanese if it should seem relevant to count it among southern polysyllabic languages). All these languages are true polysyllabics; phonology is more complicated in Formosan languages than in the families to the east and west. Some Indonesian languages (including Malay) have a kind of vowel harmony in which the aperture of the vowel of the first syllable determines that of the following vowel. A few cases of laryngeal phonation types are found (as in Java) and a few rudimentary tonal or register systems (in New Guinea). These phenomena are probably too isolated to count as prestages toward groups 2 or 1.

[2] For the description of a Mon-Khmer language with no traces of tone or phonation types, see Egerod 1982a.

GENETIC CLASSIFICATION ACCORDING
TO WORD CORRESPONDENCES

In Figure 3 languages, language groups, or language families are connected by means of stippled or solid lines. The stippled lines indicate
that genetic relationship has been posited based on word correspondences. The solid lines show typological relationship (indicated only
when it is not evident from the arrangement of the illustration). We
have already called attention to some of these relationships, but
more are commented upon in the following.

From Viet-Muong one stippled line goes up to Sinitic, one connects with Tai on the right, and one with Mon-Khmer below. The
extensive connections to Sinitic are reasonably explained through
successive waves of borrowings from Sinitic during the long periods
when (North-)Vietnam was politically and culturally dependent on
China. On the other hand, there has been great doubt whether the
Tai or the Khmer correspondences were older and of a genetic nature. It is, however, now a matter of general consensus that Vietnamese has borrowed heavily from Tai but is fundamentally related
to Khmer (Haudricourt 1953). But also Tai has three stippled lines
(besides the one to Viet-Muong), one to Sinitic, one to Mon-Khmer,
and one to Malayo-Polynesian. These facts have likewise given rise
to much dispute (Egerod 1976). The Khmer connection can be explained through rather late borrowing by Thai (Siamese) from Khmer.
The relationship between Tai and Sinitic is much more complicated.
The conclusions of Benedict 1942 and Haudricourt 1948 seem to
stand, that Chinese-Tai word correspondences represent borrowings
(although sometimes of a strikingly fundamental nature, which is
also true of the Tai loans in Vietnamese), whereas on the other hand
Tai-Austronesian correspondences represent originally shared vocabulary (Benedict 1942). But as the number of good Tai-Austronesian
correspondences increases, the count goes up at the same rate for
Tai and Sinitic (Manomaivibool 1975). Also it becomes increasingly
clear that a considerable number of words were borrowed very
early by Chinese from Tai (Benedict 1975). The stratification of Chinese loanwords in Tai (and Thai) is by no means easy to work out,
but certain semantic groups can be dated with relation to each other
(Egerod 1957, 1958, 1959, 1961). The inescapable conclusion must be
that although Austro-Tai, of course, includes Tai and although Austro-Viet, of course, includes Viet, the symbiosis of the two groups

with each other and with Sinitic (probably in China) (Terrien de La-couperie 1887) has been so long and so intense that it has almost but not quite broken down and extinguished the original genetic patterning.[3]

Between Oceanic and Ainu[4] and between Oceanic and Japanese, correspondences have been postulated. Much more radical is Benedict's claim that Japanese belongs to the Austro-Kadai branch of Austro-Tai (Benedict 1990). His word comparisons, if accepted, would finally do away with the status of Japanese as the one and only *Mischsprache* (Murayama 1976; Egerod 1980) in this universe.

Finally Figure 3 shows stippled lines from Ainu (Naert 1958) and from Altaic to Indo-European, both connections having been postulated. For Altaic the way goes via Uralian (Finno-Ugric), which shows certain correspondences with Indo-European. In setting up such long chains of languages, where each link is based on word correspondences, we need not imagine that all languages are genetically related from one end of the chain to the other. The connections get to be so remote that we cannot be sure where original relationships leave off and where loan connections take over, and it is characteristic that when one language or language group has more than one link it is not always the same words that bind in both directions. The chain from East Altaic (which actually can be started already with Oceanic) through West Altaic and Uralian to Indo-European can be continued through Hamito-Semitic (including Arabic and Hebrew) to Bantu (Hjelmslev 1963). In doing this we do not postulate that Hawaiian is related to Zulu, only that each link on the way is established through word correspondences that have to be explained.

Tibeto-Burman and Muṇḍa are connected to Indo-European by solid lines, indicating typological, especially grammatical parallels. Tibetan has ablaut (vowel alternation) in the verbal inflection, just as Indo-European does, and furthermore in both families a central vowel indicates the extrovert or centrifugal (outward movement, transitivity, or dependence), and a back vowel indicates the introvert or centripetal (inward movement, intransitivity, or independence) (Pulleyblank 1965a, 1965b). This is also true of certain Caucasian lan-

---

[3]For a discussion of whether and when this happens, see Egerod 1980, especially p. 130.

[4]Ainu-Altaic relationship was postulated by Patrie in 1982.

guages. Whether this is ultimately to be explained by genetic relationship, diffusion, or spontaneous (archetypal?) creation is in no
way certain.[5]

Certain Tibeto-Burman languages such as Tibetan and Lolo (=
Yipho, in the border regions of China and Burma) possess a so-called
ergative sentence structure; that is, they have neither active nor passive constructions but only an impersonal construction, with the
agent of a transitive verb marked as a kind of instrumental and the
agent of an intransitive verb expressed the same way as the object of a
transitive verb. The ergative sentence construction is often restricted
to past tense, whereas the present tense is differently structured.
Ergative sentence structure was found in the oldest Indo-European
and is still common in Indian languages. Ergative constructions are
also found in the Caucasus and in Basque (non-Indo-European).

Modern North Sinitic to a large extent avails itself of ergative constructions. Spoken North Sinitic was not written and therefore not
much heard of after the Archaic period. Archaic North Sinitic of the
Zhou dynasty (first millennium B.C.) had phonological and grammatical peculiarities that still surface in the north of China today
(Demiéville 1950; Egerod 1971, 1972). The oldest Archaic Sinitic used
a special set of personal pronouns in subordinate sentences that
were construed ergatively (Egerod 1989) (see more below).

In some Tibeto-Burman languages that use ergative it is regular
to express in a single verbal particle the same three semantic elements that are usually contained in one Indo-European verbal ending, namely, tense, mood, and grammatical person. In the Lolo language Akha (Egerod 1985) the particle *e* in the sentence *ŋá nɔ̀ áŋ dì e*
'I will beat you' expresses the information that the agent is first person, that the tense is nonpast, and that this is inherent knowledge,
not the result of seeing, hearing, or feeling (cf *-e* in German *ich
komme*, which indicates first person agent, nonpast tense, and indicative). A construction in Akha that corresponds to the English
present participle has active meaning, whereas a construction cor-

---

[5] If genetic relationship should some day be accepted as the explanation for Indo-
European and Sino-Tibetan word correspondences (and secondarily the grammatical
similarities), we are approaching a patterning of two great superstocks and four language families, which could be viewed as the four "Indos":

Hesperic $\begin{cases} \text{Indo-European} \\ \text{Indo-Sinitic (Sino-Tibetan)} \end{cases}$

Austric $\begin{cases} \text{Indo-Oceanic (Austro-Tai, Austronesian)} \\ \text{Indo-Viet (Austro-Viet, Austroasiatic)} \end{cases}$

responding to the past participle has passive meaning (constructed with an ergative agent as also used in the finite past tense), with an active-passive alternation as in many Indo-European languages. It is reasonable to imagine that these typological similarities may be the result of mutual influence (cf. the solid line in Figure 3 from Burmic to Indo-European).

In a number of Sino-Tibetan, especially Himalayan, languages the personal pronouns enter into insoluble compounds with verbs in constructions that are reminiscent of noun plus possessive pronoun (also in the oldest Sinitic, agentive pronouns are possessives). This phenomenon is known as "pronominalizing" or "pronominal incorporation" and is also found in Muṇḍa (Austro-Viet) and Indo-European. Mutual influence must have taken place, but it is not certain in which direction, although it seems a good guess that Sino-Tibetan provides the donor languages in this respect.

We have found that the languages under consideration can be divided according to word structure into three major typological groups that do not coincide with the language families arrived at on the basis of word correspondences. Furthermore we have seen that between the typological groups there are languages in intermediary stages on their way from one group into another and that in each group there are languages that have made a complete change from one type to another. In some cases I have drawn connecting lines to languages outside the groups and families treated here, and it has not always been possible to distinguish between genetic relationship, mutual influence, or loans, or between genetic and typological relationship, and it has not always been possible to tell which way the influence has been working.

TYPOLOGICAL CLASSIFICATION ACCORDING TO SENTENCE STRUCTURE

In classifying languages we have used word correspondences and word structure. We shall now avail ourselves of a third criterion, sentence structure.

Three major sentence types turn out to be relevant. European languages make use of all three types:

Sentence Type	Examples
1. Impersonal (or existential)	It is raining (cats and dogs). *Il y avait une fois un certain Blaise Pascal.*

2. Personal (or narrative)   She ate the cake. *Der Hund ist von seinem*
                                    Herrn geprügelt worden.
3. Determinative (or predicative) Peter is the one who can eat the most.
                                    "Ich bin ein Berliner."

The impersonal sentences indicate a state and are single peaked in that all information is part of the verb phrase. The determinative sentences contain a predication and are double peaked, by necessity containing a subject and a predicate. The personal sentences express a process and are multipeaked, with a changing number of satellite noun phrases indicating the direction of the process. Many East Asian languages insist on one sentence type to the partial or complete exclusion of the others. One more sentence type is, however, found in most (all?) languages, namely, the thematic sentence, in which one noun phrase is introduced or exposed as a theme (topic), with the rest of the sentence serving as rheme (comment). In some languages a theme is marked differently from a noun phrase that is part of the state, or the predication, or the process. In others the difference may not be explicit, at least not in the written language (French regularly exposes the theme, so that *"mon père, il est . . ."* contains both a theme and a subject, whereas German never allows it: *"Mein Vater ist . . ."*). It is a matter of debate if and how Chinese (Sinitic at all stages) distinguishes theme, subject (and agent), and sentence adverb (Egerod 1982b).

Most languages have determinative sentences. I shall discuss only the cases where they are the only or the predominant sentence type.

In the discussion of sentence structure I will use the following abbreviations for some technical terms.

A   Agent
H   A head that has modifiers
Is   Instrument
It   Intransitive, verb that cannot have both agent and object
L   Locus, place (in some languages includes beneficiary)
M   Modifier of a head
N   Noun
O   Object, patient
P   Predicate to a subject
Pt   Particle
R   Rheme, comment to a theme
S   Subject that has a predicate
St   Sentence
StPt Sentence particle

T   Theme, topic for a rheme
Tr   Transitive, verb that governs an object
V   Verb
X   Focus, starting point for process, agent in active sentences, patient, locus, or instrument in passive sentences
Y   Terminus, end of process, patient in active sentences

In West Altaic languages all verbs are impersonal and stand at the end of the sentence followed only by an existential sentence particle or suffix with the meaning of 'there is': *"es gibt"* and *"il y a"*. Agent and patient are both verb modifiers, marked or unmarked. Manchu normally marks the object: *Bi bithebe arambi* 'I am writing a letter' < 'as for me (*bi*) writing (*ara*) takes place (*-mbi*) having as goal (*-be*) a letter (*bithe*)'. Modern Japanese distinguishes theme from agent: *watashi wa* 'as for me' whereas *watashi ga* 'I'. This difference is not marked in West Altaic and is recent in this form in Japanese (*ga* was formerly a possessive particle marking the agent as the owner of the action).

The Altaic main type can be written

$$A_{(M)} \; O_{(M, \; accusative)} \; V_{(H)} \; StPt$$

that is, agent and patient both modify the verb; patient can be marked as accusative object; the sentence ends in an existential particle after the verb.

In the same way as Altaic languages place verb modifiers before the verb, they also place noun modifiers before the noun, and just as they place sentence particles after the sentence, they place particles after nouns and verbs as their heads. This can be written "MH" and "HPt" (modifier before head, particle after head).

Some Tibeto-Burman languages have a sentence structure very reminiscent of Altaic. The Tibetan sentence ends with an existential particle after the verb, which again follows its modifiers. But whereas in Manchu the patient is marked (as accusative), in Tibetan the agent is marked as an instrument. This is the ergative construction mentioned earlier: Tibetan *Saŋs-rgyas kyis chos bstan to* 'The Buddha has taught us the law' < 'By (*-kyis*) the Buddha (*saŋs-rgyas*) there has been (*to*) learning (*bstan*) of the law (*chos*)'.

The Manchu verbal sentence is impersonal (existential) accusative; the Tibetan is impersonal (existential) ergative. We can write the Tibeto-Burman main type as

$$A_{(M, \; ergative)} \; O_{(M)} \; V_{(H)} \; StPt$$

that is, agent and patient both modify the verb; the agent is marked as ergative; the patient is unmarked (or marked as the place where the action strikes or unfolds; cf. "pound meat," "pound on the door," "knock at the door"), and the sentence ends in an existential particle after the verb. The Tibetan particles are the same for verbs and nouns (the verbs are construed in the sentence as nouns), but the verbs have a special set of prefixes, which I include in the formulas with particles. Tibetan modification can then be written

$$MH_V, MH_N (H_NM), PtH_V, H_{V>N}Pt, H_NPt$$

that is, modifier precedes the verb and usually also the noun (but sometimes it follows the noun), and particles precede the verb but follow the noun and the nominalized verb.

I shall now turn to the other main branch of Tibeto-Sinitic, that is, Sinitic. Modern North Sinitic (such as Modern Northern Chinese) possesses two main sentence types. Modern North Sinitic *ràng wǒ bǎ shū mài le* 'I sold the book' is constructed: I (*wǒ*, marked as ergative by means of *ràng*) the book (*shū*, marked as patient or inert by means of *bǎ*) sell (*mài*); the whole sentence is marked as accomplished and complete by means of the particle *le*: 'By-me take book sell-completed'. In the sentence *Wǒmen bǎ ge zhū pǎo le* 'A pig has run away from us' the construction is 'as for us (*wǒmen*, theme) a pig-directed (*zhū*, marked as inert by means of *bǎ*) running away (*pǎo*) has taken place (*le*)'.

In this sentence type North Sinitic has the same word order as Tibeto-Burman and Altaic: agent, patient, verb, sentence particle. In the other main sentence type of Modern North Sinitic the patient follows the verb and no final particle is necessary. One can say *Wǒ mài shū* 'I sell books', where the unmarked agent *wǒ* precedes and the unmarked patient *shū* follows the verb *mài*. Some such sentences can be turned into passives (usually of unpleasurable processes): *Wǒ dǎ tā* 'I beat him'; *Tā bèi wǒ dǎ le* 'He was beaten by me', where *bèi* marks the agent in a passive sentence. Such sentences are personal (narrative). In personal sentence types the agent can be marked as an instrumental only in passive sentences, which are counterposed to active sentences.

The North Sinitic sentence types can be written, respectively,

Ergative: $A_{(M, ergative)} O_{(M, inert)} V_{(H)} StPt$
Active: $A_{(X)} V_{(Tr)} O_{(Y)} StPt$
Passive: $O_{(X)} A_{(M)} V_{(Tr)} StPt$

The North Sinitic modifier precedes its head, and particles precede nouns (except for the possessive *de*, as in *fùqin de* 'father's') but follow verbs (except for *bèi* and *gěi*, which indicate that a patient or a beneficiary are involved in the verb phrase).

South Sinitic languages prefer the personal (narrative) construction to the impersonal (existential). In sentences with two noun phrases (one accusative and one dative) after the verb, North Sinitic places dative before accusative, whereas South Sinitic does the opposite. In certain compounds the South Sinitic modifier is placed after the noun. In these respects South Sinitic approaches Tai (just as it does phonologically), which can be written with the formulas:

$$A_{(X)} \ V_{(Tr)} \ O_{(Y)} \ (StPt), \text{ and HM}$$

Like Sinitic, Tai can form a passive:

$$O_{(X)} \ A_{(M)} \ V_{(Tr)}$$

In the active, neither agent nor patient is marked.

Among the Tibeto-Karenic languages only Karen follows the South Sinitic model. The Karenic languages, which genetically are usually placed closer to Tibeto-Burman than to Sinitic, typologically form an intermediary stage between Tibeto-Burman and Sinitic, just as Tai is intermediary between Sinitic and the southern polysyllabic languages. The Tai word order is the same as that of Viet-Muong and Mon-Khmer, whereas we have seen that word correspondences place Tai with Malayo-Polynesian (and secondarily with Sinitic).

The large group of languages that have developed personal sentence structure with transitive verbs and passive constructions derived from active are mostly tonal monosyllabic languages. It is a reasonable supposition that the grand whittling down (Terrien de Lacouperie 1887) through which words have become single syllables with laryngeal phonation types and tones has worked hand in hand with a grammatical refinement (Egerod 1976, 1978) giving birth to fixed word order without marking of noun functions. The construction in which patient follows the active verb is in agreement with neighboring Malayo-Polynesian languages like Indonesian and Formosan, even though the relationship of nouns to verbs is of a totally different nature in these languages.

The oldest Sinitic language, Early Archaic Chinese (before and after the beginning of the first millennium B.C.), shows reminiscences of a sentence type in which all pronouns are placed before the verb irrespective of function, as in Tibeto-Burman. In this language agents are either subjective or ergative, the latter only in certain embedded usages, displaying pronominal forms that are alienable and inalienable possessives (see below) when used with nouns (Egerod 1989). In Late Archaic Chinese (latter half of first millennium B.C.) pronominal agents are either themes or possessives, and noun agents are marked as possessives in subordinated sentences. These possessive agents can be compared with both pronominalized Himalayan and Malayo-Polynesian. Different Archaic Chinese populations have no doubt had linguistic contacts with peoples in all directions (Eberhard 1979; Benedict 1972), including Austro-Tai and Austro-Viet.

Indonesian and Formosan languages possess neither impersonal (existential) nor personal (narrative) sentence structure, but only the determinative (predicative) type. The word that contains the verb must always be construed as a noun. One cannot say "I eat" but only "I am the one who eats" or "The one who eats is me"; not "He eats the rice" but "He is the one who (rice-eats =) eats the rice" or "What he eats is rice"; not "He felled the tree with his axe" but "The one who (tree-felled =) felled the tree with an axe was he"; "What he felled with his axe was the tree" or "What he (tree-felled =) felled the tree with was his axe". There is always a subject and a predicate, but sometimes the verb phrase contains the subject, sometimes the predicate (depending on language and available structures). Therefore the sentence is either a subjectivization "He is the one who . . ." or a predicativization "The one . . . is . . .". Also thematization (exposure) occurs in these languages "As for that man he is . . .".

There is one active and three passives (direct, indirect, and instrumental passive) (Egerod 1965, 1966). In Maranao (Philippines) one can say (McKaughan 1962):

Somombali? so mama? sa karabao.	'The man killed the water buffalo'. < 'The killer of the water buffalo was the man'.
Sombali?in o mama? so karabao.	'The water buffalo was killed by the man'. < 'The man's goal for killing was the water buffalo'.
Sombali?an o mama? so maior sa karabao.	'The man kills the water buffalo for the chief'. < 'The man's place (beneficiary) for the killing of the water buffalo was the chief'.

Isombali? o mama? so gelat ko karabao. 'The man killed the water buffalo with his knife'. < 'The man's instrument for the killing upon the water buffalo was his knife'.

As appears in the above examples the one who is identified with the verbal noun ("killer," "goal for killing," "place for killing," or "instrument for killing") carries the case particle *so* ('nominative'). The agent in the passive types and the patient in active as well as in direct and indirect passive types are in possessive cases, marked *o* for the agent and *sa* for the patient. These two possessives are subjective (or dominating) genitive and objective (or dominated) genitive (also known from Latin). In Maranao as in many Malayo-Polynesian languages the two kinds of genitives are used with nouns as well as with verbs: *so sapi? o solotan* 'the sultan's cow' has a dominating genitive because the sultan can decide about his cow, whereas in *solotan sa mandeian* 'the Sultan of Mandeia' we find Mandeia in the dominated genitive, since Mandeia does not dominate its sultan (but the other way round). With verbs we get (as above) *sombali?an o mama? sa karabao* 'the man's place for the killing of the water buffalo . . .' with "the man" in the dominating (subjective) and "the buffalo" in the dominated (objective) genitive.

In almost all Polynesian languages that have the genitives it is the one containing the vowel /a/ that is dominating and the one with the vowel /o/ that is dominated (that is, opposite of Maranao). By chance the same two vowels are contained in the Japanese possessive markers *ga* and *no*, which have usages reminiscent of the dominating/dominated distribution when they modify nouns. Modifying verbs, *ga* is subjective; *no* is, however, not objective but subordinating. I have mentioned the existence in Early Archaic Chinese of two series of pronouns, one dominating (and subjective), the other dominated (and ergative).

The four sentence types of Maranao can be written:

$V_{(H) (S, source)} A_{(P)} O_{(M)(dominated\ genitive)}$
$V_{(H) (S, goal)} A_{(M)(dominating\ genitive)} O_{(P)}$
$V_{(H) (S, place)} A_{(M)\ (dominating\ genitive)} L_{(P)} O_{(M)\ (dominated\ genitive)}$
$V_{(H) (S, instrument)} A_{(M)\ (dominating\ genitive)} Is_{(P)} O_{(M)\ (place)}$

In all four types the verb is a head with modifiers (agent, object, or place). The verb contains the subject, whose predicate can be agent, object, locus (beneficiary), or instrument. When the predicate is an instrument, the object is not a dominated genitive but a locative.

The Indonesian main rule is for modifiers to follow the head and for particles to follow verbs but precede nouns:

$$HM, \; H_V Pt, \; PtH_N.$$

Modern Malay (Bahasa Malayu, Bahasa Malaysia, Bahasa Indonesia) appears to be simplified compared to the system described above. Only with pronouns does the genitive enter into the verb phrase, as agent of passive verbs preposed in first and second persons but postposed in third person and also postposed when there is a third person patient of active verbs:

Rumah<u>ku</u>	'My house'	kutolong	'is helped by me'.
Rumah<u>kau</u>	'Your house'	kautolong	'is helped by you'.
Rumah<u>nya</u>	'His house'	ditolong<u>nya</u>	'is helped by him'.
		menolong<u>nya</u>	'helps him'.

Malay word order is otherwise like that of Tai: agent before and patient after the verb. Malay is an intermediary type between southern monosyllabic and southeastern polysyllabic languages.

Sentences in Oceanic languages are impersonal (existential) as those we saw in Altaic and Tibeto-Burman. Like those other languages Oceanic languages have existential sentence particles, but some of the languages mark the agent as ergative and some mark the patient as accusative. The word order is, however, the exact opposite of that of the previously treated existential languages, in that the sentence is opened with the existential particle and then the verb follows and finally the various noun phrases. Maori among the Peripheral Polynesian (or East Polynesian) languages provides an example of accusative sentence structure, whereas Samoan among the Central Polynesian languages possesses ergative sentence structure.

In Maori one can say, '*Ka patu te tangata i te poaka*' 'The man killed the pig' < 'there was (*ka*) man (*tangata*)-killing (*patu*) affecting (*i*) the pig (*poaka*)', where *te* is the definite article. The agent *te tangata* is unmarked, and the patient *te poaka* is marked as accusative by means of the particle *i*.

In Samoan one can say, "*Sā ʔave e le fafine le taʔavale*" 'The woman drove the car' < 'there was (*sā*) automobile (*taʔavale*)-driving (*ʔave*) by (*e*) the woman (*fafine*)', with *le* being the definite article. The patient *le taʔavale* is unmarked, but the agent *le fafine* is marked as ergative by means of the particle *e*.

TABLE 1
Schematic Overview of Classifications

Language group	Syntax
Altaic	$A_{(M)}$ $O_{(M,\ accusative)}$ $V_{(H)}$ StPt; MH, HPt
Tibeto-Burman	$A_{(M,\ ergative)}$ $O_{(M)}$ $V_{(H)}$ StPt; MH_V, MH_N, (H_NM), PtH_V, $H_{V>N}Pt$, H_NPt
North Sinitic	$A_{(M,\ ergative)}$ $O_{(M,\ accusative)}$ $V_{(H)}$ StPt $\Big\}$ MH, (PtH_V), H_VPt, PtH_N, (H_NPt)
	$A_{(X)}$ $V_{(Tr)}$ $O_{(Y)}$ (StPt)
South Sinitic	$A_{(X)}$ $V_{(Tr)}$ $O_{(Y)}$ (StPt); MH, (H_NM), H_VPt, PtH_N, (H_NPt)
Tai, Khmer	$A_{(X)}$ $V_{(Tr)}$ $O_{(Y)}$ (StPt); HM, PtH
Indonesian	$V_{(H)\ (S,\ source)}$ $A_{(P)}$ $O_{(M)}$ (dominated genitive)
	$V_{(H)\ (S,\ goal)}$ $A_{(M)}$ (dominating genitive) $O_{(P)}$
	$V_{(H)\ (S,\ place)}$ $A_{(M)}$ (dominating genitive) $L_{(P)}$ $O_{(M)}$ (dominated genitive)
	$V_{(H)\ (S,\ instrument)}$ $A_{(M)}$ (dominating genitive) $Is_{(P)}$ $O_{(M)}$ (place)
Central Polynesian	StPt $V_{(H)}$ $A_{(M,\ ergative)}$ $O_{(M)}$; HM, H_VPt, PtH_N
Peripheral Polynesian	StPt $V_{(H)}$ $A_{(M)}$ $O_{(M,\ accusative)}$; HM, H_VPt, PtH_N

The Indonesian rows are braced together with: HM, H_VPt, PtH_N

See pp 220–221 for abbreviations.

Both Maori and Samoan can apply the two genitives (vowel /a/ and vowel /o/) in subordinate clauses to mark agent and patient. As far as modification is concerned, the word order is as in Indonesian-Formosan. In formulas Oceanic can be rendered:

Central Polynesian: StPt $V_{(H)}$ $A_{(M,\ ergative)}$ $O_{(M)}$; HM, H_VPt, PtH_N
Peripheral Polynesian: StPt $V_{(H)}$ $A_{(M)}$ $O_{(M,\ accusative)}$; HM, H_VPt, PtH_N

SCHEMATIC OVERVIEW OF CLASSIFICATIONS

The results of the preceding discussions are summarized in Table 1. This figure shows how sentence structure changes step by step as we move from one language group to the next and how we end up with a system that is the opposite of the one we started out with in practically all its features.

The picture is even more striking if we restrict ourselves to the main types, as in Table 2.

Finally we can set up single distinctive features as in Table 3. This

TABLE 2
Syntax of Main Far Eastern Language Groups

Language Group	Syntax					
Altaic main type	AOV	MH	VPt	NPt	St	StPt
Tibeto-Burman main type	AOV	MH	PtV	NPt	St	StPt
Mon-Khmer main type	AVO	HM	PtV	PtN	St	StPt
Malayo-Polynesian main type	VAO	HM	VPt	PtN	StPt	St

TABLE 3
Three Distinctive Features of Far Eastern and Oceanic Languages

Language Group	Sentence structure	Noun phrase marking in relation to verb	Place of verb in sentence
Altaic	Existential	Accusative	Verb final
Tibeto-Burman	Existential	Ergative	Verb final
North Sinitic	Existential	Ergative-inert	Verb final
South Sinitic, Mon-Khmer, Tai	Narrative	Neutral	Verb central
Indonesian	Determinative	Possessive	Verb initial
Central Polynesian	Existential	Ergative	Verb initial
Peripheral Polynesian	Existential	Accusative	Verb initial

table read downward shows three distinctive waves: From existential sentence structure we move through narrative and determinative back to existential. The marking of nominal phrases in relation to verb phrases begins with accusative marking and moves through ergative, inert, neutral, and possessive back to ergative and accusative marking. Finally the placement of the verbal phrase moves from verbfinal through verb-central to verb-initial. So we return to the original elements in the opposite order.

We have seen that among the middle-zone languages, tonal monosyllabics, we find languages with ablaut (meaningful vowel alternation), whereas north and south of this zone we find umlaut (assimilation of vowels in different syllables). We have also seen that in the northern (and eastern) languages of the middle zone, assimilation or dissimilation takes place from syllable to syllable (sandhi), but chiefly concerning laryngeal and tone phenomena, in connection with which also vowels can change. In southwestern polysyllabic languages (Mon-Khmer) there are tonal registers connected with laryngeal phenomena, whereas the southeastern polysyllabic languages (except for a couple of enclaves), just like the northern polysyllabic languages, lack both tones and laryngealization. So we have a movement from umlaut and tonelessness through ablaut and tones, via tonal registers and umlaut with tonelessness, to tonelessness. Finally I mention again the existence between tonal monosyllabic languages, on the one hand, and polysyllabic languages with free choice of vowels, on the other, of an intermediary zone (Mon-Khmer) whose first syllable in bisyllabic words is excluded from the full use of the phonological inventory.

Recall from Figure 3 how the languages of the Far East and Oceania form a chain of language relationships based on the criteria of word correspondences and how this chain ends with the regular correspondences between Japanese and Oceanic. An arrangement of languages based on criteria of word structure also forms a chainlike pattern. Finally the typology of sentence structure takes us back where we started with a beautiful mirror image of the initial type.

REFERENCES CITED

Benedict, P. 1942. "Thai, Kadai, and Indonesian: a New Alignment in Southeastern Asia." *American Anthropologist* 44: 576–601.

———. 1972. *Sino-Tibetan: a Conspectus*. Ed. by J. Matissoff. Cambridge: Cambridge University Press.

————. 1975. *Austro-Thai Language and Culture*. New Haven: Human Relations Area Files Press.

————. 1990. "Japanese/Austro-Tai." *Linguistica Extranea*, Studia 20. Ann Arbor, Mich.

Catford, J. 1964. "Phonation Types, the Classification of Some Laryngeal Components of Speech Production. In honor of Daniel Jones," pp. 26–37. London.

Demiéville, P. 1950. "Archaïsmes de prononciation en chinois vulgaire." *T'oung Pao* 40: 1–59.

Eberhard, W. 1979. "Kultur und Siedlung der Randvölker Chinas." *T'oung Pao* 36: supplement.

Egerod, S. 1957. "The Eighth Earthly Branch in Archaic Chinese and Tai." *Oriens* 10: 295–299.

————. 1958. "Swatow Loanwords in Siamese." *Acta Orientalia Hafniensia* 23: 137–156.

————. 1959. "A Note on Some Chinese Numerals as Loanwords in Tai." *T'oung Pao* 47: 67–74.

————. 1961 (unpublished). *Tai, Chinese, and Indonesian*. Study Group on Problems of Linguistic Comparison in South East Asia and the Pacific. London: School of Oriental and African Studies.

————. 1965. "Verb Inflexion in Atayal." *Lingua* 15: 251–282.

————. 1966. "Word Order and Word Classes in Atayal." *Language* 42: 246–368.

————. 1970. "Distinctive Features and Phonological Reconstructions." *Journal of the American Oriental Society* 90.1: 67–73.

————. 1971. "Phonation Types in Chinese and South East Asian Languages." *Acta Linguistica Hafniensia* 13.2: 159–179.

————. 1972. "Les particularités de la grammaire chinoise." *Festschrift Haudricourt* (*Langues et Techniques*. Ed. by J. M. C. Thomas et al.), pp. 101–109. Paris: Editions Klincksieck.

————. 1974. "Sino-Tibetan languages." *Encyclopaedia Britannica*, 15th edition.

————. 1976. "Benedict's Austro-Thai Hypothesis and the Traditional Views on Sino-Thai Relationship." *Computational Analyses of Asian and African Languages* 6: 51–61.

————. 1978. *Typology of Chinese Sentence Structure*, pp. 89–99. Copenhagen: Les amis du Prince Pierre.

————. 1980. "To What Extent Can Genetic-Comparative Classification be Based on Typological Considerations." In Thrane et al. 1980.

————. 1982a. "An English-Mlabri Basic Vocabulary." *Annual Newsletter of the Scandinavian Institute of Asian Studies* 16: 14–20.

————. 1982b. "Differentiation and Continuity in Classical Chinese." *Bulletin of the Institute of History and Philology* (Academia Sinica) 53.1: 89–112.

————. 1983. "China: Melting Pot of Languages or Cauldron of Tongues?" In *Hong Kong–Denmark Lectures on Science and Humanities*, pp. 37–51. Hong Kong: Hong Kong University Press.

————. 1985. "Typological Features in Akha." *Festschrift Benedict*. Pacific Linguistics Series C 87, pp. 96–104.

————. 1989. "Possessives in Early Archaic Chinese." *Proceedings of the Second International Conference on Sinology.* Taipei: Academia Sinica.

Egerod, S. C., and M. J. Hashimoto. 1982. "Concord, Vowel Harmony, and Accents: a Typo-geographical View of Suprasegmental Government." *Computational Analyses of Asian and African Languages* 19: 1–21.

Haudricourt, A. G. 1948. "Les phonèmes et le vocabulaire du Thai Commun." *Journal Asiatique* 236: 197–238.

————. 1953. "La place du viêtnamien dans les langues austro-asiatiques." *Bulletin de la Société linguistique de Paris* 49: 122–128.

Hjelmslev, L. 1963. *Sproget.* Copenhagen: Berlingske Forlag.

Karlgren, B. 1915–1926. *Études sur la phonologie chinoise.* 4 vols. Uppsala: K. W. Appelberg.

————. 1956. "Compendium of Phonetics in Ancient and Archaic Chinese." *Bulletin of the Museum of Far Eastern Antiquities* 22: 211–367.

Lacouperie, Terrien de. 1887. The Languages of China before the Chinese. London: David Nutt. 1966. Taipei: Ch'eng-wen, 148 pp.

Manomaivibool, P. 1975. *A Study of Sino-Thai Lexical Correspondences.* Ann Arbor, Mich.: University Microfilms.

McKaughan, H. 1962. "Overt Relation Markers in Maranao." *Language* 38.1: 47–51.

Murayama, S. 1976. "The Malayo-Polynesian Component in the Japanese Language." *Journal of Japanese Studies* 2.2: 413–436.

Naert, P. 1958. "La situation linguistique de l'aïnou." *Lunds Universitet Årsskrift* 53.4: 1–234.

Patrie, J. 1982. *The Genetic Relationship of the Ainu Language.* OC Special Publications 17. Honolulu, Hawaii.

Pulleyblank, E. G. 1965a. "The Indo-European Vowel System and the Qualitative Ablaut." *Word* 21: 86–101.

————. 1965b. "Close/Open Ablaut in Sino-Tibetan." *Lingua* 14: 230–240.

Thrane, T., et al. 1980. *Typology and Genetics of Language.* Copenhagen: Travaux de cercle linguistique de Copenhague 20.

The Classification of Caucasian Languages

J. C. CATFORD

By "Caucasian languages" we mean those languages spoken in the Caucasus Mountain region of the USSR between the Black Sea and the Caspian Sea that (unlike other languages of the region) are neither Indo-European, Turkic, Mongolic, or Semitic. In Russian they are generally called "Ibero-Caucasian"—*iberijskokavkazskie jazyki*. The first part of this Russian designation refers to Caucasian Iberia—an ancient Transcaucasian state that from the third century B.C. was one of the two units composing the kingdom of Georgia, the other being Colchis—not to the Iberian peninsula at the opposite end of Europe. It is true that the term "Ibero-Caucasian" has sometimes been used to refer to a presumed wider grouping of languages (for example, by Holmer 1947) implying a typological or genetic relationship of Caucasian with Basque—a relationship, incidentally, that has long been posited and is currently accepted by some Soviet linguists.

The diversity of peoples and languages in the Caucasus has been notorious since antiquity. Herodotus writing in the fifth century B.C. says that "many and all manner of nations dwell in the Caucasus". Four centuries later, Strabo, referring to the Greek city of Dioscurias, on the Black Sea near present-day Sukhumi (capital of Abkhazia), states that "seventy tribes come together there, though others who care naught for the facts say three hundred. All speak different languages, because they live in scattered groups not associating with each other, by reason of wilfulness and ferocity."

Shortly after Strabo, Pliny tells us that, according to Timosthenes, Dioscurias had been the gathering place of 300 tribes, all speaking different languages, and that later the Romans had used 130 interpreters there. Medieval Arab travelers and geographers continued to report on Caucasian polyglossia. In the tenth century, the geographer al-Mas'udi, who named the Caucasus "*Jabal al-Alsun*", the 'Mountain of Tongues', speaks of "seventy-two peoples, each with its king and speaking its own language", adding, incidentally, like Strabo, that the peoples of the Caucasus do not communicate with each other but, unlike Strabo, attributing their lack of communication to the extreme ruggedness of their mountain terrain. There can be little doubt that the extreme difficulty of the terrain was a factor contributing to the development of numerous different languages and dialects in the area.

Another tenth-century Arab traveller, Ibn Haukal, notes that "they say that [on Mt. Caucasus] there are 360 languages. I formerly disbelieved this, till I myself saw many towns, each having its own language as well as Azerbaijanian and Persian". A later Arab scholar, the fourteenth-century geographer and historian Abul Feta (Abū 'l-Fidā'), also speaks of 300 languages in the Caucasus.

At the present day it is usual to count 37 Caucasian languages. These clearly fall into two major groups, *North Caucasian* (Abkhazo-Nakho-Dagestanian) and *South Caucasian*, which is also known as "Kartvelian," from *Kartveli* (pl. *Kartvelebi*), the self-designation of the Georgians, whose language is called *kartuli ena*. Each group falls into subgroups, as indicated in Table 1. At the time of the October Revolution the only Caucasian language with its own ancient writing system was Georgian; since then eleven more languages have been provided with orthographies and have developed literary norms. Languages are numbered consecutively from 1 to 37 in Table 1, and the names of literary languages are in boldface type.

The various subgroupings are the generally accepted ones, based partly on generally recognizable likenesses and differences between languages rather than on relationships established on a completely systematic basis.

The total number of languages listed here, 37, is somewhat arbitrary, since it depends in part on particular decisions about what to count as languages or dialects. In the numbered list the only dialects I have named are 37a and 37b, the two main dialects of Zan, Megrelian and Laz. The reason is that they are sometimes listed as separate languages in the specialist literature. The numbers of speakers of these languages ranges from about 3 million speakers of Georgian, through about half a million speakers of Chechen and Avar, down to only 200 speakers of Ginukh, and only one speaker of Ubykh.

TABLE 1
Classification of Caucasian Languages

NORTH CAUCASIAN			
ABKHAZO-ADYGAN (Northwest Caucasian)			
Abkhazan	1. **Abkhaz**	2. **Abaza**	
Ubykh	3. Ubykh		
Adygan (Circassian)	4. **Adyghe**	5. **Kabardian**	
		(Kabardino-Cherkess)	
NAKHO-DAGESTANIAN (Northeast Caucasian)			
NAKH			
Veinakh	6. **Chechen**	7. **Ingush**	
Batsbi	8. Batsbi, or Ts'ova Tush		
DAGESTANIAN			
Avaro-Andi-Dido		9. **Avar**	
Andi	10. Andi	11. Botlikh	12. Godoberi
	13. Karata	14. Akhwakh	15. Bagwali
	16. T'indi	17. Chamalal	
Dido (or Tsez)	18. Tsez	19. Khwarshi	
	20. Ginukh	21. Gunzib	22. Bezhta
	(Hinukh)	(Hunzib)	
Central Dagestanian		23. **Lak**	24. **Dargi**
LEZGIAN			
Samurian	25. **Tabasaran**	26. Agul	27. Rutul
	28. Tsakhur	29. **Lezgi**	
Shah Dagh	30. Budukh	31. Kryz	
Peripheral	32. Khinalug	33. Archi	34. Udi
SOUTH CAUCASIAN (KARTVELIAN)			
	35. **Georgian**		
	36. Svan		
	37. Zan	37a. Megrelian (or Mingrelian)	
		37b. Laz or Chan	

The list does not give a picture of the real linguistic diversity within the Caucasian language group, since most Caucasian languages have many noticeable dialectal variants, often differing widely from each other, in some cases to the point of mutual unintelligibility. Thus, for example, the dialect of Dargi spoken in the *aul* (mountain village) Kubači, famous for its master goldsmiths and metal workers, is mutually unintelligible with Literary Dargi, based on the dialect of Akuša—only about 30 kilometers distant as the crow flies, but much more by mountain road. Indeed Kubači has sometimes been treated as a separate language, as witness the title of the book by Magometov 1963.

The highly divergent Avar dialect spoken in the Zakataly region of northern Azerbaijan is said to be unintelligible to speakers of Literary Avar, based on a northeastern dialect. To take another example, which is even more striking since it concerns a relatively "small" language, Magomedbekova 1967 (p. 9) tells us with respect to Akhwakh, a language of the Andi group spoken by about 5,000 people, that the divergences between the northern and southern dialects are so considerable that "the speakers of these dialects converse with each other not in their dialects but in the Avar language." Again, the straight-line distance between these dialect areas is negligible, but the mountainous terrain made communication between them, before the advent of helicopters, enormously difficult.

In view of the persistent ancient reports of 300 or so languages in the Caucasus, it is interesting to note that a list I recently made of different Caucasian dialects mentioned in the specialist literature yielded a total of more than 350. If, as is likely, something like this degree of dialectal diversity goes back to antiquity, those whom Strabo scathingly accused of "caring naught for the facts" may have been reporting more accurately than he thought!

The dialectal fragmentation of Caucasian languages is one of the circumstances that makes detailed comparative study difficult, particularly for scholars outside the USSR who do not have access to speakers of all dialects and must rely on dictionaries and other works that often deal only with the literary variety of the language.

CAUCASIAN "FAMILY TREE"

Figure 1 is a "family tree" showing the relationships between the Caucasian languages in a more graphic form. Some of the nodes in this tree diagram are marked by numbers. These represent lexico-statistical percentages, based on the Swadesh 100-word list. As pointed out in Catford 1977, these are to be regarded as quite tentative, but they provide some quantitative support to the accepted groupings.

It will be noted that the North Caucasian languages and Kartvelian (South Caucasian) are joined by a dotted line, unlike the full lines joining other groups. This indicates the uncertainty, or improbability, of a genetic relationship between these two branches of Caucasian. The circled figure 6 represents an average of about 6% shared vocabulary—specifically shared between Georgian and Abkhazo-

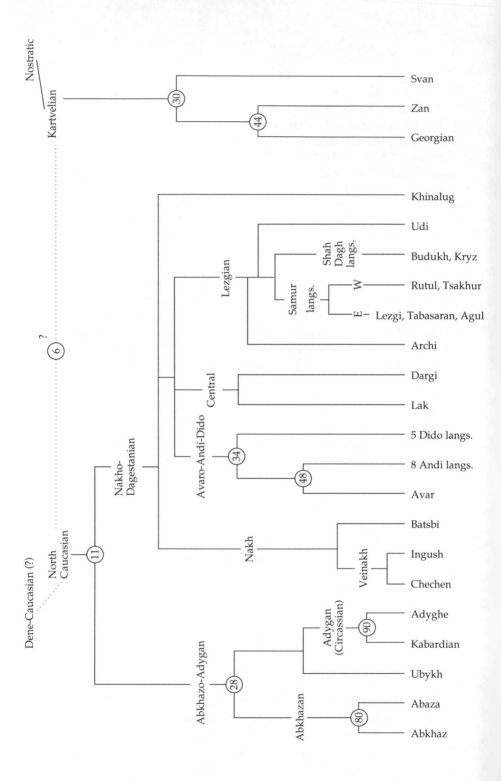

Adygan (about 6.3%) and Georgian and Avar (about 5.5%). Some proportion of this, possibly all, is no doubt due to borrowing.

The Abkhazo-Adygan languages very clearly break down into two subgroups of closely related languages, Abkhazan (Abkhaz and Abaza) and Adygan, also known as Circassian (Adyghe, or West Circassian, and Kabardian, or East Circassian). In addition to these groups we have the language isolate, Ubykh, which I have some-what arbitrarily indicated in the tree diagram as closer to Adygan than to Abkhazan. In point of fact, Ubykh is lexicostatistically about equally related to both (about 36% to 40% shared cognates). Phono-logically it is closer to Abkhazan, but grammatically probably closer to Adygan.

All the remaining North Caucasian languages belong to the North-east Caucasian, or Nakho-Dagestanian group. This consists of two distinct subdivisions, namely, the small close-knit Nakh group and the much larger and more diverse Dagestanian group. The two more closely related Nakh languages, Chechen and Ingush, are sometimes known (as here) as Veinakh, or Vejnakh, languages.

There are generally reckoned to be three major groups of Dage-stanian languages, so-called because for the most part they are spoken in the Dagestan Autonomous Soviet Socialist Republic. Among the Lezgian languages, Archi, spoken in an isolated posi-tion, flanked by Avar and Lak, is something of an outlier, as is Udi, spoken in two villages in northern Azerbaijan and one village in eastern Georgia. Another small subgroup of Lezgian languages is spoken in northern Azerbaijan and is known as the "Shah Dagh group" because they are located near the mountain of that name. The most compact group of Lezgian languages is spoken largely along the course of the Samur River (hence "Samur languages"), chiefly in Dagestan but with some slight spillover into Azerbaijan.

GEOGRAPHICAL DISTRIBUTION
OF CAUCASIAN LANGUAGES

Map 1 is a sketch map of the Caucasus region showing the locations of the four main groups of Caucasian languages (Abkhazo-Adygan or Northwest Caucasian, Nakh, Dagestanian, and Kartvelian) and of some particular subgroups (Andi, Dido, and Lezgian—written "Lezgi" on the map) and languages.

Virtually all the North Caucasian languages are, not surprisingly, spoken on the northern slopes of the Great Caucasus range, except

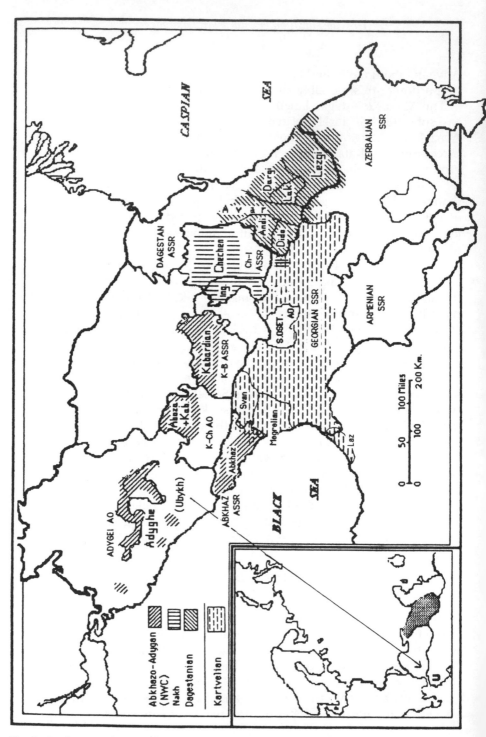

For legend see opposite page.

for Abkhaz, spoken on the Black Sea coast in the Abkhaz Autonomous Soviet Socialist Republic, a province of the Georgian Soviet Socialist Republic.

The Abkhazo-Adygan languages are, as can be seen, now spoken in somewhat scattered pockets, though formerly they were widely spread throughout the Northwest Caucasus. Adyghe is spoken in the Adygei Autonomous Oblast' (AO) and in a few scattered locations nearer the Black Sea coast: Kabardian is chiefly spoken in the Kabardino-Balkar Autonomous Soviet Socialist Republic and also in the Karachay-Cherkess AO (where the Kabardian speakers are known as "Cherkess", hence the official Russian name of the language *kabardino-čerkesskij jazyk*). Abaza is spoken alongside Kabardian in the Karachay-Cherkess AO. In both these territories the Caucasian language is spoken in the north, while in the southern part we find a Turkic language, Karachay-Balkar, the two dialects of which are, of course, spoken respectively in the Karachay-Cherkess AO and the Kabardino-Balkar ASSR.

One language, Ubykh, formerly spoken approximately where indicated on the map, is no longer spoken in the Caucasus because all its speakers left in the 1860s. I am happy to report (1991) that the last fully competent speaker of Ubykh, Tevfik Esenç (principal informant for Dumézil and Vogt), is alive and well and living near Manyas, in Anatolia, just south of the Sea of Marmora. Manyas is the place indicated by the letter *U* on the map and described rather ominously as the "terminal location" of Ubykh. The story behind the removal of Ubykh (and other languages) to Turkey is as follows. About 1864 the Russians invaded and finally conquered Circassia in the northwestern Caucasus. A great number (estimated at nearly half a million) of Northwest Caucasian Muslims migrated to Turkey when their homeland was invaded. A great many were settled in Turkey, where their descendants, including the last speaker of Ubykh, still live. The Turks settled many others around the eastern borders of the Ottoman Empire as policemen and frontier guards. Hence the present-day large colonies of so-called Circassians (which include some other North

Map 1. Caucasian language groups and some languages. AO = Autonomous Oblast', ASSR = Autonomous Soviet Socialist Republic, SSR = Soviet Socialist Republic, K-CH = Karachai-Cherkess, K-B = Kabardino-Balkar, Ch-I = Chechen-Ingush, (Ubykh) = approximate former location of Ubykh, U = terminal location of Ubykh, in Turkey.

Caucasians, such as Abkhaz, Chechen, and Lezgi) throughout the Middle East, particularly in Iraq, Syria, Jordan, and Israel. Incidentally there are about 2,000 Circassians in New Jersey, mostly immigrants from Syria.

When the great Circassian Diaspora occurred, the Adygan languages were unwritten, and so the dispersed Circassians of the Middle East were largely illiterate in their own language, except for some ingenious local attempts at devising an orthography. One of the most interesting of these was the Roman orthography devised in Damascus by a Circassian (Bzhedugh) schoolmaster, Harun Batokw, in the 1930s, an orthography that had a certain local currency certainly into the 1940s. More recently, members of the Circassian community (nearly 3,000) in Israel petitioned the Israeli Ministry of Education to have their children introduced to reading and writing in Adyghe. In the summer of 1973 in Israel I had the interesting and rewarding task of conducting an intensive seminar for a small group of Circassian schoolmasters on the Soviet Cyrillic orthography, on Adyghe grammar, and on the problem of designing a reading primer and other materials. As a result of our work, children in the two Circassian villages in Israel now learn to read and write in their own language. As far as I know, they are the only Middle East Circassian community that has this advantage.

To return to the map—the two principal Nakh languages are spoken, as indicated, in the Chechen-Ingush ASSR. The third language of the group, Batsbi, is spoken in one village in Georgia.

The remaining North Caucasian languages, the Dagestanian group, are, as I have said, spoken mainly in the Dagestan ASSR and chiefly in the extremely mountainous southern and western part of the ASSR. The flatter northern and coastal area is chiefly populated by speakers of the Mongolic language Kalmyk and the Turkic languages Nogai and Kumyk. The latter language is called by the Avars ɬaraʕ matš', or 'plains language', as opposed to Avar itself, which is maʕarul matš' or 'mountain language.' As the map shows, the Andi and Dido languages are spoken in the western salient of Dagestan, where pockets of Avar are also found and where Avar is the *lingua franca* of the area.

The Lezgian languages are spoken in southern Dagestan, and as the map correctly indicates, both they and Avar spill over into northern Azerbaijan.

CAUCASIAN TYPOLOGICAL FEATURES

Already in a letter written in 1864, printed in 1888, the great Russian caucasologist Baron Pjotr K. Uslar had noted the family resemblance of all Caucasian languages, despite their diversity, in these words: "It is already possible to state affirmatively that to the great language families of the old world—Semitic, Cushitic (Coptic, Ethiopic), and Ural Altaic—we must add a completely independent family of *Caucasian* languages, since all these languages, despite an amazing diversity, present deep kindred traits. The Armenian language is Indo-European; Georgian, apparently, is a Caucasian language and, in all probability, the most remarkable of the whole family."

Here Uslar posits a single Caucasian family, uniting the Kartvelian language Georgian with the North Caucasian languages that he had studied so deeply and effectively. This, until recently, has probably been the most widely accepted view, but more on that below. Meanwhile, let us look more closely at some of those "kindred traits," or general typological features, within the diversity of Caucasian languages.

PHONOLOGICAL FEATURES:
THE CONSONANTAL COMMON CORE

Looking first at phonetics and phonology, we see that there is a characteristic "core" type of consonant system common to all Caucasian languages but that this common core is expanded and elaborated in several different ways, which are to some extent differentially characteristic of the various subgroups of Caucasian.

Among the core consonantal features found in all Caucasian languages are (1) *stops* articulated at *labial*, *dentalveolar*, *velar*, and *uvular* locations (types p t k q), (2) *affricates* at two locations (types ts and tʃ), and (3) *fricatives* at *alveolar*, *postalveolar*, and *uvular* locations. It is a characteristic and unusual feature of Caucasian languages that if there is only one posterior dorsal fricative it is always uvular rather than velar. In addition to these types of obstruents, all Caucasian languages also have a small number of nonobstruents—a bilabial and a dentalveolar nasal, a bilabial or labiodental approximant or semivowel (sometimes alternating with a labiodental fricative), a palatal semivowel, and a lateral approximant, that is, an "ordinary" l-sound, except in the Adygan literary languages, in which all three

TABLE 2
Georgian Consonant System

	1	2	3	4	5	6
Obstruents						
Stops						
Voiced	b	d			g	
Voiceless aspirated	p	t			k	
Glottalic	p′	t′			k′	q′
Affricates						
Voiced		dz	ʤ			
Voiceless aspirated		ts	tʃ			
Glottalic		ts′	tʃ′			
Fricatives						
Voiced	(v)	z	ʒ			ʁ
Voiceless	f	s	ʃ			χ
Nonobstruents		r				
	w	l		j		
	m	n				

Numbered series are: 1, Labial (including labiodental); 2, dentalveolar; 3, postalveolar; 4, palatal; 5, velar; 6, uvular.

laterals, the voiced one as well as the voiceless and glottalic ones, are fricatives not approximants (ɮ ɬ ɬ′).

In all Caucasian languages the stops form triads of *voiced, voiceless aspirated,* and *glottalic* sounds of the types (d t t′) without exception at the dentalveolar and velar locations, though one or more members of the triad may be missing at the labial or uvular locations. These triadic series extend to the affricates in more than half the Caucasian languages and also to some of the fricatives in the Adygan languages and in dialects of two Andi languages (Bagwali and Chamalal).

Almost exactly this "common-core" system of consonants is realized in the Kartvelian languages, which have the simplest consonant systems of Caucasian languages. Table 2 displays the 29-consonant system of Georgian, which exemplifies this Kartvelian type.

ELABORATIONS OF THE COMMON CORE

The *common core* is elaborated to a greater or lesser degree in other Caucasian languages, right up to the system of 80 consonants of the virtually extinct Ubykh. Of the fully living and functioning Caucasian languages, the most extensive consonant system is that of the Bzyb dialect of Abkhaz. This is a system of 67 consonant phonemes, which are displayed in Table 3.

TABLE 3
Abkhaz (Bzyb dialect) Consonant System

	1	2	3	4	5	6	7	8	9	10	11	12	13	14	15	16	17	18
Obstruents																		
Stops																		
Voiced	b	d	d^w						ǵ	g	g^w							
Voiceless aspirated	p	t	t^w						ḱ	k	k^w							
Glottalic	p'	t'	$t^{w'}$						ḱ'	k'	$k^{w'}$	q̇'	q'	$q^{w'}$				
Affricates																		
Voiced		dz	dz^w	dẑ		dz̦	dz											
Voiceless		ts	ts^w	tŝ		tŝ	tɕ											
Glottalic		ts'	$ts^{w'}$	tŝ'		tŝ'	tɕ'											
Fricatives																		
Voiced	v	z		ẑ	$\hat{z}^w$	z̦	z	z^w				ʁ́	ʁ	$ʁ^w$				
Voiceless	f	s		ŝ	$\hat{s}^w$	ŝ	ɕ	$ɕ^w$				χ̇	χ	χ^w	χ^{ς}	$\chi^{w\varsigma}$	ʜ	$ʜ^w$
Nonobstruents																		
	w	r																
		l					j	ʕ										
	m	n																

Numbered obstruent series: 1, Labial (bilabial stops, labiodental fricatives); 2, dentalveolar; 3, dentalveolar labialized (stops have simultaneous dental and labial closure; affricates are actually labiodentalized); 4 and 5, postalveolar (loosely "retroflex") "hard" hushing sibilants; 7 and 8, plain and labialized laminopostalveolar "soft" hushing sibilants; 9, 10, 11, velar palatalized, plain, and labialized stops; 12, 13, 14, uvular palatalized, plain, and labialized stops and fricatives; 15 and 16, plain and labialized pharyngealized uvular fricatives; 17 and 18, plain and labialized deep pharyngeal fricatives.

It can be seen that the Bzyb system augments the common core in two chief ways—by the addition of articulatory locations for affricates and fricatives and by secondary articulations. The added articulatory locations are, first, among the sibilants, the opposition of two types of postalveolar articulation: *apicopostalveolar* (or loosely "retroflex") (column 6) with tongue-tip slightly turned up toward the extreme back of the alveolar ridge (like the "hard" ʃ-type sounds of Russian, Polish, and Mandarin Chinese) and *laminopostalveolar* (columns 7 and 8) with the tip down and the highly convex blade and anterodorsum of the tongue forming a channel just behind the alveolar ridge (like "soft" ʃ-type sounds).

There is a third type, characterized as *hissing-hushing*—that is, auditorily between the hissing s-type sibilants and the hushing ʃ-type sibilants. These sounds, which are particularly characteristic of the Adygan languages, are, in fact, articulatorily intermediate between the ʃ- and s-types, being produced with a ʃ-like laminopostalveolar channel at the extreme back of the alveolar ridge but with the tip and rim of the tongue touching the backs of the *lower* front teeth. This effectively abolishes the *sublingual cavity*, the small cavity in front of and beneath the blade of the tongue, which is characteristic of ʃ-type sibilants.

The other additional articulatory location is *pharyngeal* (columns 17 and 18). In this dialect, as in Literary Abkhaz, these deep pharyngeal phonemes have no voiced counterparts (ʕ, ʕʷ) as they do in Abaza: in Abkhaz these are represented by the vowel a and the labial-palatal semivowel ɥ.

The secondary articulations are *labialization*, actually realized as double articulation, with complete simultaneous dental and labial occlusion in the case of dʷ tʷ tʷ' and as labiodentalized affrication in the case of dzʷ tsʷ tsʷ' and *pharyngealization* (the two features co-occurring in the simultaneously labialized and pharyngealized χʷˤ). These secondary articulations are not confined to Abkhazan. Both are very well developed in Ubykh, which has a set of five pharyngealized labials, as well as pharyngeals, which together with other additions brings the Ubykh consonant inventory up to 80. Labialization is also characteristic of the two Adygan languages, and both features, pharyngealization and labialization, are quite common in Dagestanian languages, notably in the Lezgian languages and in Lak and Dargi. In the Kumukh dialect of Lak, for example, occlusive labialization occurs with velar stops and the dentalveolar affricate: thus, for example, the numeral kʷ'i 'two' and the word tsʷaχ 'fear' are pro-

TABLE 4
Akhwakh (Northern Dialect) Consonant System

	1	2	3	4	5	6	7	8	9
Obstruents									
Stops									
Voiced	b	d				g	q		(ʔ)
Voiceless									
aspirated	p	t				k	q		
Voiceless									
fortes						k̄	q̄		
Glottalic	(p')	t'				k'	q'		
Glottalic									
fortes						k̄'	q̄'		
Affricates									
Voiced			ʤ						
Voiceless		ts	tʃ	tɬ					
Fortes		t̄s	t̄ʃ	t̄ɬ					
Glottalic		ts'	tʃ'	tɬ'					
Glottalic									
fortes		t̄s'	t̄ʃ'	t̄ɬ'					
Fricatives									
Voiced		z	ʒ				ʁ	ʕ	
Voiceless		s	ʃ	ɬ		x	χ	ħ	h
Fortes		s̄	ʃ̄	ɬ̄			χ̄		
Nonobstruents		r							
	w			l	j				
	m	n							

Numbered series are: 1, Labial; 2, dentalveolar; 3, postalveolar; 4,alveolar lateral; 5, palatal; 6, velar; 7, uvular; 8, pharyngeal; 9, glottal.

nounced [p͡k'i] and [p͡tsaχ], respectively, both with complete, light, endolabial closure.

Our third specimen of Caucasian consonant systems is the Andi language Akhwakh, Table 4. Akhwakh illustrates other North Caucasian typological features, that is, the occurrence of so-called *strong*, or *geminate*, or, as I shall call them, *fortis* consonants (represented by a macron over the relevant symbol), and the occurrence of *obstruent laterals*.

Fortes occur in all Dagestanian languages except the Dido languages and two of the Shah Dagh languages, Kryz and Budukh. Outside of Dagestanian, fortis-like unaspirated and long stops and sibilants occur in two dialects (Bzhedug and Shapsug) of Adyghe. In the Russian language literature on these dialects they are generally referred to as *preruptivnye*, that is, 'preruptives,' a term apparently coined to contrast with *abruptivnye* 'abruptives,' meaning '*ejectives*' (glottalic sounds).

In Dagestanian languages the plain versus fortis opposition is realized in two distinct ways. In Avar and some of the Andi languages (including the one variety of Akhwakh that I have heard) fortis stops have a long and strong affricated release; thus there are oppositions such as [kʰ] versus [kxx], [k'] versus [kxx'], and [q'] or [qχ'] versus [qχχ'] among the affricates, with the plain members of the pairs having short (and sometimes aspirated) affrication and the fortes having long, tense unaspirated affrication, thus [ts] or [tsʰ] versus [tss], [tɬ] or [tɬʰ] versus [tɬɬ]. Analogously plain fricatives are short, lax, and aspirated, whereas fortis fricatives are tense, long, and unaspirated, thus [sʰ] versus [ss], and so forth.

In the Central Dagestanian and Lezgian languages, on the other hand, the opposition is usually realized differently, most noticeably with respect to stops, where the plain members of pairs are aspirated, and the fortis members are unaspirated and often very noticeably geminate when intervocalic, thus [-tʰ-] versus [-tt-], and so forth.

With respect to the obstruent laterals, Akhwakh is exceptionally well endowed, having preserved what is assumed to be the full complement of Proto-Avaro-Andi-Dido laterals, that is, four lateral affricates (two plain and two fortis, voiceless and glottalic) and two lateral fricatives (plain and fortis). Literary Avar has three obstruent laterals (ɫ, ɫ̄, and tɬ'), with a fourth (tɬ) in some variants, but the Avar dialects vary in their degree of preservation of laterals down to complete absence of obstruent laterals in the Zakataly dialect of northern Azerbaijan, where literary ɫ and ɫ̄ are represented by palatal ç and ç̄ respectively and tɬ' by k'.

The only Dagestanian language outside of the Avaro-Andi-Didi group that has obstruent laterals is the somewhat aberrant or at least unusual Lezgian language Archi, which has the affricates tɬ and tɬ' and the fricatives ɫ and ɫ̄. Incidentally, an unusual feature of these laterals in Archi is that they are not dentalveolar laterals but velar, or slightly palatalized velar, laterals. That is, the median oral closure that forces the airstream into a lateral channel is not formed by the tip of the tongue against the alveolar ridge but by the dorsal surface of the tongue against the roof of the mouth.

Among the Nakh languages only Batsbi has one obstruent lateral (ɫ), but both the Adygan languages, Adyghe and Kabardian, have generally three lateral fricatives, voiced (ɮ), voiceless (ɫ), and glottalic (ɫ'), although there are some deviations from this in some dialects. Thus the voiced fricative is occasionally replaced by a lateral approximant (l) and the glottalic member of the triad may be realized as an affricate (tɬ') in the Beslenei dialect of Kabardian, as it is in Ubykh, which has the same triad as Adygan. Lateral obstruents have been posited for Proto-Dagestanian by Bokarëv, Gigineišvili, and others and for Proto–North Caucasian by Nikolaev and Starostin.

Another characteristic North Caucasian feature, not fully illustrated in the examples I have given, is the proliferation of *deep throat* sounds, namely, *pharyngealized uvulars*, such as those we have seen in Bzyb and also those found in Dagestan, for example, in the Lezgian languages Tsakhur and Rutul and in dialects of Agul; *upper pharyngeal fricatives* varying to approximants (types ħ ʕ) as in Avar; *lower pharyngeal*, or *epiglottal*, stop (ʡ) contrasting with glottal stop (ʔ) in Chechen and in dialects of Agul such as Burkihan and Burshag; *lower pharyngeal raucous fricatives* (H and ʕ) with some epiglottal trilling in the same dialects and also in some Northwest Caucasian (Abkhazo-Adygan) languages; and so on.

Many of the consonantal characteristics of Caucasian languages that we have been examining obviously can be compared with those in American Indian languages, particularly some of the languages of the American Northwest. Those shared Caucasian and American phonological features include triadic consonant series, the proliferation of velars and uvulars, labialization, particularly as a feature of back consonants, and the existence of lateral obstruents. Some of these and other typological similarities were studied in detail in Milewski 1955, and they may possibly have had some influence on the postulation of a distant genetic relationship between North Caucasian and Na-Dene embodied in the Dene-Caucasian hypothesis.

CONSONANT CLUSTERS

Before going on to consider Caucasian vowel systems I might mention *consonant clusters*. Here the Kartvelian languages, particularly Georgian, are preeminent. Georgian has initial clusters of from two to six consonants and final clusters of from two to five. The majority of Georgian consonant clusters consist of a sequence of two homogeneous obstruents (that is, both voiced, both voiceless, or both glottalic) with or without one or more nonobstruents before, between, or after them (types dʁ tχ bʁ pk tkr dzʁv brdz pχv pkn, and so on).

The most interesting feature of these clusters from the typological point of view is that the regular ones, that is, those conforming to rules of initiatory and phonatory homogeneity and of permitted participating articulatory types, are also normally *recessive*—that is, they *recede* into the mouth, with the initial obstruent being articulated further forward than the following one. This is a most unusual rule of consonant cluster structure, and it is therefore significant that exactly the same rule is found in the Adygan languages. In these languages, too, except for some systematic exceptions, morpheme-initial consonant clusters consist of a homogeneous sequence of two obstruents that are recessive with respect to articulation (types ps pɬ px pχ pɬ' bz bʒ bɣ bʁ tx tχ, and so on).

Basically the same cluster rules apply to Ubykh, Abkhaz, and Abaza. In the Nakh languages there are fewer clusters, but for the most part they, too, conform to the same rules as the Georgian and Adygan clusters do, including that very unusual recessive sequencing rule. This then is a feature of phonological typology that, though not pan-Caucasian, characterizes subgroups of both Kartvelian and North Caucasian. Consonant clusters are virtually absent from Dagestanian languages, except for Lezgi, and there they do not conform to the rules I have just discussed.

CAUCASIAN VOWEL SYSTEMS

With respect to vowels, there are fewer general Caucasian features. As is well known, the Northwest Caucasian languages as a group are characterized by the possession of minimal vowel systems of an unusual linear or, better, vertical type. It was suggested by Jakovlev as long ago as 1923 that Kabardian might at one time have had only one vowel phoneme, and there have been later claims that present-day Kabardian and also Abkhaz and Abaza are monovocalic (Jakovlev 1923; Kuipers 1960, 1976; Allen 1956, 1965). In fact, Kuipers 1960 suggests that Kabardian may be vowelless. However, for reasons adduced in Catford 1984 and Choi 1990 it seems to me that the monovocalic hypothesis is untenable and that the vowel systems of the Abkhazo-Adygan languages are more appropriately described as systems of two vowels (type ə-a) in Abkhaz, Abaza, and Ubykh and systems of three vowels (type ə-e-a) in Adyghe and Kabardian.

Other Caucasian languages have more orthodox vowel systems, some even exhibiting a certain exuberance. Thus Chechen is said to have 30 distinct vocalic nuclei, fifteen vowels and fifteen diphthongs. Those fifteen vowels, however, do not represent fifteen distinct vowel qualities but rather nine basic vowels, six of which also occur long.

Among Dagestanian languages Avar and all eight of the Andi languages have five-vowel systems (type i-e-a-o-u), though most of the latter group augment their vowel systems with long vowels or nasalized vowels, or both. Apart from Tsez, the Dido languages have slightly more complex systems. Lak has basically a *triangular* three-vowel system (i-a-u) augmented by three slightly pharyngealized vowels (types eʕ æʕ ɵʕ), whereas Dargi has a *square* system (i-e-a-u + pharyngealized æʕ).

The Lezgian languages generally have slightly more elaborate vowel systems; several of them include some pharyngealized vowels: Tsakhur completely duplicates its six-vowel system (i-e-a-o-u-ɤ) with a set of six pharyngealized vowels, and Udi has an eight-vowel system (i-e-a-o-u+y-ø-æ), of which only the first five have pharyngealized counterparts.

Of the Kartvelian languages, Georgian and Laz have simple five-vowel systems (type i-e-a-o-u), whereas Megrelian has a sixth vowel (unrounded central to back ɤ). Svan has basically a seven-vowel system (i-e-æ-a-o-u-ɤ), but various dialects of Svan apparently augment the system with front rounded vowels (y-ø) and with a length opposition.

This rather long summary of Caucasian phonetics and phonology shows that the Wittgensteinian *family resemblance* that Uslar pointed out in 1864 is tempered by considerable diversity, a diversity that is not without a certain amount of fairly compact *zoning*, which, whatever its genetic implications, enables us already at the level of phonological typology to make some kind of classification of subgroups. The Kartvelian languages are fairly well differentiated from the North Caucasian languages by the relative simplicity of their sound systems, although Georgian appears curiously united with the Abkhazo-Adygan languages (and perhaps also Nakh) by that very unusual articulatory recessive characteristic of homogeneous consonant clusters, which it shares with them.

The Abkhazo-Adygan languages have common consonantal traits but, above all, are unified (and differentiated from other groups) by their unusual minimal- and vertical-vowel system. The Nakh languages have consonant systems that lack many of the exuberances of Abkhazo-Adygan and Dagestanian but unusually rich vowel systems, particularly in the case of Chechen.

Among the Dagestanian languages, simple vowel systems and among consonants the existence generally of a set of lateral obstruents tend to mark off Avar and the Andi languages, though this latter trait appears to associate Archi with them. Proliferation of *deep throat* sounds characterizes the Central Dagestanian and to some extent the Lezgian languages.

A useful listing and synoptic table of phonological traits of all Caucasian languages is to be found in Kibrik and Kodzasov 1978 (pp. 113 to 117).

SOME GRAMMATICAL FEATURES

I turn now to a brief consideration of grammatical traits that characterize Caucasian languages. Here I am essentially summarizing remarks made on this topic in Catford 1977, where it is pointed out that few of these are common to all Caucasian languages, although some may have formerly been widespread or general Caucasian traits. A case in point is noun classification. This feature, in all probability once more widespread or universal in Caucasian, is present today in 28 of the 37 Caucasian languages. The greatest number of classes are found in the Nakh languages (where Batsbi has eight classes, Chechen and Ingush six each) and in two of the Dido languages, Khwarshi and Gunzib, each with six classes. Classes are absent from Kartvelian and only minimally represented in Abkhaz-Abaza.

Another characteristic that partially unites, partially divides Caucasian languages is their handling of locative expressions. Apart from postpositions, of which some use is made by all Caucasian languages, there is a sharp distinction between Abkhazo-Adygan and Nakho-Dagestanian, the former operating with locational preverbs (that is, locational prefixes on verb forms), the latter with locational case morphemes. Thus, for 'The man is in the house' Abkhazo-Adygan says the equivalent of 'The man the house in-stands', whereas Nakho-Dagestanian has 'The man house-in is'.

In the Dagestanian languages, the locative cases are expressed extremely systematically, generally by means of a sequence of two suffixes, the first carrying the *orientational* meaning (*in, on, under,* and so on) and the second specifying *directional* meaning (*static* relation, *approach, departure,* and so on). In the Abkhazo-Adygan languages the orientational meaning is expressed by the preverb, with the directional meaning being expressed by selection of a particular verb. Thus, despite an obvious surface difference there is an underlying resemblance between the two groups in that in both of them the two aspects of relational-locational meanings are systematically but separately expressed.

There is at least one other underlying similarity between the locative expressions of Abkhazo-Adygan and Dagestanian that concerns two obligatory semantic distinctions that are not too common in languages. These are (1) the distinction between *IN an empty space and IN a filled space* and (2) *ON a horizontal surface* and *ON a nonhorizontal surface*. These distinctions are found in the Adygan languages and in at least a dozen Dagestanian ones.

Another general North Caucasian trait is the absence of relative pronouns and adverbs, together with a paucity of conjunctions, so that virtually all sentential conjoining and subordination is carried out by the use of conjunctive verb forms, participles, verbal nouns, and so on. The Kartvelian languages are anomalous, since they make use of conjunctions and relative pronouns.

Probably the best known syntactical feature of Caucasian languages is the *ergative* construction of transitive sentences, in which the subject is in an oblique case while the object is in the same unmarked or nominative case that the subject of an intransitive verb is. All Caucasian languages have an ergative construction with one exception—the Megrelian dialect of Zan.

In the Kartvelian languages Georgian and Svan the ergative transitive construction occurs only with verbs in the aorist set of tenses. In the Zan dialects the ergative construction has been generalized from exclusive use with aorist transitives in two ways. In Laz, *all transitives*, present as well as aorist, take the ergative construction. In Megrelian *all aorists*, intransitive as well as transitive, have their subject in the ergative case. Consequently Megrelian cannot be said to have an ergative construction any longer, since the ergative caseform is completely dissociated from transitivity.

Although all Caucasian languages, with this one exception, have an ergative construction, there is a sharp distinction between the Kartvelian and North Caucasian languages with respect to ergativity. In Georgian and Svan the ergative construction is obligatory with all transitive aorists, and the nonergative construction occurs with intransitives and nonaorists. In these languages then, ergativity is a purely *formal* and meaningless feature of transitive aorists.

In North Caucasian, on the other hand, we find that in many, perhaps all, languages there is an opposition between an ergative and a nonergative, or *nominative* construction (that is, one in which the subject of the transitive verb is in the nominative case). The speaker is free to select one or the other and thereby to convey a *different meaning*. The following are examples from North Caucasian languages:

Kabardian: 'The youth is reading the book'.

(1) Ergative construction:	š'ale-m	txəłə-r	jedʒe
	boy[E/O]	book[N]	reads
(2) Nominative construction:	š'ale-r	txəłə-m	jewdʒe
	boy[N]	book[E/O]	reads

In (1) the subject (S) is in the ergative/oblique (E/O) case (that is, a case that has both the ergative and other, especially dative-like, oblique functions), while the object (O) is in the nominative (N) case. In (2) the case-forms of S and O are reversed. The meaning-difference is that (1) implies that the youth is assiduously reading right through the book, and in (2) he is reading superficially, or merely dipping into the book. Some authors describe type (2) as *intransitive*, regarding *book* in the oblique case as a kind of circumstantial, or locative, complement or adverbial ("The youth is reading— in the book"). But this is to overlook that in a genuine Kabardian intransitive the pronominal prefix on the verb would be *ma-*, hence *madʒe*: the construction is simply a *weak* transitive.

Comparable examples can be found in Nakh and Dagestanian languages, as follows:

Dargi: 'I am reading the book'.

(3)	nuni	ʒuz	butʃ'ulra
	I[E]	book[N]	read
(4)	nu	ʒuzli	utʃ'ulra
	I[N]	book[E]	read

These examples from Abdullaev 1971 convey approximately the same difference of meaning as the Kabardian examples do. Abdullaev claims that (3) is not transitive, since it has the verb-noun concord pattern of intransitives, but nevertheless he refers (p. 206) to the ergative noun in (4) as "the object of action."

In other examples of transitive constructions with a nominative S, the O may be in some other oblique case, for example, in the *instrumental* in Gunzib (E. A. Bokarëv 1959: 63). In yet other languages, such as Chechen, Avar, Tsakhur, and Khinalug, the O in the *nominative transitive* construction is in the same case as the S, namely, the nominative. The following Avar example is from A. A. Bokarëv 1949:

Avar: '. . . they are making a road'.

(5)	hez	nuχ	habuleb	bugo
	they[E]	road[N]	making	are
(6)	hel	nuχ	habulel	rugo
	they[N]	road[N]	making	are

Of these examples Bokarëv says that (5) "expresses primarily the action of the subject upon a definite object. . . . (6) primarily indicates the occupation of the subject . . . it characterizes it in terms of this action, laying no stress upon what particular object the action is directed to".

In these examples from North Caucasian languages it is clear that the ergative construction is no mere obligatory and meaningless peculiarity of transitive sentences as it is in Georgian but is a term in a meaningful opposition of *ergative* versus *nominative* construction. No matter what form is taken by its surface manifestation, the ergative construction expresses *strong transitivity*—a tight, purposeful, and effective relationship between a verbally expressed *activity and its object*. The nominative construction, on the other hand, expresses *weak transitivity*, implying a tight relationship between the *activity and its subject*: it stresses the activity of the subject rather than the effect of the activity upon the object.

Incidentally the nominative (weak) transitive construction is now often referred to as the *antipassive*. This is a totally inappropriate and misleading term, at least as far as North Caucasian languages are concerned. It carries with it the implication that the relationship between the ergative construction and the nominative construction is analogous to the relationship between the active and the passive in *nonergative* languages. The analogy, however, is totally false—the two processes (*passive transformation* and *antipassive transformation*) have nothing in common at any level—morphological, syntactic, semantic, or pragmatic.

The false analogy was originally engendered, I believe, by an article on ergativity by Kuryłowicz 1946/1973, in which he juxtaposes examples of the two transformations in the context of the outdated belief that the ergative is formally a passive construction but differing from the passive merely stylistically. This is clearly wrong, for reasons that I have adduced elsewhere (for example, Catford 1976), most cogently because in several Caucasian languages a genuine passive construction coexists with the ergative construction as an alternative option for the speaker, but there are four or five other reasons for not regarding the ergative construction as a passive.

According to Dešeriev 1959 (p. 170) a nominative transitive construction coexists with the ergative transitive construction in all Caucasian mountain languages. Whether or not the opposition, ergative versus nominative, in fact exists in all North Caucasian languages, it is certainly present in many, and this is in clear contrast to the Kartvelian languages.

As mentioned above, where an ergative construction occurs in Kartvelian, it is a purely *formal* and obligatory accompaniment to the selection of an aorist verb form. In North Caucasian it is *functional*, being in meaningful opposition to the nominative construction. In other words, although in North Caucasian languages the ergative is no doubt the *unmarked* transitive construction, the speaker has the option of selecting the marked nominative transitive construction to mean something slightly different.

The distinction between *formal* and *functional* ergativity is a general one. It can be used to characterize the ergative construction of any language in which an ergative construction occurs.

It is interesting to note that in Indo-European those Iranian, Dardic, and Indic languages that possess an ergative construction have in fact a purely *formal* ergative as an obligatory and not independently meaningful accompaniment of a past tense, just like Kartvelian. This is another typological similarity between Kartvelian and Indo-European to set alongside the morphophonological similarity of *ablaut* discussed by Gamkrelidze and Mačavariani 1965. Note, however, that Kumakhov 1981 draws attention to ablaut phenomena in Adygan, which, though differing somewhat from Kartvelian ablaut, slightly diminishes the significance of this Kartvelian parallel with I E.

On the other hand, a *functional* ergative, contrasting meaningfully with a nonergative construction, is found in Tibetan, in Chukchi-Kamchatkan languages, and in Eskimo-Aleut. This is a typological similarity with North Caucasian. Tibetan, of course, is one of the languages in the proposed Sino-Caucasian, or Dene-Caucasian, macro-family, and possibly Chukchi-Kamchatkan also belongs to the same family. Eskimo-Aleut, on the other hand, aligns with Nostratic rather than Dene-Caucasian.

We have now seen a goodly number of phonological and grammatical features of Caucasian languages, and it will be useful to summarize these in tabular form so that similarities and differences between the various groups of Caucasian languages can be seen. A detailed list of 33 phonological features, showing their distribution over all Caucasian languages, is given in Kibrik and Kodzasov 1978. Table 5 is a slightly expanded version of the table given in Catford 1977.

Clearly one cannot make a serious quantitative use of this highly selective table, but it does give some indication of similarities and differences and suggests how the *family resemblance* first mentioned

TABLE 5
Phonological and Grammatical Features of Caucasian Languages

Phonological or grammatical feature	Kart-velian	Abkhazo-Adygan	Nakh	Dage-stanian
1. Voiced-voiceless-glottalic triads	+	+	+	+
2. Glottalic fricatives	−	(+)	−	(+)
3. Pharyngeals	−	+	+	+
4. Pharyngealized consonants	−	+	−	+
5. Apico- vs. lamino-postalveolars	−	+	−	+
6. "Hissing-hushing" ŝ	−	+	−	−
7. Lateral obstruents	−	+	−	+
8. Voiced lateral fricative	−	+	−	−
9. Labialized consonants	−	+	−	+
10. Fortis consonants	−	(+)	−	+
11. Recessive consonant clusters	+	+	+	−
12. Minimal vowel systems	−	+	−	−
13. Pharyngealized vowels	−	−	−	+
14. Noun classes	−	(+)	+	+
15. Numerous local cases	−	−	(+)	+
16. Directional preverbs	(+)	+	−	(+)
17. *Orientator* and *direction* separately expressed	−	+	−	+
18. Unusual semantic distinctions of *on* and *in*	−	+	−	+
19. Conjoining, relativization, etc. by verb	−	+	+	+
20. Ergative construction—formal	+	−	−	−
21. Ergative construction—functional	−	+	+	+

by Uslar is based on rather few features common to all Caucasian languages.

MATERIAL CORRESPONDENCES

So far we have looked at some general typological characteristics. We must now turn our attention to material correspondences such as might be the basis of a genetic classification of the Caucasian languages. Before we go on to consider some of the attempts that have been made to establish regular sound correspondences between members of various groups of Caucasian languages, it will be useful to look at Table 6, which is a list of sample Caucasian words in 34 North Caucasian languages and in the three Kartvelian languages. The words in this list are among those stable forms that one might expect to exemplify genetic relationships rather than borrowing.

TABLE 6

Sample Caucasian Word List

Language	I	Thou	We excl. / incl.	You	One	Two	Three	Four	Five
1. Abkhaz	sa	wa/ba	ħa	çʷa	za	ʃʷ-	χ-	pçˁ	χʷ
3. Ubykh	sə-	wə-	çˁə-	ŝʷə-	za	tqʷˁa	ŝa	pɬˀa	ecŝ
4. Adyghe	se	we	te	ŝʷe	zə	ɕʷˀə	cˁ	pɬˀə	tʃɨ
5. Kabardian	se	we	de	fe	zə	tˀʷˀew	ŝə	pɬˀə	eᵐχɨ
6. Chechen	suo	ħuo	tχuo / waj	ʃu	tsha?	ʃiˀ	qoˀ	diˀ	pχiˀˀ
8. Batsbi	so	ħo	tχo / waj	ʃu	tsha	ʃi	qo	dʃiw	pχi
9. Avar	dun	mun	niʒ / niɬ	nuʒ	tso	kˀi-	ɬab-	unqˀ-	ʃu-
10. Andi	din/den	min	iʃˁi / iɬi	biʃi	se-	tʃˀe-	ɬob-	boqˀo-	ĩʃˀdu-
11. Botlikh	den	min	iʃˁi / iɬi	biʃti	tse-	kˀe-	habu-	boʁu-	ijdu-
13. Karata	den	men	iʃˁi / iɬi	biʃdi	tse-	kˀe-	ɬab-	boʔo-	ĩʃdu-
16. T'indi	de	me	iʃa / iɬɬa	biʃi	tse-	kˀe-	ɬab-	boʔˀu-	ĩʃtu-
17. Chamalal	dĩː	mĩː	iʃi / iɬti	biti	se-	etʃˀiˀi-	ɬaɬa-	boʔˀu- (+ boː)	iʃu-

18. Tsez	di	mi	eli	meʒi	sis	qʼaʕ-no	ɬoʕ-	uj-	ɬo-
20. Ginukh	de	me	eli	meʒi	hes	qʼo-	ɬo-	uqʼi-	ɬe-
21. Gunzib	də	mə	ile	miʒ	hə̃s	qʼa-	ɬχ-	oqʼe-	ɬi-
23. Lak	na/ʈu-	ina	ʒu	zu	tsə	kʷi	ʃam	muqʼ	x̄œʕ
24. Dargi	nu	hu	nuʃa	ħuʃa	tsa	kʼe	ħæb-	aw-	ʃe-
Kubachi	du	u	nuša	uša	sa	kʷe	ʕæb	oʁʷ	xu
25. Tabasaran	uzu	uvu	utʃu / uxu	utʃʕu	sa-b	qʼø-	ʃubu-	juqʼu-	xu-
28. Tsakhur	zə	vu (ʁu)	ʃi	ʃu	sa-	qʼoʕ-	xeb-	joqʼ-	xo-
29. Lezgi	zun	wun	tʃun	kyn	sa-	qʷʼe-	pu-	qʼu-	wa-
32. Khinalug	zu	vu	jir / kin	zur	sa	kʼu	pʃo	onʁ	pxu
33. Archi	zon	un	nen / nentʼu	ʒʷen	os	qʕʷe	ɬeb	ebqʼ	ɬo
34. Udi	zu	un	jan	vaʕn	sa	pʼaʕ	χib	bipʼ	qo
35. Georgian	me	ʃen	tʃʃwen	tkwen	erti	ori	ʕami	otχi	χuti
36. Svan	mi	si	næj	sgæj	eʃχu	jori	ʕemi	woʃtχw	woχuʃd
		('our' = niʃgwej / gwiʃgwej)							
37a. Megrelian	ma	si	tʃʃki	tkwa	arti	ʒiri	s.ɪmi	otχi	χuti

The phonological forms of most of the items in the list, even without comparison with other unlisted items, clearly fall into certain groups, and I do not intend to comment on them in much detail. It is clear that the Kartvelian forms differ sharply from the North Caucasian forms, with the exception of the numeral 'five'.

In discussing the Proto-Kartvelian form of this word, *xu(s₁)t, Klimov, in his [*Etymological Dictionary of the Kartvelian Languages*] (1964), points out that Bork 1907 had already drawn attention to the similarity of this form to numerous North Caucasian forms and of the numeral 'three' (Proto-Kartvelian *sam-) to North Caucasian forms such as Avar ɬab- (dial. sab-), Dargi ħab-.

In addition, it may be noted that, though the Proto-Kartvelian form for 'two' is *jor-, there is another Proto-Kartvelian root, *t'qub-, meaning 'twins', which matches the North Caucasian forms for 'two'. It may well be borrowed from Abkhazo-Adygan. Among the 1,050 or so items in Klimov's dictionary, 42, or about 4%, exhibit a resemblance to Abkhazo-Adygan forms.

The Proto-North Caucasian form for 'two' has been reconstructed by Nikolaev as *q'[ül] or *q'$_+$il, that is, in IPA, *qʷ'(yʕ) or *qʷ'iʕ (with labialized glottalic [q] followed by a pharyngealized vowel) and by Starostin as *q'ʷla, that is, *qʷ'ʕa (with pharyngealized consonant). All these forms are somewhat suggestive of borrowings from Indo-European—plausibly *kʷ' or *qʷ' could be assimilated and glottalized forms of *dw- (in the even more IE-looking Ubykh and Adygan forms the initial t- is a prefix).

Incidentally, one might speculate that Dagestanian forms for 'three' such as ɬa-b, ɬo-, and so on might also be of IE origin: a voiceless lateral fricative is a plausible reflex of *tr-. One thinks of those Central Dardic languages in which precisely this development has occurred: Gawar ɬe, Wotapuri pa 'three'; Wotapuri puɬ- 'son' (< putr-); and so on. Both Nikolaev and Starostin have reconstructed Proto–North Caucasian 'three' with an initial lateral affricate as (Nikolaev) *ǩelbʌ [= tɬeʕb + unknown vowel] and (Starostin) *ǩe/H/e-bʌ [= tɬe + unknown postuvular consonant + e]. The IE parallel is to be found in the Indic Bhadarwahi dialects of Jammu and Kashmir where both *pr- and *tr- have resulted in an initial (retroflex) voiceless lateral affricate, thus 'three' ʈɬa. In introducing these reconstructions by Nikolaev and Starostin at this stage I have anticipated somewhat: I will have more to say about these scholars soon.

The setting up of lists of sound correspondences leading to the reconstruction of Caucasian protolanguages (and particularly Proto–

North Caucasian) is a task that has been pursued most intensively since the early 1960s. Kuipers (1963a) gives a good summary of the work done in both descriptive and comparative studies of Caucasian up to that time.

The comparative study and the reconstruction of proto–sound systems for Caucasian languages have progressed at different rates, related to the relative intractability of the material of different branches of Caucasian. We can confidently accept Kartvelian as a genetically related group. The Proto-Kartvelian sound system was reconstructed with some confidence by Klimov 1960, and the same author's [*Etymological Dictionary of the Kartvelian Languages*] (1964) is an invaluable resource.

The comparative study of the North Caucasian languages and the reconstruction of Proto–North Caucasian have presented much more difficulty. This, of course, is due largely to the phonological complexity of North Caucasian languages. This complexity in itself renders the establishment of sound correspondences difficult, but there is an additional problem, that is, that Caucasian languages have probably been spoken in approximately their present locations for three or four millennia. It is probable that during this long period of symbiosis genetic relationships have been to some extent overlaid and obscured by borrowing.

As early as the 1960s some progress had been made in establishing the genetic relationships of Dagestanian languages. E. A. Bokarëv, after bringing out his comparative study of the Dido languages in 1959, published his pioneering [*Introduction to the Comparative-Historical Study of Dagestanian Languages*] in 1961. In this he set up a rather simple Proto-Dagestanian sound system consisting of 49 consonants, including fortis stops, affricates, and fricatives, and five lateral obstruents, including a voiced lateral affricate (which, unlike the other lateral obstruents, is not preserved in any Dagestanian language) to account for correspondence sets in which Lak, Dargi, and some Lezgian languages have voiced reflexes in certain positions, as opposed to the voiceless or glottalic reflexes of other laterals. Bokarëv's reconstruction did not include labialized consonants or pharyngeals. In a later, posthumously published work (Bokarëv 1981) he extended his reconstruction to include Nakh.

In an important work published in 1964 Gudava established detailed consonantal correspondences between the Andi languages. The next major step in Dagestanian reconstruction was Gigineišvili's [*Comparative Phonetics of Dagestanian Languages*] of 1977. This reduced

TABLE 7
Transliteration of Proto-Lezgian Consonant System

```
p   t   tʷ          k   kʷ   q    qʷ    qˤ    qˤʷ
p̄   t̄   t̄ʷ          k̄   k̄ʷ   q̄    q̄ʷ    q̄ˤ    q̄ˤʷ      ʔ   ʔʷ   ʔ   ʔʷ   ʔˤ   ʔˤʷ
p'  t'  tʷ'         k'  kʷ'  q'   qʷ'   qˤ'   qˤʷ'
b   d               g   gʷ   q̄'   q̄ʷ'   q̄ˤ'   q̄ˤʷ'

ts  tsʷ  tʃ  tʃʷ  tɬ  tɬʷ
t̄s  t̄sʷ  t̄ʃ  t̄ʃʷ  t̄ɬ  t̄ɬʷ
ts' tsʷ' tʃ' tʃʷ' tɬ' tɬʷ'
t̄s' t̄sʷ' t̄ʃ'       tɬ' tɬʷ'

s   sʷ   ʃ   ʃʷ   ɬ   ɬʷ          χ   χʷ   χˤ   χˤʷ    H   h   hˤ
s̄   s̄ʷ        ɬ̄   ɬ̄ʷ          χ̄   χ̄ʷ   χ̄ˤ   χ̄ˤʷ
z        ʒ   ʒʷ                    ʁ   ʁʷ   ʁˤ
+m m̄ n ñ v w r j l ī and i iˤ e eˤ æ æˤ ə əˤ u o oˤ a aˤ
```

the number of Proto-Dagestanian consonants to 44 *inter alia* by abolishing p' (a rare sound, possibly nonexistent in Proto-Dagestanian) and voiced fricatives, which he takes to be secondary developments in the languages (specifically Avaro-Andi) where they occur.

Talibov 1980 established a Proto-Lezgian sound system of 35 consonants. This includes fortis affricates but no labialized, pharyngealized, or pharyngeal consonants—the Agul pharyngeals, for example, being, according to Talibov, derived from uvulars. A different picture is presented by the Proto-Lezgian sound system included in Alekseev's 1985 [*Questions of the Comparative-Historical Grammar of the Lezgian Languages*]. Although Alekseev's book deals with morphology and syntax, he nevertheless provides a chart of the reflexes of Proto-Lezgian sounds, and the Proto-Lezgian reconstruction that he uses is that of S. A. Starostin. This consists of an inventory of no fewer than 101 consonants and 13 vowels. The consonant system, transliterated as best I can (there are a few obscurities), is given in Table 7. It may be questioned whether this vast array with nearly complete sets of *plain* versus *fortis* (p vs. p̄ etc.) and *labialized* obstruents and with large numbers of *pharyngealized* obstruents (such as qˤ χˤ ʔˤ ʔˤʷ) is plausible. It certainly represents the array of correspondence sets for the nine Lezgian languages displayed on the chart (the tenth language, Khinalug, formerly regarded as Lezgian, is omitted for a reason to be mentioned in a moment). It is, however, a little difficult to believe that this was the actual sound system—101 consonants and 13 vowels—of spoken Proto-Lezgian. Nevertheless it has the merit of accounting for all the *exotic* sounds of the Lezgian languages.

As I just indicated, Khinalug is not counted as a Lezgian language for the following reason. Alekseev classifies the Lezgian languages on the basis of a lexicostatistical study. Using the Swadesh 100-word list, he establishes the number of cognates shared by all pairs of Lezgian languages, including Khinalug and also as a kind of external control Avar and Lak. Alekseev presents a table of cognates for all pairs of the languages studied. On the basis of this he shows that the most closely related language pairs are Tabasaran and Agul (69 cognates), Budukh and Kryz (63), Lezgi and Agul (53), Lezgi and Tabasaran and Tsakhur and Rutul (50). Udi and Archi are clearly more remote.

By calculating the average cognate percentage for all the pairings of a given language with all the others in the list, one can get a kind of index of the centrality of that language in the Lezgian group as a whole. By this method the non-Lezgian languages Avar and Lak are seen to have average percentages of cognates shared with Lezgian languages of 29 and 28 respectively. Khinalug, by the same method, has a percentage of shared cognates of only 26! In other words, Khinalug appears to be even less Lezgian than Avar and Lak. Average percentages of cognates shared with other Lezgian languages for other languages are Tabasaran and Agul 45, Lezgi 41, Budukh 40, Tsakhur 38, Archi 36, and Udi 34.

Alekseev points out that Khinalug differs from Lezgian languages not only lexically but also in terms of unusual phonetic developments and peculiar morphological features, and this is additional evidence of its peripheral status. One interesting point in Alekseev's table is that it shows the cognate percentage for Avar-Lezgi as 27. This is precisely the figure for Avar-Lezgi given independently in Catford 1977 (p. 310) and is encouraging evidence of the consistency, if not the validity, of the method.

The Central Dagestanian (Lak-Dargi) sound correspondences were studied in Gaprindašvili 1966 and more recently in Akiev 1977. The latter work presents a series of word lists showing correspondences between Lak and Dargi rather than setting up a Proto–Central Dagestanian. It demonstrates the close relationship between Lak and Dargi.

The Nakh languages are clearly closely related, and the sound correspondences between them have been worked out and discussed by Sommerfelt 1934–1947, Dešeriev 1963, and Imnaišvili 1977.

For the Abkhazo-Adygan languages no completely worked out proto-language has been established. It is clear that the Adygan languages, Adyghe and Kabardian, are very closely related, as the lexi-costatistical cognate percentage of 92 indicates. The Abkhazan languages, Abkhaz and Abaza, are likewise closely related (cognate percentage 80). Consequently, it has proved relatively easy to establish sound correspondences within each subgroup, particularly within Adygan. Here we have, first, the pioneering work of Jakovlev 1930, followed by Kuipers' detailed working out of Proto-Adygan (Proto-Circassian) (1963b), followed by his *Dictionary of Proto-Circassian Roots* (1975), which is a most valuable reference work. The most recent work is Kumakhov 1981, a detailed comparative-historical study of Adygan phonetics. Information about the sound relations within Abkhazan are more sketchy, but some can be obtained from, for example, Genko 1955 and Lomtatidze 1976.

No full reconstruction of Abkhazo-Adygan (Northwest Caucasian) as a whole has been published, but Shagirov's [*Etymological Dictionary of the Adygan (Circassian) Languages*] (1977) provides useful information, and his [*Common Material and Structural Features of the Abkhazo-Adygan Languages*] (1982) lists 379 cognates. These illustrate many sound correspondences, but Shagirov does not explicitly set up a complete Proto-Abkhazo-Adygan. As Kuipers pointed out in 1963, the problem of establishing regular sound correspondences is very great when one is dealing with languages in which virtually all roots consist of a single consonant or consonant cluster, particularly when there are many homonyms and the consonant systems are extremely rich.

The most ambitious work on the reconstruction of North Caucasian as a whole is that of the two young Soviet linguists, who have already been mentioned, S. Nikolaev and S. A. Starostin. Nikolaev kindly supplied us at the University of Michigan with a list of over 2,000 Proto–North Caucasian roots. These exemplify over 180 different consonantal sound correspondences, which would seem to imply a Proto–North Caucasian consonant inventory of 180 items. They include practically complete sets of labialized and fortis stops, affricates, and fricatives, no fewer than 18 pharyngeal and laryngeal sounds, 16 lateral affricates, and 5 lateral fricatives. Presumably these numbers will be reduced as correspondence sets are conflated as a result of further research, since even for highly consonantal North Caucasian, 180 consonants seems excessive. Unfortunately we have no information from Nikolaev about the specific items in the various North Caucasian languages and language groups upon which this reconstruction is based. What can be learned from such published sources as are available to us (dictionaries of some of the North Caucasian literary languages and the like) is inadequate for the purpose of evaluating the reconstructions.

Some slightly different reconstructions have been published by Starostin; we have in fact already used some in the discussion of the sample word list (Table 6). Starostin used his reconstructions of Proto–North Caucasian and of proto-languages of several subgroups of North Caucasian in an article published in the *Ketskij sbornik* (1982). We use that as a source of some examples in Table 8, given as a sample of the reconstructions in question. I have chosen to illustrate examples of Proto–North Caucasian dentalveolar affricates, and the numbers at the head of each column refer to the numbered items in Starostin's list.

In Table 8 I have retained Starostin's transcription. This is reasonably self-explanatory, except for the representation of lateral obstruents by symbols for velars with a *háček* (wedge) on top—x̌ = ɬ, ǩ = tɬ, ǧ = dɮ. This way of transcribing laterals derives from Kibrik and Kodzasov, who in an article published in 1970 recommended some modifications of IPA script for the transcription of Caucasian languages. These included the introduction of a diacritic to indicate *lateralization*, originally a subscript tilde. Their original intention was to promote flexibility, in particular the possibility of distinguishing between "normal" dentalveolar laterals, which they represented as ʃ̰ ʒ̰ tʃ̰ = ɬ ɮ tɬ, and velar laterals (such as occur in Archi), which they represented as x̰ ɣ̰ kx̰ = velar lateral fricatives and velar lateral affricate (such as occur in Archi). In their 1977 work on Archi, Kibrik and Kodzasov changed over to the wedge diacritic, representing the Archi (palatalized) velar laterals as ǩ, ǩ', x̌, ɣ̌, and so on. This is the usage Starostin and Nikolaev have generalized, using ǩ, x̌, and so on for all lateral obstruents, not merely for the Archi velar laterals. The use of symbols for postalveolar ʃ and velar x and so on as the basic symbols to which the lateral diacritic is attached captures more or less the *acoustic* characteristics of obstruent laterals. Spectrograms of Archi lateral affricates and fricatives show a concentration of acoustic energy at low frequencies (around 1.5 to 3.0 kHz), corresponding roughly with the frequency concentration of slightly palatalized velar fricatives, whereas more "normal" (as in Avar and Adyghe) dentalveolar obstruent laterals exhibit frequencies from 2.5 or so kHz upwards, more like those of postalveolar ʃ-type fricatives.

Starostin's reconstructions in Table 8 require little comment, although there are some apparent anomalies for which, no doubt,

TABLE 8

Some Starostin North Caucasian Reconstructions

Group and Language	147 'One'	73 'Weasel/Mouse'	134 'Autumn/Winter'	144 'Prickle'	67 'Anger'	71 'Bear'	146 'Ox'
PNC	*cʰə	*cʰarg̃ʷ/a/	*c̄ʰow/i/lHʌ	*cacʌ	*cʷamʔi	*cʰʷaʔnʌ	*jəmcʰo
PDag.	"	*cʰarg̃ʷʌ	+c̄ʰ/i/wolHʌ	*cace	"	"	"
PLezgian	*ša	*sʌ(r)k̃ʷ	*cowol	*c̄ač	*šam-	*sʷe'	*jamc
Lezgi	sa		čvul	zaz	seb	sev	jac
Tabasaran	sa-b			cac	seb	šve'	jic
Agul	sa-d	sok	so͡t-aql	zaza	seb/sev		jacʷ
Archi	os/šej-		civil	cac	šam	šo	ans
Tsakhur			cuvaž	zaza	sem	psi	
Khinalug etc.							
Avar	co	cak'u		zaz	čin	ci	os
PAndi	*ce/se	*cak̃'u	*c̄ibʌrʌ	*zaza	*šimi	*sin'i	*'umco
Andi	se/ce	sark'u	sibiru	zaz	šim	sēj	unso
Akhwakh etc.	ce-be		c̄ibera	žaža	šimi	šin/šij	unča
			(T'i.) c̄ibar	zaza	"	sī	musa
Dargi	ca	(Kar.) sak'u	šut	cače/zanzi /čanči	himi/sume	šin-ka	u(n)c
Lak	ca				ši	cu-ša	nic
PTsez	*hə-s/si				*simə	*sih	*'ŏs
Tsez	sis				semi	ze(j)	is/os
etc.	(Hun.) hŏs				(Hun.) simi	(Bezh.) sih	(Hun.) jĕtt ('cow')
PNakh	*c-Ha	*šʌrtq'a	*st'abo	*ʒéʒ	*stim	*ča	*jĕtt jett [1]
Chechen	cHa	šatq'a	(Bats st'abo)	zéz	stim	ča	
	cHa	šurtq'a					
PNWC	zʌ	*c̄əγwʌ/-γ-	*b-ž'ʌ	*čača	*ž'ʷə	*məš̃ʷʌ	*c̄ʷə
Ubykh	za	*cəyə/c'-	bž'a	caca	gə-ž'ʷə	məš̃ʷa	cʷə
PAbkhazan	*zə	a-cəʀ/-c'-	*bźə-Ha		*e-g-ž'-	*məš̃ə	*cʷə
Abkhaz	z-nə ('once')	c'əʀ	bźə-Ha		a-gʷə-žv-	a-mš̃v	a-čv
Abaza	za-k'ə	*c̄əʀʷa	bźə-Ha	*čača	gʷə-ž'ə	mš̃ə	č̄ʷə
PAdygan	*zə	cəʀʷa		cáča	*gʷə-e-ž'-ə	məša	č̄ʷə
Adyghe	zə	ʒəʀʷa		cáča	e-gʷə-ž-ə	məša	cʷə
Kabardian	zə			ʒása	gʷə-ʒə	məša	və

PNWC, Proto Northwest Caucasian; T'i. T'indi

Starostin could give explanations. For example, in item 73, why is Proto–North Caucasian initial *cʰ represented by *š in Proto-Nakh and *c in Proto-NWC when its reflexes in these languages in item 147 are *c and *z respectively? And there are a few other similar problems. A more specific question has to do with item 146 and is indicated in the list by [1]. Here it will be seen that the Proto-Nakh and Chechen reflexes of *jəmcʰo 'ox' are given as *jett and *jett respectively, meaning 'cow', but the Chechen word for 'ox' is *stu*, and this is presumably the correct reflex of *(jəm)cʰo; compare items 134 and 67.

EXTERNAL RELATIONS OF CAUCASIAN

There has long been speculation about the external relations of Caucasian, but no serious *rapprochements* were possible until some form of Proto-Caucasian or Proto–North Caucasian was set up. For example, Lafon's 1952 comparison of Basque and Caucasian was less convincing than it might have been because the sound correspondences that he adduced were set up between Basque and various different isolated Caucasian languages: there was no Proto-Caucasian with which to make the sort of comparisons that are necessary in setting up a distant, interfamily relationship: but see now Čirikba 1985.

The well-established Proto-Kartvelian made possible the detailed comparison of Kartvelian with other languages, and, as is well known, Illič-Svityč 1971 showed convincingly that Kartvelian can be included in the Nostratic macrofamily. On this, see Shevoroshkin's chapter in this volume. The possible external relationships of North Caucasian, however, remained uncertain, although Basque, Burushaski, Paleo-Siberian, and, among ancient languages, Sumerian and Urartian had all been suggested as possibly related to North Caucasian.

Recently, however, Starostin has suggested that North Caucasian belongs to a macrofamily consisting of North Caucasian, Yeniseian (represented at the present day only by Ket), Sino-Tibetan, Chukchi-Kamchatkan, and probably also Na-Dene, known as Sino-Caucasian, or, if Na-Dene is included, Dene-Caucasian. On this also see Shevoroshkin's chapter.

The data in Table 8, which I have used as a sample illustration only of North Caucasian reconstructions, are actually taken from an article by Starostin on external relations of Yeniseian, though I have extracted from it only data relating to North Caucasian.

Although Illič-Svityč's assignment of Kartvelian to Nostratic seems very plausible, the Dene-Caucasian hypothesis is less convincing so far, partly because of uncertainties about the methods used by Nikolaev and Starostin in the reconstruction of Proto–North Caucasian. Nevertheless, the work of such linguists as Nikolaev and Starostin is extremely important, and we look forward to the forthcoming publication of their *Etymological Dictionary of North Caucasian Languages*.

REFERENCES CITED

Abdullaev, Z. G. 1971. *Očerki po sintaksis darginskogo jazyka*. Moscow: Nauka.
Akiev, A. S. 1977. *Istoriko-sravnitel'naja fonetika darginskogo i lakskogo jazykov*. Makhachkala: Učpedgiz.
Alekseev, M. E. 1985. *Voprosy sravnitel'no-istoričeskoj grammatiki lezginskix jazykov*. Moscow: Nauka.
Allen, W. S. 1956. "Structure and system in the Abaza verbal complex." *Transactions of the Philological Society*, pp. 127–176.
———. 1965. "On one-vowel systems." *Lingua* 132: 111–124.
Bokarëv, A. A. 1949. *Sintaksis avarskogo jazyka*. Moscow: Akademija Nauk.
Bokarëv, E. A. 1959. *Tsezskie (didoiskie) jazyki Dagestana*. Moscow: Akademija Nauk.
———. 1961. *Vvedenie v sravnitel'no-istoričeskoe izučenie dagestanskix jazykov*. Makhachkala: Dagestanskij Gosudarstvennyj Universitet.
———. 1981. *Sravnitel'no-istoričeskaja fonetika vostočnokavkazskix jazykov*. Moscow: Nauka.
Bork, F. 1907. *Beiträge zur kaukasischen Sprachwissenschaft*. Teil I. *Kaukasische Miscellen*. Königsberg.
Catford, J. C. 1976. *Ergativity in Caucasian Languages*. ERIC, Documentation Reproduction Service, no. ED112704.
———. 1977. "Mountain of Tongues: the Languages of the Caucasus." *Annual Review of Anthropology* 6: 283–314.
———. 1984. "Instrumental Data and Linguistic Phonetics." Topics in Linguistic Phonetics in Honour of E. T. Uldall. *New University of Ulster Papers in Linguistics and Language Learning* 9: 23–48.
Čirikba, V. A. 1985. "Baskskij i Severokavkazskie jazyki." In Piotrovskij, B. B., ed. *Drevnjaja Anatolija*, pp. 95–105. Moscow: Nauka.
Choi John-Dongwook. 1990. "Kabardian Vowels Revisited." *UCLA Working Papers in Phonetics* 74 (Feb.): 1–15.
Dešeriev, Ju. D. 1959. *Grammatika xinalugskogo jazyka*. Moscow: Akademija Nauk.
———. 1963. *Sravnitel'no-istoričeskaja grammatika naxskix jazykov*. Grozny: Čečeno-inguškoe Knižnoe Izdatel'stvo.
Gamkrelidze, Th. V., and G. Mačavariani. 1965. *Sonant'ta sist'ema da ablaut'i kartvelur enebši* [The System of Sonants and Ablaut in Kartvelian Languages]. Tbilisi: Mecniereba.
Gaprindašvili, Š. G. 1966. *Fonetika darginskogo jazyka*. Tbilisi: Mecniereba.
Genko, A. N. 1955. *Abazinskij jazyk*. Moscow: Akademija Nauk.
Gigineišvili, B. K. 1977. *Sravnitel'naja fonetika dagestanskix jazykov*. Tbilisi: Izdatel'stvo Tbilisskogo Universiteta.

Gudava, T. E. 1964. *Konsonantizm andijskix jazykov*. Tbilisi: Izdatel'stvo Akademii Nauk Gruzinskoj SSR.

Holmer, N. M. 1947. "Ibero-Caucasian as a linguistic type." *Studia Linguistica* 1: 11–44.

Illič-Svityč, V. M. 1971, 1976, 1984. *Opyt sravnenija nostratičeskix jazykov (semitoxamitskij, kartvel'skij, indoevropejskij, ural'skij, dravidijskij, altajskij)*. Moscow: Nauka.

Imnaišvili, D. S. 1977. *Istoriko-sravnitel'nyj analiz fonetiki naxskix jazykov*. Tbilisi: Mecniereba.

Jakovlev, N. F. 1923. *Tablicy fonetiki kabardinskogo Jazyka*. Moscow: Travaux de la section des langues du Caucase septentrional de l'Institut oriental à Moscou.

———. 1930. "Kurzer Überblick über die tscherkessischen (adygheischen) Dialekte und Sprachen." *Caucasica* 6: 1–19.

Kibrik, A. E., and S. V. Kodzasov. 1970. "Principy fonetičeskoj transkripcii i transkripcionnaja sistema dlja kavkazskix jazykov." *Voprosy Jazykoznanija* 6: 66–78.

———. 1977. *Opyt strukturnogo opisanija arčinskogo jazyka*. Tom 1. *Leksika. Fonetika*. Moscow: Izdatel'stvo Moskovskogo Universiteta.

———. 1978. "Fonetičeskie obščnosti." In *Strukturnye obščnosti kavkazskix jazykov*. Moscow: Nauka.

Klimov, G. A. 1960. *Opyt rekonstrukcii fonemnogo sostava obščekartvel'skogo jazyka-osnovy*, pp. 22–31. Moscow: Izdatel'stvo Akademii Nauk.

———. 1964. *Ètimologičeskij slovar' kartvel'skix jazykov*. Moscow: Akademija Nauk.

Kuipers, A. 1960. *Phoneme and Morpheme in Kabardian (Eastern Adyghe)*. Janua Linguarum Ser. Min. 8. The Hague: Mouton.

———. 1963a. "Caucasian." Ed. by T. A. Sebeok, *Current Trends in Linguistics* 1: 315–344.

———. 1963b. "Proto-Circassian Phonology: an Essay in Reconstruction." *Studia Caucasica* 1: 56–92.

———. 1975. *A Dictionary of Proto-Circassian Roots*. Lisse: The Peter de Ridder Press.

———. 1976. "Typologically Salient Features of Some North-West Caucasian Languages." *Studia Caucasica* 3: 101–127.

Kumakkov, M. A. 1981. *Sravnitel'no-istoričeskaja fonetika adygskix (čerkesskix) jazykov*. Moscow: Nauka.

Kuryłowicz, J. 1946. *Ergativnost' i stadial'nost' v jazyke*, 5: 387. Moscow: Izdatel'stvo Akademii Nauk.

———. 1973. "La construction ergative et le développement 'stadial' du langage." *Esquisses linguistiques*. Munich: W. Fink Verlag.

Lafon, R. 1952. *Études basques et caucasiques*. *Acta Salmaticensia Filosofia Letras* 5(2): 5–91.

Lomtatidze, K. V. 1976. *Apxazuri da abazuri enebis ist'oriul-šedarebiti analizi: 1. Ponologiuri sist'ema da ponet'ik'uri p'rocesebi* [Historical-comparative analysis of the Abkhaz and Abaza languages: 1. Phonological system and phonetic processes]. Tbilisi: Mecniereba.

Magomedbekova, Z. 1967. *Axvaxskij jazyk*. Tbilisi: Mecniereba.

Magometov, A. 1963. *Kubačinskij jazyk*. Tbilisi: Izdatel'stvo Akademii Nauk Gruzinskaja SSR.

Milewski, T. 1955. "Comparaison des systèmes phonologiques des langues caucasiennes et américaines." *Lingua Posnaniensis* 5: 136–165.

Nikolaev, S., and S. A. Starostin. (forthcoming). *Etymological Dictionary of North Caucasian Languages*.

Shagirov, A. K. 1977. *Ètimologičeskij slovar' adygskix (čerkesskix) jazykov*. Moscow: Nauka.

——. 1982. *Material'nye i strukturnye obščnosti leksiki abxazo-adygskix jazykov*. Moscow: Nauka.

Sommerfelt, A. 1934, 1938, 1947. "Études comparatives sur le caucasique du nord-est." *Nordisk Tidskrift för Sprogvidenskap* 7: 178–210, 9: 115–143, 14: 141–155.

Starostin, S. A. 1982. "Praenisejskaja rekonstrukcija i vnešnie sv'azi enisejskix jazykov." *Ketskij sbornik*. Leningrad: Nauka.

Talibov, B. B. 1980. *Sravnitel'naja fonetika lezginskix jazykov*. Moscow: Nauka.

Uslar, P. K. 1888. *Ètnografija kavkaza. Jazykoznanie. II. Čečenskij jazyk*. Tiflis.

Recent Research on the Relationships of Japanese and Korean

SAMUEL E. MARTIN

There is no general agreement on the genetic relationships of either Japanese or Korean. For both languages we have seen numerous hypotheses relating them to each other, to the adjacent Altaic languages (Tungusic, Mongolian, Turkic), or to both, and a fair number of attractive etymological comparisons have been proposed. Claims of relationship with Ainu, with Nivkh (Gilyak), and with Inuit (Eskimo) have also been made. Farther afield, each language has been compared with one or all of the Dravidian languages, the most recent attempts being those of Fujiwara and Ōno Susumu for Japanese and of Morgan Clippinger for Korean. Some Japanese scholars have drawn comparisons between Japanese and Malayo-Polynesian; in recent years Murayama Shichirō has published extensive research on that subject, though lately he has redirected his attention to an earlier interest in possible ties with Korean and Altaic. I believe the majority view today would hold that Japanese and Korean are more likely to be related to each other than to any other language and that the historically adjacent Tungusic languages are the likeliest candidates for further relationship.

This study continues a long-standing interest I have had in pursuing the prehistory of the lexicon and grammar of each of these two languages within a framework that seeks to explore similarities of form and function that may be argued to result from something other than chance resemblance or universal trends and that are unlikely to be accounted for as loanwords. Twenty years ago (Martin 1966) I offered 320 etymologies, some original, others inspired by earlier researchers. I attempted to establish regular phonological correspondences, independent from those that might be attributed to borrowing. Largely for mnemonic reasons, I offered letter values for the correspondences, but these "reconstructed phonemes" were intended as abstract entities and were motivated by phonetic considerations only in part. If I were revising that paper, I would now pay more attention to the phonetic assumptions underlying the posited correspondences and to the relative ordering of rules that they imply. I would also begin from a much better morphophonemic reconstruction of the etyma of Proto-Japanese than was available at that time (see Martin 1987) and a view of pre-*Hankul* Korean that has been enriched by the research of a number of perceptive scholars, especially Lee Ki-Moon, Kim Wanjin, and S. R. Ramsey; my revision would also be based on a better understanding of the language of the fifteenth century (see Martin 1983).

The earliest forms of written Japanese, *ca.* A.D. 700, show that two dialects were already in existence and the morphophonemic complexities of these, together with morphological structures surviving in modern dialects (especially those of the Ryūkyū islands and of the Hachijō islands), permit us to reconstruct a still earlier form of the language, particularly with respect to derivational morphology and the verb inflections. Our best sources for Korean are regrettably modern, the *Hankul* evidence from the second half of the fifteenth century (sometimes called "Middle Korean" but better termed "Early Modern Korean") and later, but there are also words written in Chinese phonograms from *ca.* 1350 and, though scanty, even earlier, *ca.* 900–1200. Moreover, there are Korean place names and references in Chinese sources, but it is not always clear to what extent these are from an ancestral version of what we call Korean today, since we know there were other languages also spoken on the peninsula, such as the "Koguryŏ" language, as attested in at least 82 words written in phonograms, words that resemble Old Japanese about as much as they do what we can surmise of the Silla language, directly ancestral to later Korean (K. M. Lee 1964: 20). Morphophonemic complexities in the language of the fifteenth century allow the internal reconstruction of the phonology of an ancestral language that is earlier by perhaps 300 to 500 years, and whenever possible that is the starting point for lexical comparisons with Japanese. The farther back we go, of course, the more speculative the venture becomes.

This chapter is divided into three parts: first, a brief presentation of work on segmental phonology, focusing on the conclusions of the 1985 dissertation by John Whitman; second, an examination of problems of relating the accentual systems, with particular attention to some recent papers by Murayama; and finally, a comparison of certain grammatical elements, as an updated and expanded version of Martin 1968.

PHONOLOGICAL CORRESPONDENCES

In his dissertation, Whitman reconstructs a realistic set of phonemes to account for the major correspondences posited between Middle Korean and Old Japanese. He proposes the array of vowel correspondences in Table 1.[1]

Whitman argues a more specific source for the OJ vowels *uy* (written "*iy*" in Martin 1987), *wo*, *ey*, and *ye* that presumes two processes: loss of medial **r* after short vowels and loss of medial **m* after short vowels that show up as OJ *u* (that is, PKJ **u*, **ü*, and word-internal **o*). The vowel-length environment is based on treating the low initial register of Middle Japanese (MJ) (attested by a *low dot* in the eleventh century and so marked below) as distinctive vowel length, an interpretation first suggested by Hattori and developed in Martin 1987. It is necessary to specify this negative environment (whatever its phonetic interpretation) in order to account for the OJ retention of -*r*- in some examples that would otherwise be exceptions to the elision of *r*:

MK ·*poy* 'belly' : OJ *para* > MJ .*fa.ra* 'belly' = PKJ **po:ra* (+ K suffix -*i*)
MK .*ko·lay* 'walnut' : OJ **kuruy* (*kuri*, *kuru*-) > MJ .*ku.ri* 'chestnut', *kuru-mi* 'walnut' = PKJ **koro* (+ K suffix -*i*)

And the narrower environment for the elision of **m* is needed so as to account for examples of retained -*m*- that would otherwise be exceptional:

MK ·*twu·lwu·mi* 'crane' : OJ *turu* > MJ .*tu·ru*. (a high-low fall on the last syllable) = PKJ **türüm* (+ K suffix -*i*)
MK .*a·chom* 'morning' : OJ *asa* > MJ .*a·sa.* = **asom* (+ K -*h*- secondary)

Where a MK monosyllable has the "rising tone" marked with a *double dot* in *Hankul* texts of the fifteenth century (and written with a preposed colon below), the cognate does not lose the medial -*r*- or -*m*-:

[1] Abbreviations used in this chapter are, *adn* adnominal; *aux*, auxiliary verb; *Ch*, Chinese; *F*, falling pitch; *H*, high pitch; *inf*, infinitive; *J*, Japanese; *K*, Korean; *L*, low pitch; *MCh*, Middle Chinese; *MK*, Middle Korean; *MJ*, Middle Japanese; *OJ*, Old Japanese; *PJK*, Proto-Japanese-Korean = *PKJ*, Proto-Korean-Japanese; *R*, rising pitch; *Skt*, Sanskrit. Accentual information is omitted for the causative and passive formants (17.1 to 17.4).

TABLE 1

PJK	MK	OJ
*i	i	i
*a	a	a
*$ü$	wu	u
*$ö$	u	o
*o	o	u word-internally; a in long syllables
*u	wo	u
*e	e	a but o when final, or with other o

MK *:kwom* 'bear' : OJ *kuma* > MJ *.ku.ma* 'bear' = PKJ **ku:m*
MK *:kwol* 'valley' : OJ *kura* 'valley' = PKJ **ku:r*

But some cases of the MK rising tone are secondary, the result of compressing a disyllabic low-high sequence under monosyllabification, and these lose the medial resonant:

MK *:woy* (< **.woʻi*) > modern K *oi/oy* 'melon' : OJ *uri* > MJ *.uʻri* 'melon' = PKJ **uri*

And for certain words, notably a group of verb stems analyzed in Ramsey 1975, the MK rising tone is the result of a low tone that has absorbed the high tone of a second syllable with an elided final vowel (for the value of which, in the absence of external information, we can assume nothing more than the minimal quality of MK *u/o*). Should the PKJ reconstructions be **kuma* 'bear' and **kura* 'valley'? Compare MK *:syem* 'island' : OJ *sima* > MJ *.si.ma* = PKJ **sima* (with Korean vowel breaking).

The correspondence of MK /o/ to OJ /a/ when final but to /u/ when nonfinal may be explained, as Whitman points out, if we assume that final vowels were regularly lengthened in pre-OJ, as is generally assumed to be the case for the vowels of OJ monosyllabic nouns not followed by a suffix. (A similar situation holds today in Kyōto and in the Ryūkyūs.) That explanation may be inadequate; further study is in order.

Given the proposed rules, Whitman proceeds to show that the OJ diphthongal vowels in certain words resulted from the elision of *-r-* or *-m-*:

OJ	pre-OJ	Examples
uy	< **u[m]i*	MK *ʻmwom* 'body' : OJ *muy* > MJ *ʻmi* = PKJ **mum* + J *-i*
	< **u[r]i*	MK *ʻpul* 'fire' : OJ *puy* > MJ *.fiʻ* (with rise) = PJK **por* + J *-i*
		MK *.kwo.kwoʻli* 'stem' : OJ *kukuy* > MJ *.ku.ki* = PJK **kukuri*

wo < **u[r]o*   MK *kwulek* (with suffix *-k*) 'basket' : OJ *kwo* > MJ .*ko* 'basket'
                 = PJK **küle* (> pre-OJ **kuro*)

ey < **a[r]i*   MK .*ta.li* 'leg, limb' : OJ **tey* > *te, ta-* > MJ .*te* = PKJ **tari*

   *o[r]i   MK ·*mol* 'seaweed' : OJ *mey, mo* > MJ (?.)*me*, ·*mo-·fa* = PJK
                 *mor (with J suffix *-i*)

ye < **i[r]a*   MK *pol*, modern K *pel*, Koguryŏ phonogram PYEL < **pilo*
                 'layer' : OJ *pye* = PJK *pir(o)* > pre-OJ **pira*

The last etymology calls for closer scrutiny (compare OJ *pira* 'flat, flat thing, petal'); there are so few etyma with the OJ vowel *ye* that parallel cases are hard to come by, though Whitman offers two others, each of which involves problems that will have to be taken up elsewhere.

Whitman reconstructs a system of initial consonants in Table 2. The most doubtful of these are **g* and perhaps **z*, which is based on only two etymologies: MK :*sil* 'thread' : OJ *ito* > MJ .*i·to* 'thread' = PJK **zitör?* and MK :*sel* 'new year; year of age' : OJ -*zo* (?< -*so*) in *ko-zo* 'last year' or (= *ki-so*) 'last night'. I find the four etymologies used to support **g* unconvincing. Whitman, on the other hand, rejects my attempt to reconstruct a proto **g-* to account for the correspondence of MK *k-* to OJ zero (Ø), and there are indeed problems with most of the etymologies in Martin 1972; even 'bathe' (MK :*kam-* : OJ *amuy-* < **amu-i-*) merits reconsideration. This question I will explore on another occasion.

TABLE 2

PJK	MK	OJ
*p	*p*	*p*
*t	*t*	*t*, but *s* before PJK **i* or **y*
*k	*k*	*k*
*c	*c*	*t*, but *s* before PJK **i* or **y*
*s	*s*	*s*
*š	*h*	*s*
*m	*m*	*m*
*n	*n*	*n*
*b	*p*	*w*
*d	*t*	*y-, [y]i-*
*g	*n*	*k*
*j	*c*	*y-, [y]i-*
*z	*s*	*[y]i-, -z-*
*y	*y*	*y-*
*-r-	*l*	*r*
*-l-	*l*	*s*

Whitman presumes a plausible sequence of changes in pre-MK:

1. Devoicing of *o, *u, and *i in noninitial syllables
2. Aspiration of obstruents before devoiced vowels in final position
3. Deletion (elision) of devoiced vowels in final position
4. Voicing of obstruents between sonants (vowels, semivowels, resonants):
   a. Plain obstruents become voiced
   b. Aspirated obstruents become voiced spirants

What about initial aspirated obstruents? The aspiration is correlated with loss of an initial devoiced vowel, the weak or minimal-quality *o or *u. It is to be noted that the MK weak vowels do not appear in word-initial position, except for *ustum* 'top, leader', an oddly shaped word of uncertain etymology.

   Granted this background, Whitman neatly accounts for the following comparisons:

MK ˙*pho˙lo-* (etc.) 'blue, green' : OJ *awo(-)* > MJ *.a˙wo.(-)* 'blue, green' = PKJ **o:bol-(/*ö:bör-)*
MK ˙*phul* 'grass' : OJ *awi* > MJ *awi, .awi-* 'indigo' = PKJ **o:bol/*öb:öl)*
MK ˙*phol(-˙i)* 'fly' : OJ *amu/abu* > MJ *.a˙bu.* (fall inferred) 'gadfly' < PKJ **o:mbor*
MK ˙*tho-* 'burn' : OJ *atu-* > MJ *.a.tu-* 'hot'
MK ˙*tho-* 'get, be sensitive/susceptible to' : OJ *ata-r-* (etc.) > MJ ˙*a˙tar-* (etc.)

And, assuming **hm* > *m* in Korean, even these (among others):

MK ˙*mah* 'yam' : OJ *umo* > MJ *umo/.imo* [?< **.i.mwo*] = PKJ **omogo* or **omago*
MK ˙*mas* (< **˙ma-s*) 'flavor' : OJ *uma-, ama-* > MJ *.u.ma-* 'delicious', ˙*a˙ma-* 'sweet' = PKJ **oma-*
MK *mah* 'rainy season' : OJ *amey* > MJ *.a˙me.* (with fall) 'rain' (< **.a˙ma-.i-*) = PKJ **o:mago*
MK ˙*spol-* 'suck' : OJ *sup-* > MJ *.su.w-* (spelled "*suf-*") 'suck' = PKJ **sopor-*
MK ˙*swusk* < **swuck* 'charcoal' : OJ *susu* > MJ *.su˙su(?.)* 'soot' = PKJ **süsük*

   Inevitably, many questions remain in the details of Whitman's treatment. For example, the vowel correspondences as stated do not seem to account for the vowels in two excellent etymologies that he cites without comment:

MK *.ep-* 'bear' : OJ *op-* > MJ *.ow-* (spelled "*of-*") 'bear'
MK *.cek* 'time' : OJ *toki* > MJ *.to.ki* 'time'

   In many respects, however, Whitman's conclusions are sound, and his productive approach opens up an exciting era of more rigorous and realistic comparison and reconstruction that promises to lift research on the genetic relationship of these two languages above the level of mere speculation.

ACCENT

One of the striking similarities between Korean and Japanese is that of the accent systems. From attestations of the eleventh century we know that late-Heian Japanese had a system of pitch accent patterns that differentiated words and phrases. To show that a syllable was low in pitch a dot was written at the lower left of the *kana* symbol; the upper left corner got the dot if the syllable was high pitched. In addition, a few words are noted with a dot in the upper right corner, and that is taken to have been a rise in pitch; in some texts there is evidence of a subtle notation (slightly raised low-left dot) that is believed to indicate a final fall in pitch. Both the rises and falls appear to be secondary in nature, often clearly the result of a compression of two syllables into one, so that sequences of high and low were realized on a single syllable. The patterns comprise two distinctive elements: the distinctive initial pitch and (optional) change of pitch at some later point; these are called, respectively, "register" and "locus" in Martin 1987. These patterns differentiated shorter words (of one to three syllables), which fall into accent types (at least five for disyllables) in a largely unpredictable way. Many longer words took canonical patterns, which were to some extent predictable, as was the accentuation of paradigmatic forms, given the basic accent assignment of the stem. The Middle Japanese accentual system survives in the modern language, but major changes merged certain types for most of the dialects, including those spoken in prestigious Kyōto and Tōkyō, and the phonetic realization of the distinctions vary. A few dialects, such as those of Kumamoto in Kyūshū and of Ibaraki in eastern Honshū, have independently lost the distinctions altogether.

Hankul writing of the fifteenth century was usually annotated with a similar system of dots to indicate pitch accent. The inspiration for these dots came from Chinese phonologists who, as early as the seventh century, developed a system of marking one of the four corners of a character to indicate its tone, which was an integral part of the pronunciation of a Chinese morpheme. With the names chosen less for descriptive than for mnemonic reasons (the words were themselves examples), the three tones of Middle Chinese were called "even," "rising," and "going," and the abrupt pronunciation of syl-

lables with a final unreleased stop (-*p* -*t* -*k*) were treated as a fourth
type, the "entering" tone. Where Japanese used both the high left
dot of the Chinese "rising" tone notation to mark their high pitch
and the low left dot of the Chinese "even" tone to mark their low
pitch, the Koreans left the low pitch unmarked and used the high
dot (the position of the dot is now irrelevant) to mark the high pitch.
They also marked certain syllables with a double dot, which we will
indicate with a colon before the romanized syllable; these syllables
were pronounced with a long rise, and often that can be shown to
come from a compression of two syllables (low-high) into one (rise)
either by crasis or by an apocope that leaves a stranded high pitch
to be realized as part of the surviving syllable. Many features of the
accent system of Middle Korean (= early Modern Korean) survive
in some of the modern dialects in the south and the east, but in the
central and northwestern parts there are only vestiges in the form
of vowel length (for the long low-rising), and even that has disappeared among younger Seoul speakers, who have vowel length only
from newer sources, such as contractions or English loanwords.

It should be emphasized that although the Japanese and Korean
adapted notational devices and used terminology ("even tone" for
the low pitch, "rising tone" for the high) developed in China, the
pitch accent systems of the two languages were not borrowed from
China, nor were they monosyllabic "tone" systems like that of classical Chinese. Throughout their history, Japanese have typically borrowed foreign words, including the vast horde of Chinese monosyllables, by adapting them to the polysyllabic open-syllable structure that characterizes historic Japanese and assigning them canonical
patterns that ignore accentual or tonal distinctions in the source language. Korean, on the other hand, was better suited to acquire the
Chinese monosyllables more or less intact, and they preserved the
major distinction of "even" versus "oblique" tones, of such importance in Chinese poetry. Chinese words that were of the "even" class
(over half the vocabulary of Middle Chinese) were pronounced with
the Korean low pitch and those of the "rising" and "going" tones
were generally given the long rising pitch marked by the double
dot; this distinction is partly preserved by older Seoul speakers,
who lengthen the first vowel of a word that begins with a Chinese
morpheme of the "rising" or "going" tone. The other kind of Chinese "oblique" tone was the abrupt "entering" tone, for syllables
ending in -*p* -*t* -*k*; unlike the Japanese (who generally added an epenthetic vowel), Koreans kept these words as closed monosyllables

ending in -*p*, -*l*,[2] and -*k* and in the fifteenth century marked them with the single dot that represented the high pitch. (We lack specific knowledge about the phonetic nature of the tones in Middle Chinese, which may have varied considerably in different dialects of the language, as they do in China today.)

Can we find correspondences between the pitch accent patterns of Korean and Japanese? Looking for that in lists of putative cognates, I came to negative conclusions in Martin 1975b, as earlier in Martin 1966, where I suggested that the accentual systems would have to be accounted for separately. The MJ system of patterns is much richer than that of the MK system, since each type has a mirror image in each of the two registers. Has Korean merged accentual distinctions of an earlier, richer system? Or is the MK system merely a continuation of earlier, nondistinctive prosodies that acquired some degree of distinctiveness as the result of changes in nonprosodic features, such as segmental shape? The skewness of distribution of the MK accent types, especially in the verb stems, indicates that many of the assignments earlier may have been predictable on the basis of morphophonemic shapes, as Ramsey's research has shown.

And yet two recent approaches offer new possibilities worth exploring. We have seen that Whitman, by using the interpretation of MJ low-initial register as vowel length, is able to set up a negative condition for the loss by Japanese of PKJ medial **r* and **m*. Can other phonological changes be found that require Korean high or low pitch as a condition? The second approach is found in recent work by Murayama who observes that:

1. Takayama's discovery of a correlation between the traditional Chinese tones of *Man'yō-gana* (phonograms) used to write poems in parts of *Nihon-Shoki* (720) with the tone marks in *Myōgi-shō* (1081) is taken to indicate that the phonetic accent of the Nara period was similar to that of the Heian: "even" was Low, "rising" was High.

---

[2] On the Korean treatment of MCh -*t* as -*l*, see K. M. Lee 1981 (p. 77), referring to an observation by Ligeti 1970 that the "Northern Wei had -*r* not -*t*". Staël-Holstein 1914 (p. 646) notes that the Chinese word for *Buddha* is transcribed in Tibetan as *phhur* and the word for *Boddhisattva* is transcribed as *sar* by the Uighur. It should be observed that the -*l* in the relatively unassimilated Chinese loans of the learnèd vocabulary in the fifteenth century was prescriptively written -*lq*, with addition of the symbol associated with the MCh glottal-stop initial—a spelling also given the native imperfect adnominal marker -(*u*)*lq* but not (normally) the accusative marker (*u*)*l*, perhaps because of the peculiar obstruent tensification that is projected by the adnominal suffix, a possible indication of absorption of the genitive -*s* (or -*t*), on which see Martin 1983.

TABLE 3

	Japanese	Korean[1]
LL (low atonic)		
'Buddha'	.fo.to.ke < *potokey	.pwu.thye
'district'	.ko.fo.ri < *kopori	.ko.wolh < *kopolh[2]
'ramie'	.mu.si	? .mo.si[3]
'bowl'	.fa.ti < *pati	.pa.li[4] (?< *pati) < Ch pwat < Skt pātra
LH (low tonic)		
'magpie'	.ka·sa-.sa.gi[5]	:ka·chi (?= .ka·[ ]·chi)
HH (high atonic)		
'ax'	*·na·ta 'ax'	·nat 'scythe'
HL (high tonic)		
'temple'	*·te.ra	·tyel[6]
'like'	·go.to(-) < *-n- koto	.kot (ho-)

[1] Since the low pitch was left unmarked in the Korean texts, the low dots in the citations are inferred. For Japanese words unattested in *Myōgi-shō* the accent is reconstructed from modern dialects or taken from Kamakura sources. I have reinterpreted, adapted, and supplemented some of Murayama's data. In the Korean reconstructions *u* and *o* are the unrounded *y* and *ǫ* and *wu* and *wo* are the rounded versions; I have ignored the vowel shift *wo* < *wu*. For both languages a low dot before a syllable marks the low pitch (L), and a high dot marks the high (H); double dots (.. and ··) indicate Japanese prenasalized initials; the preposed colon (:) marks the Korean low-rising tone R (= LH). The Old Japanese "*kō*" vowels are written as Cwo, Cye (or Ce), and Ci (= Cyi); the "*otsu*" vowels as Co (= Cǫ), Cey, Ciy.
[2] Cf. *cwokhoWol* (Lyong text 2: 22b) = *cwoh koWol[h]* 'Millet District'.
[3] Compare .*mo.si* ·*pwoy/woy* (Pak cho ?1517⁻).
[4] Murayama mistakenly gives this as .*pa·li*, perhaps following the mistake in Nam Kwangwu's dictionary. (The texts confirm [1]Yu Changton's version.)
[5] "A pair brought in from Shilla as a gift [in 598]" (*Nihon-Shoki*). Although -*sagi* has been taken as 'heron', perhaps this is a four-syllable borrowing that reflects earlier Korean *kacacakhi LHLL > *kaca[ca]hi LHL/LHH > *kac[a]hi RH.
[6] Probably from something like Middle Chinese *tsrhat* (→ Sino-Korean *chalq*) from Sanskrit *kṣetra*.

2. For several words probably borrowed from Korea before the eighth century, Murayama finds phonetic similarity between the eleventh-century Japanese accent and the fifteenth-century Korean accent (see Table 3). Murayama concludes that the phonetic accent patterns of earlier Korean were similar to those of the fifteenth century.

3. Murayama finds similar correspondences for words that may be early borrowings but perhaps are cognate (see Table 4).

Murayama has provided striking examples, but a word of caution is in order with respect to his conclusions. In the case of the probable loans, it should be kept in mind that throughout its history Japanese has imposed canonical accent patterns on foreign words, including those borrowed from China, disregarding the prosodic features of the source language. The history of each accentual system includes independent developments, such as the suggestion

TABLE 4

	Japanese	Korean
LL[1]		
'thing'	.ko.to 'fact'	.kes 'thing; fact'
'bear'	*.ku.ma[2]	:kwom ?< *.kwo˙ma
'island'	.si.ma[3]	:syem ?< *.sye˙mV[4]
'house'	.i.fe < ifye < *ifey < *ipa-Ci[5]	.cip
LH		
'melon'	.u˙ri	:woy < *.wo˙[C]i
'needle'	.fa˙ri < fari[y] < *paru-Ci	.pa˙nol
'field'	.fa˙ta < *pata[6]	.path
'spider'	.ku˙mo < *kunpo/*konpo	.ke˙muy
'shepherd's purse'	.na˙du-na < *nantu	.na˙zi
'not'	.a˙ni 'how . . .?!'	.a˙ni 'no, not'
	.na˙ni 'what; (not) anything'	
'morning'	.a˙sa (.ga) ?< *asa-CV LHL	.a˙chom
'father'	.o.fo-˙˙ti < *opo -n- ti[7]	.e.pe˙zi 'parent', .a˙pi 'father'
	'grandfather'	
'whale'	.ku˙˙ti.ra ?< *kunti-ra	.kwo.lay (?< *kwota[C]i LHL)
HH[8]		
'body'	˙mi < miy < *mu-Ci	˙mwom
'mouth'	.if- < *ip[a]- 'say'	˙ip 'mouth'

[1] Murayama compares the "low" accent of Korean pwok 'blowfish' with the "LL" of Japanese fuku (> fugu), but the lone attestation for the Korean accent is ˙pwok .kwo˙ki (Kup 2: 57b), which is high. The Japanese accent is hard to infer from available data: Tōkyō HL and Kyōto LF indicate *pukù, but Kagoshima "A" indicates the high register (*puku or *pūku). He also compares Korean .tak 'paper mulberry' with Japanese taku, for which he assumes LL because in Man'yō-shū 1233 it puns with the verb (kakagey) taku 'comb up into a bundle; row hard', but we have no way of knowing whether that verb stem was low register (type B) or high (type A). The Japanese noun is probably borrowed from the Korean, which in turn is borrowed from the Old Chinese *thiag (> Beijing chú).

[2] Compare .ku.ma-..taka ('bear hawk' =) 'crested eagle'.

[3] Paykcey *syema (To 1981: 29) is thought to be the source of the variant sema found in Nihon-Shoki. The Japanese word sima also meant 'quarters, territory' and may be related to sime- < simey- < *sima-Ci- 'occupy, stake out'.

[4] From *sima with vowel breaking, according to K. M. Lee 1959.

[5] This assumes that the eastern (Azuma) OJ version ifa < ipa was basic and the vowel -ye of central OJ was partially assimilated to the first vowel. The -Ci is a widely used noun suffix, which Whitman (among others) treats as just -i, like the Korean counterpart; the assumed consonant, which elided by the time of historic Japanese, was perhaps minimal, but I put it in my reconstructions for reasons set forth in Martin 1987. In that work I also call attention to the possibility that OJ ifo < ipo 'hut' is related and that OJ ya (together with the common Ryūkyū etymon for 'house') may have originated as a contraction i[w]a < ipa. But Whitman suggests that OJ ifye < ipye was likely contracted from a compound of *ip + ya, implying a separate etymology for the latter.

[6] Or fatake LHL < fatakey < *patakaCi is usually taken to be -ka(-Ci) 'place', but perhaps fata is a truncation of fatake. Notice -tVkey : -th in 'Buddha'.

[7] From *opo 'big' + adnominal marker + ti < *tiy < *to-Ci 'father'.

[8] Murayama offers 'mother' ˙e˙mi (also ˙e.ma-:nim) and omo 'mother' as HH, but there is no evidence for that accent. A hapax variant amo LH has been postulated from phonograms in Nihon-Shoki, but that may instead be a graphic quirk intended to be read as ame 'heaven'. Murayama also compares the word for 'rice field' ˙nwon with Japanese numa 'marsh', for which he reconstructs *HL accent, but the accent of numa (despite Kagoshima "A") should probably be reconstructed *LL on the basis of the short forms nu R = nuu LH, both in Myōgi-shō, and the compound numa-midu, Kamakura LLLL/LLLH. (Yet if this is from nu[ra]-ma 'wet place', we would expect the high register.) Korean nwon has also been compared with Japanese no < nwo 'field', clearly low register and so attested in Nihon-Shoki manuscript markings. This word interestingly belongs to a small group of short nouns in Hateruma (Yaeyama) that unexpectedly have a final nasal: /nuun/.

TABLE 5

	Japanese	Korean
HH(H) ≠ LH(H)		
'pot'	˙ka˙ma	.ka˙ma
'bee'[1]	˙fa˙ti	:pel ?< *pe˙lV
'star'	˙fo˙si	:pyelh ?< *.pyel˙hV
'mallow'	˙a˙fu˙fi < *apupi	.a˙wok (dial. apok, apuk; akwuk, akwok)[2]
HL(L) ≠ LH(H)		
'stone'	˙i.si	:twolh ?< *.twol˙hV
Additional examples, however, can be adduced to support his accent correspondences, such as		
(HH)		
'bamboo'	˙ta˙ke < *takey < *taka-Ci	˙tay < *˙ta˙(C)i[3]

[1] Whitman suspects that the accent of MK :pel indicates a contraction. Since the rising pitch is also given for the variant :pel-i, attested 1517 (Pak cho) and 1520 (Pen.yek Lo), that cannot be the source; :pel must have later attached the common suffix -i. Whitman compares the Japanese word for 'bee' with MK .pa˙to:li 'wasp', assuming a pre-MK doublet *˙pa˙tol/*˙pe˙tul (the latter version leading to the contraction in :pel(-i)) and reconstructing PKJ *patori/*petöri. (To what extent final -i in the various forms is to be treated as a suffix is unclear; a noun suffix -i is common in both languages and must have been present in the proto-language as well.) The Yonaguni form has the final fall of pitch that characterizes nouns that may have had a long vowel in Proto-Japanese, and so it is perhaps a similar but independent contraction.
[2] In phonograms of ca. 1350 (Hyangyak kwukup-pang) "a-pwu".
[3] Cf. Old Chinese tiog.

that Japanese low register came from distinctive vowel length and that the low-rising tone of Korean resulted from compression. The relative time depth of a proto-language ancestral to Japanese and Korean raises a serious question, in view of the relative instability of accentual systems in general and historically in these languages in particular. The statistical preponderance of certain types and the attraction of canonical forms increases the likelihood of accidental resemblances. Moreover, there are counterexamples to the correspondences that Murayama posits (see Table 5).

GRAMMATICAL ELEMENTS[3]

The grammars of Japanese and Korean are remarkably similar, so that it is easy to make word-to-word and even morpheme-to-morpheme translations between the two. The dissimilarities turn out to be relatively trivial or to disappear when older varieties and dialects of each

[3] In the earlier part of this chapter V stood for "vowel" (as opposed to C consonant), but in this discussion and in Table 6 it means "verb".

language are taken into account. The syntax is a model example of the object-verb language, with modifier preceding modified, with the predicate at the end, and with the relationship between the adjuncts (the noun phrases) and the predicate shown by postpositional particles, by ellipted postpositions, or (as with adverbs) left unmarked. A set of "adverbial" particles mark the focus of the adjunct beyond its predicate, contrasting or entailing the adjunct(s) or possible adjunct(s) of other predicates or possible predicates, as exemplified by the Japanese particles *mo* 'even, also, . . .' and *wa* 'as for, with respect to, when it comes to, . . .'. The order of adjuncts is relatively free within the simplex, so that the subject can follow the object though the semantically unmarked order is the other way. Nouns, being names, can occur without markers, but the predicating parts of speech are stems that normally must be followed by suffixes to form the predicate. These parts of speech are the verb, the adjective, and the essive, which functions as simply a noun predicator, a kind of semantically minimal way to turn a noun into a predicate. The Korean essive serves as the modern "copula" stem *i-*; historically the Japanese copula is a complex structure that incorporates the auxiliary *ar-* 'be' to the essive infinitive *ni* or its extension *ni-te*, with later contractions to the modern irregular paradigm of *da*, *de*, *ni*, and so on. Ellipsis of the copular expression is common in Japanese, often leaving behind an emphatic sentential particle such as *yo* 'mind you' or *zo* 'indeed' as the only marker. The paradigms of the three Korean predicators are virtually identical, except that the adjective and the copula lack certain verbal categories, such as imperative 'do it!'; hortative 'let's do it!'; and processive 'is doing'. Although the paradigmatic categories of the Japanese adjective seem similar to those of the verb, the suffixes themselves are quite different, and the paradigm appears to have developed largely out of contractions of nominalizers (*-ku*, *-sa*, and earlier *-mi*) in construction with the auxiliary verb *ar-* 'be', as explained in Martin 1987, Chapter 7. In addition to the expected adnominalizations of the predicated adjectives, Korean has a fair number of adnouns, such as say 'new', which may be directly preposed to modify a noun, since one noun may directly modify another noun without recourse to the "genitive" particle *uy* or the adnominalized copula *in*. These phenomena are not obvious in modern Japanese, except insofar as they can be said to underlie compound nouns, but in Old Japanese the adjective stem was relatively free and could modify the noun by direct juxtaposition or with the mediation of "genitive" particles, as well as by using the adnominalizing suffix of the paradigm (*-ki*).

The verbal suffixes relate the predication to the speaker's perception of the situation (time, aspect, likelihood, deference toward predicate subject or toward listener, affirmation/interrogation, command/exhortation) or to its place in the discourse: finality, nominalization and its handmaiden adnominalization, adverbialization, and various kinds of conjoining ('and also', 'and then', 'and so', 'and yet') that are often ambiguous, vague, or elusive in meaning. The developmental history of the verbal paradigms in each language shows considerable variation, with new shapes replacing old forms in familiar categories, with new categories arising, and with changes in the function and meaning of old categories. The verbal paradigms are intermittently enriched by the contraction of complex structures that incorporate auxiliary stems: the contemporary past-tense suffixes Japanese -*ta* and Korean -*ess*- incorporate the respective existential stems (*ar*- and *iss*- 'be') by compressions that took place at different times and, it seems, quite independently.

The etymological relationship of particular verbal suffixes may be obscured by the migration of shapes and functions through time and in different dialects. That is true also of the noun postpositions, such as the case-marker particles, where disparate elements can be seen to overlap or totally share a functional area: in Japanese the particles *ga* and *no* serve to adnominalize (the "genitive" case), to nominalize (extruded 'the one that'; summational 'the fact that'; direct 'the doing/being'), or to mark a particular valence ("nominative case"), and the exact differentiation between them varies from dialect to dialect throughout the history of the language. In modern Korean the nominative marker has two shapes that are in complementary distribution, *i* after a consonant and *ka* after a vowel; but four centuries ago the shape *i* was used after vowels too, and there it normally lost its syllabicity (. . . $i \rightarrow$ . . . *y*), while the other shape *ka* went virtually unattested in written Korean before foreign missionaries noticed it in the nineteenth century. The instability of the categories and the volatility of the shapes pose problems in the comparison of the grammatical elements of the two languages. In Table 6 I list certain groups of grammatical morphemes that deserve investigation. Under each group the cogent forms are cited for both languages when a common prehistory of the shapes seems likely. By its very nature, the material poses many problems, some of which are addressed in the notes, and I have not hesitated to temper my judgments with question marks.

TABLE 6
Grammatical Elements

Korean	Japanese
1. Genitive/nominative particles	
1.1. $\cdot^u/_oy$?< [G]y < *ka i[1]	
1.2. ka[2] ?< ·ka(/·kwo) 'question' or (= ·kwot) 'place'; ? ''borrowed from Japanese ga''	ga < n ka (?< ka 'question' or -ka 'place')
1.3. ·i < postadnom. i 'one/fact/ person' (9.2) ?< ·i/ywo 'this (one)'	(i)[3]
1.4. s ?< [ke]s, ?< postadnom. so/to 'fact'	tu[4]
NUMERAL -s[5]	NUMERAL -tu
1.5. —	no ?< [mo]no 'thing'[6]; ? Azuma adominal of essive ni 'be'; ?< n[-i ar-]o essive inf. + existential/aux. adnominal

---

[1] Just the opposite of the later (pleonastic) . . . i ka → y ka, as in nay ka < na i ka 'I'. The -G- represents a voiced laryngeal (or velar) fricative that was only indirectly evinced by the fifteenth-century orthography; it vanished early but left traces by blocking an expected liaison in the spelling of l followed by i, y, or z.

[2] The origin of the suppletive relationship between ka and i in modern Korean is a perplexing question; orthographic use of . . . i (or "y") after a vowel obviously continued long beyond the period in which this was the spoken norm. Whether the substitution of . . . ka was brought in by Hideyoshi's invaders is a difficult question. Kim Hyengkyu 1954 imputes two instances to the Koryŏ songs (sok.ka) "Twongtwong" and "Sekyeng pyelkwok," but this has not been confirmed. There is but a single example in the early Hankul texts: ·qilq-·chyey ·ka 'all [believe]' (1463 Pep-hwa 1: 120), explicating a Chinese passage in which the Hankul grammar annotation places the emphatic subject marker yza (< i za). The next attestations are a few from the latter half of the seventeenth century, such as poy ka wol kes in i 'the boat will probably come' (1676 Chep-hay sin-e 1: 8), translating a Japanese sentence. I am tempted to think that . . . ka was there all along, perhaps as a colloquial emphatic. Modern -uni-kka (n) = -uni 'because' is believed to be a semantic extension of -ni-s-ka (question), and -ta-ka = -ta 'and then; only when' is said to be a direct attachment of the infinitive of taku- 'bring near', but a reexamination of those etymologies may be in order. Compare the development of the meaning 'but' for Japanese ga and the antithetical uses of nominative- and accusative-marked nominalizations in both languages. On the Korean i/ka see Kim Panghan 1957; Nam Kwangwu 1957; L. S. Lee 1958; Kim Hyengkyu 1954 and 1964, who attributes the modern rise of ka to avoidance of hiatus; Hamada 1970; Hong Yuncak 1975; and S. U. Lee 1981, who would derive ka from the verb ka- 'go'. See also Se Cengmok 1982 on subject marking in MK subordinate clauses and, on the genitive particles, An Pyenghuy 1968 and Kim Sungkon 1971.

[3] A particle i meaning 'in particular (that . . .)' has been postulated as an emphatic subject marker for Old Japanese; in the Man'yō-shū examples it is usually followed by the focus particles fa or si. Later it was used only in Kanbun reading aids (annotations). Etymologically this can be identified with the postadnominal (9.2); aru-i-wa 'or; perhaps' is a relic of the structure. And maybe the morpheme is present in the verb form . . . ey [-ba/-do] < *. . . a-i (?< *-Ci).

[4] Already fairly fossilized in Old Japanese, the particle tu is often treated as specifically a "locative genitive" (nifa tu tori 'the bird in the yard' = 'chicken'), but there are a few examples that point to a wider use (such as asatuki 'chives' < asa tu ki 'mild onion' with the adjective stem asa-).

[5] Korean :seys 'three', :neys 'four', and .ye·les 'several' occur without the -s before a noun (and Japanese numerals usually lack the -tu before a noun), but tases < .ta·sos 'five' and yeses < *.yo·sos 'six' are usually intact. Matters are further complicated by the occurrence of -h rather than -s in .ho.nah 'one' (just .hon before a noun), :twulh ?< *.twu·pel 'two' (:twu before a noun), ·su·mulh 'twenty' (·su·mu before a noun, and yelh 'ten'; also, by earlier versions with -h and -k (:sek = :seh 'three', :nek = :neh 'four') or just -h (.ye·leh 'several').

[6] Perhaps the postadnominal no 'one, fact/thing/person/ . . .', which is a kind of resumptive pro-

(continues)

TABLE 6
(*Continued*)

Korean	Japanese
1.6.　?— (cf. 8.1, 13.4)	n^7; *n tu* > -*zu*- 13.4; *n ka* > *ga* 1.1
1.7.　$\stackrel{\cdot}{\text{—}}$	*na* ?< *n[i] a[r-]*
2. Accusative[8] particles	
2.1.　$(\,)l^9$?< [*ho*]-*lq* 'to say/do/be';	
?< $(\,)lwo$ 'to/toward; as'	
2.2.　—	[*w*]*o* ?< **bo*[10]; *wo si-te*
2.3.　—	[*wo*] *ba* < *n pa* (see 5.2; focus)
3. Allative/dative particles	
3.1.　$\cdot^e/_ay$?< $\cdot[G]ay$ < $\cdot^*ka$ 'place' *i*	—
(= 1.1)[11]	
3.2.　*kkey* < *skuy* < *s k[u-ngek]* $\cdot ey$	—
(< . . .)	
3.3.　*eykey* < $^u/_oykey$ < $^u/_oy$-*kungey*	—
$^u/_oy$ (< . . . 1.1) *ku-ng[ek] ey*	
(< . . . 3.1)	
3.4.　*hanthey* < *hant* $^e/_ay$ < *hon·toy* =	—
.ho.n[ah] ·toy 'one/same place'	
3.5.　—	*ni* < essive (infinitive)
3.6.　—	*e* < *fe* < *fye* < **pe* 'direction, vicinity'
3.7.　—	*sa* (dial.) ?< *sa[ma]* 'way, direction'
3.8.　—	*made* (*ni*) < *mante* ?< **ma n *ta-Ci* 'both
	hands > completely'
3.9.　*kkaci* < *skoci* (1600s) < *.sko·cang*	— (Amami *kati* probably not related)
< *s .ko·cang* 'its end/limit'; cf.	
:*kos* 'brink' < **.ko·so* ? =	
*.ko·co (cf. J *.ki.si* 'cliff, shore')	

noun, has a different source from the particle in its other uses (and from the copula alternant). But notice that all uses of *ga* and *no* are shared by each in one dialect at one time or another. (Kōchi uses *ga* as the postadnominal.)

[7] The Proto-Japanese particle *n* (not necessarily a contraction of the genitive /*no*/), is the major source of *rendaku*, a device realized in later Japanese as voicing and/or nasality in the initial obstruent of the second element of a compound.

[8] In Korean sometimes used for dative or allative: *Na l cwe* 'Gimme!'; *Hak.kyo lul ka* 'Go to school!'

[9] Miller 1977 would give us an Altaic etymology based on the "Old Korean accusative *hel*," but that is a ghost form based on mistaking noun-final -*h* for the initial of the particle. The answer must lie elsewhere. The interpretation of the early songs is highly controversial, and we would do well to treat forms claimed to be "Old Korean" with caution. On the case markers in this material, see Pak Pyengchay 1965, who has no *h*- for the accusative. (If the *h*- were genuine, it could be used in favor of my highly problematic hunch that the accusative may have developed from a contraction of the verb form *ho-lq*.)

[10] Japanese *wo* has been treated as an expletive ('lo . . . !'), but the Manchu accusative particle *be* is a likely cognate. Notice also Korean *pwo*- 'look' ('lo' is short, after all, for 'look!'). An outside possibility is that *wo* may simply be an assimilated version of *wa* < **pa* despite the problems of chronology *wa* < ?*fa* < **pa*.

[11] This treats $\cdot^u/_ay$ and $\cdot^e/_ay$ as variant reductions of the same string but leaves open the question whether *ka* is from 'place' in the genitive as well as the dative. An alternative explanation of the

TABLE 6
(*Continued*)

Korean	Japanese
3.10. Others (*tele, pwokwo,* etc. < verb forms)	(phrasal *ate ni, ni si-te, ni —-te,* etc.)

4. Ablative (/locative) particles

4.1. (*ey*) *se* < ·*sye* < [.*i*]·*sye* < *pisi-e

4.2. (*ey*) .*pu·the* < .*puth-·e*

4.3. —   *kara* ?< ·*ka.ra* 'trunk; shell; handle'

4.4. —   .*yori, yuri; yo, yu* (also traversal) < ?

4.5. —   *ni-te* (locative) < 'being', etc.

5. Focus particles: subdued focus

5.1. *n*(*Vn*) ?< [*ho*]*n* 'say' (*cf. ilan* <   See adnominalizers (8)
     i-la [*ho*]*n*)

5.2. -*n* ·*pa* 'situation'   ·*wa* < *fá* < *pa 'as for'; cf. . . . (*no*) *ba-ai*
                           'as for' < *n pa + *afyi* < *ap[*a-C*]*i, ba*
                           'place' < *(*V-i*) *n pa* (e.g., *ari-ba*)

6. Focus particles: highlighted focus

6.1. ·*two* 'even; also; indeed; yet,   (*V-ey*) *do* < *n to* 'even if (*V*)' (?= .*to*
     but'   'that' 9.6)
                              ?*zo* (> Ryūkyū *du*) 'indeed, indeed be'
                            (or = ·*so* 'that' 9.6, 12.3) ·*to*[·*ko*(·*ro*)]
                            'place/situation; but'

6.2 (-)·*toy* 'even though' ?< ·*toy*
     'place'

6.3. — ? cf. 13.6 .*mu*(·*es*)   *mò* 'even; also; indeed; yet, but' ?<
                            mo[*no*] '[very] thing';[12] ?< *mu[-*Ci*]
                            'body, self' (> *miy* > *mi*)

6.4. —   *mai* (Miyako) ?< *madi* < *made* (= 3.7)

7. Focus particles: spotlighted focus

7.1. ·*kwos* 'precisely, just'   *koso* 'precisely, just' (? .*kosò*, ? ·*ko.so*)

7.2. *ya*/*iya* < ·*i*[·*z*]*a*, dial. *sa* < (*i*/*l*)   ?*zo* < *so*/*zo* < (*n*) *so* 'indeed, is indeed;
     za < *sa 'precisely, just,   (?< *so* 'that'); OJ *si* 'indeed' (?< *si ga*
     indeed'[13]   'that; you')

8. (Ad)nominalizers

8.1. -*n* (perfect) 'done, been'   -*n* (Amami *a-n, wu-n*)

8.2. -*lq* (imperfect) '(to) do/be'   -*r* (Amami *a-r, wu-r*)

---

genitive would treat it as a junctured variant of the nominative *i*, with the minimal vowel ᵘ/ₒ, as usual, epenthetic.

[12] A derivation *mo* < ·*mo.no* would be supported by the Heian accent, F < HL. But the noun 'thing' was .*mo.no* LL in the eleventh century and only became Kyōto ·*mo.no* HL around 1350.

[13] Ross King calls attention to the Turkish particle *ise* 'as for . . .', which "is used . . . to direct attention to the preceding word" (Underhill 1976: 416). The Turkish particle is said to be the conditional auxiliary -*sᵉ*/ₐ attached to "the stem *i*-" (*Ibid.* 412) so that the underlying meaning appears to be 'if it be'; the Korean particle sometimes means 'only if it be'. I have assumed that the first syllable of *iza* is the nominative *i*, since all the examples appear to be subjects; the few direct-object examples are with *za* (Sek 19: 30) or (*o*)*l za* (Kok 52).

(*continues*)

TABLE 6
(*Continued*)

Korean	Japanese
8.3. -*m* (future[14]/definite) '(will) do/be'	-*m* (Amami *a-m*, *wu-m*) -(*a*)-*mu* > -*an*/*aũ* > -ɔɔ[15] (future/ hortative/tentative)
9. Postadnominal nominalizers	
9.1. .*kes* (abstract/concrete)	.*ko.to* (abstract only)
9.2. ·*i* (abstract/person),[16] cf. 1.3	·*i* (abstract) in *aru-i-wa* 'or; perhaps'; cf. 1.3
9.3. ·*pa* (situation, circumstance)	See 5.2
9.4. *tey* (place, circumstance; but) < ·*toy*; ·*theh* 'site, place; intention'	·*to·ko*[·*ro*] 'place, circumstance; but'
	?*to* '(felt/said to) be; as; and' (subjective essive)
	?*to* 'with' (reciprocal)
9.5. —	*no* 'fact/thing/one that' ?< [.*mo*].*no*
9.6. *so*/*to* (fact; cf. ·*to* = ·*toy* 'place')	*so*/*su* (Shimane, Yamaguchi) 'thing/one that'; Ryūkyū *si* < *su* (Amami *na-si* 'yours', *qar ga si* 'his'; Okinawa V-*și ga* 'but')
	to (Kagoshima) 'thing/one that'
9.7. *ci* < ·*ti* < *to* + ·*i*	—
9.8. ·*ka*/·*kwo* (question)	*ka* (question)
9.9. ·*ya*/·*ywo*/·*i* (question)	*ya* (question)
9.10. ·*ta* (question)	— (cf. 13.2)
9.11. .*cek* 'time (when)'	.*to.ki*
9.12. ·*kwot* 'place'[17]	·*ko-·ko* 'here'; .*so-·ko* 'there' (cf. 12)
10. Nominalizer/adverbializer	
10.1. -·*kwo*[18] Cf. ·*kwot* 'place' (9.12)	(Adj)-*ku* '(so as) to be; being' (V*a*)-*ku* ?= V-*r*[*u*] *aku* 'doing'
10.2. -·*ki* ?< -·*ti*[19]	—
10.3. -*key* < -·*k*ᵘ/ₒ*y* ?< *-ka i* (cf. 1.1)	—

[14] As in *Cwum a* 'I will give it to you'. As a literary nominalization, -*m* is equivalent to modern (-*n*) *kes* and can serve as a sentence-final form. The connective -*mye* (= -*kwo*) is -*m* + copula infinitive *i-e*, and -*mulo* 'because' is -*m* + particle ( )*lwo*.

[15] The modern allomorph -*yoo* was created by analogy with *si-yoo*, a conflation of Muromachi *syoo* < *sye-u* < *se*-[*m*]*u* 'will do'.

[16] The postadnominal *i* 'fact' is used in the nominalization that serves as the favorite sentence form in sixteenth-century Korean with or without the copula: *·n i* ([*i*]*la*), *-l i* ([*i*]*la*), and so on. The suffix *-i* makes derived nouns or adverbs in Korean; Japanese derives nouns from the infinitive V-*i* (?< *-Ci*).

[17] But .*ke·kuy* 'there', .*ce·kuy* 'there', and .*ye·kuy* 'here' are not simply contractions of .*ku ·kwot ey* and so on but require a more complicated derivation: .*k*[*u*.*nge*]·*kuy* (also .*ku·ng*[*ek*]*uy*) from .*ku .ngek ·uy*, with a mysterious bound noun *ngek* 'place' (cf. .*nyekh* 'direction').

[18] The function of Korean -*kwo* is mostly equivalent to Japanese -*te*, though the infinitive (-*e*) is used, as -*i* in earlier Japanese, in many structures where modern Japanese would have -*te*. The form -*te* is taken to be a particle derived from the infinitive of the auxiliary *tu*(*ru*), but that is open to question. Earlier the particle was limited to *si-te*, *ni-te*, *to-te*, and *sa-te*; only the first two have the particle attached to an infinitive ('do' and 'be' respectively).

[19] In modern Korean the nominalizations -*ki* and -*ci* (< -*ti*) are complementary in syntactic distri-

TABLE 6
(*Continued*)

Korean	Japanese
11. Quotative particle	
11.1. *kwo* < [.*ho*-]·*kwo* 'saying'	—
11.2. (—)	*to* 'that (it be)' ?< 9.4.; ?< *to* = *so* 'that'
12. Deictics/anaphorics (semantically skewed)	
12.1. ·*i* / *yo* 'this' (cf. 1.3, 9.2)	— (cf. 9.2)
12.2. .*ku* (?< *ke*) / *kwo* 'that; it, he/ she'	·*ko* 'this'
12.3. *ce* < ·*tye* / *cwo* 'yon; obvious'	·*so*, *to* 'that' but .*so*·*ko* 'there' (despite ·*so*·*re*)
12.4. —	[*k*]*a*(-) 'yon; obvious'
12.5. .*e*·*nu*, :*en*- 'which; (not) any'	*i*-, *i*-*n*- 'which; (not) any': see 13.3, 13.4
13. Indeterminatives (= interrogative/ indefinites)	
13.1. ·*nwu* 'who; (not) anyone' (·*nwu* .*kwo* → *nwukwu*)	.*na*·*ni* 'what' ?< *na(*n*), ?< *na ani; ·*na-zo*; Ryūkyū *nuu, noo, nau, nayu* < *na-[*d*]*u* < *na-do = *na-zo*
13.2. — (cf. 9.10)	·*ta*(-·*re*) 'who' (→ *dare* 1800s); Ryūkyū *taa, too* < *ta[*r*]*u*, *taru* < *ta-du < *ta-do < *ta-zo = *ta* ³/₍*o*²⁰
13.3. *e*- 'wh. . .'; *e-ti* < .*e*- ·*toy* 'where'	*i*- 'wh. . .'; .*i*-*tu* < *i-to[*ki*] 'when'; ·*i*-.*ku*-.*ra* 'how much' (?< *i- *ika* -[*a*]*ra*), *i-ku-tu* (?< *i- *ika* - *tu*)²¹
13.4. .*e*-·*nu* 'which'; :*en.cey* < .*e*·*nu.cey* < .*e*-·*nu* .*ce.k uy* 'when'	*i-n*- 'wh. . .'; *i -n-tu - ko* > .*i*·*du*·*ko* (→ *idoko* → *doko*) 'where'; *i-n-tu - ti* > *iduti* (→ *duti → *doti* → *dotti*) 'which way'; *i -n-tu -re* > .*i*·*du*·*re* (→ *dure → *dore*) 'which one'²²

bution, as elegantly shown by S. C. Song, but the phonological environment is irrelevant; that indicates probable suppletion (morphemes of different origins sharing a function) or a doublet, with two competing versions of the same morpheme now used in complementary structures. The latter is probably the case. What seems to have happened is that there were dialects in the fifteenth century, as there are today, with a tendency to palatalize a velar before *i* or *y*. As a reaction to that assimilation (perhaps felt to be sloppy?) there were back-formations giving a false velar for an original apical affricate (*ci* → *ki*) or stop (*ti* → *ci* > → *ki*), for which there are other examples, such as modern *kimchi* (first attested around 1834) ← (·)*tim*·*choy* (attested 1527) < *cim-choy from Sino-Korean morphemes *chim* 'submerge' (hence 'pickle') + :*choy* 'vegetables'. The early texts offer very few examples of -*ki* (+ case particle), but structures that would have -*ki* in the modern language had -*ti* (without the case marker, in the examples I have seen). The first edition of ^*Nokeltay* (known as "*Pen.yek* ⌐*Nokeltay*"), to be dated before 1517, has examples of -*ti* for -*ki*, but it also has examples of -*ki* with the negative auxiliary *mal*-, where one would expect -*ti*. The two forms may have been competing: ·*ka*·*ki* (:)*mal*·*la* (1: 26) = [·]*ka*·*ti* :*mal*·*la* (2: 7) 'don't go!' The palatalization of *ti* (and *ty*) to *ci* (and *cy*) is said to have taken place around the end of the seventeenth century (K. M. Lee 1962b: 269) but An Pyenghuy 1957 found examples of *c* for *ty* (and *chy* for *thy*) in the 1632 edition of *Twu-si enhay*. What relationship, if any, may exist between -*ti* and the postadnominal *so/to* (9.6) is unclear.

²⁰ Cf. *tasokare-doki* 'twilight, dusk < time when [one must ask] who he?'

²¹ Cf. *ika-hodo* 'how much', (*do*-)*ika*- 'huge'; *iku*- = *nan*- 'how much/many . . .'.

²² The suffix -*re* is a truncation < *are[*y*] < *ara-Ci 'the existent'; a variant reduction yielded

(*continues*)

TABLE 6
(*Continued*)

Korean	Japanese
13.5. :*es-·ti* < .*e-·s·ti* 'how' (?< 9.7); :*es-te* < :*es·tye* < .*e-·s·ti* [*ho-*]*ye*	—
13.6. .*mu·es* < .*mu·es* < .*mu·ses* < .*mu·su* [.*k*]*es* (also .*mu·su* *k*[*es*]) 'what' (= .*mu·sus*)	—? cf. *mono, mo*
13.7. ·*myech* 'how much/many' ?< .*mu i ech*	
13.8. :*a.mwo*, :*a.mo* 'any' ?< *.*a·ni* .*mu* 'not what'	—? cf. *nani mo* 'nothing'; *nani-mono* 'what thing'
14. Negatives	
14.1. .*a·ni* 'not'	?.*a·ni* 'how . . . ?!'; .*na·ni* 'what; (not) anything' ·*na-*(.*ku*) 'be(ing) lacking, nonexistent' V*a-n*(*a*)- 'not V'; -*ni*, -*nu*, -*zu* < *-*ni su*, -*zi* < *-*ni si na* V *so* = V-*u na* 'don't V!'
14.2. :*eps-* 'not be' < *:*e-.p*[*i*]*si-* ?< .*a·*[*n*]*i* ?= 13.3 (but accent?), ?— 13.4	
14.3. :*mwot* 'not possibly, not at all' ?< .*mwo·tV* = .*mwot-·a* 'altogether'	.*mo·da sù* 'be silent, decline to speak' ?< *monta*
14.4. :*mal-* ?< *.*ma·lo-* 'cease, finish; desist, refrain, don't!'	·*ma.na* 'don't' (Heian *Kanbun* reading aid); V-*u mai* < ·*ma··si* ?< *ma*[*si*]-*zi* (? = V*a-ma-* future + *si* + -*n*[*i*]-*si* neg.) 'let's not; probably not' ·*ma-·ma* 'as is, undisturbed' (postadnominal)
15. Existential verbs; perfect auxiliary	
15.1. *iss-* < .*is-* < .*i.si-* < *pisi-* 'be' V-*ess-* < V-·*es-* < V-·*e* .*is*[*i*]-	·*wi*[*y*]- ?< *bᵘ/₀-*Ci*- (or ?< *bida-*) 'be, stay, sit' [dial.] V*yoru* < V-*i wor-* (< *wi*[*y*] *ar-* < . . .)
15.2. — (? perhaps .*a-* of .*a·ni* 14.1, or :*a-* of :*a.mo* 13.8	.*a-*(*r*)- 'be' OJ V-*er-* < V-*i ar-* V(*i*)-*ta* < V-*i ta*[*r-*] < V-*i te ar-* (< . . .)
16. Proverb	
16.1. ·*ho-* (inf. ·*ho·ye*) 'do; say; be' ?< *hyo-* < *syo-* *sikhi-* < .*si·ki-* 'cause to do/be' ?= *si-ki-* < *syo-ki-*	·*su-/si-/se-* < *so-* 'do; [dial.] say; (be)'[23]

---

*ari > -*ri* in *hito-ri* 'one person' (< *fitori* < *pito* [*a*]*r*[*a*-*C*]*i*) 'one person'. *Dore* is attested 1216.
The adnoun *do-no* 'which' (attested 1264) < *do*[*re*] *no*. The /u/ → /o/ in these words is by analogy
with (*i*)*doko*, where the penultimate vowel assimilates to the color of the final vowel. For the
double genitive -*n-tu*- see 1.6, 1.4.
[23]Korean *ho-* is used to predicate both verbal and adjectival nouns (including the -*ti* nominaliza-

TABLE 6
(*Continued*)

Korean	Japanese
17. Causative/passive formants	
17.1. -*ki*-, -*hi*-, -*Gi*-, -*i*- (= *-$y^u/_o$-) / -*y*-	V*e*[*y*]- < V*a*-[C]*i*, V*i*[*y*]- < V*o*-C*i* or V*u*-C*i*-
17.2. -$G^u/_o$-, -$Gw^u/_o$-, -$w^u/_o$-, -$hw^u/_o$-	—
17.3. -*y*-*Gi*-, -*y*-*Ga*-, -*y*-$Gw^u/_o$-, -*y*-*hwo*-	
17.4. -*hi*-*i*, -*Go*-*y*-, $Gw^u/_o$-*y*-	
18. Bound auxiliary: honorific (subject-exalting)	
18.1. -$^u/_o$*si*-	V*a*-*s*(*a*)- ?< *-*si*-
19. Personal pronouns	
19.1. ·*na* 'I/me' (?← 19.4)	—
19.2. —	*wa* ?= *wá*, .*wa*-·*re*, *wanu* < *ba(*n*) 'I/me'
19.3. .*ce* '(I my)self' < Ch (= Sino-Korean *ca* of *ca*-*ki*, *ca*-*sin* 'oneself')	— (Sino-Japanese *zi* of *zi*-*ko*, *zi*-*sin*, *zi*-*bun*, etc.)
19.4. ·*wu*·*li* 'we' ?< *uti, ?< :*wulh i* 'fence[-inside] person'	·*u*·*ti* 'in(group), home'
19.5. .*ne* 'you'	(·)*na*, ·*na*·*n*·*zi* < *na*-*muti* 'you'
20. Plural markers	
20.1. ·*tolh* 'group (of people/things)'	?.*ta*·*ti* 'group (of people)'; OJ . . . *doti* 'like folk, fellow . . . s' ?< *[*tomo*]*doti* < *tomo*-*dati* < *tomo n tati 'friends'
20.2. -:*huy* of .*ne*-:*huy* 'you all' and .*ce*-:*huy* 'we all'	—
20.3. —	(-)*ra* 'group (of people/demonstratives)' < -*ra* 'quantity'[24] (*iku*-*ra*) < *[*a*]*ra* 'existent' noun < verb 'be'

tions); adjectives are differentiated from verbs only by lacking such forms as imperative, hortative, and processive (-*no*-*n*, -*n*-*ta*). Japanese *su*-/*si*-/*se*- predicates verbal nouns (but some may have stative meanings 'be . . .'), and adjectival nouns attach the copula *ni ar*-. The verb infinitive can be predicated with (V-*i*) . . . *suru*, but the adjective is predicated with (A-*ku*) . . . *aru*. Nouns are predicated with the copula *i*- in Korean and with *ni* (*ar*-) in Japanese. I trace the irregular allomorphs of the Japanese verb back to a stem *so, found in the old prohibitive *na* V-*i so* 'don't': *si* < *s[*o*-C]*i*, *su*(*ru*) < *s[*o*]-*u*(*ru*); *se*-*mu* < *so-*mu*, *se*-*nu* < *so-*nu* (vowel fronted).

[24] As in *iku*-*ra* 'how much'. There are a goodly number of nouns that incorporate the suffix -*ra*, essentially meaning 'that which is . . .', such as *takara* 'treasure' < 'that which is high/costly', *sakura* 'cherry tree' < 'that which blooms', and *makura* 'pillow' < 'that which one pillows oneself with'; also *ko*-*ti*-*ra* 'this direction/way' (and deictic set). Related is the use of the infinitive-derived noun *ari < *ara-[C]*i* 'that which exists' in two contracted versions: the -*re* of *ko*-*re* 'this one' (and deictic set) and the -*ri* of *hito*-*ri* 'one person', for which there is a parallel in Old Turkish *er* 'man' and *er*- 'exist', a likely cognate of *ar*-. Attempts to find cognates for Japanese -*ra* in Altaic (or other) "plural suffixes" are ill advised.

290 S. E. MARTIN

REFERENCES CITED

An Pyenghuy. 1957. "Cwung-kan Tu-si enhay ey nathanan t kwukay-
umhwa ey tay-ha.ye." *Ilsek [1] Yi Huysung sensayng songswu kinyem [1] nonchong* 329–342.
———. 1968. "Cwungsey kwuk.e uy sok.kyek emi ey tay-ha.ye." *[1] Yi Swungnyeng paksa songswu kinyem [1] nonchong* 337–411.
Hamada Atsushi. 1970. "Shukaku-joshi *ka* seiritsu no katei." *Chōsen-shiryō ni
yoru Nihon-go kenkyū* 255–286.
Hong Yuncak. 1975. "Cwuqkyek emi '-ka' ey tay-ha.ye." *Kwuk.e-hak* 3: 65–92.
Kim Hyengkyu. 1954. "Cwuqkyek tho 'ka' ey tay-han soko." *Choy Hyenpay
sensayng hwankap kinyem [1] nonmun-cip*, 93–107. Seoul: Sasangkyey-sa.
———. 1964. "'Ka' cwuqkyek tho uy tay-han kochal," *Kwuk.e-sa yenkwu*, ed.
3, 199–211. Seoul: Sasangkyey-sa.
Kim Panghan. 1957. "Kwuk.e cwuqkyek cepmi-sa 'i' ko caylon." *Hakswul-en
[1] nonmun-cip* 5: 32–61.
Kim Sungkon. 1971. "Tho-ssi 'oy/uy' uy palqtal ul salphim." *Hankul Hak.hoy
50-tol kinyem [1] nonmun-cip* 185–200.
Lee, Ki-Moon [= [1] Yi Kimun]. 1959. "On the Breaking of *i in Korean."
Aseya Yenkwu 11 (2): 131–137.
———. 1964. "Materials of the Koguryo Language." *Journal of Social Sciences
and Humanities, Korean Research Center* 20: 11–20.
———. 1972. *Kwuk.e-sa kaysel*. Revised ed. Seoul: Mincwung Sekwan.
———. 1980. "Arutai-syogo to Kankoku-go—sono hikaku-kenkyū ni tsuite
no shōken." *Kyōto Sangyō-daigaku Kokusai Gengo-kagaku Kenkyū-jō shohō*
1 (3): 104–112.
———. 1981. "[1]Itwu uy kiwen ey tay-han il-kochal." *Cintan hakpo* 51: 65–78.
Lee, Seung-Uk [[1]Yi Sunguk]. 1981. "Putongsa uy hesa-hwa—cwuqkyek
celmi-sa 'ka' uy palqtal ey tay-ha.ye." *Cintan hakpo* 51: 183–202.
Lee, Soong-Nyong [= [1]Yi Swungnyeng]. 1958. "Cwuqkyek 'ka' uy palqtal
kwa ku haysek," *Kwuk.e-kwuk.mun-hak* 19: 53–57.
Lewin, B. 1976. "Japanese and Korean: The Problems and Prehistory of a
Linguistic Comparison." *Journal of Japanese Studies* 2 (2): 389–412.
Ligeti, L. 1956. "Le tabghatch, un dialecte de la langue sien-pi." *Mongolian
Studies, Bibliotheca Orientalis Hungarica* 14.
Martin, S. E. 1966. "Lexical Evidence Relating Korean to Japanese." *Language* 42: 185–251.
———. 1968. "Grammatical Elements Relating Korean to Japanese." *Proceedings of the Eighth Congress of Anthropological and Ethnological Sciences* B.9:
405–407.
———. 1972. "A Voiced Velar Stop for Proto-Korean-Japanese." Unpublished manuscript.
———. 1975a. *A Reference Grammar of Japanese*. New Haven: Yale University
Press.
———. 1975b. "Problems in Establishing the Prehistoric Relationships of
Korean and Japanese." *Proceedings of the International Symposium Commemorating the Thirtieth Anniversary of Korean Liberation* 159–172. Seoul:
National Academy of Sciences.
———. 1978. "On Comparing the Accentual Patterns of Korean and Japa-

nese." *Nwunmoy He Wung paksa hwankap kinyem nonmun-cip* 563–579. Seoul: National University Press.

———. 1981. "The Nature of Accentual Distinctions in Earlier Japanese." *Proceedings from the First Nordic Symposium in Japanology* 84–105. University of Oslo, East Asian Institute, Occasional Papers No. 3.

———. 1983. "Consonant Distinctions in Earlier Korean." New Haven: Private printing. Revised and expanded from *Hangeul* [= *Hankul*] 175: 59–171, 1982.

———. 1987. *The Japanese Language Through Time.* New Haven: Yale University Press.

Miller, R. A. 1977. "The Altaic Accusatives in the Light of Old and Middle Korean." *Memoires de la Société Finno-Ougrienne* 158: 157–169.

Murayama Shichirō. 1957. "Vergleichende Betrachtung der Kasus-Suffixe im Altjapanischen." *Studia Altaica* 126–131.

———. 1984a. "Chikagoro shitta koto." *Mado* 48: 1.

———. 1984b. "Nikkan-go hikaku to akusento." *Kankoku Bunka* 1984 (4): 4–9.

———. 1984c. "Nihon-go to Kankoku-go to no kankei: atarashii apurōchi no kokoromi." *Etonosu* 24: 120–124.

———. 1984d. "Akusento o kōryo shita Nikkan-go hikaku." Paper presented at Yūrashia Kenkyū-kai 7: 3. *Kankoku Bunka* 1984 (5): 27.

———. 1986a. Nihon-go no hikaku-keitairon-teki kenkyū. *Kyōto Sangyō-Daigaku Kokusai Gengo-kagaku Kenkyū-jō Shohō* 7 (2): 176–183.

———. 1986b. "Kankoku-go no gogen—'ue' o arawasu go o chūshin ni." *Kankoku Bunka* 1986 (5): 4–9.

Nam Kwangwu. 1957. "Cwuqkyek cosa 'ka' ey tay-ha.ye." *Cwungan Tayhak.kyo Munliq-kwa Tayhak Munkyeng* 4: 11–17. Reprinted in his 1960 *Kwuk.e-hak* [1] *nonmun-cip* 371–378 (also remarks 310–311).

Pak Pyengchay. 1965. "Kotay kwuk.e uy kyek-hyeng kwukyeng" [Studies of the Case-Forms of Ancient Korean]. *Korea University Commemorative Theses, Humanities* 119–181.

Ramsey, S. R. 1975. "Middle Korean *W*, *z*, and *t/l* verb stems." *En.e yenkwu* 11 (1): 59–67.

———. 1978. *Accent and Morphology in Korean Dialects.* Seoul: Tower Press.

Se Cengmok. 1982. "15-seyki kwuk.e tongmyeng-sa naypho-mun uy cwue uy kak ey tay-ha.ye." *Cintan hakpo* 53 (4): 171–194.

Sohn Ho-min. 1980. "The State of the Art in the Historical-Comparative Studies of Japanese and Korean." *Korean Studies* 4: 29–50.

Staël-Holstein, A. von. 1914. "ΚΟΔΑΝΟ und Yüeh-shih." *Sitzungsberichte der Königlich Preussischen Akademie der Wissenschaften* 21: 629–650.

Street, J. 1981. "Remarks on the Phonological Comparison of Japanese with Altaic." *Bulletin of the International Institute for Linguistic Sciences (Kyōto Sangyō University)* 2 (4): 293–307.

Takayama Michiaki. 1981. "Gen'on seichō kara mita Nihon-Shoki on-gana hyōki shiron." [*Kyūshū-Daigaku*] *Gobun-kenkyū* 51: 12–20 and charts.

———. 1982. "Shoki kayō on-gana to gen'on seichō." [*Kyūshū-Daigaku*] *Bunken-tankyū* 10: 1–6.

Underhill, R. 1976. *Turkish Grammar.* Cambridge, Mass.: M.I.T. Press.

Unger, J. M. 1977. *Studies in Early Japanese Morphophonemics.* Bloomington:

Indiana University Linguistics Club. (Yale University dissertation 1975.)

Whitman, J. 1985. *The Phonological Basis for the Comparison of Japanese and Korean*. Harvard University dissertation.

[1]Yi Kimun; *see* Lee, Ki-Moon.

[1]Yi Sunguk; *see* Lee, Seung-Uk.

[1]Yi Swungnyeng; *see* Lee, Soong-Nyong.

Yoshitake Saburō. 1929. "The History of the Japanese Particle *i*." *Bulletin of the Society of Oriental and African Studies*. 5 (4): 889–896.

Genetic Connections Among the Altaic Languages

ROY ANDREW MILLER

Almost 165 years after the address by Sir William Jones to the Asiatic Society of Bengal that is furnishing us with the theme for this symposium, another Englishman—and, like Sir William, also a knight of the realm—found himself confronted by a concatenation of linguistic evidence from Asia that was, *mutatis mutandis*, parallel in many ways to the data whose details and symmetry had over a century and a half earlier attracted Sir William's interest and attention.

This time around the Englishman was Sir Gerard Clauson (1891–1974). The languages were Turkic, Mongolian, and Tungus,[1] or, more precisely, the several hundred languages belonging to these three families that had long been regarded by European scholarship as being genetically related members of a larger linguistic unity. The idea that this was the case goes back at least to the time of Philip J. T. von Stralenberg (1676–1747), who suggested something of the sort in 1730,[2] some six decades earlier than Sir William's lecture. Various terms were subsequently used for the original language thus postulated. "Scythian" and "Tatar," or "Tartar," were popular for a while. These were succeeded by the designation "Altaic," which from *ca*. 1850 becomes all but universal for the hypothesis of genetic relationship in question.[3]

---

[1] I retain the somewhat inconsistent but traditional language-name terminology of the field, thus "Turki*c* (but distinguished from Turki*sh*), Mongoli*an*, and Tungus" (also sometimes called "Tungusi*c*" in the literature).

[2] This celebrated Swedish adventurer spelled his name "Stra*h*lenberg" in his German-language writing (1730, 1738). It has become customary in the literature to credit him with first arranging the principal Altaic languages into a system that indicated, largely by implication, some idea of their relationship with one another.

[3] I defer to some other occasion an account, long overdue, of the genesis and implications of the term "Altaic" itself, as well as a study of the long-standing terminological association of Altaic with Uralic under the "Ural[o]-Altaic" rubric.

We all know Jones's conclusions about what today are called the Indo-European languages. But with Clauson, a century and a half later, it emphatically was not a case of similar stimuli exerted under similar circumstances producing similar results. Far from inferring that in the case of the Altaic languages he too had to deal with many now quite different languages that had, however, probably "sprung from some common source," Clauson for his part reached just the opposite conclusion.

Clauson decided that the linguistic data available from the attested forms of Turkic, Mongolian, and Tungus did not constitute evidence for the existence of an earlier linguistic unity. Not only did he himself thereafter never depart one iota from his position, but also his views bearing upon this issue have come today virtually to dominate Altaic historical linguistic scholarship throughout the world. To this general statement the existence of a few stubborn pockets of resistance, that is, of adherents to the Altaic hypothesis [4] scattered here or there in the world, provide only a minor exception.

Luckily enough, Sir Gerard has described for us the exact circumstances under which he lost his faith in the until-then widely accepted Altaic hypothesis and the reasons why for the rest of his life he would work so untiringly to refute, as best as he could, what appeared to him to be the tremendous error of this view:

As a young man I had always accepted the theory that the Turkish and Mongolian languages were genetically related. It seemed *prime facie* probable, but I was not greatly moved by the subject; it was Turkish, and not Mongolian, that interested me. But I did accept it, and so when a Romanized text of the *Secret History of the Mongols*,[5] a work that I did expect to interest me, became available, I tried to read it. I did not begin to understand it, and I could find nothing Turkish about the language in which it was written. And so I came

[4] The "Altaic hypothesis" is the assumption that the Turkic, Mongolian, and Tungus languages are all later, changed forms of an original linguistic unity that we call "Proto-Altaic." I retain the term "hypothesis" in all Altaic contexts, whether pro or con, in the belief that all linguistic relationships of this order inevitably remain on the level of hypothesis and are not propositions susceptible of proof.

[5] The *Secret History of the Mongols*, our most important and most substantial text in Middle Mongolian (thirteenth and fourteenth centuries), survives only in a Chinese transcription, accompanied by two Chinese translations, one an interlinear trot, the other a smooth version, so that the Middle Mongolian text proper has had to be reconstructed. The first attempt at this, published by E. Haenisch in 1937, is probably the publication to which Sir Gerard had reference, but there have been several others (details in Poppe 1955: 11–12).

to the conclusion that the theory that the Turkish and Mongolian languages were genetically related—the Altaic theory—was almost certainly wrong (1962: xii).[6]

In this, as in everything, Sir Gerard was as good as his word. The opening salvo in his attack upon the Altaic hypothesis took the form of a reply (Clauson 1956) to a review of a Mongolian textbook (Posch 1956), followed in close succession by Chapter XI of Clauson 1962, which, in his own words, "attack[s] the whole subject again *de novo*" (1962: xiii).

Of course, Clauson was hardly the first person in Europe to have questioned the earlier existence of an Altaic linguistic unity, that is, the ultimate genetic relationship of Turkic, Mongolian, and Tungus. As early as 1820 the French Orientalist Abel-Rémusat had entertained doubts on the matter. He was especially troubled by what appeared to him to be a lack of commonly shared basic vocabulary among all the languages concerned. Some three decades after Sir William Jones, the essential concept that sets and systems of similarities might possibly be open to explanation by the languages in question having "sprung from some common source" had yet to reach the Orientalist circles of Paris. Sir Gerard for his part appears not to have been familiar with Abel-Rémusat's work.[7] Nevertheless, much of what the French scholar wrote in 1820 reads like an epitome of what Sir Gerard would write in the 1950s and 1960s. Sir William's insights and science are as absent from the one as they are from the other.

At any rate, Sir Gerard's particular contribution was to focus attention almost entirely upon the so-called basic vocabulary issue. This he did to the virtual exclusion of all other questions, phonological as well as morphological, that might otherwise also have been expected to play their own role in these discussions. This they have

[6]Clauson 1962 was incidentally the author's own *Festschrift*. In his Introduction Sir Gerard remarks that although he was by then at the age when scholars customarily receive such tributes from their students and colleagues it appeared highly unlikely that he would be so honored, and he arranged for this, his own publication of his own work instead.

[7]Doerfer too seems to have noticed Abel-Rémusat's doubts somewhat after the fact (1974: 108). The interesting problem of the extent to which his own subsequent reading of the *Recherches* reflects his own convictions on the topic and of how accurately it reproduces the sense of the original is one of the many that we must set aside for another occasion (especially such problems as those posed by Abel-Rémusat 1820: 138 versus Doerfer 1974: 106).

not done. And that they have not is due, almost entirely, to the vigor and thrust of Clauson's anti-Altaic arguments, as also to the all-but-universal approval with which his position was soon greeted.

Eventually Clauson's views were to be cast into definitive form in 1969, when he argued almost entirely upon the basis of translations into the various languages of what Sir Gerard felt to be basic vocabulary,[8] followed by his subsequent comparison of these translations among themselves. When his translations into Turkish, Mongolian, and Tungus for "basic vocabulary" item x did not look anything like the same item in the other languages—which was, to be sure, more often than not the case—this was interpreted by Clauson as proving that the languages involved were not genetically related to one another.

Thus, for 'eye', Clauson brought together Tkc. $k\bar{o}z$, Mo. $nid\ddot{u}n$, and Ma. $yasa$,[9] each of which translates 'eye'; similarly, for 'foot', Tkc. $adaq$, Mo. $k\ddot{o}l$, Ma. $bethe$;[10] and so forth. In neither of these cases (nor in many other similarly generated sets) did the translations for any individual item look even remotely alike. In short order, then, Sir Gerard drew from all this the far-reaching conclusion that the languages cited could not possibly have "sprung from a common source"; otherwise their basic words for such basic things as 'eye' and 'foot' ought naturally to be far more like one another than his lists of translation equivalents showed them actually to be.

The Indo-Europeanist will most likely find this argument pathetically puerile. English 'arm' is translated by French *bras*, 'face' by Ger-

[8] Much of the discussion here formally centered upon the assumptions and canons of 'lexicostatistics' and 'glottochronology,' which unfortunately contributed their own considerable ramifications of confusion to the entire problem. Ligeti (1975: 103, 112) appears to have been the only participant to take the trouble to familiarize himself with the built-in limitations of both sets of assumptions.

[9] Tkc. = Turkic (as customary in the Altaic literature when one is citing a kind of "Common Turkic" but specifying no individual language in particular, hence not "Turkish"); Mo. = Mongolian (when not specified, Written [or Literary] Mongolian); and Ma. = Manchu, here as a representative for the Tungus family of Altaic; in other contexts, Ev. = Evenki is instead cited for Tg. = Tungus; Alt. = Altaic; OTk. = Old Turkish; Tu., tü = Turkish.

[10] Actually, "the names of the parts of the human body represent one of the most stable groups of words in the vocabulary of the Altaic languages" (Poppe 1974: 127). This is demonstrated, *inter alia*, by the data and reconstructions in Kolesnikova 1972, which establishes common and inherited Altaic forms for 'mouth' (*bis*), 'breast', 'spine' (*bis*), 'shoulder', 'collar bone', 'internal organs', 'hand, arm', 'wrist', 'hip joint', 'vein', and 'occiput', plus five additional etyma for various specific portions of the collarbone, shoulder bone, and spine. Even within the limited context of the 'eye' and 'foot' words cited above, Doerfer is far from the mark when he dismisses

man *Gesicht*. None of these words look in the least alike. But who would use these and similar translation equivalents to argue against the genetic relationship of the Indo-European languages? The professional scholar will also find it difficult to believe that this doctrine of "disproving genetic relationship by comparison of translations" ever found its way into print in the pages of serious scholarly journals, much less that it was (and still is) believed and maintained by reputable scholars in many parts of the world, particularly in Germany, the homeland of comparative linguistics and of the neogrammarians. But even there, it was to be Sir Gerard's technique for disproving a proposed genetic relationship by the comparison of translations that stuck in the minds of most as having sounded the death knell of the Altaic hypothesis: "Sir Gerard im Grunde das richtige Gespür hatte" ['Sir Gerard was basically on the right track'] (Doerfer 1974: 133).

The year 1960 saw the publication of Teil 1, *Vergleichende Lautlehre*, the only part yet to appear of Nikolaus N. Poppe's *Vergleichende Grammatik der altaischen Sprachen* (Poppe 1960).[11] This compact, succinct handbook, written largely with the needs of his students in mind,

the Altaic evidence with a brusque *"hier ist einfach nichts zu machen"* (1974: 119). In the 'eye' words, Tg. Olcha *nasar* shows by its initial that we must reconstruct Proto-Tungus *ñā̆.sa* and not, with Doerfer, * iāsa* (thus also answering the question "warum *n*-?" posed for the Olcha form by Benzing 1955: 973). This brings the Tungus evidence into correspondence with the Mongolian and also with Korean *nun* 'eye' (the details are clear but cannot be treated here). Tkc. *kȫz* is a secondary nominal formation going with Tkc. *kȫ-r-* 'to see' (Menges 1968: 158), to be compared in turn with Ma. *hoi-* 'to see, look' in Ma. *hoilaca-* 'to look to both sides' and *hoilala-* 'to glance backward' (and incidentally supplying the missing Tungus root *kö, concerning the alleged absence of which Doerfer 1974: 119 makes much!). Further cognate is Old Japanese *körö* 'a die (for gambling)'; cf. the semantics of Eng. *snake eyes*. For 'foot' the Altaic etymologies of the Turkic and Mongolian forms have long since been established by Poppe (1960: 52, 110, 124). Ma. *bethe* goes with Proto-Tungus *bäl- (cf. Tg. Solon *beldir*), a root that may be directly compared with Middle Korean *pal* 'foot' (Lee 1958: 106, no. 10). Etymological evidence for these superficially disparate body-part terms is not lacking. The difficulty is that, in general, it has not been adequately and comprehensively studied.

[11] Professor Poppe celebrated his 93rd birthday on August 8, 1990; it seems unlikely that any more of the several originally planned parts of his *Vergleichende Grammatik* will ever appear. To some extent this great and unfortunate lack may be supplemented by several of his papers published subsequent to 1960 in which he has dealt, piecemeal, with the morphology. But the effectual termination of the *Grammatik* at the point where he left it in 1960 has nevertheless been a major disaster for Altaic historical linguistics. This in turn has been due in large measure to the almost uniformly unfavorable reception afforded Teil 1.

drew in a large degree upon the body of Poppe's own earlier work, which by the early 1960s already extended over three and a half decades. Particularly important in this connection had been Poppe 1926, a pioneering contribution bringing much needed order and system into the previously piecemeal comparisons that had long distinguished the field. In the main, it was the principal task of Poppe 1960 to refine, amplify, and further illustrate the findings of Poppe 1926.

Poppe 1960 also drew upon the work of G. J. Ramstedt (1873–1950),[12] the scholar whom Poppe himself has long considered to be the true founder of modern Altaic comparative linguistics. But Ramstedt's *Einführung in die altaische Sprachwissenschaft* had had to be published posthumously (Ramstedt, edited by Aalto 1957, 1952, 1966). As a consequence his work abounds in problematic forms and questionable data, particularly in many sections where it is apparent that the aging and infirm author was all too frequently forced to cite words and their meanings from memory, often with disastrous consequences.[13]

Always more than willing to acknowledge Ramstedt's accomplishments, Poppe nevertheless has also never hesitated to point out, when necessary, the problems and difficulties that confront the user of the *Einführung*.[14] From this there logically followed his resolve to present, in his own *Lautlehre*, a rigorous sifting out of the good grain from the chaff in Ramstedt. At the same time he so elaborated and refined the Finnish master's view of Proto-Altaic phonology that, in Poppe 1960, the reader finds a tightly organized, thoroughly consistent system of rigorous phonological correspondences linking together all the Altaic languages—Turkic, Mongolian, and Tungus alike.[15]

But by the time of Poppe 1960, Sir Gerard's views had already turned the tide in Altaic historical linguistics. No substantial reviews of Poppe 1960, correctly evaluating its importance to the field, were published. Only a few brief notices appeared, none of them enthusiastic.

[12] See the important obituary notice of Ramstedt by Poppe 1951.
[13] See the discussion of Ramstedt's Korean comparative work in Miller 1984.
[14] Poppe 1953 provides important examples of Poppe's carefully considered criticisms of some of the positions taken in Ramstedt/Aalto 1957. His talent for combining a proper respect for Ramstedt's enormous accomplishments in the field with meticulous attention to the many problems and questions raised by the posthumous text of Ramstedt/Aalto as published is notable.
[15] Poppe 1960 does not include expressly overt writings for all the Proto-Altaic forms implicit in its reconstruction; these may conveniently be consulted in Street 1974.

Typical of the monograph's reception was Sinor 1963. Sinor dismissed the overall accomplishment of the *Lautlehre* out of hand: "On rails that had been laid far back in the nineteenth century he [Poppe] went as far as anyone can go. It is not his fault that they have led him to a dead end" (1963: 144). He took particular exception to the use of reconstructed forms symbolizing earlier stages of the various languages being treated therein. For Sinor, all these carefully asterisked preforms and protoforms were just handfuls of sand cast into the eyes of the reader. He saved particularly biting contempt for one passage in which he found Poppe painstakingly explaining a regular system of developments in a set of cognate forms in terms of three different earlier and necessarily reconstructed stages of linguistic history—Pre-Mongolian, Proto-Mongolian, and Proto-Altaic. Of this he wrote: "With three Jokers in hand it is easy to win any game" (1963: 134).

The result of reviews of this sort, especially when their impact was reinforced by the sudden and spectacular ascendancy of Sir Gerard's views, was predictable. Instead of now building upon Poppe 1960, the mainstream of European studies in Altaic linguistics turned instead with renewed vigor to documenting the details of its disillusionment with the entire concept of an original Altaic linguistic unity, the same disillusionment that Sir Gerard had experienced when he tried, unsuccessfully, to read the Middle Mongolian *Secret History*.

This disillusionment found its most important initial expression in a work that is still its most impressive single monument, the four thick volumes of G. Doerfer 1963–1975, a reworking and elaboration of his *Habilitationsschrift* submitted to Göttingen in February 1960. Ostensibly Doerfer 1963–1975 is a lexicological study of the Turkic and Mongolian loanwords (these are *Elemente* of this title) in various later stages of Iranian, but actually it proves to be principally concerned with an item-by-item refutation of all Altaic etymologies in the literature, particularly those earlier proposed by Ramstedt and Poppe. For each item studied, Doerfer 1963–1975 always reaches a definitive negative decision on the ultimate etymological identity of the non-Iranian elements he studies.

If the Mongolian words he studies happen to look somewhat like Turkic words and at the same time mean much the same thing as they do, this similarity is always held to be solely because these forms were earlier and separately borrowed into Mongolian from Turkic. So also for any Tungus forms encountered along the way. Parallels in forms and similarities in meanings between Tungus on the one hand and Turkic and Mongolian on the other are always, according to Doerfer, to be interpreted as pointing to borrowings from Turkic into Mongolian and then from Mongolian into Tungus. Otherwise we would have to talk about inheritances from Proto-Altaic, which is impossible, because Proto-Altaic never existed. Sir Gerard was right.

Finally, any words that appear to have—as Ramstedt and Poppe had long held that many do—common representation in all three branches of the traditional Altaic classification (and hence also were believed by Ramstedt and Poppe to represent later, changed forms of linguistic materials variously inherited from an original Proto-Altaic) must, according to Doerfer, necessarily be assigned instead to some other cause or reason—most often, to historical-linguistic *Zufall* when they are not, as he attempts to point out in many instances, simply the result of mistakes and misunderstandings of the materials on the part of Doerfer's predecessors.

In a word, the ultimate message of the four volumes of Doerfer 1963–1975 is a simple one. Gerard Clauson was right. The Altaic hypothesis was wrong and misleading.

For all the massive bulk of its format and the ominous air of finality inherent in its hundreds of negative etymological judgments, Doerfer 1963–1975 is not unduly inconsiderate of the reader. For anyone not prepared to plough through its four thick volumes with their hundreds of involved lexicographic-etymological studies, the initial volume had already included a hefty section entitled *Bemerkungen zur Verwandtschaft der sog[enannten] altaischen Sprachen* (1963: 51–105). In this early introductory section of his monograph, Doerfer already draws up his battle lines in clear and unmistakable if somewhat prolix detail.

These magisterial *Bemerkungen* upon which all the rest of the four volumes of Doerfer 1963–1975 depend teach, to begin with, that the existence of ostensible sets of formal and semantic parallels that we may sometimes observe in linguistic evidence from "the so-called Altaic languages" is always due to one of six different factors, no more, no less: "(1) der Zufall; (2) Urwörter: Onomatopoetika, Lautgebärden usw.; (3) Zufällige Konvergenz; (4) Entlehnung; (5) Adstratwirkung; (6) Urverwandtschaft, d. h. mehrere Sprachen stammen aus einer gemeinsamen Ursprache" ['(1) chance; (2) primeval words: onomatopoeia, phonetic symbolism and the like; (3) accidental convergence; (4) borrowing; (5) substratum effect; (6) ancestral affinity, that is, several languages originate from a common ancestral language'] (1963: 54–55).

Thus true genetic relationship, of the type postulated for Altaic by Ramstedt and Poppe, is not absolutely ruled out as a possibility. But it finds itelf only in sorry sixth place, after all other possible "explanations" for similarities in forms and their meanings have been ruled out. It is also important to understand at this point that throughout his study Doerfer employs the term *Urverwandtschaft*, not in its generally accepted sense of a larger, superstock relationship, but merely for the more usual situation in which "mehrere Sprachen stammen aus einer gemeinsamen Ursprache," that is, for Sir William's "sprung from a common source."

Otherwise, there is little in this list that calls for comment. "*Zufall*" embraces such linguistic look-alike curiosities as Ma. *sefu* 'master' and Fr. *chef*.[16] "*Zufällige Konvergenz*" is a little more involved. Essentially, by this term Doerfer categorizes instances in the literature in which he believes others have made mistaken morpheme analysis or incorrect morpheme division in the attested languages and hence have been able to produce comparisons that appear to point in the direction of Proto-Altaic, but, as he believed, this is of course impossible, since Proto-Altaic never existed. "*Adstratwirkung*" is also a bit involved. This is what is at issue when it would appear that both Turkic and Mongolian have borrowed the same word from some unknown, unattested other language. The uninformed have frequently identified this other unknown as Proto-Altaic, but that is of course impossible, since Proto-Altaic never existed. And finally, there is that well-known Arabian phoenix "*Urverwandtschaft*."

These six canonically permissible *Erklärungen* ('explanations') for observed similarities and parallels among languages are, in their turn, conveniently amplified under the headings of sixteen *Bedingungen* ('conditions'). These teach the essential conditions for any demonstration of genetic relationship, if such a demonstration is to have a hope of being convincing, for any language family or group in the world, but again it is clear throughout, with particular application to the situation in the "so-called Altaic languages."

All or most of these sixteen *Bedingungen*, Doerfer decrees, must be satisfactorily met if languages are to be considered cognate. The

[16] A rather contrived example for *Zufall*, at best: the history of both words is perfectly well understood (Ma. *sefu* is a quite recent loan from Chinese *shih-fu* 'id.') nor has anyone ever suggested that Manchu and French *were* related. If *Zufall* has any value at all in such discussions, it is only when the forms at issue involve languages that reasonable men *have* considered as possibly related and at the same time forms whose histories are obscure, at least as concerns their ultimate etymological connections (Eng. *have*, Lat. *habere*; Eng. *day*, Lat. *dies*; and the like).

fewer of these conditions a given historical-linguistic problem satisfies, the less convincing will be the putative demonstration of genetic relationship. Altaic, he goes on to say, satisfies at best only
four out of the sixteen—or at the worst, perhaps only a single one
of these essential conditions. In all the other sixteen, Altaic is found
lacking. *Ergo* there never was an Altaic linguistic unity. Hence also
there are no Altaic languages.

The first of these sixteen essential conditions—and the only one
in the list that Doerfer is at all sure we find satisfied in the case of
Altaic—is probably also the simplest. To demonstrate a linguistic relationship convincingly, "we must first find similar-sounding words
[*ähnlich klingende Wörter*]." The second condition is, surprisingly
enough, stated partly in English: "Es müssen Lautgesetze aufgestellt
und diese strikt beachtet werden (make a Lautgesetz and stick to
it)" (1963: 77). The several pages of discussion that follow this second somewhat startling pronouncement make it clear that the gradual process of successive refinement and subsequent amplification
of sound laws with which we are all familiar from Indo-European
studies, specifically the process of increasingly precise statements
involved in such famous episodes of Indo-European scholarship as
the discovery of Grassmann's law and Verner's law, are not to be
permitted in conducting Altaic studies. Here to the contrary we are
enjoined to "make a Lautgesetz and stick to it," that is, first arrive at
our conclusion and then reject or otherwise discard all evidence that
does not happen to fit that earlier *a priori* solution.

The complete list of Doerfer's additional fourteen *Bedingungen* is
too long and involved to permit detailed recapitulation here. But a
careful reading of each item is recommended, to the Indo-Europeanist
in particular, who will find that almost every one of these criteria
would, if literally applied to the Indo-European languages, also
lead to the inevitable conclusion that Indo-European, like Altaic, is
a wrong and misleading myth.

Reviewing the record of the literature from the vantage point provided by the passage of over two decades, one is struck more than
anything else by the unexpected silence that greeted Doerfer's massive attack, with its more than 50 pages of *Bemerkungen* and sixteen
elaborately amplified *Bedingungen*.

Poppe himself reviewed each volume of Doerfer's *Elemente* as it
appeared (Poppe 1965, 1966, 1968, 1978). But the uninformed reader
of the brief notices he devoted to the monograph would hardly guess
that the principal thrust of the volumes at issue was the wholesale

refutation of the lifework of the reviewer. Poppe's only specific reference to the Altaic controversy in his reviews of the *Elemente* is laconic to the point of obscurity: of the *Bemerkungen* he wrote only, "The main point is . . . the whole first part of Doerfer's work, in which he discusses the weaknesses of the Altaic theory, is out of place" (1965: 78). So also in his brief notice of the concluding volume of the *Elemente*, where Doerfer once more took the opportunity further to denigrate the Altaic hypothesis. Of this too Poppe wrote simply, "This portion of Doerfer's work has little bearing on the main subject, *i.e.*, Mongolian and Turkic elements in Persian" (1978: 141).

Elsewhere, however, Poppe was somewhat less orphic in recording his opinion of all this. In Poppe 1973, one of several papers he wrote during the 1970s as preliminary versions for the second volume on morphology of his *Vergleichende Grammatik*, he described with considerable directness the problems that logically ensue if, with Clauson and Doerfer, we insist upon explaining everything in the Altaic languages as resulting either from Turkic loans into Mongolian, or from Mongolian loans into Turkic.

The specific example that Poppe employed in this connection was one that had earlier appeared in his *Vergleichende Grammatik*, where, among other features of the reconstruction there proposed, it particularly illustrated the regular phonological devlopments of Proto-Altaic *p- (yielding Tkc. $\emptyset$-, Middle Mo. [MMo.] h-, Written Mo. [WMo.] $\emptyset$-, Monguor f-, and so on) and Proto-Altaic *-r_2- (yielding Tkc. -z-, Chuvash -r-, Mo. -r-, and so on):

WMo. *urtu*, MMo. *hurtu* 'long', Monguor *fudur* 'id.', Chuvash *vărăm* 'id.', OTkc. *uzun* 'id.' (Poppe 1960: 81) [17]

To those who would explain even this variety of closely interlocking phonological correspondences as having resulted entirely from loans out of Turkic into Mongolian, Poppe directed the following quite blunt reply:

Die Wurzel ist also mo. *ur-* = türk. *uz-*, wo *r* und *z* regelrechte Entsprechungen sind. Wenn dies ein Entlehnung aus den Türksprachen ist, so müssen die Mongolen nur die Wurzel *uz-* entlehnt, *z* in *r* "verwandelt" . . . und

---

[17] A Tungus cognate appears to be lacking for this set, but the etymology is nicely complemented by Old Japanese *Furu-* 'be old' (Murayama 1962: 111; Miller 1971: 149), which is also phonologically regular in its treatment of the original *-r_2- (Miller 1975: 158). Attempts to relate Turkic *uzun* to, for example, Japanese *oy-* 'to age' (thus Martin 1966: 235, no. 129) are best abandoned, since they take no cognizance of the original initial *p- of the form.

ausserdem ein prothetisches *p angesetzt haben, *was gewiss ganz absurd ist*. Möchte man auch in diesem Falle die Möglichkeit einer Verwandtschaft bestreiten, so ist es bestimmt einfacher die ganze Etymologie abzulehnen und eine zufällige Ähnlichkeit anzunehmen ['The root thus is Mo. *ur-* = Tkc. *uz-*, where *r* and *z* are regular correspondences. If this is a loan from the Turkic language, the Mongols must have borrowed only the root *uz-*, "changed" the *z* to *r* . . . , and moreover affixed a prothetic *p, which certainly is completely absurd*. Should one wish to contest the possibility of a relationship here as well, it is decidedly easier to remove the whole etymology and to assume an accidental resemblance'] (Poppe 1973: 120, italics added).

It would be difficult to put the matter more directly.

Miller 1971 renewed scholarly interest, dormant for several decades, in the possibility that Japanese and Korean might also, in one way or another, be languages that represented some variety of inheritance from the same Altaic proto-language with the reconstruction of which Poppe, Ramstedt, and their predecessors had been concerned. The suggestion, particularly with respect to Japanese, was by 1971 already of some hundred years standing in the literature. Obviously the time had arrived to evaluate it in terms of subsequent advances in Altaic historical-linguistic studies. Naturally, too, such an evaluation, which was the overall goal of Miller 1971, had to be met with massive resistance on the part of the anti-Altaicists. If indeed there never had been an Altaic linguistic unity, as Clauson and Doerfer claimed to have proved, how in the world could Japanese—or Korean, or anything else—be "an Altaic language"?

The response was quick to appear. Doerfer 1974 was a lengthy anti-Altaicist polemic particularly aimed at Miller 1971. Actually it said very little about the Japanese language, and what little it did have to say on that subject was mostly wrong.[18] Rather, it took the position that "Ohne die Lösung der altaischen Frage ist also ein Vergleich des Japanischen mit 'dem' Altaischen nicht sinnvoll" ['without a solution to the Altaic question a comparison of Japanese with "the" Altaic is thus meaningless'] (1974: 107). From that point it then embarked yet once again upon a full-scale exposition of the falseness and folly of the Altaic hypothesis, reaffirming the essential correctness of Sir Gerard's position.

[18] Miller 1976 notes some of the more obvious errors of Doerfer 1974 and corrects a few of his more striking miscitations and erroneous quotations. But it was not possible there actually to enter upon a discussion of his essential criticism against the Altaic hypothesis.

The principal innovation of Doerfer 1974 was its increasing tendency to rely upon arguments from silence. This or that form in this or that language, we are told over and over again, cannot be "Altaic" because it is attested *only* in language *x*, never in languages *y* or *z*. This made the crime of someone else's suggesting that perfectly plausible cognates for many of the forms in question existed elsewhere, specifically in Japanese, especially heinous. Such suggestions clearly had to be put down at the outset. Otherwise they might threaten to shake the entire carefully erected structure of the anti-Altaicist positions.

Another important feature of Doerfer 1974 was its renewed emphasis upon the suggested importance, as evidence against the Altaic hypothesis, of the alleged existence of a relatively small number of words common to Turkic and Tungus in comparison with the larger numbers of look-alikes that may be identified between Turkic and Mongolian on the one hand and Mongolian and Tungus on the other. To many observers, this particular situation within the data might equally well be interpreted as evidence *for* the Altaic hypothesis. If there had been an original Altaic language, it need not necessarily have left identifiable cognates for every original feature in all three subfamilies.

Peripheral retention (in this case, in Turkic and Tungus) of inherited features that happened, for one reason or another, to be altered out of recognition or simply replaced in the central areas of the later descendent languages (in this specific example, Mongolian) is the only explanation necessary to account for the instances of Turkic-Tungus sets of cognates that happen to lack Mongolian representation. But, of course, the existence of these sets does pose problems for those who would argue that everything without exception in all these languages started with the Turks, from whom it was then borrowed by the Mongols and from whom it in turn passed on to the Tungus.

Doerfer 1975–1976 initially appeared to represent a startling *volte-face* on the part of its author. Those who had followed the literature up to this point were more than a little startled, to say the least, to read Doerfer expressing himself in terms such as the following: "I must confess that in most points I enjoy agreeing with the classical view of such men as Ramstedt and Poppe" (1975–1976: 3). Even Sir Gerard now comes in for some lumps. He had dismissed the Ramstedt-Poppe reconstruction of Proto-Altaic *p- as a feature in the original language that would account for the later reflexes, including Tkc. Ø-, MMo. *h*-, WMo. Ø-, Tg. *f*-. According to Clauson

1961 what really had happened here was that the Turkic forms in initial Ø- were (of course, as always) original, but when the Mongols borrowed these words, they took them over with a rather inelegant, low-class quasi-cockney variety of pronunciation. In the process they added the initial *h*- so characteristic of all vulgar locutions, and these vulgar cockney-oid *h*- forms of the Mongolians were later and further disfigured by the secondary Tungus borrowers in their turn.[19]

Doerfer 1975–1976 cuts himself free from all this. Ramstedt and Poppe, he admits, were right but only about the sequence of the phonetic changes thus symbolized. On the all-important question of what these changes signify, in the sense of what the particular segment of linguistic history is to which they are to be assigned, it turns out that Ramstedt and Poppe were always wrong and that Clauson was right after all, even though now bereft of his cockney-speaking Mongolians.

Doerfer (1975–1976: 25) accepts the Ramstedt-Poppe sequence of events for **p*-, but for him all those events occurred in "Turkic." After all, there never *was* an Altaic in which they could have taken place. And so also for all the other ostensible evidence in Doerfer 1975–1976 for this or that *volte-face*. Each, upon inspection, turns out to be only apparent, not real. Nothing has really changed. Major elements of the Ramstedt-Poppe phonological reconstruction have been taken over. But the essential conceptual position out of which that reconstruction grew and upon which it was entirely based is still regarded as incorrect and misleading. Everything still comes from Turkic. There is not, nor ever was, an Altaic.

According to Doerfer, "words common to Tu. and Mo. are neither Alt. words nor relatively modern Tu. loanwords in Mo. . . . , but they are PTu. loanwords in PMo., *a situation quite close to real relationship*. (More precisely: These were loanwords of a very old Tu. dialect which must have been quite close to PTu.)" (1975–1976: 6–7, italics added). Much of this paper may be read with profit, simply by altering Doerfer's "PTu." throughout to "PA" for Proto-Altaic. But to do that would be to do its author a gross injustice. The entire point of Doerfer 1975–1976 is precisely the opposite; that is, the Proto-Turkic that he reconstructs and uses to explain observed data in Mongolian

---

[19] A justly celebrated early Turkological contribution by W. Bang (1916–1917: 119, footnote) suggested a quasi-cockney origin for certain Eastern Turkic forms in initial *h*-, reminding us that Bang was quite equally as famous an Anglicist as he was a Turkologist. But this is a far cry indeed from suggesting that such accidents of articulation could have been responsible for the hundreds of cognates that are at hand to document Proto-Altaic **p*-.

and Tungus was precisely that, that is, only an early form of Turkic and not an early common or original language; that is, it was *not* Turkic. *Plus ça change, c'est plus la même chose.*

Lexical evidence played a major role in Sir Gerard's original and discouraging discovery. Even though he knew Turkish well, he could neither read nor understand the Middle Mongolian of the *Secret History*. He could not read the text because he did not recognize enough of the words. His problem was lexical. From this he went on in logical succession to attack this entirely lexical problem through entirely lexical means. This in turn led him to his concern for "basic vocabulary" and for what historical-linguistic process might be "expected to have happened," that is, to considerations of common sense.

The Altaic field has no genuinely old written records, nothing of the time depth that texts such as those available from Indo-Iranian provide for the Indo-Europeanist. Even for later stages of the Altaic languages, when written records do become available for certain parts of the family, we continue to lack the kind of involved, interlocking documentation that frequently makes it possible to arrive at those nice decisions about the direction and frequency of lexical loans that so brilliantly and so frequently distinguish, for example, the work of our colleagues in the Romance languages. And for most of the Tungus group there are no written records at all, at least nothing earlier than nineteenth- and twentieth-century field records.

This situation meant that all of Sir Gerard's decisions about just how borrowing took place, once he had made up his mind that borrowing *had* taken place, necessarily had to be implemented in the absence of documentary evidence. This is where intuition and common sense had to come into the picture. For Sir Gerard, common sense in this connection meant very simply that he had here to deal with "the kind of words . . . which less advanced peoples [that is, for Sir Gerard, the Mongols] might be expected to borrow from more advanced peoples [that is, the Turks]" (1962: 216). Nothing that he encountered on the lexical level—the only level he considered—appeared to him to provide evidence that the languages he was concerned about had ever "sprung from some common source." There is no evidence in his work that, indeed, Sir Gerard was even familiar with this concept as such. But even if he had been, to invoke it in his studies would have left his much-admired and "more-advanced" Turks uncomfortably close relations to his "less-advanced" Mongolians, for whose well-known history of excesses and record of past barbarisms he was always only partly successful in concealing his fastidious disdain.

But historical linguistics, like all other aspects of linguistic science, may never properly be limited to the level of lexicon alone. Phonology, morphology, and syntax are always also to be considered. The overall syntactic parallels and similarities among all the Altaic languages are so great and so immediately striking that—in a curious variety of the logic of inverse argumentation—they are, today at least, virtually never mentioned in any of the literature, whether pro- *or* anti-Altaic.[20] But this still leaves morphology and phonology. The way in which each of these equally critical levels of linguistic structure has or has not played its specific role in the controversy surrounding the genetic relationship among the Altaic languages must now also be mentioned if we are to present an even moderately rounded view of the issue as a whole.

Under the rubric of morphology the student of the literature is immediately struck by its almost total absence from the entire Altaic controversy in modern times. This is particularly striking in view of the fact that Doerfer has ruled, as his seventh condition for genetic relationship, that "in urverwandten Sprachen müssen auch morphologische Merkmale zum Vergleich herangezogen werden" ['morphological characteristics must also be cited for comparison in cognate languages'] (1973: 83). Precisely so. But in his four-page exegesis of this particular condition, where he attempts to demonstrate only how far short of the mark the "so-called" Altaic languages fall in this connection also, Doerfer makes no mention of one of the most important and also one of the earliest monographs in the field, Ramstedt 1912. This work almost single-handedly established the comparative studies of the Altaic languages on the basis of a large number of morphological correspondences between the various attested languages in the forms and formations employed by those languages for the derivation of secondary verb stems. Ramstedt 1912, with its detailed tracing of an involved system of derivational morphology

---

[20] Unfortunately, virtually all the literature, if it mentions syntax at all, contents itself with the generalization that "all the Altaic languages" (or, for the anti-Altaic camp, "all these languages") are uniformly of the SOV order." This generalization is by and large as false as it is misleading. All the Altaic languages (and Japanese also, for its part) are characterized *not* by SOV syntax but rather by a highly specific variety of nominal predication: "[apart from the imperatives, and (perhaps) an inherited optative] *all anderen Verbalformen, die in den verschiedenen altaischen Sprachen als prädikative Formen oder Tempusbildungen dienen, . . . sind geschichtlich und meisten auch begrifflich nur verschiedenartige verbale Nomina*" ['all other verbal forms that serve as predicates or tense forms in the different Altaic languages are historically and usually also conceptually nothing but heterogeneous verbal nouns'] (Ramstedt/Aalto 1952: 85–86, §52). Overlooking this simple fact of Altaic syntax has led to many extremely misleading generalizations both historical and typological (cf. Miller 1979).

across the entire spectrum of the Altaic domain but particularly in
the then better-documented Turkic and Mongolian families, was—
and in the view of those few who now espouse the Altaic hypothesis, still is—the keystone of Altaic comparative linguistics.

This is particularly true now that Poppe 1973 has fleshed out the
sections of Ramstedt's original monograph dealing with Tungus, for
which in 1912 Ramstedt had only a few mostly unsatisfactory sources
at his disposal. Taken together, Ramstedt 1912 and Poppe 1973 document a complex system of secondary deverbal and denominal verb-
stem derivation. Reflexes of the same original morphemes may be
identified as operating in the same inherited morphological processes in many different languages. This morphological evidence
testifies to a system so intricate and so detailed that in sum total it
unquestionably argues for the ultimately common origin of the languages involved, no matter how greatly their subsequent individual
histories have been complicated by borrowings and other potentially
obscuring factors.

In more than one way, Ramstedt 1912 will be sure to remind the
Indo-Europeanist of Bopp 1816. Indeed, the role of the former in
Altaic historical linguistics is closely and significantly parallel to the
role of the latter in Indo-European. The only possible exception to
this generalization is the unfortunate fact that, unlike Bopp 1816,
Ramstedt 1912 has all too frequently been forgotten, ignored, or at
least overlooked in the swirl of controversy concerning the genetic
relationship among the Altaic languages. Clauson ignored it, just as
he ignored phonology and everything else in all linguistic structures
except "words which less advanced peoples might be expected to
borrow." But so also has Doerfer, a somewhat more surprising matter.

Ramstedt 1912 is never cited in the pages of Doerfer's *Elemente*,[21]
and none of its many convincing etymologies unquestionably dem-
onstrating cognate morphemes operating in inherited formations
involving the derivation of secondary verb stems in Turkic, Mongolian, and Tungus are ever mentioned by him, or by any of the other
anti-Altaicists. Nevertheless, Ramstedt 1912, precisely as Bopp 1816
did, brings together evidence from the details of the morphology of
the languages involved that documents the operation of what must,
if they are to be explained at all, be acknowledged to be cognate morphemes in different descendant languages. Only the fact of the lan-

---

[21] One hesitates to make claims for the thousands of unindexed pages of Doerfer
1963–1975. But certainly one does not encounter Ramstedt 1912 in those specific contexts of that study where one would expect it to be cited, nor does it appear in its
expected place in the *Literatur* (1963: xxxv).

guages concerned having "sprung from some common source" can possibly be the solution to the patterns presented by the data. Borrowing, particularly, as Clauson and Doerfer would insist, borrowing by Mongolian from Turkic and then by Tungus from Mongolian, is out of the question once we inspect the forms and their functions within the morphology.

Poppe 1973 reconstructs eight formants for those secondary verb stems that, in describing the Altaic languages, are generally termed "*Genera verbi*," citing for each a large number of cognate formations from a wide range of languages in all three families of Altaic. But many such formations may also be recovered from Ramstedt 1912, where despite the sketchy coverage of Tungus materials (completely treated in Poppe 1973), substantial numbers of these formations are documented for Turkic and Mongolian, many of which now prove also to have cognates in Japanese and Korean, unknown and unnoticed by Ramstedt.[22]

Thus in both Indo-European and Altaic the initial exhibition of the most important morphological evidence for the genetic relationship among the languages involved was in fact by and large carried out long before the details of the comparative phonology had been established—or in the case of Indo-European, even before the necessity for establishing such details was generally recognized. In a sense, the phonology of Altaic was not completely set forth until Poppe 1960. This has led to the mistaken impression in many quarters that the ultimate goal of Poppe 1960 was to demonstrate, through its reconstruction of the phonology, that the Altaic languages are genetically related to one another.

To understand Poppe 1960 in this fashion is to do it considerable injustice. Poppe 1960 took the genetic relationship of the languages involved in its reconstruction as a matter that had already largely been demonstrated in quite satisfactory detail and to a substantial degree of credibility by the morphological materials assembled in Ramstedt 1912, as well as by the large body of other literature that had preceded it. It was not intended to be and indeed is not a starting point but an intermediate summing up along our road of gradually understanding what can be learned about the original linguistic unity that ultimately underlies the attested languages.

As with morphology, so also with phonology, even though in this sector of the grammar the problems presented by the materials avail-

[22] For examples (actually, only a sampling of the evidence) see Miller 1983.

able are slightly different and hence also slightly different have been the approaches of the anti-Altaicist camp.

One of the potential difficulties in the classical Ramstedt-Poppe reconstruction of Proto-Altaic phonology is that only a few of its segmental phonological units are necessarily reconstructed into shapes significantly different from the bulk of their reflexes in the later attested languages. Most of the reconstructed phonology consists of narratives of the following order: Proto-Altaic *t- :: Tkc. t-, Mo. t-, Tg. t-, and the like. In other words, even though there is good reason, in the light of the morphological findings of Ramstedt 1912, for initially assuming genetic relationship among the languages at issue, there is on the face of the matter no intrinsic reason why the putative cognate forms cited in support of these reconstructions might not be loans in one direction or another, at least no reason insofar as such correspondences as that of t- to t- to t-, and the like, back and forth among the three major subgroups of Altaic is concerned.

The other important consideration that imposes itself in the historical phonology of Altaic in this particular connection is the fact that, with one important exception, virtually no context-sensitive variation in the phonology of the reconstruction, of the type that, for example, in Indo-European is treated under the rubric of Verner's law, makes itself apparent.

Nevertheless, there is one segment within the comparative phonology of the Altaic languages where the nature and structuring of the sound correspondences appear, at least to anyone accustomed to the usual assumptions and operating procedures of the Indo-Europeanist, absolutely to rule out even the remote possibility of explaining all the similarities to be observed in forms and their meanings entirely through a scenario of borrowing. This segment is that of the liquids, where for decades it has been realized that the following sets of regular correspondences hold true for substantial numbers of forms:

	Mongolian	Tungus	Turkic (generally)	Except Chuvash[23]
1.	-l-	-l-	-l-	-l-
2.	-l-	-l-	-š-	-l-
3.	-r-	-r-	-r-	-r-
4.	-r-	-r-	-z-	-r-

[23] Chuvash is one of the Turkic languages, chiefly notable for having -l- and -r- for *-l₂- and *-r₂-. This and other specific features of Chuvash had long led to its mis-

For the Indo-Europeanist, the data above are seen as illustrating a textbook case of the sort of historical-phonological system in which it is necessary, if we are to implement the assumptions and practices of the comparative method, to postulate an original system of liquids more complex than that surviving in any of the later languages.[24] The Indo-Europeanist will also more likely than not find it difficult to believe that the elegant simplicity of the historical solution virtually implicit in the data above has escaped the grasp of most Altaicists for nearly 80 years, during which period the significance of these data has continued to be hotly debated.

But in actual fact Ramstedt and following him Poppe have been virtually alone in the field in postulating four separate, contrasting liquids for the original language in order to account for the above correspondences. These they have reconstructed as (1) $*l$, (2) $*l_2$, (3) $*r$, and (4) $*r_2$. They have also speculated, at different times in the literature and at different stages in the study of the question, on what the specific articulatory features may have been that originally distinguished, for example, $*l$ from $*l_2$, similarly $*r$ from $*r_2$. But the principal thrust of the Ramstedt-Poppe historical solution for the aforementioned data has been, as must be true of any historical-linguistic solution if it is to carry conviction, essentially structural and contrastive. Given the data, they have argued for the prior existence of four distinctive and significantly contrasting phonemes in this portion of the original phonology. From the reflexes, we may safely assume that these reflexes fell into two larger sets (the l's and the r's). But within each of these sets, only the numbering technique explicit in such writings as $*l_2$ and $*r_2$ may safely serve to distinguish and identify the original contrastive units.

Apart from the work of Ramstedt and of Poppe, a truly bewildering and linguistically unedifying swelter of speculation has surged about and continues to threaten to engulf this simple set of historical-phonological correlations.

There has been, for example, much talk in the literature of "rhotacism" and "lambdacism," particularly on the part of those who, like Sir Gerard, have insisted that the Turkic forms must always represent the original system on the grounds, when grounds are sug-

---

classification, but today there is little question about its membership in the Turkic family of Altaic.

[24] For example, Hamp 1975, which unequivocally demonstrates the Indo-Europeanist reaction to these Altaic correspondences.

gested at all, that since it is "well known" that Turkic provided the starting point for the borrowings that explain away all the similarities and parallels between the "so-called" Altaic languages anyway, so here also, among the liquids, the same pride of place must necessarily be assigned to Turkic.

The logical contradiction concealed in this "rhotacism" and "lambdacism" argument will again hardly escape the Indo-Europeanist. If indeed, as Sir Gerard and the others have consistently argued, there never was an Altaic linguistic unity and if indeed all parallels and similarities in forms and meanings to be observed among the "so-called" Altaic languages are to be explained simply by everybody's having first borrowed everything from Turkic, or else later from Mongolian (which had itself first borrowed it all from Turkic), then there *is* no system. There *are* no correspondences. And "-*l*- = -*l*- = -*š*- = -*l*-" and the other sets of phonological juxtapositions summarized earlier simply do not exist except as marks on paper.

It is only when we begin with a hypothesis of genetic relationship, and then proceed to attempt to provide evidence that argues for or against the hypothesis, that $x = y$ phonological correlations of this variety have linguistic reality, not to mention even the possibility of historical significance. To deny *a priori*, with Sir Gerard and the others, even the possibility of a genetic relationship among these languages and then at the same time to feel compelled to explain why or how or under what circumstance "Mo. -*l*- corresponds to Tkc. -*š*-" is a fatal internal contradiction. If the languages are not genetically related, no explanation is necessary, which is indeed fortunate because in that case none is possible. But if they are, only the explanation of Ramstedt and Poppe is necessary, or indeed possible.

Unfortunately for the polemicists no amount of "lambdacism" or "rhotacism" is able to conceal the evidence that this particular sector of the Altaic phonology preserves, evidence that shows how, in case after case, the attested forms effectively rule out the possibility of explaining documented similarities in forms and their meaning solely by hypotheses of borrowings in any or all directions.

Either forms such as OTk. *taš* 'stone', Mo. *cilaɣun*, and Tg. Ev. *ǰolo* 'stone' have some historical connection with one another (apart from their common meaning), or they do not. If they do not, well and good. But few in the history of the Altaic literature, including the most vocal of the polemicists, have been willing to settle for that. If these forms, on the other hand, do have some historical connection among themselves, that connection either may be the result of genetic relationship among the languages cited (that is, they are all later changed forms of some form in an earlier common language) or may have resulted from borrowing back and forth among the languages. If borrowing is to be the explanation, we must explain why, when Mongolian borrowed its word for "stone" from Turkic, it settled for such a grossly incompetent phonetic imitation of the original. Why borrow a form in final -š and reproduce it with a form in -l-? Or, if Mongolian is here the original and Turkic the borrower, why reproduce a form in -l- with a form in -š?

All this, of course, leaves aside what is an even more important and an even less frequently asked question. Why should any of these peoples have been under a compulsion to borrow from one another a word for something as common, ordinary, and well known to their everyday lives as "stone"? No matter how highly one may regard the Turks or how meanly one may think of the Mongolians and the Tungus peoples—and equally disregarding the reasons, if any reasons there actually may be, for all these ethnic biases—the entire loan hypothesis quickly approaches the point of reducing itself to its own inherent absurdity when the semantic content of the lexical items involved is on this particularly ordinary level.

At any rate and refreshingly unlike most of his copolemicists, Doerfer has occasionally been sensitive to the phonological conundrum with which this segment of the Altaic evidence would confront anyone determined to argue against an original genetic relationship among the Altaic languages.

In the *Elemente* he frankly admitted defeat at the hands of "-l- = -l-," but "-l- = -š-" and the other correspondences from the system cited above: "Ob für das Urtü[rkische] z und š oder r und l gelten, dürfte *eine unentscheidbare Frage sein*" ['Whether z and š or r and l were the values for the earliest stage of Turkish is probably *an unresolvable question*'] (1963: 99, italics added). But just over a decade later, he was "now convinced that r', l' (or similar forms [sic]) may be somewhat more likely than z, š" and expressed himself as now willing to settle this once *unentscheidbare Frage* in terms of what is, in effect (though he does not so distinguish it), a variety of internal reconstruction performed upon Proto-Altaic (a difficult operation, at best, if Proto-Altaic did not ever exist), in terms of which original *-r- would have yielded Turkic -r- in certain phonetic environments but -z- in others, especially when followed by different vowels or diphthongs or both (Doerfer 1975–1976: 33, 36). But unfortunately these different vowels or diphthongs are not attested, and so he must reconstruct them—and does, writing such strange-looking bundles as *li̯ɛ and *ri̯ɛ—in the process breaking his own strict rule against the folly of *teleologischen Sternchenformen* ['teleological asterisked forms'].

All in all, the involved tangle of internal contradictions to which all this leads truly makes one wonder all the more why the very simplicity of the original Ramstedt-Poppe solution for the four liquids is such a stumbling block for the anti-Altaicists. Whenever they attempt to tamper with it, the solutions they suggest are always far more riddled with unresolved complications than is the notably elegant four-liquid reconstruction to whose minor elaboration they so greatly object.

What is most important, however, is that in this last-cited paper one finds signs that Doerfer has tended to move, in many details and over the decades, closer and closer to the position of Ramstedt and Poppe, at least in certain elements of the reconstruction of Proto-Altaic, but without ever essentially changing his opinion, as set forth in his 1960 *Habilitationsschrift*, that Proto-Altaic never existed. Comparison of Turkic with Mongolian and Tungus merely provides, according to Doerfer, a means by which we may "reconstruct an early stage of Tu[rkic]" (1975–1976: 3); "the words common to Tu. and Mo. are neither Altaic words nor relatively modern Tu. loanwords in Mo. . . , but they are PTu. loanwords in PMo., *a situation quite close to real relationship*. (More precisely: These were loanwords of a very old Tu. dialect which must have been quite close to PTu.)" (1975–1976: 6, 7, italics added).

Finally, even for the much-mooted problem of the four liquids, by this time Doerfer was willing to accept in all its essentials the Ramstedt-Poppe solution but, once more, without admitting that this solution in any way argued for the earlier existence of an Altaic linguistic unity. Proto-Turkic, he now decreed, had indeed had r, r_2, l, and l_2. But when Mongolian borrowed its words from Proto-Turkic, it simply changed all the r_2 and l_2 words into ordinary r and l, and then, sometime later, Turkic changed its own r_2 and l_2 into z and $š$ (1975–1976: 33–36).[25] In a word, by 1975–1976, hardly anything apart from its name and a few details of reconstruction (more frequently details of symbol usage than genuine differences in inventory and structure of the reconstruction itself) separated Doerfer's

---

[25] Róna-Tas (1971: 395 footnote 18) collects a sampling of Doerfer's frequently shifting and contradictory views on the *-l_2-, *-r_2- question.

Proto-Turkic from the Proto-Altaic of Ramstedt and Poppe. But the
name "Proto-Turkic" was no mere detail. Above all else, it indicated
and indicates clearly and unequivocally that everything that appears
to be common within the "so-called Altaic languages" does not come
from Proto-Altaic: it comes instead from Turkic. In short, nothing at
all has changed a whit since Sir Gerard Clauson and the 1950s.

Much, perhaps almost everything, about the position taken by
Clauson and Doerfer with respect to the Altaic hypothesis is almost
certain to strike the Indo-Europeanist as strange if not inexplicable.
For Ramstedt and Poppe, the principles of Indo-European historical reconstruction were part and parcel of the historical study of the
Altaic languages. The methods and assumptions of the neogrammarians were givens upon the basis of which they set about their
own work.

They were, of course, involved with non-Indo-European languages. But this did not lead them to conclude at the outset that
methods and assumptions that had demonstrated their validity over
two centuries of Indo-European studies were, by that very token,
invalid for Altaic any more than, in a particularly famous example,
L. Bloomfield had abandoned the principle of regular sound change
merely because he was working with Algonquian and because Algonquian was not Indo-European.

Ramstedt had begun the introduction to his unfortunately posthumous *Einführung in der altaischen Sprachwissenschaft* with the following memorable lines:

Die altaische Sprachwissenschaft ist ein Zweig der allgemeinen vergleichenden Sprachforschung. Ihr besonderes Gebiet ist, die Gesetze, die in
der Altaischen Sprachfamilie festzustellen sind, zu erforschen, zu erklären
und darzustellen ['Altaic linguistics is a branch of general comparative linguistics. Its special field is to investigate, explain, and state the rules that
are to be identified in the Altaic linguistic family'] (1957: 13).

In undertaking the comparative study of perhaps any other non-
Indo-European family in the world, none of this would have had to
be said. But in Altaic, as we have seen, it still apparently cannot be
said too often.

This does not mean that in the polemical literature we do not find
frequent invocations of Indo-European and of Indo-European materials. For example, Indo-European data prove to be the principal
weapon in his arsenal of argumentation when Doerfer attempts to
vindicate Sir Gerard's original idea that it is possible to disprove ge-

netic relationships among languages by comparing the translations of "basic-vocabulary" items into the languages concerned. Some may counter, Doerfer admits, that the mere fact that, for example, Turkic, Mongolian, and Tungus all have different words for "moon" tells us nothing about the genetic relationships that may or may not exist among these languages. After all, French *lune*, Irish *gealach*, and German *Mond* are also all different, and surely no one would argue on this basis against the relationship among the Indo-European languages. Of course not, admits Doerfer. But why? Because the French, Irish, and German words cited all go back to "gut ind[o-europäischen] Wurzeln" (1974: 107). *That* is the great and operative difference. In Altaic, of course, we can hardly expect to find "good Indo-European roots"—and we do not.

To many it will seem that Doerfer has here not addressed himself to the central issue. Where do the "good Indo-European roots" that so neatly solve the problem of *lune*, *gealach*, and *Mond* come from? How were they established and reconstructed? What assumptions were implemented by the scholars responsible for these "good Indo-European roots," and where is it written that the same assumptions, if followed through to their logical extension in other languages in other parts of the world, would not lead to equally "good" roots, even if not Indo-European?

So also for the apparent problem presented by sets of Altaic cognates that appear to show reflexes only in Turkic on the one hand and Tungus on the other.[26] Here I must stress the qualifying "apparent," lest we too fall into the perils of the argument from silence to which we must return below. Many of these supposed "Turkic-Tungus only" sets are actually fleshed out, to considerable historical significance, by forms in Japanese and Korean. But for the moment and purely for the sake of the argument involved, accepting these sets as they are usually presented in the anti-Altaic literature, the Indo-Europeanist will hardly see in them the supposedly fatal contradiction to the Altaic hypothesis that they are so often taken to be.

One need only mention J. Schmidt 1872 and his wave theory in order to clarify the mechanism through which it becomes perfectly

[26] Doerfer (1974: 124 footnote 51) claims that Poppe has established only six Turkic-Tungus etymologies. Like all the other statistics in this study, the figure is not to be taken at face value. It represents not a true accounting of the evidence but rather merely the result of Doerfer's sifting and sorting of what is available—processes that provide much opportunity for concealing, when not actually discarding, everything that might otherwise prove embarrassing.

R. A. MILLER

possible for certain forms to have survived only on the periphery of the original Altaic linguistic domain. Again, this becomes particularly important when Japanese and Korean evidence is introduced into the discussion. If, as I have argued elsewhere,[27] Old Japanese *s* and Old Korean *s/š* do indeed continue the same pattern of develment for Proto-Altaic *l_2* as the *š* that we find in Turkic, the true periphery of the Altaic domain is finally established. The jumping-off place in the east was not Tungus, which has *l* for *l_2*, but Old Japanese and Old Korean with their *s* and *š*, just as Turkic in the west, at the other extreme of the periphery, also has *š*. The *l* languages, Mongolian, Chuvash, and Tungus, are thus all found inside the *s/š* periphery.

In these and many other particulars the Indo-Europeanist who takes the trouble to become familiar with the frequently sordid details of the Altaic controversy will often have occasion to reflect upon how frequently this dispute demonstrates a surprising lack of familiarity, on the part of the anti-Altaicists, with the basic elements of the historical method of the neogrammarians, even today, 200 years after Sir William Jones. If we persist, with Sir Gerard, in explaining everything in Mongolian that "looks like Turkish" by borrowing, we are eventually back in the days of trying to explain Latin as somehow being a borrowed, altered form of Greek, since it is well known that the Romans had borrowed (or more often stolen) so much from the Greeks that common sense argued that their language must also have originated in the same unedifying fashion. Until Sir William Jones and his vision of "some common source, which, perhaps, no longer exists," that was all that could be said on the subject. For the anti-Altaicists, who mostly appear never to have heard of Sir William, it still is.

Indeed, if we persist in the anti-Altaic approach as exemplified in the work of Sir Gerard and Doerfer, we must go much further back in time than the 200 years that separate us from Sir William. We are back with Michael of Lithuania, who in 1615 attempted to explain the forms he had noticed that appeared to be "similar" in Latin and Baltic—what we today would call the "Italo-Balto-Slavic isoglosses"— by conjuring up a wholly imaginary band of Roman colonists. These soldiers of Caesar's British invasion force he imagined must have been shipwrecked on their way to England and settled as a result in Lithuania.[28] So also have the anti-Altaicists frequently conjured up

[27] For the Old Korean reflexes of *-l_2- as -*s*- or -*š*-, see Miller 1979b.
[28] The story is told in Kretschmer 1896: 4 note 1.

"Proto-Bulgars"[29] and other wholly imaginary peoples, their languages as unknown to linguistics as their putative speakers are unknown to history, for the sole purpose of explaining away the $*l_2$ and $*r_2$ correspondences in a manner that would make it unnecessary to postulate the existence of an original Altaic language.

Can anything be done to facilitate a breakthrough in Altaic historical-linguistic studies? Ever since Sir Gerard's disillusioning experience with attempting to read the *Secret History*, positions have increasingly hardened on both sides. Everyone who is likely to be persuaded by the work done until now is apparently already persuaded, in one direction or another. Nothing that is published now seems to change anybody's mind, in either direction.

Perhaps one way out of all this is to leave aside the "Altaic hypothesis" and the entire controversy that has grown up concerning it in the literature for the time being and instead to approach the question from a new quarter. This new approach will involve focusing initially upon the possibilities presented by an investigation of a genetic relationship between what we may call the "outer Altaic languages," principally Japanese and Korean, and the longer-studied and more frequently cited Turkic, Mongolian, and Tungus languages, which in the proposed scheme would become, as a group together, the "inner Altaic languages." Decades of polemic on the relationship among the inner languages have hardly advanced our understanding of what was really happening here in history, particularly since, ever after Sir Gerard's disillusionment, the consensus has been that indeed nothing happened. Perhaps it is time then to turn to the outer languages.

The crux of the matter, which is at the same time why the future study of the outer languages may well prove to be a way out of the Altaic impasse, is that the variety of loanword operations that Doerfer, Clauson, and the others have postulated to account for attested data in Turkic, Mongolian, and Tungus are clearly ruled out as possibilities as soon as Japanese—or, for that matter, as soon as any other outer language—is introduced into the problem.

No one knows the earliest histories of the Proto-Turkic, Proto-Mongolian, and Proto-Tungus speakers—where they lived, how fre-

---

[29] The Volga Bulgars are, of course, historical, with fragments of their language attested in inscriptions from the late thirteenth and early fourteenth centuries. But the "*frühbolgarisch*" so frequently cited in the anti-Altaic literature are no more than *populus linguaque ex machina*, invented to explain everything in Altaic phonology that cannot otherwise be explained.

quently they changed sites, or how often their paths crossed and recrossed. There are no early written records. There are no genuinely early histories. The situation, which is familiar to the Amerindianist, is one in which all reliance must be put upon the assumptions and methods of the neogrammarians if the problem is to be studied at all. The Mongolians *could* have borrowed all their vocabulary from Proto-Turks. The Tungus speakers *could* have borrowed virtually everything they have from the Mongolians. A neogrammarian interpretation of the linguistic data makes these assumptions highly improbable, but it does not actually rule them out as downright impossible. It *might* all have happened, sometime, somewhere in Greater Eurasia. There is really no way to be sure that it did not, particularly when we abandon all known historical-linguistic methods and assumptions.

But the moment that Japanese is introduced into the discussion, all this changes. Now the most elementary considerations of time and geography immediately rule out the loanword explanations with which Clauson and Doerfer have attempted to account for the similarities between Turkic, Mongolian, and Tungus. How could the Japanese, who have been living in their isolated islands at least since the first millennium before our era, possibly have borrowed words, morphology, and syntax from the Turks—whether from Old Turks, or Proto-Turks, or any other variety of Turks?

Much the same is also true about Korean, though here the issue is slightly clouded by the geographical situation of the Korean language during those relatively minor portions of its chronological span for which we have reliable data. The Koreans might very well have had contacts with other peoples upon the Asian mainland in prehistoric times that could have resulted in massive linguistic borrowing. We know that they certainly did have this variety of contact in historical times, though by then the degree and importance of the resulting borrowing are clearly of minor importance.

None of these reservations attaches to the case of Japanese. We know where the Japanese are now and also that they have been there for a very long time. The length of time and the location both rule out the remotest possibility of a Doerfer-Clauson hypothesis of linguistic parallels and similarities solely through loans, in the case of Japanese *vis-à-vis* the inner languages. If we discover linguistic evidence that appears to indicate significant similarities between Japanese and the inner Altaic languages, it either means nothing, or it indicates a genetic relationship of very long standing, a genetic rela-

tionship in the sense that the Japanese language is a later changed
form of the same original linguistic unity that must be responsible
for the similarities among the inner languages. The importance that
Japanese necessarily assumes in future discussions of the Altaic hypothesis is inescapable.

Doerfer has frequently dwelt in some detail on the alleged significance of the nonattestation of more than one etymon in this or that
sector of Altaic. A particular favorite of his in such discussions has
been the Turkic verb *ör-* 'weave, plait':

> Es gibt Wörter wie tü. *örmäk* = mo. *örmege* 'Mantel'. Nun ist aber die Wurzel,
> *ör-* 'weben', rein türkisch (im Mo. nicht belegt), und ebenso ist das Suffix
> rein türkisch. . . . Da nun aber s o w o h l die Wurzel als auch das Suffix
> rein türkisch ist (beide im Mongolischen nicht belegt), ist natürlich das
> ganze Wort türkisch ['There are words like Turkish *örmäk* ('plait') = Mon-
> golian *örmege* 'cloak'. But here the root *ör-* 'to weave' is pure Turkish (not
> attested in Mongolian), and so also is the suffix pure Turkish. . . . And since
> the root and the suffix as well are pure Turkish (both unattested in Mongo-
> lian), the whole word is of course Turkish'] (1974: 111).

Even on the simplest level of dictionary attestation, there are severe problems with all this. Both Mongolian *ör-* and (apparently a
doublet) *er-* in the sense required may easily be isolated from some
dozen entries in the standard lexical sources.[30] But the outer languages have still more surprises awaiting anyone who would try to
make capital of what is "not known" and what "does not exist" in
this etymology. Old Japanese has *ör-* 'weave, plait', and Middle
Korean had both *olk-* and *ŏlk-* (another apparently parallel doublet) in
the same sense. The overall congruity of these outer forms with
Turkic was noticed by Martin years ago (1966: 246, no. 259).

It is one thing to claim that "since *ör-* 'to weave' is solely attested
in Turkic, Mo. *örmüge* must be a loan into Mongolian from Turkic"
and that as a consequence Proto-Altaic never existed. But to explain
away the evidence from the outer languages is quite another. How
ever did the Japanese manage to borrow their word from the Turks,
or the Mongols, especially since the form is attested in Japanese written records from periods so early that one cannot yet speak historically to either Turks or Mongols? And from whom and from where
did the Koreans borrow their doublet (no pun intended)?

---

[30] Lessing 1960, *s.vv.*, registers a large number of obviously secondary formations
all involving original **er-* 'weave, twist, plait', including *ergimel* 'spinning', *erükle*, *örke*
'felt flap covering yurt smoke hole', *ercile-* 'to spin', among many others.

Poppe has compared Mo. *siɣuryan*, Khalkha *šūrya* 'snowstorm' with Tg. Ev. *sigir* 'rain with wind and storm' (1960: 61, 115, 131), implying an original Proto-Altaic *sïgūr* (Street 1974: 26). Japanese has *šigure* (*shigure*) 'cold rain in autumn or early winter'.[31] It is of course possible that the Tungus form is a borrowing from Mongol, though this leaves unexplained why the Tungus speakers would have had to go to another language family to borrow a term with such a semantic referent; nor is there anything in the phonology that would indicate a borrowing.

But in that case and if indeed there never was a Proto-Altaic *sïgūr*, then from whom did the Japanese borrow their *šigure*? The problem is a nasty one for the anti-Altaicists. Most recently Doerfer solves it by still further expanding the argument from silence. Now he simply deletes both Mo. *siɣuryan* and Ev. *sigir* from the list of forms that he claims includes all Mongolian-Tungus "parallels" (1985: 304). By neglecting to include this set of Mongolian-Tungus lexical items in his materials, he deftly sidesteps in silence the entire issue presented by Japanese *šigure*. But like all arguments from silence, the technique, carefully crafted though it is, falls apart the moment one begins to explore the outer languages. One has now only to look into dictionaries (though this too has been forbidden to the anti-Altaicists, cf. Doerfer 1974: 141, §7.3[5]!) to find forms of the Old Japanese *ör-* 'weave' and Japanese *šigure* 'rain storm' variety. One is then at liberty either to dismiss everything that one finds as *"Zufall"* or to try and make some sense of it. And now, also, behind the dictionaries there is fortunately a growing body of literature. This in particular will be increasingly difficult to relegate to a permanent zone of silence, no matter how many carefully eviscerated *Materialsammlungen* of the type of Doerfer 1985 are published.

Today, 200 years after Sir William, one thing at least is clear. The essential task of Altaic historical linguistics remains unchanged. Unfortunately, it also largely remains unachieved. That principal task is and for some time in the future apparently will continue to be redirecting Altaic historical-linguistic studies back into the mainstream of comparative linguistics, the mainstream from which Sir Gerard Clauson diverted them in the 1950s, with the consequences that we have surveyed in the present paper.

Of course, even though this essential task for the future is essentially simple, it has more than one facet. In particular, the following

---

[31] The significance of the semantic shifts in the various attestations of later changed forms for Proto-Altaic *sïgūr* is discussed in Miller 1986.

four come immediately to mind, listed largely if not entirely in the order of their urgency:

1. Much remains to be learned about the nature, course, and direction of the historical connections underlying the histories of all the Altaic languages, "inner" and "outer" alike. But the long-standing hypothesis of their genetic relation and the hypothesis of their descent in some way from a common proto-language, other than merely by a set of lateral borrowings from Turkic into Mongolian and from Mongolian into Tungus, has *not* been disproved. As far as the historical linguist is concerned, it has not even seriously been cast into question. The genetic hypothesis remains to be explored, verified, expanded where possible, rejected where unsound, reframed where necessary. But it has not been demonstrated to be invalid, unworkable, or intellectually unsound.

2. *All* the lexicon and *all* the morphology of *all* the languages at issue, "inner" and "outer" alike, must be rescrutinized. This time around the work must be done, not with a view to seeking out what can be disproved, but rather with the aim of finding out what new can be learned. If, as in Doerfer 1985, we persist in discarding whatever linguistic evidence threatens to prove inconvenient or embarrassing for this or that special, preconceived view of how these languages are related among themselves, we will continue only to run in place, exerting great energy but in actual fact getting nowhere.

3. As we go about this work of rescrutinizing the total linguistic evidence now available, we must actively develop reliable techniques for distinguishing loans from genetically related forms. This can be done only by identifying overt features, either phonological, morphological, or cultural-semantic, not by following to their illogical conclusion racist preconceptions about how "advanced" the Turks were or how "backward" the Mongolians must have been. It is probably also high time to cease all talk, in these as well as in other connections, of the putative linguistic roles of "ein Herrenvolk mit höherer Kultur" ['a master race with higher culture'] (Doerfer 1974: 116). The very expression is calculated to set too many teeth on edge to be of future utility for Altaic studies, or indeed for anything else in the world.

4. Linguistically speaking, almost everything still remains to be done with virtually every aspect of the historical study of the outer languages. What we do not know about the history of Japanese and Korean and about how they may possibly fit in with the inner Altaic languages presently far outweighs what we do know. But surely it is

the height of folly to attempt, *ab initio*, utterly and absolutely to rule out all consideration of even the possibility that the study of these languages too may eventually contribute to the clarification of long-standing problems in the Altaic field, solely on the grounds that "it has been proved that there *are* no Altaic languages."

Doerfer simply puts down the fiat that until we first achieve the solution of the Altaic question it is "senseless" to attempt to compare Japanese with Altaic (1974: 107). In historical linguistics there are no final solutions. The Indo-Europeanists have not yet solved all their problems. But does this mean that no one should have taken up the comparative study of the Tokharian languages or of Hittite solely on the grounds that Indo-Europeanists still had their disputes and their unresolved difficulties?

R. K. Merton has written of what he calls "the fallacy of the latest word," in a study that attempts to account for "the resiliency exhibited by some theories or derived hypotheses, despite their periodically 'conclusive' refutation" (1984: 1091). The anti-Altaic position of Clauson and Doerfer is, to be sure, the "latest word" in many, perhaps in most, Altaic scholarly circles today. Whether the Altaic hypothesis will also eventually exhibit the "resiliency" of which Merton writes remains for the future to tell.

In the meantime, it cannot be stressed too strongly that the Clauson-Doerfer approach, for its part, rests on the same variety of "common but untenable tacit assumptions" with which Merton's study is concerned. It consistently confuses linguistic meaning with bilingual translation. It ignores morphological connections. It denigrates the gradual process of refinement and sorting-out by means of which sound laws are slowly and gradually established in all language-relationship studies. It denies the validity of all reconstructions, except when invoked to "disprove" someone else's postulated etymology. Most important of all, it persists in accounting for sets of systematic parallels among data in different attested languages by "deriving" one attested language from another.

Accordingly, it largely misunderstands the essential nature of postulated earlier linguistic relationships, in particular the extent to which these are not susceptible to "proof." It does not attempt to distinguish between "proof" and the painstaking accumulation of evidence that argues with ever more and greater force of conviction by reason of its several interlocking levels, not only involving vocabulary, but phonology, morphology, and syntax as well. What cannot actually be proved can hardly be disproved.

In short, Sir Gerard tragically overlooked the great discovery of Sir William that this symposium commemorates. In the final analysis, he was simply unwilling to admit—or perhaps he simply did not realize—that what are now different languages may in fact have "sprung from some common source."

REFERENCES CITED

Abel-Rémusat, J. P. 1820. *Recherches sur les langues tartares, ou Mémoires sur différents points de la grammaire et de la littérature des Mandchous, des Mongols, des Ouigours et des Tibétains.* Paris: Imprimerie Royale.

Bang, W. 1916–1917. "Über die türkischen Namen einiger Grosskatzen." *Keleti Szemle* 17: 112–146.

Benzing, Jh. 1955. "Die tungusischen Sprachen, Versuch einer vergleichenden Grammatik." *Abhandlungen der geistes- und sozialwissenschaftlichen Klasse, Akademie der Wissenschaften und der Literatur, Mainz* 11: 949–1099.

Bopp, F. 1816. *Über das Konjugationssystem der Sanskritsprache.* New York and Hildesheim: G. Olms, reprint 1975.

Brockelmann, C. 1954. *Osttürkische Grammatik der islamischen Litteratursprachen Mittelasiens.* Leiden: E. J. Brill.

Cincius, V. I., ed. 1972. *Očerki sravnitel'noj leksikologii altajskix jazykov.* Leningrad: Nauka.

Cincius, V. I., et al., eds. 1975, 1977. *Sravnitel'nyj slovar' tunguso-man'čžurskix jazykov: materialy k ètimologičeskomu slovarju.* 2 vols. Leningrad: Nauka.

Clauson, G. 1956. "The case against the Altaic theory." *Central Asiatic Journal* 2: 181–187.

―――. 1962. *Turkish and Mongolian Studies.* (Prize Publication Fund, Royal Asiatic Society of Great Britain and Ireland, vol. 20.) London: Luzac & Co.

―――. 1969. "A Lexicostatistical Appraisal of the Altaic Theory." *Central Asiatic Journal* 13: 1–23.

―――. 1969b. Leksikostatističeskaja ocenka altajskoj teorii." *Voprosy Jazykoznanija* 5: 22–41.

―――. 1972. *An Etymological Dictionary of Pre-Thirteenth-Century Turkish.* Oxford: Clarendon Press.

Doerfer, G. 1963–1975. *Türkische und mongolische Elemente im Neupersischen, unter besonderer Berücksichtigung älterer neupersischer Geschichtsquellen, vor allem der Mongolen- und Timuridenzeit.* 4 vols. Wiesbaden: Franz Steiner.

―――. 1973. *Lautgesetze und Zufall, Betrachtungen zum Omnicomparativismus.* (Innsbrucker Beiträge zur Sprachwissenschaft, Bd. 10.)

―――. 1974. "Ist das Japanische mit den altaischen Sprachen verwandt?" *Zeitschrift der Deutschen Morgenländischen Gesellschaft* 124: 103–142.

―――. 1975–1976. "Proto-Turkic: Reconstruction Problems." *Türk Dili Araştırmaları Yıllığı Belleten* pp. 1–59.

―――. 1985. *Mongolo-Tungusica.* (Tungusica, Bd. 3.) Wiesbaden: Otto Harrassowitz.

Hamp, E. 1975. "The Altaic Non-obstruents." In Ligeti, L., ed. 1975, pp. 67–70.

Kolesnikova, V. D. 1972. "Nazvanija častej tela čeloveka v altajskix jazykax." In Cincius, V. I., ed. 1972, pp. 71–103.

Kretschmer, P. 1896. *Einleitung in die Geschichte der griechischen Sprache*[2]. Göttingen: Vanderhoeck u. Ruprecht, reprinted 1970.

Lee Ki-moon. 1958. "A Comparative Study of Manchu and Korean." *Ural-Altaische Jahrbücher* 30: 104–120.

Lessing, F. D., et al., eds. 1960. *Mongolian-English Dictionary*. Berkeley & Los Angeles: University of California Press.

Ligeti, L., ed. 1975. *Researches in Altaic Languages*. Papers read at the 14th Meeting of the Permanent International Altaistic Conference Held in Szeged, August 22–28, 1971. (Bibliotheca Orientalis Hungarica, 20.) Budapest: Akadémiai Kiadó.

———. 1975. "La théorie altaïque et la lexico-statistique." In Ligeti, L., ed. 1975, pp. 99–115.

Martin, S. E. 1966. "Lexical evidence relating Korean to Japanese." *Language* 42: 185–251.

Menges, K. H. 1975. *Altajischen Studien, II. Japanisch und Altajisch*. (Abhandlungen für die Kunde des Morgenlandes, 41,3.) Wiesbaden: Franz Steiner.

Merton, R. K. "The Fallacy of the Latest Word: the Case of 'Pietism and Science'." *American Journal of Science* 89: 1091–1121.

Miller, R. A. 1971. *Japanese and the other Altaic languages*. Chicago: University of Chicago Press.

———. 1975. "Altaic Lexical Evidence and the Proto-Turkic 'Zetacism-Sigmatism'." In Ligeti, L., ed. 1975, pp. 157–172.

———. 1976. "Wissenschaftliche Nachrichten." *Zeitschrift der Deutschen Morgenländischen Gesellschaft* 126: *56*–*76*.

———. 1979. "Japanese, Altaic, and Indo-European." *Journal of Indo-European Studies* 7: 307–313.

———. 1979b. "Old Korean and Altaic." *Ural-Altaische Jahrbücher* 51: 1–54.

———. 1981. *Origins of the Japanese Language*. Seattle: University of Washington Press.

———. 1981b. "Altaic Origins of the Japanese Verb Classes," in Arbeitman, Y. L., and A. R. Bomhard, eds. *Bono Homini Donum: Essays in Historical Linguistics in Memory of J. Alexander Kerns*. pp. 845–880. Amsterdam: John Benjamins.

———. 1983. "Japanese Evidence for Some Altaic Denominal Verb-Stem Derivational Suffixes." *Acta Orientalis Hungarica* 36: 391–403.

———. 1984. "Korean and Altaic." *Journal of Korean Studies* 5: 143–171.

———. 1986. "Linguistic Evidence and Japanese Prehistory." In Pearson, R. J., ed. *Windows on the Japanese Past: Studies in Archeology and Prehistory*, pp. 101–120. Ann Arbor, Michigan: Center for Japanese Studies.

Murayama Shichirō. 1962. "Etymologie des altjapanischen Wortes *irö* 'Farbe, Gesichtsfarbe, Gesicht'." *Ural-Altaische Jahrbücher* 34: 107–112.

Poppe, N. N. 1926. "Altaisch und Urtürkisch." *Ungarische Jahrbücher* 6: 94–121.

———. 1951. "Gustav John Ramstedt." *Harvard Journal of Asiatic Studies* 14: 315–322.

———. 1952. "Review of Ramstedt/Aalto 1952." *Studia Orientalia* 19 (5): 1–22.

————. 1955. "Introduction to Mongolian Comparative Studies." *Mémoires de la société finno-ougrienne* 110. Helsinki: Suomalais-Ugrilainen Seura.

————. 1960. *Vergleichende Grammatik der altaischen Sprachen*, Teil 1, *Vergleichende Lautlehre*. (Porta Linguarum Orientalium, n.s., 4.) Wiesbaden: Harrassowitz.

————. 1965. "Review of Doerfer 1963–1975, Bd. 1." *Central Asiatic Journal* 10: 75–79.

————. 1966. "Review of Doerfer 1963–1975, Bd. 2." *Central Asiatic Journal* 11: 222–227.

————. 1968. "Review of Doerfer 1963–1975, Bd 3." *Central Asiatic Journal* 12: 156 158.

————. 1973. "Über einige Verbalstammbildungssuffixe in den altaischen Sprachen." *Orientalia Suecana* 21: 119–141.

————. 1974. "Remarks on Comparative Study of the Vocabulary of the Altaic Languages." *Ural-Altaische Jahrbücher* 46: 120–134.

————. 1975. "Review of Doerfer 1973." *Central Asiatic Journal* 19: 158–159.

————. 1978. "Review of Doerfer 1963–1975, Bd. 4." *Central Asiatic Journal* 22: 140–141.

Posch, U. 1956. "Review of Grønbech and Krueger." *Central Asiatic Journal* 2: 76–79.

Ramstedt, G. J. 1912. "Zur Verbstammbildungslehre der mongolisch-türkischen Sprachen." *Journal de la Societé finno-ougrienne* 28 (3): 1–86. Helsingfors.

————. (Pentti Aalto, ed.) 1952. "Einführung in die altaische Sprachwissenschaft. II. Formenlehre." *Mémoires de la Société finno-ougrienne* 104: 2. Helsinki: Suomalais-Ugrilainen Seura.

————. (P. Aalto, ed.) 1957. "Einführung in die altaische Sprachwissenschaft. I. Lautlehre." *Mémoires de la Société finno-ougrienne* 104: 1. Helsinki: Suomalais-Ugrilainen Seura.

————. (P. Aalto, ed.). 1966. "Einführung in die altaische Sprachwissenschaft. III. Register." *Mémoires de la Société finno-ougrienne* 104: 3. Helsinki: Suomalais-Ugrilainen Seura.

Schmidt, J. 1872. *Die Verwandtschaftsverhältnisse der indogermanischen Sprachen.* Weimar: H. Böhlau.

Sinor, D. 1963. Observations on a New Comparative Altaic Phonology." *Bulletin of the School of Oriental and African Studies.* 26: 133–144.

Strahlenberg, P. J. T. von. 1730. *Das nord- und ostliche Theil von Europa und Asia. . . .* Stockholm. (Studia Uralo-Altaica, 8, Szeged & Amsterdam: reprint 1975.)

————. 1738. *Russia, Siberia and Great Tartary, an Historico-geographical Description of the North and Eastern Parts of Europe and Asia. . . .* (New York: Arno Press, reprint 1970.)

Street, J. 1974. *On the Lexicon of Proto-Altaic: a Partial Index to Reconstructions.* Madison, Wisconsin: the author.

The Amerind Phylum and the Prehistory of the New World

MERRITT RUHLEN

Ever since European explorers first reached the New World almost five centuries ago and found that the two entire continents were already inhabited, there has been great interest in the indigenous peoples of the Americas. In the past two centuries in particular these native peoples have been the subject of intensive research by anthropologists, archeologists, biologists, and linguists. Among the many questions that have been investigated by such scholars are the following: (1) When did these peoples first arrive in the New World? (2) Where did they come from? (3) How are the various groups related to each other? There has been substantial progress on some of these questions and very little on others. It is now apparent that the initial immigration was fairly recent because all hominid remains so far discovered in the New World belong to the species *Homo sapiens sapiens*; there are no archaic varieties of *Homo* such as those widely found in the Old World. Furthermore, there is no trace of human occupation in the archeological record before 100,000 B.P., and indeed the few putative dates before around 14,000 B.P. are open to serious question. Before this date alleged traces of humans are meager; after this date they rapidly become plentiful. Many anthropologists consider the earlier dates as simply spurious results of carbon-14 dating.

We also know that the Native Americans are biologically closest to Asiatic peoples. Physical similarities are apparent even to the untrained eye and are confirmed by genetic studies. It has thus long

I would like to acknowledge the many valuable conversations I have had with Joseph Greenberg concerning the internal structure of the Amerind phylum. Similarly, I am indebted to L. L. Cavalli-Sforza of the Stanford University School of Medicine for the statistical analysis of the data. The able counsel of both has been invaluable in this preliminary study of the internal structure of the Amerind phylum.

been accepted that the Native Americans migrated from East Asia, in all likelihood at a time when the Bering land bridge connected northeast Asia with Alaska. From this point the immigrants would have gradually moved east and south, eventually populating all of North and South America. Suggestions that the initial immigration took place in South America, followed by an expansion northward, are fanciful and unsupported by the evidence. The Polynesian occupation of the Pacific Islands is of very recent date, and so even if some Polynesians did reach as far as the New World, they would have found it already occupied. And in any case, as we shall see later, the linguistic evidence points to a north-south expansion.

Despite the fact that scholars have made remarkable progress on the questions of when and from where these peoples migrated to the New World, there have remained many questions on the internal relationships of the Native Americans and on the number of distinct migrations that they represent. But with the publication of Greenberg 1987 these questions too have begun to yield answers. Using the methodology of *multilateral comparison* that he pioneered so successfully in regard to the classification of African languages over three decades ago, Greenberg classifies all the languages of the New World into but three phyla: (1) Amerind, (2) Na-Dene, and (3) Eskimo-Aleut. We cannot entirely discount the possibility that there were other migrations that have left no trace in the linguistic record, but the lack of any tangible evidence for such groups means that it is *just* a possibility, one that must always remain open.

The distribution of these three phyla, which is shown in Map 1, indicates that the initial migration was that of the Amerind people, followed by the Na-Dene and the Eskimo-Aleut in that order. Such a relative chronology agrees well with the internal diversity of each family. The Amerind family is so diverse that its unity and bounds went largely unnoticed before Greenberg's work. Most Amerindian linguists to the present day have clung to the belief that the New World contains dozens if not hundreds of independent linguistic groups, among which there are no known genetic relationships (Campbell and Mithun 1979). The underlying causes of such linguistic myopia are discussed fully in Ruhlen 1987, to which the interested reader is referred. By contrast, the unity of the Eskimo-Aleut family is so clear that it was first recognized by Rasmus Rask early in the nineteenth century and has since that time been universally accepted. In the matter of unity the Na-Dene family lies some-

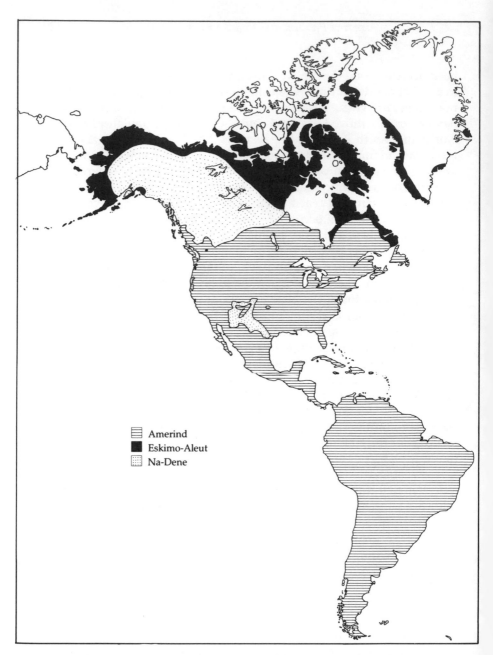

Map 1. Language Families of the New World. (Reprinted from Ruhlen, M. 1987. *A Guide to the World's Languages*. Vol. 1: *Classification*. Stanford, Calif.: Stanford University Press.)

Amerind
Eskimo-Aleut
Na-Dene

where between the obvious Eskimo-Aleut family and the largely unnoticed Amerind family. Like Eskimo-Aleut, it was first noticed in
the nineteenth century and was given firm support by Edward Sapir
early in this century, but despite this history, it is by no means universally accepted even today.

What evidence is there that there were in fact three separate migrations from the Old World to the New World and not simply one
migration with subsequent diversification within the New World?
Probably the strongest evidence is that the Eskimo-Aleut group is
most closely related to languages of northern Asia and Europe (see
Greenberg, this volume), whereas the Na-Dene group is closest to
Sino-Tibetan, Ket, and the North Caucasian languages (see Shevoroshkin and Manaster-Ramer, this volume). It thus appears highly
unlikely that the three New World phyla form a valid genetic grouping at any level, though of course all three may ultimately be related
if the three phyla to which they belong are related. A few roots common to all three argue for an interpretation of this sort. Beyond this
linguistic evidence, studies of human dentition and genetics support the same tripartite classification (see Greenberg, Turner, and
Zegura 1986).

In light of the known archeological, biological, and linguistic
data the most plausible scenario for the peopling of the New World
appears to be the following. At some time between 20,000 and
12,000 B.P. the initial immigration took place, and these people came
to occupy most of North and South America in a short period of
time (several millennia). It was this population that ultimately gave
rise to all of the diverse Amerind tongues. Considerably later, though
the timing is difficult to determine, the second immigration occurred,
giving rise to the modern Na-Dene languages. Finally, at some time
after 4,000 B.P. the ancestors of the modern Eskimo-Aleut group appeared on the scene, completing the pre-Columbian penetration of
the Americas. Zegura 1985 provides an excellent survey of these
questions.

The present paper is entirely prospective; for a detailed retrospective account of Amerindian classification see Ruhlen 1987. Furthermore, I focus here entirely on the initial Amerind immigration.
Using the data of Greenberg 1987, I investigate the internal subgrouping of the Amerind phylum, and from this subgrouping I try
to deduce the relative chronology of its disintegration. Much of the
evidence I have not yet had time to investigate thoroughly, and this
paper should be considered a report on work in progress rather than

a definitive statement. Nevertheless, even at this preliminary stage some of the results do seem to be well supported, other results less so. All the proposals should be considered working hypotheses, subject to refinement and revision as the analysis proceeds. In this sense they differ from Greenberg's tripartite classification of New World languages, which I consider established beyond a reasonable doubt.

INTERNAL STRUCTURE OF THE AMERIND PHYLUM

Greenberg 1987 divides the Amerind phylum into eleven subgroups and provides supporting etymologies for each. These eleven stocks are Almosan-Keresiouan, Penutian, Hokan, Central Amerind, Chibchan-Paezan, Andean, Equatorial, Macro-Tucanoan, Macro-Carib, Macro-Panoan, and Macro-Ge. The distribution of these eleven subgroups is shown in Maps 2 and 3. Greenberg also suggests, without explicit evidence, that (1) Almosan-Keresiouan, Hokan, and Penutian form a higher-level grouping, which he calls Northern Amerind, (2) Equatorial and Macro-Tucanoan go together in a grouping called Equatorial-Tucanoan, (3) Macro-Ge and Macro-Panoan together form a Ge-Pano group, and (4) this Ge-Pano group is closest to Macro-Carib in a grouping called Ge-Pano-Carib.

As a first step in investigating Amerind subgrouping, I constructed a matrix showing the distribution of the 329 etymologies found in two or more of the eleven Amerind subgroups. This matrix, which appears as Appendix C of Greenberg's book, is necessarily imperfect in several respects. First, better documented language families are more likely to show cognates than poorly documented ones. Second, families with many languages have a greater chance of retaining ancestral Amerind roots than families with relatively few languages. Third, because his pioneering effort covered an enormous number of languages over a vast geographical territory, Greenberg cannot be expected to have noted every possible cognate even when such documentation does exist. Despite these caveats, however, the matrix is sufficiently rich and detailed to warrant further investigation.

If two or more of the eleven Amerind subgroups do constitute a valid genetic node within Amerind, we should expect to find exclusively shared innovations that define such nodes. Therefore, as a first step in the analysis I compiled a list of two-way and three-way exclusively shared etymologies in the Amerind matrix. The results,

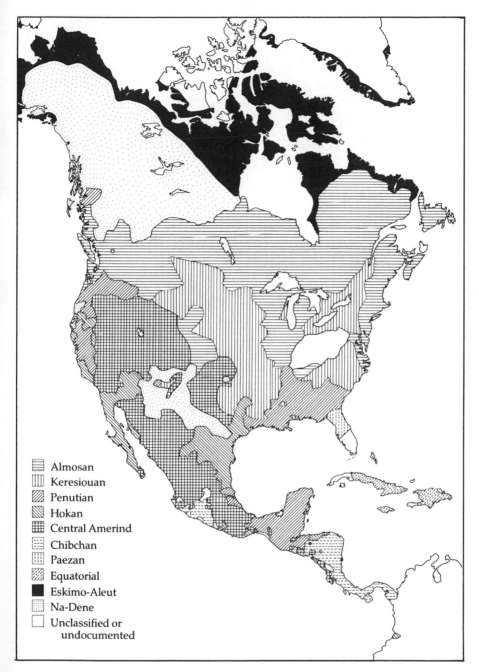

Legend:

- ▦ Almosan
- ⊞ Keresiouan
- ▨ Penutian
- ◨ Hokan
- ▦ Central Amerind
- ⠿ Chibchan
- ▥ Paezan
- ▩ Equatorial
- ■ Eskimo-Aleut
- ⠿ Na-Dene
- ☐ Unclassified or undocumented

Map 2. Amerind subgroups, North and Central America. (Reprinted from Ruhlen, M. 1987. *A Guide to the World's Languages*. Vol. 1: *Classification*. Stanford, Calif.: Stanford University Press.)

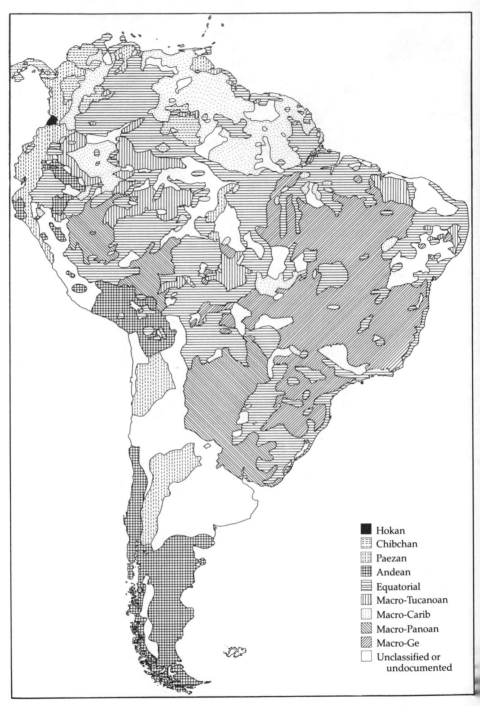

■	Hokan
▤	Chibchan
▥	Paezan
▦	Andean
▤	Equatorial
▥	Macro-Tucanoan
▦	Macro-Carib
▧	Macro-Panoan
▨	Macro-Ge
☐	Unclassified or undocumented

Map 3. Amerind subgroups, South America. (Reprinted from Ruhlen, M. 1987. *A Guide to the World's Languages*. Vol. 1: *Classification*. Stanford, Calif.: Stanford University Press.)

TABLE 1
Exclusively Shared Etymologies

Number	Groups
	TWO-WAY
9	Almosan-Keresiouan & Penutian, Equatorial & Andean, Equatorial & Macro-Tucanoan
8	Penutian & Hokan
7	Almosan-Keresiouan & Hokan
5	Penutian & Chibchan-Paezan
4	Equatorial & Macro-Ge, Macro-Tucanoan & Macro-Ge, Chibchan-Paezan & Macro-Panoan, Macro-Ge & Macro-Panoan, Macro-Carib & Macro-Panoan, Macro-Carib & Macro-Ge, Chibchan-Paezan & Equatorial
3	Hokan & Macro-Ge, Central Amerind & Chibchan-Paezan, Hokan & Chibchan-Paezan, Hokan & Andean, Penutian & Andean, Andean & Macro-Carib
2	Penutian & Central Amerind, Chibchan-Paezan & Macro-Carib, Almosan-Keresiouan & Central Amerind, Andean & Macro-Tucanoan, Hokan & Macro-Tucanoan, Hokan & Macro-Carib, Andean & Macro-Panoan, Chibchan-Paezan & Andean, Almosan-Keresiouan & Andean
	THREE-WAY
5	Almosan-Keresiouan, Penutian & Hokan
4	Macro-Ge, Macro-Panoan & Macro-Carib
3	Andean, Macro-Ge & Macro-Panoan; Penutian, Central Amerind & Chibchan-Paezan
2	Hokan, Central Amerind & Macro-Ge; Hokan, Andean & Macro-Panoan; Chibchan-Paezan, Andean & Macro-Ge; Almosan-Keresiouan, Macro-Panoan & Macro-Ge; Equatorial, Macro-Tucanoan & Macro-Ge; Penutian, Central Amerind & Macro-Ge

which are shown in Table 1, support all of Greenberg's suggested higher-level groupings. The most strongly supported, perhaps somewhat surprisingly, is the Northern Amerind grouping.

As a second step in the analysis, Cavalli-Sforza applied certain standard statistical tests to the Amerind matrix. These tests construct "maps" and phylogenetic trees based on the data contained in the matrix. Two variations of the tests were used. In the first (Figures 1 and 2) only the presence of shared traits was counted; that is, similarity between groups is based solely on shared cognates. In the second (Figures 3 and 4) both the presence and absence of shared traits are taken into account; in this case similarity is based not only on shared cognates but also on the failure to participate in an etymology.

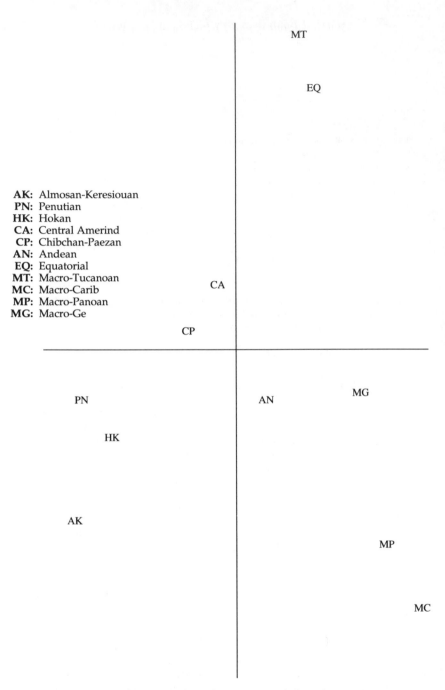

Figure 1. Similarity of Amerind stocks in terms of shared cognates

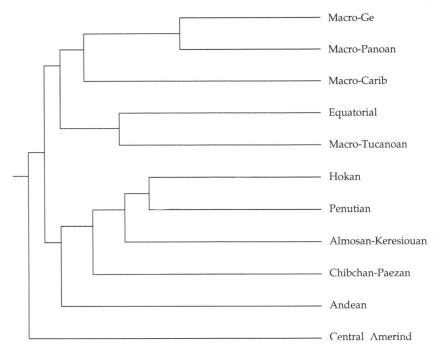

Figure 2. Phylogenetic tree of the Amerind phylum based on shared cognates.

The two phylogenetic trees are similar and support those higher-level groupings suggested by Greenberg. In addition, they both support a grouping of Equatorial-Tucanoan with Ge-Pano-Carib in a node I call Southeastern Amerind. Chibchan-Paezan and Andean are intermediate between Northern Amerind and Southeastern Amerind, slightly closer to Northern Amerind in Figure 2 but closer to Southeastern Amerind in Figure 4. The one major difference in the two plots was Central Amerind, which was the most divergent branch of Amerind in Figure 2 but was placed with Ge-Pano-Carib in Figure 4. The source of this anomaly is not readily apparent, but evidence discussed below supports the idea that Central Amerind is in fact the most divergent branch of Amerind. Its curious position within Ge-Pano-Carib in Figure 4 may result from a confusion of traits that are indeed absent in Central Amerind with traits in Ge-Pano-Carib that are absent because of poor documentation.

Finally, taking into account the subgrouping evidence outlined above, I went through the 329 Amerind etymologies and made the most restrictive hypothesis possible for each. For example, an ety-

AK: Almosan-Keresiouan
PN: Penutian
HK: Hokan
CA: Central Amerind
CP: Chibchan-Paezan
AN: Andean
EQ: Equatorial
MT: Macro-Tucanoan
MC: Macro-Carib
MP: Macro-Panoan
MG: Macro-Ge

Figure 3. Similarity of Amerind stocks in terms of shared cognates and the absence of shared cognates.

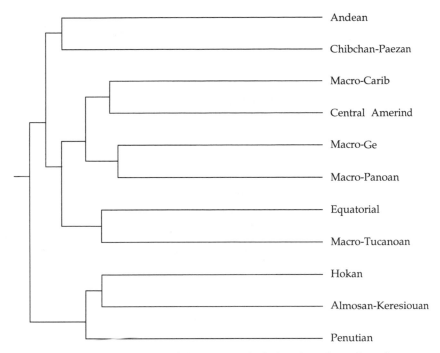

Figure 4. Phylogenetic tree of the Amerind phylum based on shared cognates and absent shared cognates.

mology restricted to Macro-Ge and Macro-Panoan is considered to be an innovation of Ge-Pano and is ascribed no higher status within the Amerind phylum. The result of this partition of the Amerind etymologies is shown in Table 2, and the phylogenetic tree that best accounts for the distribution of the Amerind etymologies is shown in Figure 5. The Amerind phylum thus appears to consist of three basic subgroups—Northern, Central, and Southern—with Northern and Southern together being coordinate with Central at the highest level of Amerind classification. Northern Amerind and Central Amerind each consist of three subgroups, but there appears to be no evidence at present for further subgrouping. Southern Amerind also seems to consist of three subgroups, but in this case Chibchan-Paezan appears to be coordinate with the other two, Andean and Southeastern Amerind. The subgroup consisting of these latter two groups I call South American Amerind, since it encompasses the six basic Amerind stocks confined to South America.

TABLE 2
Distribution of the Amerind Etymologies

AMERIND [71/10]*
I. Central [90/2]
II. Northern and Southern [101/17]
   A. Northern [24/5]
      1. Almosan-Keresiouan [77/4]
         a. Almosan [75/4]
         b. Keresiouan [57/3]
      2. Penutian [211/7]
         a. Gulf-Mexican [35/0]
            i. Gulf [41/0]
      3. Hokan [168/9]
   B. Southern [24/5]
      1. Chibchan-Paezan [121/6]
         a. Chibchan [45/3]
         b. Paezan [60/0]
      2. South American [26/1]
         a. Andean [129/6]
         b. Southeastern [17/2]
            i. Equatorial-Tucanoan [6/3]
               (1) Equatorial [133/2]
               (2) Macro-Tucanoan [107/1]
            ii. Ge-Pano-Carib [11/1]
               (1) Macro-Carib [79/3]
               (2) Ge-Pano [1/4]
                  (a) Macro-Panoan [63/9]
                  (b) Macro-Ge [124/0]

*The first number represents the number of *lexical* etymologies supporting this group; the second number, the number of *grammatical* etymologies supporting the group.

EVIDENCE FOR THE DIVERGENCE
OF CENTRAL AMERIND

In the preceding section I give preliminary quantitative evidence for the Amerind subgrouping shown in Figure 5. This evidence has consisted solely in the distribution of the etymologies; the intrinsic linguistic content of the etymologies has not yet been brought into play. It is of course significant that of the 329 etymologies Greenberg offers in support of the Amerind phylum 101 are apparently confined to Southern Amerind. Each of these represents a potential innovation within the group, and taken together they serve to define the Southern Amerind group. Inevitably, as research proceeds, some of the etymologies that now appear confined to Southern Amerind

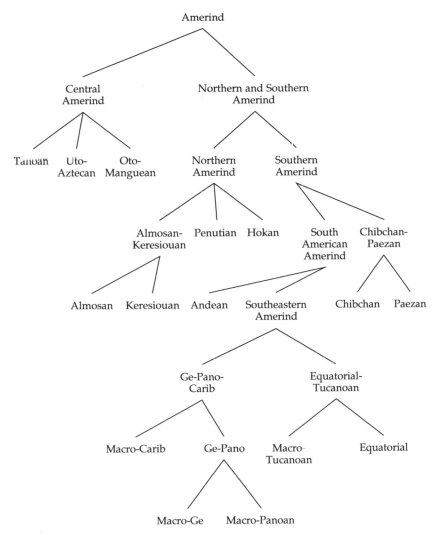

Figure 5. Phylogenetic tree of the Amerind phylum.

will be found to have cognates in Northern or Central Amerind, or both, just as some etymologies now restricted to Northern or Central Amerind will be found to have cognates elsewhere in the Amerind phylum. Some of the etymologies will no doubt turn out to be spurious and will have to be discarded. In short, there will be an inevitable shuffling of the etymologies as their scope is either broadened or restricted. At the same time, however, it is to be expected that for each Southern Amerind etymology that turns out to have Northern or Central congeners additional Southern Amerind etymologies will be found so that even a considerable shuffling of the etymologies will not necessarily lead to a different subgrouping of the Amerind phylum.

If the subgrouping proposed in Figure 5 is correct, we should expect to find corroborative linguistic evidence, in the form of phonological or semantic innovations, that represents the same period of independent historical development responsible for the lexical and grammatical innovations. Such qualitative evidence should be marshaled in support of each of the nodes posited in Figure 5. I will comment only briefly on the divergence of Central Amerind.

The statistical divergence of Central Amerind is indeed dramatic. There are 118 etymologies exclusive to Northern and Southern Amerind but only eighteen exclusive to Central and Southern Amerind and a mere five exclusive to Northern and Central Amerind. The qualitative evidence appears to run in the same direction, where we may cite three possible phonological innovations and eight possible semantic innovations separating Central Amerind from the remainder of the Amerind phylum.

The first phonological innovation concerns the shape of the root. Central Amerind is characterized by a CVC structure, whereas both Northern and Southern Amerind frequently show an initial vowel, a final vowel, or both. Thus in a significant number of the etymologies Central Amerind CVC corresponds to Northern and Southern $V_1 CVCV_2$. Furthermore, V_1 and V_2 are often similar or even identical in both the Northern and Southern groups. Etymologies showing this pattern are numerous, such as nos. 55, 61, 74, 82, 103, 104, and 112. Whether the initial and final vowels are innovations of Northern and Southern Amerind or retentions in Northern and Southern Amerind of an original Amerind trait that has been lost in Central Amerind is unclear. In either case the trait serves to distinguish Central Amerind from the remainder of the Amerind phylum.

In six of the etymologies (6, 36, 69, 185, 193, and 263) Central Amerind shows the reflex s corresponding to a stop or affricate (t, t^s, č) elsewhere in the Amerind phylum.

Finally, Central Amerind -n- corresponds to Northern and Southern -l- in etymologies 67, 140, 161, 210, and 262. In a good many

TABLE 3
Possible Semantic Innovations in Central Amerind

Etymology	Central Amerind	Northern Amerind	Southern Amerind
13	ask	seek, wish	seek, love, pleasure
55	talk	call, name	call, cry, invite
64	small	child, bear	bear, be born
104	see, find, learn, teach	eye, face, tear	eye, see, look
120	leg, thigh	foot, kick, track, sole, leg, hip, hoof, run, move	foot, ankle, shin, knee, thigh, leg
157	thigh	knee, elbow, crouch	knee, elbow, thigh, hip, foot
160	far	large, fat, all, long	large, long, all, much, many
175	work	make, do, cause	make, build, cause, work, put

cases the basic pattern seems to be Northern Amerind -*l*- = Central Amerind -*n*- = Chibchan-Paezan or Andean -*l*-, -*r*-, -*n*- = Southeastern Amerind -*r*-.

Table 3 shows eight possible semantic innovations within Central Amerind.

Taken together these phonological and semantic innovations support the notion that Central Amerind is the most divergent branch of the Amerind phylum, the possibility of which was first suggested by the quantitative evidence. I anticipate that further investigation will uncover additional evidence of this divergence.

IMPLICATIONS FOR NEW WORLD PREHISTORY

The subgrouping of the Amerind phylum shown in Figure 5, for which both quantitative and qualitative evidence has been adduced in the preceding sections, has immediate implications for the initial settling of the Americas. Indeed, a subgrouping is nothing more than a hypothesis about the relative chronology of the disintegration of a family. When we combine such information with the geographical distributions of the various subroups (Sapir's age-area hypothesis), we may deduce not only the order of the breakup of the Amerind phylum but also the geographical area in which certain divisions likely occurred.

Maps 4 to 7 summarize my preliminary conclusions regarding the disintegration of the Amerind phylum. Map 4 proposes an approximate geographical homeland for each of Greenberg's eleven basic Amerind stocks. Some of these proposals have a higher degree of probability than others. In particular, I have a fairly high degree of confidence in the positions attributed to Almosan-Keresiouan, Penutian, Central Amerind, and Chibchan-Paezan but considerably less in the case of the others. The matrices for each of these eleven Amerind branches are currently being analyzed both quantitatively and qualitatively along the lines sketched for the Amerind matrix in the present paper. Clearly the results of this analysis can be expected to shed light on the location of the original homeland of each of these groups.

Map 5 attempts to locate the homeland of the higher-level groupings that have been posited in this paper. Finally, Maps 6 and 7 show the primary and secondary divisions within the Amerind phylum that likely occurred during the early stages of its distintegration. Obviously many more such divisions would have subsequently taken place before the initial settlement of the Americas was complete.

In summary, the linguistic evidence presently available points toward the following scenario for the initial peopling of the New World. A single population, speaking a language we may call Proto-Amerind, made its way from northeast Asia across Alaska and western Canada and eventually arrived in central Montana. There is no evidence for the Amerind groups that may have been left behind during this trek, since these areas were subsequently populated by Na-Dene and Eskimo-Aleut speakers, leaving no trace of a presumed earlier Amerind population. The first basic cleavage within the family separated the Central Amerind group from the remainder of the family. Where precisely this division took place one can only conjecture; it may not have occurred until the Amerind group reached Montana, or it may have taken place earlier during the Amerind expansion. In any event, this group appears to have begun to break up in the American Southwest, where the homelands of two of its three branches can be placed (Uto-Aztecan and Tanoan).

The second basic division produced a group that would ultimately populate most of North America (Northern Amerind) and a group that would eventually occupy almost all of South America as well as portions of Central America (Southern Amerind). This second division in the Amerind family must have taken place considerably later than the first if one is to account for the special similarities (some of

1. Almosan-Keresiouan
2. Penutian
3. Hokan
4. Central Amerind
5. Chibchan-Paezan
6. Andean
7. Equatorial
8. Macro-Tucanoan
9. Macro-Carib
10. Macro-Panoan
11. Macro-Ge

Map 4. Proposed homelands of Amerind subgroups.

1. Amerind
2. Central Amerind
3. Northern and Southern Amerind
4. Northern Amerind
5. Southern Amerind
6. South American Amerind
7. Southeastern Amerind
8. Equatorial-Tucanoan
9. Ge-Pano-Carib

Map 5. Proposed homelands of higher-level Amerind subgroups.

NA: Northern Amerind
CA: Central Amerind
SA: Southern Amerind
SAA: South American Amerind
SEA: Southeastern Amerind
A: Andean
ET: Equatorial-Tucanoan
GPC: Ge-Pano-Carib

Map 6. The Amerind migration, primary divisions.

NA:	Northern Amerind
P:	Penutian
AK:	Almosan-Keresiouan
H:	Hokan
CA:	Central Amerind
T:	Tanoan
UA:	Uto-Aztecan
OM:	Oto-Manguean
CP:	Chibchan-Paezan
C:	Chibchan
PZ:	Paezan
ET:	Equatorial-Tucanoan
MT:	Macro-Tucanoan
E:	Equatorial
GPC:	Ge-Pano-Carib
MC:	Macro-Carib
GP:	Ge-Pano
MP:	Macro-Panoan
MG:	Macro-Ge
A:	Andean

Map 7. The Amerind migration, secondary divisions.

which must be innovations, others common retentions from Proto-Amerind) between Northern and Southern Amerind. Since the Northern Amerind homeland was likely in the area of Montana, the simplest hypothesis is that this was also the homeland of the Northern and Southern group. Despite the fact that the Central Amerind group branched off first, they never reached South America. Rather it was the second branch, Southern Amerind, that first reached the Isthmus of Panama, permanently blocking the entry to South America and ultimately giving rise to all the native South American Indians except the Yurumanguí, a now extinct Hokan group that formerly lived on the Pacific Coast of Colombia. With this one exception South America appears to have been populated by a single migration.

The Southern Amerind group bifurcated into the Chibchan-Paezan family, which remained generally *in situ* at the entrance to South America (though there are several important outliers), and the South American Amerind group, which moved southward to the area of northern Peru. From this region the Andean family spread southward along the Pacific Coast, eventually reaching Tierra del Fuego. The remainder of the South American Amerind group, which I call Southeastern Amerind, gave rise to the five Amerind subgroups that occupy almost all the territory east of the Andes. My main reason for locating the South American Amerind homeland in northern Peru is that five of its six constituents (all but Macro-Ge) are well represented in this region, an indication that the basic dispersal may have been from this area. Analysis of the South American matrices should clarify these problems, since at present next to nothing is known about the subgrouping of the South American stocks.

In North America the Northern Amerind grouping split into three subgroups. The Penutian group moved westward through Oregon to the Pacific Coast, whence it spread both northward into Washington and British Columbia and southward into California and at a later date to Arizona (Zuñi), the southeast (Gulf), and Mexico (Mexican Penutian). These latter two groups seem to form a subgroup within the Penutian family. The Hokan family moved southward toward Texas, around the southern end of the Rocky Mountains and then back up the Pacific Coast as far as northern California. The Almosan-Keresiouan group may be regarded as the Northern Amerind subgroup that remained in place in Montana, at least for a while. Eventually, it too bifurcated into the Keresiouan group, which spread to the south and to the east, and the Almosan group, which spread both eastward (Algonquian) and westward (Mosan, Ritwan). The Kutenai may represent the Almosan group that remained behind after the Algic and Mosan groups had branched off. The preceding scenario for the peopling of North America agrees in large measure with that outlined in Krantz (1977), which seems generally correct in its broad generalizations, though wrong on some details. Krantz's study was based on animal geography, not linguistics, and is well worth reading for anyone interested in the questions adumbrated here.

REFERENCES CITED

Campbell, L., and M. Mithun, eds. 1979. *The Languages of Native America*. Austin: University of Texas Press.

Greenberg, J. H. 1987. *Language in the Americas*. Stanford: Stanford University Press.

―――. 1988. "Some Problems of Indo-European in Broader Historical Perspective." This volume.

Greenberg, J. H., C. G. Turner II, and S. L. Zegura. 1986. "The Settlement of the Americas: a Comparison of the Linguistic, Dental, and Genetic Evidence." *Current Anthropology* 27: 477–497.

Krantz, G. S. 1977. "The Populating of Western North America." *Society for California Archaeology Occasional Papers in Method and Theory in California Archaeology*, no. 1.

Ruhlen, M. 1987. *A Guide to the World's Languages*. Vol. 1: *Classification*. Stanford: Stanford University Press.

Shevoroshkin, V., and A. Manaster-Ramer. 1988. "Recent Work on Distant Relationships." This volume.

Zegura, S. L. 1985. "The Initial Peopling of the Americas: an Overview." In Kirk, R., and E. Szathmary, eds. *Out of Asia: Peopling the Americas and the Pacific*, pp. 1–18. Canberra: Journal of Pacific History.

PART V

Methods in Genetic Classification of Languages

This section does not in any way attempt to present a general introductory treatment of methods in genetic classification. Rather, it contains papers on three different aspects of the general topic of ways of conducting research in this area. Of course, methods of investigation in this field are also discussed in some of the papers in preceding sections, including those of Greenberg and Miller.

The paper by Robert Austerlitz is a critique of some current practices of long-range comparativists, together with a suggestion that greater attention be given to other ways of explaining similarities among languages. Perhaps, as Austerlitz hints, the time has come for more serious consideration of explanations for mutual resemblance that might be said to lie between genetic relationship and the usually recognized forms of diffusion. After all, the family tree model is only a model, and it is commonly recognized to be imperfect.

Until a reasonable alternative to family-tree classification is forthcoming it must remain the basis of genetic classification. Indeed it will still be an important basis even if and when viable alternatives are developed, as the tree is the basic model for dealing with the fundamental problem in classification, the determination of degrees of relationship. Sheila Embleton presents a survey of mathematical techniques for genetic classification, using the family tree model as a primary basis but with great attention to incorporating the consideration of borrowing among related languages, an area in which much of the mathematical work she describes is her own. She is thus developing an enrichment of the family tree model.

Robert Oswalt concludes the volume by describing a computerized technique for developing and testing hypotheses of distant genetic relationships among languages. One of its welcome virtues is a simple but effective means of determining whether observed similarities among any given languages can reasonably be accounted for on the basis of chance. His technique is not intended as an alternative to the established comparative method; rather, it is a device to be used before detailed comparisons are made, that is, a method for identifying those cases in which closer comparison is most likely to yield results. Oswalt's testing procedure, like lexicostatistical studies in general, is limited by its restriction of comparisons to items with identical semantic value. It thus invites an opportunity for future development: a systematic way of dealing with semantic differences, analogous to Oswalt's method of allowing for phonological differences.

Alternatives in Long-Range Comparison

ROBERT AUSTERLITZ

In memoriam Carl and Florence Voegelin

Some contributors to this volume are exploring means for reconciling the differences among the language families of the world, if not to adumbrate one single proto-proto-language, at least to reduce the number of genetic units with which we have traditionally reckoned in comparative linguistics. This sort of search for order and simplicity, I agree, is what scientific inquiry should be. Yet, I feel that the way in which this goal has been pursued in regard to genetic classification is often counterproductive and often even harmful. I cannot say that I enjoy my role of splitter among lumpers, but since I believe in academic freedom much more fervently than I disbelieve in long-range groupings (LRGs), I will state my objections to lumping in a spirit of complete open-mindedness: I will believe the lumpers when they convince me. What is more, deep down in my heart I also believe in the *unità d'origine del linguaggio* (Trombetti 1905), but my mind balks at the thought. That is my predicament.

Meanwhile, I suggest that it is possible and preferable to do long-range comparison without long-range grouping. Alternatives to grouping as explanation for resemblances found in long-range comparison are possible.

In some earlier work (1972, 1982, 1983) I have hesitated to be convinced by attempts to connect Uralic with other language families in LRGs. I will therefore continue to use Uralic as a point of reference.

I also have another reason to be skeptical. It comes from my work with Gilyak (Nivkh), an isolate of easternmost Siberia. In all my years of fieldwork and desk work with this language I have yearned for

Sydney M. Lamb has given the manuscript that I originally submitted a thorough, critical reading and suggested changes in it, primarily to bring it into better alignment with the tenor of the conference. Some of Lamb's suggestions have led me to reconsider earlier views and to alter them, generally in the direction of moderation, consistency, and greater clarity. I accept them with thanks. They have been incorporated into the present version of the paper.

the day when comparison (long range or not) would open a door toward the resolution of the riddle of this language—where it belonged genetically. Comparison has failed me, and the more deeply I delve by means of internal reconstruction, the more enigmatic the riddle becomes.

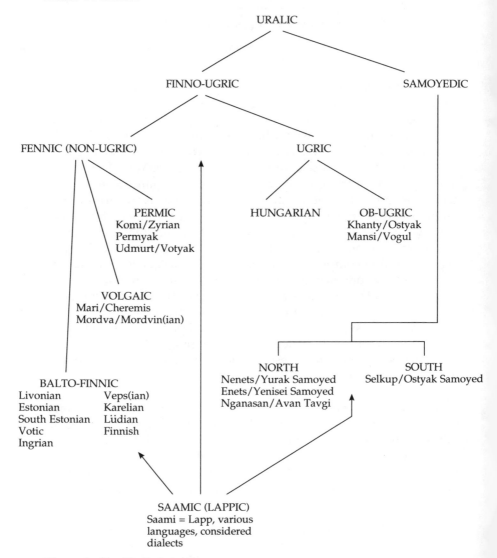

Figure 1. The Uralic languages.

The Uralic *Stammbaum* is given in Figure 1.[1] Viewed from a safe distance, Uralic is a fairly well cohering language family. According to Korhonen (1986: 154) there is agreement on from 1,000 to 1,600 etymologies. In the tree the Volgaic branch is questionable, and there is still no agreement on the precise position of Lappic (Saamic). At closer range, problems abound. Although the reconstructed vocabulary of what we think was a hunting-gathering society seems quite well attested in the reconstructed proto-language, there are problems even with this clear-cut segment. Thus the correspondence between Finnish *sydän*, inflected *sydämme-*, and Hungarian *szív* [sīv], inflected *szíve-* [sīvæ], 'heart', is irregular and has frustrated the best thinkers for two centuries. Similar problems are seen in the etymologies for "eye" and "give."

The situation in the case of a reconstruction for "sinew; nerve; blood vessel" is somewhat better. See Table 1. But there is trouble here too. Just as there are devoted partisans of LRG, there are equally devoted partisans of diffusion, an alternative in long-range comparison, who propose or maintain that this word (in Table 1) is borrowed. A simple overview of presumed loans in the Uralic languages is given in Table 2.

Table 3 provides a glimpse into the possible Indo-European etyma (or sources for etyma) of "sinew etc." What are we to make of them? The usual reconstruction for the forms in the first box (upper left) is a root with alternating forms **senw-*, **snew-*. It fits well with the Uralic forms in both form and meaning and would be a suitable source for the Uralic etymon. But does it fit as evidence for a genetic connection of Uralic and IE, as the partisan of LRGs would claim, or as a loan source? The situation is complicated by the forms in the other boxes of Table 3, which indicate the possibility of leading to a Pre-IE root consisting of **s* + vowel + root extensions **-n(-w)*, **-t*, and **-l*.

We must choose between accidental similarity between IE and Uralic, an ancient loan, or outright Indo-Uralic relatedness. Does this trilemma improve our understanding of the Uralic proto-language, of the culture of the people who presumably spoke it, or of the cultural contacts between an early form of Uralic and adjacent languages or language families?

---

[1] For a statement on language trees, see W. P. Lehmann in this volume. Still, there is no denying that trees are a valuable model, perhaps the only valuable model, for this sort of work. Let us only reflect on wave theory, which is after all a sophisticated extension or multiple of the *Stammbaum* model.

TABLE 1

Reconstruction for "Sinew, Nerve, Blood Vessel" in Uralic

FINNO-UGRIC

Lapp			Lapp	*suodnâ/suonâ*
Fennic	Balto-Finnic		Livonian	*suoń/suonə-*
			Estonian	*soon/soone-*
			Finnish	*suoni/suone-*
	(Volgaic)		Mari	*šün, śün*
			Mordva	*san*
	Permic		Udmurt	*sən*
			Komi	*sən*
Ugric			Hungarian	*ín/ina-*
	Ob-Ugric		Khanty	*ton, lan, jan*
			Mansi	*taan, tən*

SAMOYEDIC

	North		Nganasan	*taŋ*
			Enets	*ti/tino-*
			Nenets	*teʔ/ten-*
	South		Kamas	*tʼen*
			Selkup	*čɔt, tən*

Proto-Finno-Ugric: **sone, *soone, *səne*　　　**Proto-Samoyedic:** **cən*

Proto-Uralic: **səne*

From Austerlitz, R. 1990. "Uralic Languages." In Comrie, B., ed. *Major Languages*. London: Croom Helm.

TABLE 2

Presumed Sources of Presumed Loanwords into Uralic Languages

Uralic	Later Iranian	East Turkic	West Turkic	Baltic	Germanic Older	Germanic 1200+	Slavic
Samoyedic	+	+					+
Ob-Ugric	+	+					+
Hungarian	+	+	+			+	+
Permic	+	+	+				+
Mari	+	+	+				+
Mordva	+	+		+?			+
Balto-Finnic				+	+	+	+
Lappic				+	+	+	+

TABLE 3
Indo-European "Sinew etc." as Possible Etyma for Uralic

Eng. *sinew*, Germ. *Sehne/Senne* OE *sionu*, OHG *sënawa* OInd. *snávan*, *snávah* 'sinew' Latv. *pa-sain-is* 'string' Irish *sin* 'chain'	*seta* 'bristle-like part (bot.)' < Lat. *sæta* 'stiff hair, bristle' Avest. *haētu* 'dam'; ?OInd. OSl. *sětĭ* 'cord, rope' Ru. *sito* 'sieve, bolt' Ukr. *sit'* 'net snare'
Germ. *Seil* 'rope', OE *sāl* OInd. *syáti*, *sináti* 'bind' OBlg. *silo*, Ru. *silo* 'rope'	Lith. *sēta-s* 'fine sieve (esp. horsehair)' German. *Saite* '(mus.) string'
	Ru. *set'* 'net'
	Pre-IE *"*" sāi* ?

As early as 1922 Trombetti had set up an interlocking genetic grid (Figure 2) based on pronouns (1908) and numerals. His was a grand venture, on the scale of our modern Nostraticists but lacking their standards and refinements. Figure 3 is from a skeptic (Austerlitz 1983; see the commentary in Xelimskij 1985). It purports to be a report on the aggregate proposals connecting Uralic with other languages families. Some of these are the result of painstaking work; others are capricious but inspired insights. I have left out the somewhat far-fetched connections like those to Basque, Elamite, Sumerian, Muṇḍa, and Huave.

Obviously, the network shown in Figure 3 contains a set of implications. Uralic appears to have similarities to the various other groups shown, but apart from the similarities to Uralic, little or no evidence has been brought forth to support a hypothesis of genetic relationship among them. Even if two pairs of putative affines, say (1) Uralic and Eskaleut and (2) Uralic and Dravidian, can be shown independently to be cogent and credible, there is still no evidence of a cogent or credible relationship between Eskaleut and Dravidian.

There is no doubt that the most ambitious and the most admirably self-critical of the LRG schools at present is that of the Nostraticists, who are represented in this volume (see Shevoroshkin and Manaster-Ramer). Illič-Svityč 1971, 1976, 1984 and his co-workers impose the same stringent demands on their work with a large number of families as Indo-Europeanists impose on theirs (with fewer languages and within one family); in short, the Nostraticists require that their comparisons be predictive and productive: they work with sound

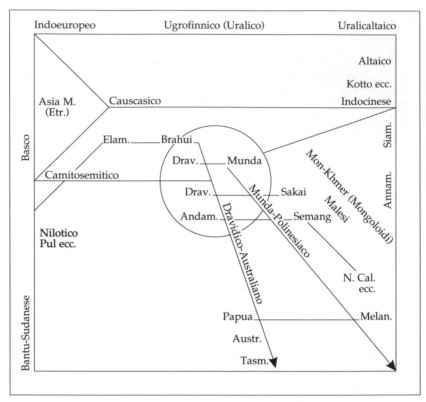

Figure 2. Schema of eastern hemisphere language relationship. *Andam.* = Andamanese; *Annam.* = Annamese (Vietnamese); *Asia M. (Etr.)* = Asia Minor (Etruscan); *Austr.* = Australian; *Basco* = Basque; *Camito-* = Hamito-; *Drav.* = Dravidian; *ecc.* = etc.; *Elam.* = Elamite; *Etr.* = Etruscan; *Kotto* = Kott; *Malesi* = Malay(sian); *Melan.* = Melanesian; *N. Cal.* = New Caledonian; *Pul* = Fula; *Siam* = Siamese (Taic?) *Tasm.* = Tasmanian. (From Trombetti, A. 1922. *Elementi di glottologia*. Bologna: Zanichelli.)

laws of the kind known from Athabascan, Semitic, Tibeto-Burman, or Indo-European studies. And yet there are flaws, just as there are flaws everywhere. I discuss here one example that opens up a broad, disturbing vista.

It is known that in IE Greek *pólis*, Old Indian *pūr* 'city' and *púriḥ* 'town', and Baltic *pilìs* and *pi'ls* 'castle' constitute the only evidence for an etymon that, for the sake of brevity, can be represented by "*polis*" here. This IE item is compared by Illič-Svityč 1984 (pp. 89–93) with a set of Altaic and a set of Uralic words. The Altaic resemblants are given in Table 4. The Buriat form seems to be a neologism. Mon-

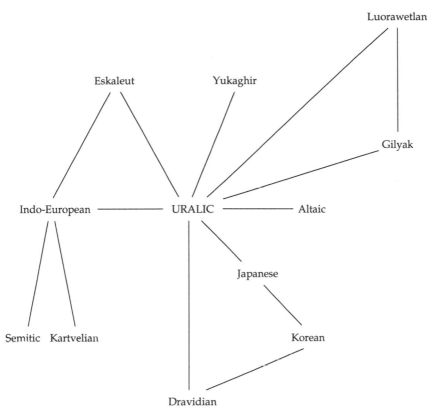

Figure 3. Uralic affinities by Austerlitz 1983.

TABLE 4
Indo-European "*polis*" Resemblants in Altaic

Turkic	Mongolic	Tungus
?Orxon *aγu*, proper noun	Buriat *alga* (neologism?)	Northern Tungus —
Turkic *aγyl*	Mongolian *ail*, *ayil*	Manchu *falga*
'sheep pen, cattle shed, village, neighbors'	'small country town, village, settlement'	'clan, tribe, folk on the same street, quarter of
	balāγān	town; group, clump, grove'

TABLE 5
Indo-European *"polis"* Resemblants in Uralic

Saam	Finn	Mrdv	Mari	Komi	Udmr
	?*palva-*				
LAPPIC	FENNIC				

golian *ail* and *balāyăn* seem to point to two different origins. Northern Tungus seems to have no forms corresponding to Manchu (Southern Tungus) *falga*. The semantic match between Mongolian and Manchu is not altogether convincing, but it is fathomable; the match between Turkic and Mongolic is better. In fact, a subtle progression seems to be at work here (going from west to east), such that Turkic and Mongolic share "village" and Mongolic and Tungusic share "settlement/same-street's-folk." This is not the place to go into the Altaic hypothesis; let me only say that I do not believe in it either. I believe that the three branches just enumerated form a continuum (from west to east, as described) that can be called a language family but is not one on the order of IE or Uralic. The answer to the question must be sought, I believe, in social (military, tribal) and economic (grazing-right) organization. Returning to Nostratic, Uralic does not fare much better than Altaic. Of the evidence adduced in Table 5, the Finnish root is attested only in a derived noun with an obscure history, and the Nenets form is a pious hope. That leaves the Ugric words, within the Ugric subgroup and with good correspondence; the presumed etymon is 'settlement, village'. Is it not more reasonable to assume that this item, which belongs to the sphere of social organization, is a loan, that it entered Proto-Ugric from an unknown source (Iranian is a good candidate, but the word is not attested in Iranian), and that it also penetrated into Turkic and perhaps from Turkic onward? Is it not more rewarding to project the question on the screen of history (or, more modestly, on a facsimile of reality) than simply to assume common origin for the IE, Altaic, and Uralic forms? (I am not competent to discuss the Dravidian and Hamito-Semitic [Afro-Asiatic] resemblants also adduced; Illič-Svityč 1984.)

For me, the lesson learned from this exercise is that this is not a convincing or gratifying way of constructing the edifice of comparative linguistics. I still ask whether there is such a way in long-range comparison. I believe that there is, namely, the exploratory rather than the dogmatic way. Examples of this approach are of two

TABLE 5
(*continued*)

Mnsi	Xnty	Hung	Nnts	Ents	Ngan	Slkp	Kms	1
powl	*pūyəl*	*falu,* *falv-*	*??pe*					2
UGRIC			SAMOYEDIC					3

kinds: (1) the Martin approach (as in this volume), which concentrates on evidence for a putative relationship between two languages without *parti pris*, and (2) the Egerod approach (this volume), which focuses on typological features over areas as large as continents. Both of these open up possibilities to the imagination without losing empirical ground.

LRGs should be self-confirming and recursive rather than additive. They should be self-corrective. If the Uralo-Yukaghir hypothesis (Figure 3) is tenable, new evidence from Yukaghir should buttress or correct what we know about Uralic. There has been no instance of such buttressing as long as there has been a Uralo-Yukaghir hypothesis. On occasion, LGRs are outright obscurantist, as when evidence from Etruscan is invoked.

What should the long-range comparativist do, if not LRG? In my opinion the following problems are more urgent and more accessible:

- *Filiation*: How do dialects become languages, if this is how languages are born?
- *Meaning change*: What are its societal preconditions?
- *Panchronic rules for sound laws*.
- *Pathways of loans*. Which foreign words (*Fremdwörter*) become loanwords (*Lehnwörter*) and which do not?

In short, I believe that the study of the forces that make a language family cohere (or the absence of such forces, which cause it to disintegrate) are a more promising investment to the profession than LRG and that comparisons of two languages at a time (of the traditional or the LRG type) are more promising than mass comparison.

Another urgent problem is that of areal diffusion and convergence, how languages grow to resemble each other (Egerod, this volume).

An ironic aspect of LRGs was almost poignantly pointed out by C. F. and F. M. Voegelin recently (1985). Many Amerindianists became accustomed to working with phyla, often established by intuiting LRGs. Eventually the question arose: Was the experiment worth the investment? The same Amerindianists (often also cultural anthropologists) who are known for their meticulous, microscopic synchronic work also invent Na-Dene and larger constructs, with which they then, often out of piety, remain saddled for generations. See Hamp 1979 and Silverstein 1979.

I now return to the societal aspect of language comparison. What is the origin of linguistic diversity? It is often assumed that separation breeds divergence. This may be so, but the contrasting fact is that contact breeds change, and faster change is, it seems, more often applicable. A bustling monolingual market town with caste dialects (merchants, warriors, bureaucrats, thieves) is a laboratory for change. By contrast, the isolated citadel of contemplation, with only philosophers, monks, and their servants, is a refrigerator. Should we not try to devise a metric for gauging divergence, fission, bifurcation—the tokens of diversity? We also need a metric for social mergers, so as to see what sort of society integrates into another society easily (in terms of language and otherwise). We need a metric for semantic splits. We need a metric for dating. We still do not know when man made his appearance in the New World; 10 or 25 or 40 thousand years ago? If Amerindian diversification took place in the New World, we would do well to design a model for how it happened in time and in space. If it happened earlier, we need another model. (One has been proposed, with little success; Austerlitz 1980; see also Nichols 1990). Or, if we approach the question from the typological side, why not build on Sherzer's 1976 thorough groundwork or use Egerod's approach (in this volume)? I have tried it for Siberia and only on a phonetic-phonological basis (1986).

Then there is the question of how realistic a given LRG is. Regardless of how convincing the Uralo-Dravidian or the Uralo-Penutian LRGs are on purely formal grounds, there is always the rock-bottom problem of how these people moved from one place to the other on the face of the earth. It is not enough simply to set up protoforms. We must remember that we are dealing with human beings who face and overcome (or are overcome by) obstacles such as mountains, the weather, and pestilence. After beginning to reconstruct Gilyak internally I found that Proto-Gilyak resembles Nootka more than modern

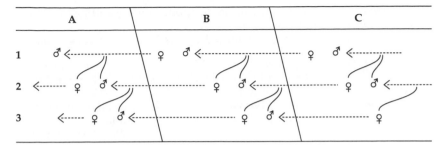

Figure 4. Schema of multilingualism.

Gilyak. Still, I would hesitate to set up a Proto-Nootka-Gilyak parent language at this point.

I have come to believe that bilingualism and even multilingualism was much more common in the past than it is now. Populations were small, the average life span was much shorter, slavery was common, and exogamy widespread. Adults probably learned languages much more easily than they learn them now (as long as there was no book learning), as in the case of slavery. In Figure 4, *A*, *B*, and *C* speak different languages. *B* gives wives to *A*, and *C* to *B*. If I am *1B*, my wife (and my son's wife) comes from *C*. My daughter, *2B*, speaks my language (*B*), she speaks her mother's language, (*C*), and when she marries, she will speak her husband's language (*A*). In this (patrilocal) society, women are trilingual and men bilingual. Such multilingualism is, to say the least, conducive to extensive transfer of vocabulary.

Finally, there is the old taboo, the question of monogenesis or polygenesis. I find it much easier to conceive of monogenesis. To imagine that the factors that conspired to give rise to human language converged more than once is mind boggling. And yet, linguistic diversity may be more easily explained by assuming polygenesis. This is just another of my dilemmas.

REFERENCES CITED

Austerlitz, R. 1972. "Long-range Comparisons of Tamil and Dravidian with Other Language Families in Eurasia." *Proceedings of the Second International Conference-Seminar of Tamil Studies* (Madras, 1968), vol. 1, pp. 254–261. Ed. by R. E. Asher. Madras: International Association for Tamil Research.

————. 1980. "Language-family Density in North America and Eurasia." *Ural-Altaische Jahrbücher* 52: 1–10.

————. 1982. "On Comparing Language Families." *Études Finno-ougriennes* 15: 45–54 (1978–1979).

————. 1983. "Genetic Affiliation among Proto-Languages." *Symposium sæculare Societatis Fenno-ugricæ* = *Mémoires de la Société Finno-ougrienne* 185: 51–57.

————. 1986. "Areal Phonetic Typology in Time: North and East Asia." In Lehmann, W. P., ed. *Language Typology 1985*, papers from the USSR-USA symposium on typology held in Moscow, December 1985. Amsterdam: John Benjamins.

————. 1990. "Uralic Languages." In Comrie, B., ed. *The World's Major Languages*. London: Croom Helm.

Campbell, L., and M. Mithun, eds. 1979. *The Languages of Native America: Historical and Comparative Assessment*. Austin: University of Texas Press.

Egerod, S. 1991. "The Genetic Classification of the Languages of East Asia." This volume.

Hamp, E. P. 1979. "A Glance from Here on." In Campbell and Mithun 1979, pp. 1001–1015.

Illič-Svityč, V. M. 1971, 1976, 1984. *Opyt sravnenija nostratičeskix jazykov (semitoxamitskij, kartvel'skij, indoevropejskij, ural'skij, dravidijskij, altajskij)*. Moscow: Nauka.

Korhonen, M. 1986. "On the Reconstruction of Proto-Uralic and Proto-Finno-Ugrian Consonant Clusters." *Journal de la Société Finno-ougrienne* 80: 153–167.

Lehmann, W. P. 1989. "The Process of Linguistics." This volume.

Martin, S. E. 1989. "Current Research on the Genetic Relationships of Japanese and Korean." This volume.

Nichols, J. 1990. "Linguistic Diversity and the First Settlement of the New World." *Language* 66: 475–521.

Sherzer, J. 1976. *An Areal Typological Study of American Indian Languages North of Mexico*. Amsterdam: North-Holland Publishing Company.

Shevoroshkin, V., and A. Manaster-Ramer. 1989. "Recent Work on Distant Relationships." This volume.

Silverstein, M. 1979. "Penutian: an Assessment." In Campbell and Mithun 1979, pp. 650–691.

Trombetti, A. 1905. *L'unità d'origine del linguaggio*. Bologna: Treves/Beltrami. (Reissued 1962, Bologna: Civitas Dei.)

————. 1908. *Saggi di glottologia generale comparata. I. Pronomi personali*. Bologna: Gamberini e Parmeggiani.

————. 1922. *Elementi di glottologia*. Bologna: Zanichelli.

Voegelin, C. F., and F. M. Voegelin. 1985. "From Comparative Method to Phylum Linguistics and Back Again." *International Journal of American Linguistics* 51: 608–609.

Xelimskij, E. A. 1985. "Review of Symposium sæculare Societatis Fennougricæ (1983)." *Sovetskoe Finno-ugrovedenie* 21: 289–294.

Mathematical Methods of Genetic Classification

SHEILA EMBLETON

There have been many attempts in the literature to develop mathematical models of genetic classification. In a survey paper such as this one, it is not possible to include them all, or even to do justice to the ones included. The methods chosen here are selected for the interest which they have generated in the literature or for their currency. For discussion and references for methods omitted here as well as for further details of those included in this survey, see Embleton 1986.

The mathematical methods used in genetic classification are usually referred to as "lexicostatistical methods," despite the fact that not all the methods involve the lexicon, simply because the best known methods are based on lexical measures. The goal of lexicostatistics then is the development of a mathematical technique for assessing the closeness of the relationship between two genetically related languages, which leads to the tentative reconstruction of the family tree for a group of languages, without using actual historical information about the language family. The perceived advantages of such a technique are the usual ones associated with quantitative methods, namely, objectivity, speed, and the ability to handle large amounts of data. The methods of course have no comment to make on the utility of the family-tree model as opposed to other possible models.

Some mathematical methods attempt to go further than merely the tentative reconstruction of a family tree by providing dates (or *time depths*) for the branching points (or *nodes*) in the tree. These methods are generally referred to as *glottochronology*, with the most celebrated such method being that of Morris Swadesh.

Although lexical measures (such as cognate counts) are often used, it should be pointed out at the outset that the mathematics in no way depends directly on the use of lexical measures. However, there is an indirect dependence in that the mathematics requires a large enough number of items on the test list or feature list for validity and that these items be independent from one another. These conditions are most easily satisfied by lexical data. Linguistic considerations favoring lexical data include the ease of measurement of similarity, the availability of word lists in large numbers of languages (including some, such as Crimean Gothic, for which little else is available), and the ease with which universals can be excluded; linguistic considerations against lexical data revolve primarily around problems associated with borrowing.

1. PAST TREATMENTS OTHER THAN BY SWADESH'S METHOD

The first mathematical method to receive any significant amount of attention in the linguistic literature is that of Kroeber and Chrétien 1937 (important later articles include Chrétien 1943, Chrétien 1956, and Ellegård 1959), based on a technique used in ethnography and physical anthropology. We take a set of languages $L_1, L_2, \ldots, L_m$ and a set of features $f_1, f_2, \ldots, f_N$, whose presence or absence can be determined for each of the languages. For each pair of languages, L_i and L_j, we can then summarize our information in a 2×2 *contingency table* (Table 1).

The amount of association between L_i and L_j is then given by

$$ r = \frac{ad - bc}{\sqrt{(a + b)(c + d)(a + c)(b + d)}} $$

which is called the *tetrachoric correlation coefficient*. This can be evaluated for statistical significance by calculating $\chi^2_{(1)} = Nr^2$. The values of r allow us to rank the closeness of the relationship for each pair of languages and subsequently to reconstruct the family tree. The method does not provide for the calculation of time depths and hence is lexicostatistical, rather than glottochronological.

There are various problems in the practical application of this method. The features must be independent of one another (particularly important for the χ^2 statistic), and the 74 features used by Kroeber and Chrétien 1937 in their work in Indo-European clearly are not (as just one example of nonindependence, f_{23} is *$\bar{a}$ and *$\bar{o}$ not assimilated, f_{24} is *$\bar{a}$ assimilated to *$\bar{o}$, and f_{25} is *$\bar{o}$ assimilated to *$\bar{a}$).

TABLE 1

	Number of features exhibited by L_j	Number of features not exhibited by L_j	Total
Number of Features Exhibited by L_i	a	b	$a + b$
Number of Features Not Exhibited by L_i	c	d	$c + d$
Total	$a + c$	$b + d$	N

There is a problem in interpreting negative correlations (such as r for Italic and Iranian is -0.66); experiments with different ways of calculating r did not solve the problem. Much of the literature on this method is devoted to discussion of whether d should be included in the calculations. The general consensus seems to be that counting d (that is, shared absence) makes sense *only* if we know that the features in question *were* in the proto-language. Since we will often want to apply the method in cases where we do not know the proto-language (as in Chrétien's 1956 Papuan data), this is a definite problem. Not counting d also raises problems in finding a valid formula for r.

The second mathematical method of importance is that presented by Alan S. C. Ross in 1950 and further applied in Davies and Ross 1975 and Villemin 1983. Although at first glance it appears quite different from the Kroeber and Chrétien model, it can be shown (Brainerd 1968) to be equivalent (even in underlying assumptions), just camouflaged by different notation, to the version of the Kroeber and Chrétien model which does not count d.

If we assume as before that we have m languages and N features, we can construct an $N \times m$ table for the language family of the form in Table 2. If a feature is exhibited in a certain language, we mark the appropriate cell in the table with a cross. The question of the relationship of L_i and L_j is then equivalent to the question: "Given the number of crosses in the two relevant columns, what is the probability of obtaining the given number of cases of a row with a cross in *each* of the two columns (or a greater number) if the crosses were placed in the two columns at random?" (Ross 1950: 27). The smaller the probability, the less likely the observed arrangement is due to chance and hence the more likely that L_i and L_j are related. The values of these probabilities can then be used to reconstruct the family tree.

TABLE 2

Feature	L_1	L_2	L_3	...	L_m
		Language set			
1	X	X			X
2		X	X		
3	X	X	X		X
4	X				X
.					
.					
.					
N	X		X		

The necessary formulae are as follows. Let

n_i = Number of features exhibited by L_i (equivalent to $a + b$ in the Kroeber and Chrétien model)
n_j = Number of features exhibited by L_j ($= a + c$)
r = Number of features exhibited by both L_i and L_j ($= a$)
R = Random variable corresponding to r

Then the probability of getting r or more correspondences is

$$P(R \geq r) = \sum_{R=r}^{N} \frac{\binom{n_i}{R}\binom{N - n_i}{n_j - R}}{\binom{N}{n_j}}$$

which (using a normal approximation) is approximately

$$1 - N_z \left(\frac{\dfrac{r - n_i n_j}{N}}{\sqrt{\dfrac{n_i n_j (N - n_i)(N - n_j)}{N^2(N - 1)}}} \right)$$

Since the Ross model is essentially equivalent to the Kroeber and Chrétien model, it should be noted that once again it is crucial that the features be independent of one another. Ross 1950 demonstrates his model using Kroeber and Chrétien's 74-feature list for Indo-European; thus his results may be suspect. Note also that the Ross model is lexicostatistical, not glottochronological.

Historically the third mathematical method of importance is Swadesh-style glottochronology, but this is treated in Section 2. The next mathematical method not in the Swadesh tradition seems

TABLE 3

Meaning	Language			
	A	B	C	D
Bone	1	1	1	1
Child	1	2	3	4
Dog	1	2	2	1
Father	1	3	2	1
Fish	1	1	1	2

to have been invented (apparently independently) three times: Gleason 1959; Dobson 1969; and Krishnamurti, Moses, and Danforth 1983. The method is to construct all possible family trees and, for each tree, to calculate the number of *rejections, trivial acceptances,* and *true acceptances.* Suppose we have the data in Table 3. For each meaning, the words in the different languages are identified by the same number if they are cognate and by different numbers if they are noncognate. The word for "bone" simply suggests that we are dealing with related languages, whereas the word for "child" simply says that we have four different languages; such words will fit any possible tree and thus are known as *trivial acceptances.* The words for "father" and "fish" are also trivial acceptances (although less obviously so).

Now consider the meaning "dog." This tells us that Tree 1 cannot be correct

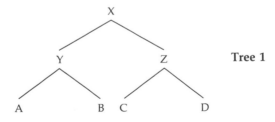

Tree 1

because *B* and *C* have cognate words and hence ought to have a common ancestor not shared by *A* and *D* (which share a different cognate). Thus "dog" is a *rejection* for Tree 1. However, "dog" would fit a tree such as Tree 2 (page 370). Thus "dog" is a *true acceptance* for Tree 2. The calculation of rejections, true acceptances, and trivial acceptances can of course be done by computer.

It is possible that several trees may fit the data more or less

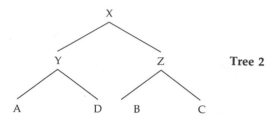

Tree 2

equally well, in which case other data (such as further linguistic data, historical or archeological evidence) must decide among them. It is also possible that *no* tree fits the data perfectly (that is, with no rejections), with borrowings being the likely cause. For example, Tree 1 might in fact be the correct representation of the genetic relationship, with C borrowing the word for "dog" from B or vice versa. If Tree 1 had accounted for perhaps all but this one meaning, with other possible trees being less successful, we could safely assume that borrowing had occurred for this meaning and that Tree 1 was indeed "correct."

The major problem with this method is the sheer number of possible trees for any reasonably sized language family. For two languages, there is 1 possible tree; for three languages, 3 trees; for four, 15; for five, 105; for six, 945; for seven, 10,395; for ten, 3.4459×10^7, and so on. Even by computer the method quickly becomes unworkable. Checking all possible trees would become unnecessary if we could narrow down the number of possible trees first. The methods to be discussed in the next few paragraphs can be used for such narrowing (or of course in their own right as tree-generating methods). Before leaving this method, it should be pointed out that it is lexicostatistical, not glottochronological.

By the early 1970s the advent of computers enabled certain types of methods requiring large-scale computation to become practical. One such method is *hierarchical cluster analysis*, a clustering technique which had already found wide application in numerical taxonomy, a subfield of biology. An early example of a linguistic application is Henrici 1973, involving Bantu. To illustrate the technique, I use here some Romance cognate data from the 215-word lists in Rea 1973.

For each pair of languages L_i and L_j, count the number of items for which L_i and L_j have *non*cognate forms and enter the resulting number in the appropriate cell of what is called the *dissimilarity ma-*

TABLE 4

	Fr	Sp	Po	Ru	Ca	It
Fr	0	64	66	97	61	49
Sp	64	0	32	99	60	63
Po	66	32	0	101	62	57
Ru	97	99	101	0	97	84
Ca	61	60	62	97	0	56
It	49	63	57	84	56	0

Fr = French; Sp = Spanish; Po = Portuguese; Ru = Rumanian; Ca = Catalan; It = Italian.

TABLE 5

	Fr	(Sp-Po)	Ru	Ca	It
Fr	0	64	97	61	49
(Sp-Po)	64	0	99	60	57
Ru	97	99	0	97	84
Ca	61	60	97	0	56
It	49	57	84	56	0

trix (which of course is always symmetric). The dissimilarity matrix for the Romance data is given in Table 4. We are now ready to begin the actual clustering procedure, which comes in three minor variations: *nearest neighbor, farthest neighbor,* and *group average*. The nearest neighbor method is as follows. Find the smallest dissimilarity in the matrix; in our case, this is 32 for Sp and Po. Thus the lowest node in the tree represents the bifurcation of Sp and Po. Then we amalgamate the Sp row and Po row into one row in the matrix, by replacing it with an (Sp-Po) row consisting of the *smaller* of the two entries; we do the same for the Sp and Po columns. The matrix becomes as shown in Table 5. We then repeat the procedure with this new matrix until all languages have been attached to the tree. For the above data, the tree will be ((Sp-Po)−((Fr-It)−Cat)−Ru), or Tree 3.

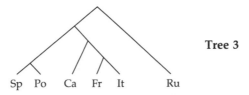

Tree 3

Sp Po Ca Fr It Ru

For the farthest-neighbor method, we use the same procedure but choose the *larger* of the two entries when amalgamating rows and

columns. The group-average method takes the *average* of the two
entries on amalgamation. In practice, all three methods usually
lead to the same family tree (as they do here).

There are several things worth noting about this method. First,
nonlexical distance measures can just as easily be used. Embleton
(1986: 35–38) demonstrates the same clustering methods on phonological distance measures, based on Romance data from Grimes and
Agard 1959, and (1986: 38–40) shows the close correlation between
trees obtained by all three clustering methods from lexical, mor-
phosyntactic, and genetic measures for seven Yanomama dialects,
based on data from Spielman, Migliazza, and Neel 1974. Second, the
method can be used on its own to generate trees or to narrow down
the number of possible trees that require evaluation with the previously described method (that is, where all possible trees are constructed). Third, although the method as described here is lexicostatistical rather than glottochronological, it can be adapted to become glottochronological by using a regression technique. Since the
mathematics involved is tedious (although not particularly complicated), the interested reader is referred to Embleton (1986: 32–40),
which includes application to Romance and to Yanomama.

Hierarchical cluster analysis is not the only mathematical technique requiring large-scale computing capacity that can be applied
to classification problems. Multidimensional scaling, factor analysis,
and principal-coordinates analysis (all available as computer package
programs) have been applied in numerical taxonomy as well as in
linguistics (Davies and Ross 1975, Henrici 1973, Dobson and Black
1979, Black 1976), although these methods are used in linguistics
more commonly for dialect classification (Linn [no date], Linn and
Regal 1984, Embleton 1985) than for language classification. In general, results of these methods show that the configurations obtained
from the linguistic data correspond closely to the actual geographical
locations of the languages (or dialects), with any distortions generally being due to borrowing. These methods are also lexicostatistical,
rather than glottochronological.

2. PAST TREATMENTS BY SWADESH'S METHOD

Swadesh 1950 and 1952 introduced a model of language change
based on a vocabulary turnover process analogous to radioactive
decay. The model claims that a standardized test list of N meanings (called *basic core vocabulary* or a *Swadesh list*) can be constructed
which are likely to be found in all cultures (such as body parts, lower

numerals, certain kinship terms, flora and fauna, and topographical and naturally occurring phenomena) and which are less subject to change and borrowing than the general vocabulary of the language. Over time, *morpheme decay* occurs; that is, in each language, some morphemes or words representing meanings on the list are replaced by others for a variety of reasons (such as taboo, semantic extension or narrowing, semantic shifts, borrowing). If one further assumes that this rate of decay is constant, one can calculate the elapsed time since any pair of languages split from their common ancestor. The mathematics involved is only summarized here; full derivations can be found in Lees 1953 and Embleton 1982, 1983, and 1986.

Let R = Rate of morpheme decay (*replacement* rate; Swadesh and Lees refer to *retention* rate, which is $1 -$ Replacement rate)
N = Number of words in the test list
$n(t)$ = Number of words unchanged since t_0

Then,

$$\frac{dn(t)}{dt} = -Rn(t) \tag{1}$$

and

$$n(t_0) = N \text{ (boundary condition)} \tag{2}$$

(1) and (2) give

$$n(t) = n(t_0)e^{-R(t - t_0)} = Ne^{-R(t - t_0)} \tag{3}$$

(3) implies

$$t - t_0 = -\frac{1}{R} \ln \frac{n(t)}{N} \tag{4}$$

which is the time depth (that is, elapsed time between t and t_0). Thus the time depth since a pair of languages split is

$$\frac{-1}{2R} \ln \frac{n(t)}{N} \tag{5}$$

R has been estimated (from languages with historical records) as approximately 19%/1,000 years for $N = 200$ or approximately 14%/1,000 years for $N = 100$; the rate of morpheme decay for the 100-word Swadesh list is lower because it is even more resistant to change and borrowing than the 200-word list. Thus for each pair of languages we simply substitute the appropriate values for R, N, $n(t)$ (note that this is the number of words unchanged in *both* languages since t_o, that is, the number of cognates for that pair) in (5) to calculate the time depth; natural logarithms (ln, or $\log_e$) can be found in tables, by slide rule, or on many pocket calculators. By calculating time depths pairwise for all language pairs in the family, we can eventually reconstruct a family tree with dates (that is, glottochronology) for the entire family.

The method is so simple and easy to apply that it seemed to offer fresh hope as well as quick results in genetic classification, particularly for families with little or no recorded history (Swadesh originally developed the method for application to Amerindian). Unfortunately, "simple" turned out to be "simplistic," a situation summarized by Oswalt (1971: 421) as follows: "inflated expectations . . . led to rapid disillusionment and deflation by the easy production of counterexamples." Few topics in historical linguistics have raised emotions as high or spilled as much ink as the debate over glottochronology, particularly in the 1950s and 1960s (for the flavor of that debate and an idea of the range of linguistic application, see Embleton 1986). The studies undertaken fall roughly into three groups, which I refer to as "pro-glottochronological," "anti-glottochronological," and "neutral." Pro-glottochronological studies typically apply the method to some language family and then either show that the results coincide with historical, archeological, or other linguistic evidence, or show how any divergence from other evidence can be explained. Although they reveal some problems with the method (such as skewing of time depths because of contact; difficulty in finding a unique equivalent for each test-list meaning), their outlook tends to be optimistic (such as belief that the method could be revised in some way; that the divergence is not serious). In contrast are the anti-glottochronological studies, which follow the same pattern and reveal the same problems but then either take a pessimistic approach to the problems encountered (for example, we can never hope for anything from mathematical methods anyway, so we should abandon all such attempts now) or blow small problems out of all proportion (for example, Swadesh does not state whether "spit" is to be taken as a noun or a verb, and so the method is therefore imprecise and useless). The neutral studies simply assume that the method is valid and then use it as a tool for some particular purpose (such as for subgrouping; to infer borrowing patterns).

Stripping away the emotion of the debate over Swadesh's glottochronology, one can see that all three types of study reveal the same sorts of problems:

1. Is R a universal (with respect to time, between languages, for different meanings)? (Some authors have suggested allowing R to vary with time, language, and meaning.)
2. The splits in the *Stammbaum* model are not "clean"; languages often influence one another after the split, and there is generally a type of drift evident immediately after a split (whereby tendencies already present in the parent language come to fruition only in the daughter languages).
3. a. Cognates may not be recognizable because of sound change (oft-cited examples are *chef–head* and *tooth–Zahn*). This leads to overestimating the time depth.
   b. Chance similarities may be interpreted as cognates (oft-cited examples are *haben–habēre* and *day–diēs*). This leads to underestimating the time depth.
   In practice, it is hoped that 3a and 3b will cancel each other.
4. It is assumed that there is a single word per language for each test-list meaning. What should be done with multiple synonyms? (Proposed solutions include choosing one at random; choosing the most frequent; consistently choosing the one that will give the highest or lowest cognate count; using fractional scoring.)
5. Is there such a thing as the "basic vocabulary"? (The usual solution here was to claim that it was extremely rare to be unable to translate a test-list meaning into the language at hand, and so one should just omit that item for that language.)

There were attempts to deal with some of these problems, but these were generally overlooked in the emotionalism of the debate. As Hymes (in van der Merwe 1966: 492) succinctly states: "It is striking how critics of glottochronology continue to discover the same criticisms, but not the constructive attempts to deal with them." But the most serious blow to glottochronology came from an article in *Language* (Chrétien 1962), which purported to disprove the mathematics of the model. This article was accepted at face value by most linguists, although mathematicians were aware of the fact that Chrétien's "disproof" itself was faulty, largely based on a misunderstanding of the difference between deterministic and stochastic (that is, probabilistic) models (a difference which had not been made clear in the original articles by Swadesh and Lees). A rebuttal to Chrétien 1962 was published by Dobson, Kruskal, Sankoff, and Savage in 1972 but unfortunately in *Anthropological Linguistics*, where it did not come to the attention of very many linguists.

Mathematicians continued to work on the model, gradually introducing more parameters. The culmination was Sankoff's 1973 *fully parametrized lexicostatistics*, in which

$$E\left(\frac{C}{N}\right) = [1 + \gamma\theta - \gamma - \theta]\,[1 + 2\beta(t - \kappa)]^{-\alpha} + \gamma + \theta - \gamma\theta \qquad (6)$$

and

$$\text{MLE}(t) = \frac{\left(\dfrac{1 - \gamma - \theta + \gamma\theta}{\dfrac{C}{N} - \gamma - \theta + \gamma\theta}\right)^{1/\alpha} - 1}{2\beta} + \kappa \qquad (7)$$

where C = number of cognates (Sankoff allowed multiple synonyms, with a fractional scoring system)

α, β are parameters of the Γ-distribution of replacement rates (introduced by Sankoff)

γ = Probability of chance recurrent cognation (in which the words at the beginning and end of the time interval are cognate, but there has been one or more noncognate replacements in the interim; introduced by Brainerd)

κ = Drift constant (introduced by Gleason)

θ = Borrowing probability (introduced by Sankoff, who laconically notes that "the mathematics become considerably more complicated" [1973: 100]).

Note how the model is now explicitly stated to be stochastic through the use of terms such as "estimated value" (E) and "maximum likelihood estimate" (MLE). Examination of limiting cases as parameters approach zero reveals the simpler Swadesh model. Also

$$\lim_{t\to\infty} E\left(\frac{C}{N}\right) = \gamma + \theta - \gamma\theta \qquad (8)$$

Thus as the time depth becomes indefinitely large, the proportion of cognates will depend on borrowing and chance cognation alone. Sankoff found that the more complex models behave remarkably similarly to the simpler ones, partially justifying the earlier (often implicit) mathematical assumptions.

3. INCORPORATING BORROWING RATES INTO A SWADESH-STYLE METHOD

A persistent concern in the construction of a test list has been the elimination of meanings susceptible to borrowing (or at least a reduction in their number). But it is by no means clear that *any* meanings exist which are completely immune to borrowing, especially in situations of large-scale contact. This uncertainty, coupled with the statistical advantages of a longer list, has resulted in an attempt to incorporate borrowing more ambitious than "fully parametrized lexicostatistics." The outline (in a biological context) was provided by Sankoff 1972a and was transferred to a linguistic context as well as extended and corrected by Embleton 1982 and 1983. Essentially, a geographical dimension is added to the family tree.

The following information is necessary for all languages in the family:

S_{XY} = Similarity between language X and language Y
  $(0 \leq S_{XY} \leq 1)$
r_X = Replacement rate for language X
b_{XY} = Borrowing rate from language X into language Y
k_X = Number of neighbors of language X (that is, those languages in contact with language X)
N_X is the set of neighbors of X.

The mathematics accepts any type of similarity measure (such as a cognate measure, a phonological divergence measure), with corresponding rates of change of similarity due to internal (r_X) and external (b_{XY}) change.

The set of differential equations used in reconstruction is given by

$$\frac{dS_{XY}}{dt} = -(r_X + r_Y)S_{XY} + \frac{1}{k_X} \sum_{Z \varepsilon N_X} (b_{YZ}S_{YZ} - b_{XY}S_{XY}) + \frac{1}{k_Y} \sum_{Z \varepsilon N_Y} (b_{XZ}S_{XZ} - b_{XY}S_{XY}) \tag{9}$$

(Full derivation and explanation is given in Embleton 1986.) The reconstruction yields a tree with dates; hence the method is glottochronological. However, the actual tree topology depends on the *relative* values of the rates only; thus the lexicostatistical use of the method is more accurate than its glottochronological use, especially if the rate estimates are at all doubtful (more on this below).

The method was extensively tested in over 5,000 simulation runs. Correlations of 0.9 and higher between generated and reconstructed trees (both in the topology and node dates) were found for computer-simulated data, even for values of r_X and b_{XY} much higher than those found in natural language. This is an important result because it gives an idea of the accuracy we can expect under the most ideal conditions; the situation will of course be worse in actual application. The improved results compared to previous methods (Swadesh's method, Ross's method, and so on, all of which had problems due to borrowing) are due to the incorporation of borrowing rates into the reconstruction process. Being able to incorporate borrowing instead of having to eliminate it lessens our dependence on the Swadesh lists; we could, for example, use different lists appropriate to different parts of the world. The results of the simulation also indicate that $N = 200$ is most appropriate (accuracy decreases badly for $N = 100$ and does not increase significantly for $N = 500$).

4. APPLICATION TO REAL LANGUAGE DATA

4.1. Germanic

The next logical step after successful testing on simulated data is testing on real language data. The Germanic family was selected because there is a consensus on most aspects of its history, and the family is large enough, with enough contact interinfluence, to

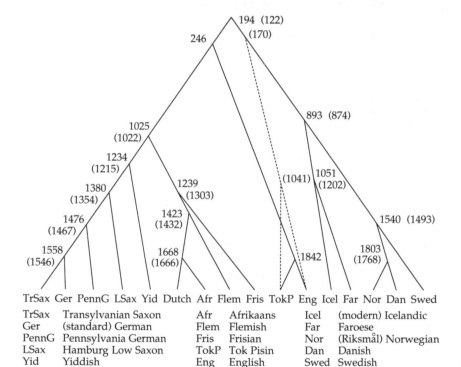

TrSax	Transylvanian Saxon	
Ger	(standard) German	
PennG	Pennsylvania German	
LSax	Hamburg Low Saxon	
Yid	Yiddish	

Afr	Afrikaans
Flem	Flemish
Fris	Frisian
TokP	Tok Pisin
Eng	English

Icel	(modern) Icelandic
Far	Faroese
Nor	(Riksmål) Norwegian
Dan	Danish
Swed	Swedish

Tree 4. Germanic. A, *Solid lines*, dates not in parentheses. **B**, *Dotted lines*, dates in parentheses.

TABLE 6
Known Historical Information, Germanic

Divergence	Reconstructed	Historical information
Nor-Dan	1803	Peace of Kiel, 1814
TokP-Eng	1842	Early to mid-nineteenth century (from migration evidence)
Dutch-Afr	1668	First European settlement, 1652; first comment on divergence, 1685
Ger-TrSax	1558	Waves of settlers from 1211 to 1846
Dan-Swed	1540	Accession of the Vasas, 1523
Ger-PennG	1476	Settlement, 1863, but admixture from other dialects and divergence from German before emigration
Dutch-Flem	1423	Both developed from thirteenth-century Low Franconian standard, but considered separate by sixteenth century
Ger-LSax	1380*	Low Saxon texts from 770, more numerous from ninth century
Dutch-Fris	1239*	First written records, fourteenth century
Ger-Yid	1234	End of the Crusade period in late thirteenth century
Icel-Far	1051*	Settled from Norway and Iceland after Norse occupation of Iceland
Ger-Dutch	1025*	Dutch "forged" out of various dialects, 1200–1500
Icel-Dan	893	Settlement of Iceland, 874 until 930
Eng-Ger	246	Traditional date for settlement of England is 449, but divergence already in continental homeland
West-North	194	Second century A.D.

NOTE: For abbreviations see Tree 4.
*Poor agreement with historical facts.

present a valid test. The 200-word Swadesh lists for sixteen present-day languages (and nine historically attested languages to aid in rate estimation) together with Equation 9 yielded Tree 4.

Some known historical dates for comparison are given in Table 6.

In looking at Tree 4,A, we see first of all that the topology of the tree (that is, the lexicostatistical aspect) is acceptable. In evaluating the glottochronological success of the method, we see that most agreements are very good. Two to note in particular are Tok Pisin (where there has been massive contact: $r = 97.7\%/1,000$ years; $b = 41\%/1,000$ years from languages outside the Germanic family) and Icelandic (often cited [as by Bergsland and Vogt 1962] as an instance of the failure of Swadesh's method). But four reconstructed dates (marked * in Table 6) are poor, postdating a more acceptable earlier historical date. These would seem to be due to undetected borrowing (as from standard German into Low Saxon), which indicates that b may need to be increased if *Verkehrsgemeinschaften* or prestige language influences are suspected. For a fuller discussion, see Embleton 1986.

Tree 4,B, is the tree reconstructed when b is set to zero (that is, that would have been reconstructed by standard glottochronology, which does not incorporate borrowing rates). Note that English is incorrectly placed with the North Germanic languages (there are sixteen Scandinavian loans in the 200-word Swadesh list) and that the date for Tok Pisin becomes absurd. This demonstrates conclusively that borrowing rates must be incorporated into any lexicostatistical or glottochronological method that aspires to validity for natural language.

4.2. Romance

A further test on a family with a relatively "known" history is provided by Romance. This is a more difficult test than Germanic because of a larger amount of interinfluence and because of the continuing influence of Latin. The tree obtained (using 200-word Swadesh lists) is Tree 5. Some known historical dates for comparison are given in Table 7.

In Tree 5,A, the topology is acceptable, as are the dates for Papiamentu, Rumantsch, and Rumanian. All the other dates are too late, with undetected borrowing as the probable cause (more on this below). Tree 5,B, is the tree reconstructed when b is set to zero; the to-

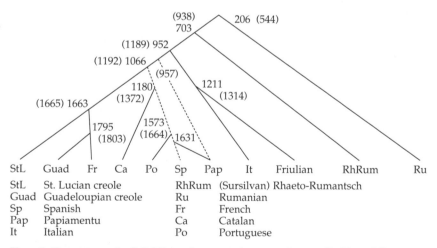

StL	St. Lucian creole	RhRum	(Sursilvan) Rhaeto-Rumantsch
Guad	Guadeloupian creole	Ru	Rumanian
Sp	Spanish	Fr	French
Pap	Papiamentu	Ca	Catalan
It	Italian	Po	Portuguese

Tree 5. Romance. A, *Solid lines,* dates not in parentheses. **B,** *Dotted lines,* dates in parentheses.

TABLE 7
Known Historical Information, Romance

Divergence	Reconstructed	Historical information
Guad-Fr	1795	Occupied by French from 1635; still French today
StL-Fr	1663	French colonization, 1650; British from 1803
Pap-Sp	1631	Curaçao first occupied by Spain, 1527; Dutch domination from 1634 to present
Po-Sp	1573	First *written* records of each in twelfth century; Portuguese separate by early eleventh century, confirmed by political events; *Poema del Cid* composed around 1140 in Castilian
Friulian-It	1211	Friuli under Langobards from 568, then Carolingian and Bavarian, under Venice from 1420, Austria from end of eighteenth century, Italy since 1866; Venice established as a city-state, 697; growth of Venetian influence from ninth century, height in fifteenth century
Ca–other "Iberian"	1180	First *written* records of Catalan in twelfth century
"Iberian"-Fr	1066	Strassburg Oaths, 842; death of last writers knowing Classical Latin and repetition of Latin liturgical formulas without comprehension in sixth to eighth centuries
It–"Fr-Iberian"	952	First *written* record of Italian 960 (Placito Capuano)
RhRum–other "West Romance"	703	Ostrogoths conquered area, 489; Franks conquered Ostrogoths in sixth century; Carolingian from mid-eighth century, beginning of influence by German rather than Rhaeto-Romanic nobility
Ru–"West Romance"	206	Dacia conquered and colonized, A.D. 101–106; last Roman troops withdrawn to south of Danube, 270; official split of Empire, 395

NOTE: For abbreviations see Tree 5.

pology and date for Papiamentu are seriously wrong, and the problem with postdating of dates becomes even more severe. Again we have proof that borrowing rates must be included in the reconstruction algorithm.

To check whether undetected borrowing could indeed be the cause of the postdatings, we multiplied by 1½ all the borrowing rates from Latin into French, Spanish, Italian, Portuguese, and

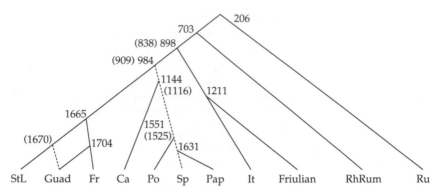

Tree 6. Romance. A, *Solid lines,* dates not in parentheses. **B,** *Dotted line,*
dates in parentheses.

Catalan as well as from French into Italian, Spanish, Portuguese,
Catalan, and Guadeloupian creole (see Tree 6,*A*). The corresponding
rates for the other languages were not increased because these languages experienced much less influence from Latin and French;
also, most of the influence was from outside the Romance family
and thus much easier to detect (such as Slavic, Greek, Turkish, and
Hungarian influence on Rumanian). The dates become better, but
there is still postdating.

A further experiment in increasing borrowing rates was attempted.
Both St Lucian creole and Guadeloupian creole have French as their
parent, and both islands have similar histories except that English
has functioned as a prestige language for St Lucian creole since 1803,
whereas French has continued to be the prestige language for Guadeloupian creole. Our calculated value of *r* for St Lucian creole is approximately 1⅔ times *r* for Guadeloupian creole, with the difference
presumably largely due to French influence (either slowing down
the normal replacement process or causing words previously lost to
be reborrowed from French). Thus we have a rough estimate of the
amount of undetected borrowing from French into Guadeloupian
creole. Tree 6,*B*, gives the result of the reconstruction with the same
selected set of borrowing rates increased by 1⅔. Agreement with
historical fact in dates and in the topology associated with Guadeloupian creole is better. Thus an arbitrary increase in borrowing
rates, perhaps even a large one, may occasionally be necessary to
handle suspected large-scale borrowing. For a fuller discussion of
Romance and the problem of undetected borrowing, see Embleton 1986.

4.3. Wakashan

The purpose of developing mathematical methods of genetic classification is primarily for application to families whose history is disputed or unknown. To see the types of problem arising in such an application, the method of Section 3 was applied to the six languages of the Wakashan family (spoken on Vancouver Island, the adjacent British Columbia coast, and northern Washington state); its further links (to Salishan, Algonquian, and so on) are uncertain and not considered here. The languages are usually given as Haisla, Heiltsuk, and Kwakwala in the North branch and Nitinaht, Nootka, and Makah in the South branch.

The 200-word lists used were not Swadesh lists but included items from the Swadesh lists as well as other meanings basic to Wakashan culture (such as flora and fauna, hunting and fishing terms). The Wakashan tribes, like many other West Coast tribes, have an established network of *potlatch* relationships (illustrated in Figure 1). Potlatches are ceremonial occasions at which many people congregate for several days to feast, sing, give gifts, and make speeches. It is at the potlatches that the various linguistic groups

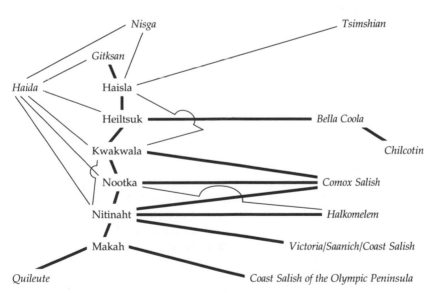

Figure 1. Wakashan potlatch relationships.
Names in italics, Non-Wakashan groups.
━━━━, Extensive potlatch relationships; ──────, less extensive potlatch relationships.

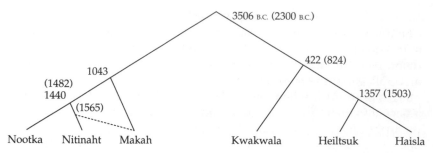

Tree 7. Wakashan. A, *Solid lines,* dates not in parentheses. **B,** *Dotted line,* date in parentheses (borrowing rates set to zero).

come into contact, and thus the potlatch relationships give a rough measure of linguistic contact.

The reconstruction obtained is given in Tree 7,*A*. The topology agrees in all respects with the opinions of Wakashanists, except in the one place where Wakashanists disagree. Klokeid (no date) and Jacobsen (1979) feel that Nitinaht is more closely related to Makah, whereas Sawyer (1982) feels that Nitinaht is more closely related to Nootka. The reconstruction here agrees with Sawyer (whose arguments were entirely phonological). In addition, Tree 7,*B*, indicates that Sawyer may indeed be correct in her claim that Klokeid and Jacobsen have been misled *by a large number of borrowings* into thinking that Nitinaht and Makah are more closely related. As for the glottochronological aspects, the figures obtained here agree with suggestions made by Sapir and Sawyer rather than with those made by Swadesh and Jacobsen (see Embleton 1986). But the glottochronological aspects of the reconstruction are much less reliable than the lexicostatistical aspects because of problems in the computation and calibration of the rate estimates.

The application to Wakashan seems to offer some additional evidence on current topics of dispute within Wakashan. But it also reveals further problems with rate estimation (both for r and for b) for languages with unknown histories. Furthermore, the determination of the borrowing relationships was fortuitously easy here because of potlatching; it would not be so easy in most cases (for example, Athapaskan).

5. PROSPECTS

The method described in Section 3 is the most reliable mathematical method for either lexicostatistics or glottochronology to appear so far, largely because it incorporates borrowing into the reconstruction process. It should also be clear that it is by no means reliable enough to be considered a substitute for any of the more usual methods but rather perhaps as a supplement to them.

There are three possible revisions to the model, all of which are easy from the mathematical or computational point of view but problematic linguistically.

1. The rates could be allowed to vary additionally between meanings and over time. Thus r_x and b_{xy} would become r_{xkt} and b_{xykt}, where k represents the meaning and t time. In practice, this will turn out to be of little use. For example, in Wakashan it was difficult enough to estimate r_x and b_{xy}, let alone r_{xkt} and b_{xykt} (although there is some evidence of potlatch relationships changing over time).

2. We could allow multiple synonyms for each meaning on the test list and have a metric to compare frequency distributions. The gains for this will be limited too. First, the situation does not arise as often as critics think it does. Second, Sankoff (1972b, 1973) showed that the results turn out about the same as allowing just one synonym per meaning. Third, this requires information about frequency which we are unlikely to have, especially for little studied languages, and raises further questions (such as, frequency in which style?).

3. There are various places in the method where weightings would be possible. For example, different items on the test list could be weighted differently (such as based on "experience"—those that have proven reliable in the past could be weighted more heavily). The weightings of course would be subjective, but at least it would be explicit as to what they are.

Perhaps the most practical solution would be simply to be aware that the reconstruction algorithm *could* be revised in these ways *if* we had additional information to utilize (such as that about rate variation over time). The danger in revising it before we have such information is that we could easily be misled into thinking our model and hence our results to be more precise than is really the case. On a more mundane level, it would be a considerable waste in computer storage and computational efficiency.

The method also needs to be tested on nonlexical data. The mathematics and the simulation results remain valid for any type of data, but the testing so far on real languages (Germanic, Romance, and Wakashan) has been done only on lexical data.

Another way in which the method could be used (although it has not yet been done) is to turn it "backwards," enabling one to experiment with different rates and topologies. For example, one could ask what borrowing rates would be necessary to produce a certain topology and then ask if such rates are plausible.

For mathematical methods in general, the future is unclear. First, there are few people working in the field because most linguists do not have adequate mathematics to develop the techniques and most mathematicians do not have sufficient linguistic expertise to test the techniques they develop (teamwork would be an obvious solution). Second, the field has been badly hurt by the emotional debates and irrational statements of the past. Both "sides" are to blame here. Those in favor of mathematical methods have sometimes been guilty of making exaggerated claims as to the potential usefulness and accuracy of their methods, even implying that the comparative method and internal reconstruction are soon to become obsolete. Many of their claims have also been premature, based on insufficient exploration of the mathematical assumptions underlying a given model, insufficient mathematical testing, and insufficient testing on "known" linguistic data. Those against the use of mathematical methods have sometimes been afraid of new methods or of their replacing the old ones, or simply of numbers in general. Sometimes the objections are to inference (if something cannot be said with 100 percent certainty, we should not say anything at all), but then these same objectors are willing to turn around quite happily to use the classical methods of inference (albeit well tested and refined). To quote Grace (1965: 4), "Historical events are not directly accessible through any means. Therefore infallible results are forever beyond our reach. The only means available in genetic classification involve inference." With mathematical methods an element of subjectivity will always be there (for example, in the rate estimates; in the counting of cognates; in the construction of a phonological divergence measure), but any arbitrariness or subjectivity must be based as judiciously and explicitly as possible on known facts (such as known intense historical contacts). It should also be obvious that lexicostatistical methods are far more reliable than glottochronological methods. A 100 percent mathematical approach is simply not possible or desirable. "Used with discretion, . . . [glottochronology] is not as worthless as is stated by some of its critics. The results must simply be interpreted appropriately. As a result of its application, linguists have further demonstration that they cannot deal with languages as though they were simply sets of physical or natural phenomena, but that they must regard languages as a social convention subject to the varied and often unpredictable influences that shape a society" (Lehmann 1984: 34). Mathematical methods should not be viewed as easy reliable shortcuts in genetic classification but rather as providing a first approximation to a tree, which can then be validated (or not) using the more traditional methods.

REFERENCES CITED

Bergsland, K., and H. Vogt. 1962. "On the Validity of Glottochronology." *Current Anthropology* 3: 115–153.

Black, P. 1976. "Multidimensional Scaling Applied to Linguistic Relationships." *Cahiers de l'Institut de linguistique de Louvain* 3: 43–92.

Brainerd, B. 1968. *Statistical Measurement of Linguistic Relationship Revisited.* Toronto: University of Toronto. (Unpublished manuscript.)

Chrétien, C. D. 1943. "The Quantitative Method for Determining Linguistic Relationships: Interpretation of Results and Tests of Significance." *University of California Publications in Linguistics* 1: 11–20.

———. 1956. "Word Distributions in Southeastern Papua." *Language* 32: 88–108.

———. 1962. "The Mathematical Models of Glottochronology." *Language* 38: 11–37.

Davies, P., and A. S. C. Ross. 1975. "'Close-relationship' in the Uralian Languages." *Finnisch-Ugrische Forschungen* 41: 25–48.

Dobson, A. J. 1969. "Lexicostatistical Grouping." *Anthropological Linguistics* 11: 216–221.

Dobson, A. J., and P. Black. 1979. "Multidimensional Scaling of Some Lexicostatistical Data." *Mathematical Scientist* 4: 55–61.

Dobson, A. J., J. B. Kruskal, D. Sankoff, and L. J. Savage. 1972. "The Mathematics of Glottochronology Revisited." *Anthropological Linguistics* 14: 205–212.

Ellegård, A. 1959. "Statistical Measurement of Linguistic Relationship." *Language* 35: 131–156.

Embleton, S. M. 1982. "Lexicostatistical Tree Reconstruction Incorporating Borrowing." *Eighth LACUS Forum*, pp. 265–272.

———. 1983. "Incorporating Borrowing Rates in Lexicostatistical Tree Reconstruction." In Brainerd, B., ed. *Historical Linguistics*, pp. 1–24. Bochum: Brockmeyer.

———. 1985. "A New Technique for Dialectometry." *Twelfth LACUS Forum*, pp. 91–98.

———. 1986. *Statistics in Historical Linguistics.* Bochum: Brockmeyer.

Gleason, H. A., Jr. 1959. "Counting and Calculating for Historical Reconstruction." *Anthropological Linguistics* 1: 22–32.

Grace, G. W. 1965. "On the Scientific Status of Genetic Classification in Linguistics." *Oceanic Linguistics* 4: 1–14.

Grimes, J. E., and F. B. Agard. 1959. "Linguistic Divergence in Romance." *Language* 35: 598–604.

Henrici, A. 1973. "Numerical Classification of Bantu Languages." *African Language Studies* 14: 82–104.

Jacobsen, W. H., Jr. 1979. "Wakashan Comparative Studies." In Campbell, L., and M. Mithun, eds. *The Languages of Native America: Historical and Comparative Assessment*, pp. 766–791. Austin: University of Texas Press.

Klokeid, T. J. (no date). *Wakashan Linguistic History: A Contribution to North West Coast Prehistory*. Victoria, British Columbia: University of Victoria. (Unpublished manuscript.)

Krishnamurti, Bh., L. Moses, and D. G. Danforth. 1983. "Unchanged Cognates as a Criterion in Linguistic Subgrouping." *Language* 59: 541–568.

Kroeber, A. L., and C. D. Chrétien. 1937. "Quantitative Classification of Indo-European Languages." *Language* 13: 83–103.

Lees, R. B. 1953. "The Basis of Glottochronology." *Language* 29: 113–127.

Lehmann, W. P. 1984. *Workbook for Historical Linguistics*. Dallas: Summer Institute of Linguistics.

Linn, M. D. (no date). *A Statistical Model for Classifying Dialect Speakers*. Duluth: University of Minnesota. (Unpublished manuscript.)

Linn, M. D., and R. R. Regal. 1984. "Numerical Taxonomy as a Tool in Dialect Research." Paper presented at the *Fifth International Conference on Methods in Dialectology*, Victoria, British Columbia.

Oswalt, R. L. 1971. "Towards the Construction of a Standard Lexicostatistic List." *Anthropological Linguistics* 13: 421–434.

Rea, J. A. 1973. "The Romance Data of the Pilot Studies for Glottochronology." In Sebeok, T., ed. *Current Trends in Linguistics*, vol. 11, pp. 355–367. The Hague: Mouton.

Ross, A. S. C. 1950. "Philological Probability Problems." *Journal of the Royal Statistical Society*, Series B 12: 19–59.

Sankoff, D. 1972a. "Reconstructing the History and Geography of an Evolutionary Tree." *American Mathematical Monthly* 79: 596–603.

———. 1972b. "Lexical Replacement Processes." *Computer Studies in the Humanities and Verbal Behavior* 4: 208–212.

———. 1973. "Mathematical Developments in Lexicostatistic Theory." In Sebeok, T., ed. *Current Trends in Linguistics*, vol. 11, pp. 93–113. The Hague: Mouton.

Sawyer, L. 1982. *A Wakashan Linguistic History*. Toronto: York University. (Unpublished manuscript.)

Spielman, R. S., E. C. Migliazza, and J. V. Neel. 1974. "Regional Linguistic and Genetic Differences among Yanomama Indians." *Science* 184: 637–644.

Swadesh, M. 1950. "Salish Internal Relationships." *International Journal of American Linguistics* 16: 157–167.

———. 1952. "Lexico-statistic Dating of Prehistoric Ethnic Contacts." *Proceedings of the American Philosophical Society* 96: 452–463.

van der Merwe, N. J. 1966. "New Mathematics for Glottochronology." *Current Anthropology* 7: 485–500.

Villemin, F. 1983. "Un essai de détection des origines du japonais à partir de deux méthodes statistiques." In Brainerd, B., ed. *Historical Linguistics*, pp. 116–135. Bochum: Brockmeyer.

A Method for Assessing
Distant Linguistic Relationships

ROBERT L. OSWALT

Proposals of relationships between languages are usually based on similarities in sound and meaning in some of the elements of the languages. The similarities may be so numerous that no linguist would dispute that there is a genetic relationship; in other cases the similarities may be sufficient to satisfy the more adventure-some, while the more cautious remain reluctant to postulate any special affinity. These borderline instances are candidates for hypotheses of distant genetic relationships. In order that the assessment of the observed similarities be shifted away from the subjective proclivities of the linguist and toward a more objective basis, the method described herein is proposed. In principle the method can be applied without machine aid, but it is exceedingly long and tedious, with hundreds of thousands of decisions required in the comparison of two languages, factors that lead to multiple human errors. These difficulties have been relieved somewhat by a computer program developed and refined over a period of years.[1]

SAMPLING

A comparable sample of each language is taken of any size large enough to lead to statistically significant results, say, over 50 independent items. For the present demonstration the sample consists

---

[1] The computer program is the result of development, necessarily sporadic, over a period of 25 years. It has undergone four complete rewrites in four different computer languages (Fortran, Fortran Assembly Program, Basic, and C), with numerous technical and conceptual improvements as their need or utility has become apparent. I am indebted to Edward R. Oswalt for programming the Basic and C series for the IBM-PC. The latest version, that used for the comparisons cited herein, is in C and is titled "Language Comparator 4.2."

of 100 vocabulary items chosen to fit a fixed semantic list; the probability of a significant relationship between the lists is measured by
means of the phonetic similarities. In most of the comparisons the
list consists of the basic Swadesh 100 words, which has the advantage of being well known and widely available.[2] With the large open
classes of the vocabulary (that is, the nouns and verbs), results can
be checked by taking a second, different 100-word sample of each
language. Since the Swadesh list is not random but is selected to
contain the elements most stable and least subject to borrowing,
no second list can be expected to reflect so well a relationship that
is genetic rather than diffusional.

CRITERIA OF SIMILARITY

I know of no way to set up criteria of semantic similarity that are
simple and consistent and will apply throughout the word list other
than to require that the forms chosen for comparison be as close as
possible to some standard meanings.[3] Affixes and elements not
involved in the basic meaning should be segmented off; the goal

[2] The semantic content of the basic list can be found in Hymes 1960. The Latin
and Sanskrit word lists were prepared from Buck 1949, and the forms were checked
in several standard dictionaries to determine if the items were the most common and
general terms. The Yurak list is from the one source Lehtisalo 1956. Modern Italian,
German, Russian, Finnish, and Hungarian lists were prepared by consulting several
educated native speakers of each language, discussing with them the segmentation of
the forms and the few instances of discrepancies in the choice of a word, in order to
come to agreement on which selections fit best into the semantic slots. The rest of the
lists were graciously furnished by experts, to all of whom I am grateful: Hindi, John
Gumperz; Estonian, Eero Vihman; Orkhon Turkic (early eighth century), Talat Tekin;
Classical Mongolian (14th century), James Bosson; Manchu (present-day speaker, Sibe
(Sibo) minority of China), Jerry Norman.
[3] It is necessary to define each semantic slot more precisely than can be given here.
Ordinarily, if a language has no general term for certain objects or acts but differenti-
ates by classes of some sort, I choose, for example, singular rather than plural, human
rather than animal or inanimate, masculine rather than feminine. In those few cases
in which there is a problem between selecting the most common of two competing
forms (as with English *stone* and *rock*, or *small* and *little*), these items can be omitted
from the comparison, or the definitions can be made more discriminating. A procedure not to follow is to allow the selection to be influenced by the shape of the word
of the same meaning in another language, because doing so would upset the impar-
tiality of the method. There has been a great deal of discussion of difficulties in filling
out a standard list (Hymes 1960 and following), but once the semantic limits for each
item are better understood, these problems are reduced to a number small enough
not to interfere seriously with the statistical determination of greater-than-chance
similarity.

is always a simple monomorphemic root. For the purposes of the demonstration herein the basic list is maintained, with no substitutions but at a cost of raising the number of chance similarities in certain instances. However, with in-depth studies, if a particular item in one language is especially long and complex, or requires a compound of two or more morphemes to render the meaning, or is otherwise troublesome to select, that semantic slot can be deleted or replaced. As for phonetic similarity, some variation is allowable, since it can be defined and measured reliably and consistently in a variety of ways. That chosen here might be called a *threshold method*: If the forms being compared satisfy a threshold number of *criteria of similarity*, they are counted as a match; if they fail to satisfy that number, they do not match.

ESTIMATION OF SIGNIFICANCE

When two vocabulary lists are aligned so that the forms with the same meaning are set against each other, a certain number of pairs are found phonetically similar; this number is the *gross score*. It is a crude measure of the degree of similarity between the two sample word lists, whose real significance can be assessed only with knowledge of the number of resemblances to be expected by chance. A *background score* is an estimate of this number; it is obtained by comparing the two lists under the same criteria of phonetic similarity used in producing the gross score but with the paired forms not of the same meaning. The *shift test* procedure produces a series of background scores through a series of essentially random arrangements: In shift 1, word 1 in the first language (call the language *J*) is compared with word 2 in the second language (call the language *K*), and word 2 in *J* is compared with word 3 in *K*, and so on down the lists until word 100 in *J* wraps around to be compared with word 1 in *K*. The number of paired forms that pass the threshold of similarity is the background score for shift 1. The comparisons can be repeated with the lists shifted relative to each other by two places, three places, on up to one place less than the length of the lists. With 100-word lists, 99 background scores can be obtained by this method, a number sufficient to reveal the important piece of information that they are not constant but may scatter surprisingly widely around a central value.

These and other points are illustrated in Figure 1, where each × results from one shift test. The location of an × on the horizontal

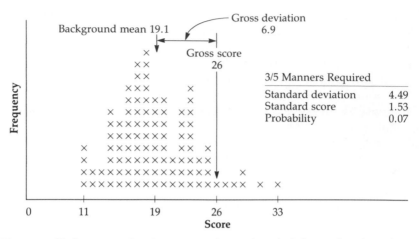

Figure 1. Shift-test results showing a relationship slightly weaker than the 0.05 level of significance.

axis indicates the value of a score (varying between 11 and 33 in this case), and the height of a stack of ×'s shows the number of times that the particular background score occurs. Marked by vertical arrows are the *background mean* (19.1, the average of all the background scores), near the peak, and the *gross score* (26), to the right of the peak. A better measure than the gross score of the degree of relationship implied in this graph is the *gross deviation*, the difference between the gross score and the background mean (26 − 19.1 = 6.9), a figure more closely representing the number of greater-than-chance similarities, perhaps even true cognates (a slight correction would have to be calculated if the relationship were stronger). A simple estimate of the significance of the situation portrayed in the graph is given by a *rank test*: Of the 100 scores, the gross score of 26 lies in seventh place, with six backgrounds greater than it. Thus there is roughly a probability of 7 out of 100 (0.07) that the gross score would be in this location, higher than 93 or more of the background scores, a suggestive figure but not enough for more cautious souls to advocate a relationship.

The distributions of background scores produced in this and other similar comparisons fall close enough to a normal (bell-shaped) curve to allow the calculation of a more refined measure of significance. The *standard deviation*, a measure of the dispersion of the background scores, is the square root of the mean of the squares of the devia-

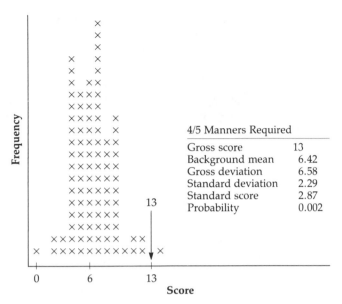

Figure 2. Shift-test results showing a relationship stronger than the 0.05 level of significance.

tions of each background score from the background mean, a lengthy calculation but built into the computer program that carries out the comparisons. The *standard score* is the gross deviation divided by the standard deviation. In the comparison of Figure 1 the standard deviation is 4.49 and the standard score is $^{6.9}/_{4.49} = 1.53$. The probability of obtaining such a score, or one higher, can be found in tables of areas under the standard normal curve.[4] A lookup in such a table yields a probability of 0.07, the same as by the rank test, although the correspondence of the two calculations will not usually be so close.

A commonly used level of significance is 0.05; the situation in Figure 1 falls short of this level. For proposals of distant linguistic relationships, when two isolated languages are being compared, I myself am more cautious and prefer a stronger resemblance, with probabilities below 0.01 (obtaining with standard scores higher than 2.3). The situation in Figure 2 surpasses this more conservative level. However, if the languages are each part of large families or stocks

---

[4]There are hundreds of suitable sources. I happen to have used the tables in Spiegel 1961.

and the members of one, in comparison to the members of the other, yield scores mostly in a marginal range (say, 1.7 to 2.3), then these scores support each other to a significance beyond that of similar scores between isolated pairs.

In much of what follows, the standard score alone, without conversion into a probability, is used as a measure of relationship. It might be pointed out that such a scale, based on the standard score, is something like the Richter scale for earthquakes: a difference of 1.0 is a big difference (for example, the change of standard score from 2.5 to 3.5 corresponds to a probability change from 0.0062 to 0.0002).

DEMONSTRATION WITH INDO-EUROPEAN

An initial demonstration of the method involves two of the languages that figured prominently in Sir William Jones's dictum that Sanskrit bears an affinity to Latin and Greek so strong as to compel the belief that they have "sprung from some common source." The trial languages are Latin and Sanskrit. I am, of course, not trying to prove that these two are related; that was proved 200 years ago by Sir William Jones and by the great body of data accumulated since by dozens of linguists. It is the sensitivity of the method that is being measured against known relationships. It turns out that the resemblances between Latin and Sanskrit are so strong that the pair provides no real test; if plotted on the scale of Figure 1, the position of the gross score would lie far off the right side of the page, 12.6 standard scores to the right of the background mean. Consequently, descendants of these two—Italian and Hindi—have been brought into comparison, because the two additional millennia of divergence should try the method more severely (some have estimated this total time depth as five to seven millennia). Here again the evidence of relationship is so strong, with a standard score of 6.5, that there is no need to apply further statistical calculations (and indeed my table of areas under the standard normal curve stops at 4.0).

The effect of varying the criteria of similarity can be illustrated with Italian and Hindi. The computer program is written so that it is possible to state the criteria narrowly or in broad terms of distinctive features. For this demonstration, the criteria are stated broadly:

1. Paired words or forms match if a sufficient number of their constituent phonemes match. The number can be made dependent on the number of consonants and vowels in each of the paired

forms. Here, the number is fixed at two consonants.[5] No vowel matches are required, although the program can handle vowels.

2.   Two phonemes match if they share a sufficient number of features. Here, two consonants match if they share

   a.   The same point of articulation[6]

   b.   A stated number of the following five manners of articulation: voicing, stoppage, nasality, friction, and laterality

The pairs of forms satisfying a criterion 2b, that all five of the manners of articulation match, are set off by the upper brace in Table 1; all thirteen pairs (the gross score) can be seen to be quite similar.[7]

---

[5] All words in these comparisons have at least two "consonants" because of the use of two special symbols: (1) ' (apostrophe) marks what would otherwise be a vowel-initial word and is defined as a laryngeal consonant matchable with ' and with ʔ (glottal stop). (2) ' (reversed apostrophe) marks the end of words that would otherwise have only one consonant and is defined to be matchable with consonants of any point of articulation and is also defined minus all the manners of articulation, with the result that, when criterion 2b is ⅗ it matches only ', when it is ⅘, it also matches voiceless consonants; when it is ⅗, it matches most consonants. This mark ' was installed not to prove or disprove any particular relationship but to reduce high backgrounds and high standard deviations resulting from unlikely matchings of the initial of a monoconsonantal word with the final of a polyconsonantal word; for example, Finnish l uu 'bone' with English b oun .

[6] The varying number of points of articulation in the languages dealt with in this paper requires some merger of distinctions. For example, Sanskrit and Hindi distinguish dental and retroflex, but the other languages do not; these two positions are therefore treated as one in these particular comparisons. Likewise for velar and uvular distinctions.

[7] Certain available keyboard symbols have been transferred to linguistic use: "$" is a palatal spirant, "7" a retroflex voiceless plain stop; "6" and "8" are vowels, and so on. But because of the great number of symbols needed to represent the sounds of the various languages, *all phonemes are written as digraphs*. The second space of a digraph may be used systematically to indicate some manner of articulation, such as aspiration (with "h") or glottalization (with "'") or palatalization (with "y"), or other common diacritics. Special digraph symbols can be created, such as "n-" for a nasal homorganic with a following stop, to be compared with other nasals, with matching not to be rejected because of a difference in point of articulation. In Finnish, "h*" represents a syllable-final /h/, which is ignored in the comparisons herein but which could be included in other comparisons; "hs" is an alternation between /h/ and /s/; "e/" an alternation between /e/ and /i/. *Often the second space of a digraph is blank*; thus /m/ is written "m plus blank." This assignment of a constant two spaces per phoneme is necessary for the processing by the computer but results in unfamiliar intervals for some of the symbols; it should not interfere with comprehension of the examples.

Length is usually represented by an asterisk, sometimes written as a separate phoneme, sometimes unified in one digraph with a preceding vowel or consonant, but, with some word lists, by doubling the basic symbol. The experimental reasons for varying the treatment are of no present importance because length, accent, and vowels are not taken into consideration herein.

More detail on the mechanics of handling data are in Oswalt 1970, where there

TABLE 1

Matching Word Pairs in Two Modern Languages of Different Branches
of the Indo-European Stock*

Gloss	Italian	Hindi	Criteria of similarity and statistical results
die	m o r	m a r	
feather	p e n *	p a n- kh	
give	d a '	d e*'	
hear	s e n- t	s u n	5/5 Manners Required
long	l u n- g	l a n- b	
name	n o m	n a*m	Gross score — 13
star	s t e l *	s i t a*r	Background mean — 2.78
stone	p i e t r	p a tha r	Gross deviation — 10.22
sun	s o l	s u*r a j	Standard deviation — 1.57
you (sg.)	t u '	t u*'	Standard score — 6.50
tooth	d e n- t	d a*n- t	
two	d u e '	d o*'	
who	k i '	k o- '	
bird	' u c e l *	c i r.	
dry	s e k *	s u*kh	4/5 Manners Required
eye	' o k * i	' a*n- kh	
hair	k a p e l *	b a*l	Gross score — 22
hot	k a l d	g a r a m	Background mean — 7.35
liver	f e g a t	k a l e*j	Gross deviation — 14.65
neck	k o l *	g a l	Standard deviation — 2.84
tree	' a l b e r	p e*r	Standard score — 5.16
what	k e '	k y a*	

See Footnote 7 for explanation of symbols.
*The lower brace marks additional word pairs found matching under relaxed criteria of similarity.

The background mean is 2.78, and the standard deviation is 1.57; both figures are low (an advantageous situation) because the criteria of similarity are so strict. The most expectable number of cognates is 10 (gross deviation: $13 - 2.78 = 10.22$). The standard score, the measure of how confident we can be that the number of resemblances is greater than attributable to chance, is a very strong 6.50 ($^{10.22}/_{1.57}$).

For a second comparison, criterion 2b is relaxed slightly to four out of five manners of articulation, with the result that there are additional matching pairs, set off by the lower brace in Table 1. In contrast with the first part there is evident some deterioration in the resemblance of the pairs. The gross score grows to 22, with nine matching pairs added to the thirteen in the first comparison. The

is also a discussion of various technical problems, many of which have now been obviated.

background mean also grows, to 7.35, so that the gross deviation does not increase by 9 but by a smaller amount, to 14.65. There are a few more true cognates found under this relaxed condition, but the proof of relationship is weaker: besides the increase in the background mean there is an increase in the standard deviation to 2.84, so that the standard score is lowered to 5.16 ($^{14.65}/_{2.84}$). This is still strong evidence but less than the previous 6.50.

For a third comparison, criterion 2b is relaxed further to three out of the five manners of articulation. There is considerably more deterioration in the resemblances of the pairs (not illustrated). The gross score grows to 37, but the background mean jumps even more to 24.71, so that the gross deviation actually falls to 12.29. This reduction in the gross deviation comes despite there being two real cognate pairs found at this stage ('drink', Italian b e v : Hindi p i*ʿ ; and 'not', n o n : n a ʿ). As always when criteria of similarity are weakened, the standard deviation rises (in this case to 3.92) and the standard score is cut more drastically to 3.13 ($^{12.29}/_{3.92}$). The resemblance between Hindi and Italian is still strong enough to show through these impediments, but not so clearly as before. As a general rule, with languages sharing this many cognates the highest standard score and strongest proof come when the criteria of similarity are most restrictive. With languages whose possible relationship is toward the limits of detectability, this is not so much the case: the greater span of time has permitted more sound changes, so that demanding near identity in two consonantal pairs may exclude real cognates to an extent greater than it reduces the background and dispersion.

Not all pairs of Indo-European languages show so great a resemblance as Italian and Hindi, but all branches clearly belong to the one Indo-European stock.[8]

URALIAN (URALIC) AND INDO-URALIAN

The method has been tried with other widely accepted stocks. Word lists in Uralian—Finnish, Estonian, Hungarian, and Yurak—have been compared binarily: Finnish and Estonian, as members of the same Baltic Finnic subgroup, show an extremely high resemblance to each other with a standard score of close to 40. Comparisons of

---

[8] Some results are published in Oswalt 1970, but the standard scores there are not so high as would obtain now because refinements in the later versions of the program have reduced certain technical factors that formerly increased dispersion in the background scores and uncertainty in the results.

these two with Hungarian yield high standard scores, in the 6 to 7 range. Comparisons of these three with the more divergent Yurak (Samoyed) also yield high scores, in the 4 to 7 range. In short the method can easily detect the relationships of the languages in the large and complex Indo-European and Uralian stocks.

All the languages dealt with in this chapter are included in the wide-ranging, hypothetical construct known as Nostratic. Less inclusive is Indo-Uralian, a special linkage of Indo-European and Uralian that has a long history of advocacy by some linguists: Pedersen (1931) accepts the connection, crediting Vilhelm Thomsen with suggesting it as early as 1869; this century, Collinder (1934, 1954) has done the most to carry the proposal forward. Nevertheless, the hypothesis is apparently not generally accepted; at least it is not discussed by most historical linguists working with these two families.

The method has been applied to testing the similarities between these two stocks. Comparisons of Russian with Uralian are the most impressive, the standard scores of Russian with Finnish and Hungarian being over 4. Comparisons of Russian and Yurak yield lower standard scores, reaching a maximum of 3 under certain conditions, not so much because of a high gross deviation, which is a mere 3, as because of an especially low standard deviation of 1. Examples of the Finnish-Russian pairs selected when five matching manners of articulation are required (with palatalization being ignored) are in the top part of Table 2, and those added when only four manners are required are in the bottom part. At the top are eleven resemblant pairs, of which about three (the background mean) can be laid to chance. The high standard score shows that for the remainder some other explanation must be sought.[9]

Comparisons of German and Finnish (Table 3) yield a score of 2.36 (probability 0.009) when five manners of articulation are re-

[9]One of the most prominent and commonly cited resemblances between Indo-European and Uralian is the set for "water." The form chosen to represent Finnish in all comparisons herein illustrates the principle that the selection be made entirely independently of whether it fits some form with which it is to be compared. An underlying representation for the Finnish, from which all alternations can be phonologically predicted is v e t e/. Because this form contains t , differing in voicing from d , the Finnish v e t e/ does not match Russian v o d when five of five manners of articulation are required, only when four or fewer are required. Since the genitive case in Finnish is v e d e n , that stem with d could have been used in the Russian comparison to increase the score under the ⅘ requirement, but such a procedure biases the result and should never be followed. Similarly the nominative case in Finnish is v e s i , a form that more easily finds a match in German v a s r , while v e t e/ does not match the German until only three of five manners are required. Here too there is no adjustment in form to influence the result.

TABLE 2

Matching Word Pairs in Two Modern Languages of Different Linguistic Stocks

Gloss	Finnish	Russian	Criteria of similarity and statistical results
bark	k aar n a	k o r	
belly	v a t s a	zhi v o t	
claw	k y n t e/	k o g o ty	5/5 Manners Required
fly (v.)	l e n t ae	ly e t	Gross score 11
heart	s y d aem *	sye r d ts	Background mean 3.09
leaf	l e h*t e/	lyi s t	Gross deviation 7.91
many	m o n e/	mn o g	Standard deviation 1.86
seed	s ie me n	sye mye ny	Standard score 4.25
that	t uo'	t '	
we	m e '	m 6 '	
yellow	k e l t a	zho l t	
breast	r i n t a	g r u dy	
cloud	p i l v e/	' o b l a k	4/5 Manners Required
man	m ie hs	m u zh	Gross score 19
neck	n i s k a	$ e i '	Background mean 7.52
one	' y k t e/	' o d n	Gross deviation 11.48
rain	s a t e *	d o zh dy	Standard deviation 2.36
sit	' i s t u	s a dy	Standard score 4.87
water	v e t e/	v o d	

See Footnote 7 for explanation of symbols.

TABLE 3

Matching Word Pairs in Two Modern Languages of Different Linguistic Stocks

Gloss	Finnish	German	Criteria of similarity and statistical results
bark	k aar n a	r i n d	5/5 Manners Required
breast	r i n t a	b r u s t	Gross score 6
cold	k y l m ae	k a l t	Background mean 2.45
leaf	l e h*t e/	b l a t	Gross deviation 3.55
name	n i m e/	n aa m	Standard deviation 1.50
seed	s ie me n	z aam n	Standard score 2.36
black	s u s t a	$ v a r ts	4/5 Manners Required
burn	p a l a	b r e n	Gross score 13
sit	' i s t u	z i ts	Background mean 6.42
tail	h aen t ae	$ v a n ts	Gross deviation 6.58
that	t uo'	d a s	Standard deviation 2.29
this	t ae '	d ii s	Standard score 2.87
yellow	k e l t a	g e l b	

See Footnote 7 for explanation of symbols.

quired, a slightly higher 2.87 ($p = 0.002$) when four are required, and a much lower 1.53 ($p = 0.07$) when only three are required. These latter two comparisons are the ones graphed in Figures 2 and 1 and illustrate well the point that taking a course (reducing the required number of matching manners of articulation from four to three) that augments the stock of found resemblant pairs (from 13 to 26) does not increase the proof of relationship, for there are concomitant increases in the background mean (6.4 to 19.1) and in the dispersion of the background scores (standard deviation change from 2.29 to 4.49) and a consequent loss of significance in the position of the gross score relative to the background mean (standard score change from 2.87 to 1.53). The two figures reveal much of this at a glance; the curve in Figure 2 is more sharply peaked, allowing a more distinct picture of the location of the gross score relative to the backgrounds.

Comparisons of German with Hungarian and with Yurak also peak at the requirement of four manners of articulation but with the marginally significant standard scores of 1.94 and 2.02, respectively ($p = 0.026$ and 0.022). Comparisons involving other modern Indo-European languages (English, Italian, Hindi) with these Uralian languages are also rather spotty, reaching a score above 2 in some comparisons but falling short in others. However, the cumulative effect, with almost all standard scores definitely positive, is that the overall situation requires some explanation.

With so many positive scores, one might wonder if these results with Indo-European and Uralian were due not so much to historical relationships as to certain universal factors that would lead to similar results between any two families. For example, if an average of two or three items on the list should be phonetically shaped by sound symbolism, or onomatopoeia, that alone could increase the standard score sufficiently to make the great majority of scores positive, even between unrelated languages. Although such a bias may occur to a minor extent, I have not yet been able to show it. Indeed, once one brings into comparison a great variety of other languages, it becomes apparent that negative standard scores are not rare: one would expect between unrelated languages, with no universal or historical factors in effect, that the standard scores would fall equally on the plus and minus sides of zero (see the Ural-Altaic comparisons below).

The remaining possible sources of the high scores are historical: either diffusional, the passage of forms from one language to the other, or genetic, descent from some common ancestor. There seems to be a definite areal effect, in the sense that with these distant comparisons the scores tend to be higher when the languages are geographically closer. That proximity creates affinity is true even within Indo-European itself, with scores tending to be higher between branches that are neighbors. Of the forms found similar in the Finnish-Russian comparisons, three—those glossed 'bark', 'seed', and 'yellow'—are listed in Hakulinen 1961 as Baltic loans into Finnish before A.D. 500; these same three also figure in the Finnish-German comparisons: Note that with 'bark (of a tree)' the Finnish form matches the Russian and German by different paths: It is the first two consonants of the Finnish k aar n a that match the two of Russian k o r , but it is the final two consonants of the Finnish that match the first two of German r i n d ; the latter comparison would seem the more likely candidate for a chance resemblance. If these three items are subtracted from the word list and the comparisons rerun, the Finnish-German score falls from 2.87 to a marginally significant 1.83, while the Finnish-Russian score drops from 4.87 to 3.82, still high enough to call for further historical explanation. It might be pointed out that eliminating known or suspected loans does not necessarily lower the standard score. In a comparison of Finnish with English, for example, the elimination of these three items raises the score from 2.45 to 2.83 because the deletion is of pairs that had not contributed to the gross score but had raised the background.

I have not searched the literature to determine whether any of the remaining resemblant pairs are considered to involve loans into Russian from Finnish or a Finnish relative. Such judgments are, in any case, better made by specialists in these stocks. The situation calls for further testing with more vocabulary samples, including use of reconstructed forms in the two linguistic groupings, to determine whether there would be, after the elimination of all known diffused forms, a residue inherited from some remote common ancestor.

ALTAIC AND URAL-ALTAIC

Of even longer history is the proposal that Uralian is related to languages in Central Asia in a hypothetical phylum called Ural-Altaic: Whitney 1867 knew the term (but preferred "Scythian") and regarded the hypothesis "an open question." He credited Castrén with holding, in 1857, to a relationship of Ugrian and Samoyed (Uralian) and Turkish (Altaic). On the validity of Altaic itself there is disagreement among those who have considered the evidence, not over whether resemblances exist between its branches but over whether they stem entirely from diffusion (there has admittedly been borrowing) or whether there is a significant corpus of shared inheritance. Most, not all, of the linguists working with the constituent languages of Altaic appear to accept the genetic validity of that grouping (see the evidence in Poppe 1960), though not necessarily of Ural-Altaic.

To test first the level of similarity among the three most accepted branches of Altaic, I acquired word lists in each in as old a form as possible (see footnote 2)—Orkhon Turkic, Classical Mongolian, and Manchu. Binary comparisons among these reveal a much lower level of resemblance than exists among the branches within Indo-European or within Uralian. Nevertheless, some moderately significant similarities can be found, especially when additional word lists are brought into consideration. Any possible genetic relationship is indeed distant.

Comparisons of the three Altaic lists with each of the Uralian lists yield no significant resemblances; the standard scores vary around zero, as many minus as plus. This is not to claim that no affinity could be found in some other part of the languages; but it is not revealed in the basic vocabulary.

COMMENTARY

Most historical linguists are accustomed to working with clearly related languages in which the prime objective is not to prove they are related but to gather sets of cognate forms in order to work out sound correspondences and reconstruct protoforms. In testing for truly distant relationships the orientation must be different: it is not simply maximizing the gross score and gathering ever more sets of resemblant forms, as many investigators seem to think; it is, rather, maximizing the standard score, sharpening the proof of greater-than-chance resemblances. Tradeoffs are necessary: Thus, as has been shown, it is usually better to tighten the phonetic criteria of similarity, giving up including some possible cognates, in order to avoid including too many spurious resemblances.

However, semantic variability, to my mind, is a more common source of failure in attempted proofs of distant relationships. Each item on the list is a semantic slot that should be filled by only one morpheme per language. If the words being compared (for example,

those meaning "see") are not phonetically similar, for many investigators there is no hesitation in accepting comparisons with less
common, or more specialized, words in the same area of meaning.
(English examples could be "gaze, glance, glimpse, leer, look, peek,
peer, stare, watch" plus dozens of others.) Or, failing to find by this
means a form sufficiently resemblant, the investigator could allow
a shift in meaning and part of speech to try comparisons with the
word for "eye." This is not to deny that these are plausible meaning
shifts nor that the word for "see" in one language may find its true
cognate in the word for "eye" in another, for one is sometimes derived from the other; but the consequence of such a procedure is
that a semantic slot, ostensibly to be filled with a single closely defined and selected form, is actually open to containing, say, five
to fifteen forms. If this be the case for each language of a binary
comparison, there is the potential of generating a number of pairings equal to the square of these figures—25 to 225—where one is
intended. Such contingent searching for resemblant forms can proceed to an extent limited only by the amount of vocabulary available
in the two languages and the imagination of the investigator. The
effect is an enormous inflation in the number of chance resemblances between any two languages, related or not. If the investigator can state precisely the limits to which he will go, the effect
might be calculated, but usually there are no fixed criteria of semantic similarity. The tendency is for the investigator to spread his net
only to the point of taking in a pair acceptably alike phonetically and
then to stop. The problem is controlled here by selecting the most
common, general, and closely fitting term for the semantic slot (see
also footnote 3), with the decision made entirely independently of
whether the chosen form is phonetically similar to its semantic mate
in some other language.

An analogous source of inflation in chance resemblances occurs in
mass comparisons of two stocks or families, each containing many
diverse languages. If, for one semantic slot, one family contains five
radically different cognate sets, and the other family a like number,
and the investigator is willing to accept and cite as possible cognates
any of the 25 combinations that happen to look alike, then there is
roughly a 25-fold increase in the probability of finding spurious resemblances over that obtaining when only one form for each family
is placed into the slot. In those instances in which the cognate forms
run through all or most of the languages of each family, cross-family
mass comparisons work well, and such resemblances constitute pow-

erful evidence for a relationship. But, as the number of cognate sets for each slot grows, the evidentiary value of any one set shrinks. It might be possible, though cumbersome, to estimate a relative value for the various patterns of cognates, but for now a simpler procedure is to reduce the mass comparison to binary comparisons, either a series of binary comparisons (as has been done here for Indo-European and Uralian) or somehow deciding which one cognate set best represents each family. This latter procedure is most facilitated by reconstruction of a proto-language, which at its best provides the double advantage of tending to isolate the surest choice for a semantic slot, eliminating many of the more recently diffused and created forms and positing a likely phonemic shape for that choice.

The comparisons presented herein have been intended as a demonstration of the power and limits of the method but concomitantly have furnished evidence of a pervasive affinity between Indo-European and Uralian whose nature would have to be clarified by deeper historical work. Such pervasive affinity is not shown, at least in the basic vocabulary, between Uralian and Altaic. There are a great many far-ranging proposals of distant linguistic relationships that could be assessed by this method, both within the Eurasian landmass and within and among other continents.

REFERENCES CITED

Buck, C. D. 1949. *A Dictionary of Selected Synonyms in the Principal Indo-European Languages.* Chicago: University of Chicago Press.

Collinder, Bj. 1934. *Indo-Uralisches Sprachgut.* Uppsala: Almqvist & Wiksells.

———. 1954. *Zur Indo-Uralischen Frage.* Uppsala: Almqvist & Wiksells.

Hakulinen, L. 1961. *The Structure and Development of the Finnish Language.* Trans. by John Atkinson. Bloomington: Indiana University Publications, Uralic and Altaic Series 3.

Hymes, D. H. 1960. "Lexicostatistics So Far." *Current Anthropology* 1: 3–44.

Lehtisalo, T. 1956. *Juraksamojedisches Wörterbuch.* Helsinki: Suomalais-Ugrilainen Seura 13.

Oswalt, R. L. 1970. "The Detection of Remote Linguistic Relationships." *Computer Studies in the Humanities and Verbal Behavior* 3: 117–129.

Pedersen, H. 1931. *The Discovery of Language: Linguistic Science in the Nineteenth Century.* Trans. by John W. Spargo. Midland Book Edition of 1962. Bloomington: Indiana University Press.

Poppe, N. 1960. *Vergleichende Grammatik der Altaischen Sprachen,* Teil 1: *Vergleichende Lautlehre.* Wiesbaden: Otto Harrassowitz.

Spiegel, M. R. 1961. *Theory and Problems of Statistics.* New York: Schaum Publishing Co.

Whitney, W. D. 1867. *Language and the Study of Language.* New York: Charles Scribner & Co.

INDEX

Casual mentions of names of languages, language families, and persons are for the most part not included in this index. Inclusion of every passing reference would have resulted in an unwieldy, overlong index that would tend to hinder rather than help the user. Entries for names are therefore limited to substantive mentions.

In this index an "f" after a number indicates a separate reference on the next page, and an "ff" indicates separate references on the next two pages. A continuous discussion over two or more pages is indicated by a span of page numbers, e.g., "pp. 57–58." *Passim* is used for a cluster of references in close but not consecutive sequence. "n" after a number indicates a footnote.

Abel-Rémusat, J. P., 295

Abkhaz, 234, 236, 238, 242–44, 248, 256, 262, 264

Accent in Japanese and Korean, 275–80

Accidental resemblance, 29. *See also* Chance resemblances

Active-passive alternation, 219

Afro-Asiatic, 123, 130, 141–62, 166, 179–84, 189, 217

Ainu, 123, 129, 137, 207, 211, 217, 269

Akhwakh, 234, 245f, 264

Albanian, 127

Aleut, 133–34. *See also* Eskimo-Aleut

Algic, 350

Algonquian, 316, 350, 383

Al-Mas'udi, 233

Almosan, 349

Almosan-Keresiouan, 332–50

Altaic, 123f, 129–38 *passim*, 179–184, 189, 202, 207–29 *passim*, 269, 293–325, 358–60; common origin proposed by Sir William Jones, 40, 42; compared with Uralic, 401–402; liquids, 311–15, 318f; morphology, 308–10; pho-

nological correspondences, 310–16; word order, 308n

Altamira y Crevea, Rafael, 11

American Indian languages, 328–34; classification, 329–31

Amerind, 178, 180, 193–95, 328–50; branches, 332–34

Anatolian, 49, 51–66 *passim*, 135. *See also* Hittite

Andean, 332–50

Animism, 68f

Anttila, Raimo, 130

Arabic, 41, 43, 167–71 *passim*

Archeological evidence for Proto-Afro-Asiatic, 141

Armenian, 127, 191

Asia, languages of, 205–29; map, 206

Asiatic Society, 23f, 34, 51

Athabaskan, 187

Australian, 180

Austric, 124, 180, 207–29 *passim*

Austronesian, 180, 202, 207, 209

Austro-Tai, 180, 207, 209–11, 217, 224

Austro-Viet, 207, 209, 211, 224

Avestan, 74–75. *See also* Persian

Bakhtin, Mikhail Mikhailovich, 19–20
Baltic, 356, 401
Band, W., 306n
Bantu, 217
Baric, 208, 211, 214f
Basic vocabulary, 39–40, 141, 207, 372, 375. *See also* Stable vocabulary
Basque, 179f, 185–86, 218, 232, 265
Batokw, Harun, 240
Bengali, 23, 26
Benveniste, Émile, 53, 59, 70ff, 78–79, 83
Berber, 143–62
Bestiality, 64–66
Bhagavad-Gītā, 37
Bilingualism, 213, 363
Bird goddess, 90–95, 102, 118, 120
Birth-giver goddess, 96–97, 119–20
Bloomfield, Leonard, 14, 32, 36, 316
Bokarëv, A. A., 259
Bopp, F., 35ff, 39, 52, 126f, 128f, 178, 309
Borrowing, 29, 39; adjusting for in lexicostatistics, 376–86; massive, 205
Boyce, Mary, 74–75
Braune, W., 14
Brown, John Pairman, 166
Brugmann, K., 128, 131f
Bryant, Jacob, 28
Bucranium, 104
Burmese, 208. *See also* Tibeto-Burman
Burushaski, 265
Bzyb, 242–44

Cassirer, Ernst, 71
Caucasian. *See* Kartvelian; North Caucasian
Caucasus, languages of, 124, 217f, 232–66
Cavalli-Sforza, Luca, 335
Celtic, 31, 52, 127, 135
Central Amerind, 332–50
Chadic, 143–62
Chambers, Sir Robert, 28
Chamorro, 135
Chance resemblances, 29; in mass comparison, 403–4; methods of estimating, 391–94
Chibchan-Paezan, 332–50
Chinese, 208, 211–29 *passim*
Chomsky, Noam, 15, 19
Chrétien, Douglas, 366–68, 375
Chukchi, 132–33, 136

Chukchi-Kamchatkan. *See* Chukotian
Chukotian, 123, 129, 132–33, 179, 254, 265
Chuvash, 137, 303, 311, 318
Circassian, 61, 237, 239–40
Čirikba, V. A., 185–86
Classification of languages. *See* Genetic classification of languages; Typological classification
Clauson, Sir Gerard, 293–313 *passim*, 316–25 *passim*
Cluster analysis, hierarchical, 370–72
Colebrooke, Thomas Henry, 28
Collinder, Björn, 128, 178, 398
Common origin, hypothesis of. *See* Genetic hypothesis
Comparative mythology, 51–52
Core vocabulary. *See* Basic vocabulary
Cornwallis, Lord, 52
Cushitic, 143–62

Dagestanian, 234, 236, 246, 249f, 252, 255, 260f, 264
Danforth, D. G., 369–70
Darwin, Charles, 15
Davies, P., 367–68
Death, symbols and omens, 99–103, 120
Degrees of relationship, 4f, 8, 131, 351, 365–87
Deities, Indo-European, 90; of Old Europe, 90–121. *See also* Female deities of Old Europe; Indo-European religion and mythology; Male deities of Old Europe
Delbrück, A., 128
Dene-Caucasian, 180, 187, 191–93, 236, 247, 254, 265
Devoto, Giacomo, 74–76
Diderichsen, P., 127
Diffusion, 201, 205f, 213f, 216–17, 219, 227–29, 351, 361–63. *See also* Bilingualism; Borrowing; Linguistic areas
Distant genetic relationships, 123–195, 202; controversy surrounding proposals of, 5–8, 124; of IE, 123–84, 189–95; proposals of, 202, 353–63; statistical assessment of hypotheses, 389–404
Doerfer, G., 295n, 296n, 299–310, 314–24 *passim*
Dolgopolsky, Aaron B., 179, 183, 188–89

Dravidian, 4, 123, 130, 179–82, 189, 202, 269, 357ff, 362
Dual inflection in IE and Semitic, 167
Dumézil, Georges, 72–74, 76, 80f
Durkheim, Émile, 69

Earth mother, 114, 119–20, 168
Edgerton, Franklin, 36
Egyptian, 143–62
Eliade, Mircea, 71f, 75f
Equatorial, 332–50
Equatorial-Tucanoan, 337, 340, 346ff
Ergative, 218, 221f, 226, 251–54
Eskimo-Aleut, 133, 254, 329–31, 333, 344; proposed external relationships, 123f, 129, 179f, 183–84, 269, 357, 359
Estonian, 354, 356, 397–98
Etruscan, 179f, 186–87
Etymology, 29, 128
Etymological speculation, 28, 40
Eurasiatic, 123, 125–38, 202; defined, 129; passive markers, 134–38; pronouns, 131–34. *See also* Nostratic
Evidence for genetic relationships, 6, 8, 29, 205–207; basic vocabulary, 39; grammatical, 29, 126ff, 129; juxtaposition of forms, 128; phonological correspondences, 128. *See also* Degrees of relationship; Distant genetic relationships; Genetic relationships, methods of determining

Factor analysis, 372
Family tree model/theory, 8, 16–17, 32, 59, 124, 201f, 235–36, 351, 365–87 *passim*
Female deities of Old Europe, 90–115, 118–20
Female symbols, 90–115
Fertility goddess, 115
Finnish, 133, 354ff, 360, 397–401
Finno-Ugric, 41, 127f, 354–56, 360–61. *See also* Uralic
Formal linguistics, 15
Formosan, 209, 211, 224, 227
Fortunatov's law, 176
Fought, John, 38
Franklin, Benjamin, 33, 52
Frazer, Sir James George, 68–71 *passim*
Freud, Sigmund, 72

Gamkrelidze, Thomas V., 79–85, 124, 129, 190–91
Generative grammar, 19f
Genesis, book of, 12
Genetic classification of languages: influence of botany on 32; mathematical methods, 365–87; methodology 125–31. *See also* Degrees of relationship
Genetic hypothesis, 1, 26–45 *passim*
Genetic relationships, methods of determining, 5–6, 12, 28–29, 126–29, 188–92, 294–325, 386. *See also* Degrees of relationship; Distant genetic relationships; Evidence for genetic relationships
Georgian, 201, 233–38 *passim*, 241f, 247–53 *passim*, 257
Ge-Pano-Carib, 337, 340, 346ff
German, 398–401
Germanic, 26, 356, 378–80
Gilyak, 123, 129, 137, 269, 353, 359, 362
Gleason, H. A., Jr., 369–70
Glottalic theory proposed for Proto-IE, 18
Glottochronology, 365, 372–87. *See also* Lexicostatistics
Gods. *See* Deities; Female deities of Old Europe; Indo-European, religion and mythology; Male deities of Old Europe
Gothic, 31
Grace, G. W., 386
Grain mother, 114
Grassmann, Hermann, 13
Grassmann's law, 13, 302
Greek, 15, 31, 55
Greenberg, Joseph, 178, 180, 193, 329–32
Grimm, Jacob, 12–13, 19, 35, 39
Grimm's law, 13, 36, 52
Guardian goddess, 98

Halhed, Nathaniel Brassey, 23, 26, 33, 44
Hamito-Semitic. *See* Afro-Asiatic
Harris, Zellig, 15
Harvest goddess, 116
Hattic, 179f, 186–87
Haudry, Jean, 79
Healing ritual, 84
Hebrew, 41, 43, 167–176 *passim*
Hedgehog goddess, 103
Herodotus, 232
Hindi, 394–97

Hirt's law, 176
Hittite, 17, 51–66, 129, 135, 190; culture, 61–66; law code, 63–66; morphology, 55, 56–60; poetry, 62; pronouns, 59; sexual relations, 64–66
Hockett, Charles F., 38f
Hoenigswald, Henry, 35, 37f
Hokan, 332–50
Holquist, Michael, 19–20
Homer, 37, 62; similes in, 62; words for prayer in, 78
Hrozný, Bedřich, 53, 129
Hübschmann, H., 127n
Hungarian, 134, 354ff, 397–98, 400
Hurrian, 179, 186–87
Hurro-Urartean, 180
Hymes, Dell, 38, 375

Iliad, 10, 37, 61f
Illich-Svitych, Vladislav M., 179, 182f, 192, 265, 357
Impersonal sentences, 220
Inalienable possession, 224
Incest, 64–66
India, 23–85 *passim*; ancient gods of, 67–85 *passim*
Indo-European 211, 217, 219, 355, 357–60, 397–402; accent, 175–76; culture, 61–66, 118–19; early vs. late, 55–56; grammar, 205; homeland, 62, 89, 201; illegal sexual relations, 64–66; laryngeal consonants of, 17, 144–62 *passim*, 168–70, 190; legal terminology, 82–84; linguistic family, 1–2, 9–10, 12–18, 25–39, 49–85 *passim*, 123–84 *passim*; major branches, 55–56; morphology, 31, 56–60; passive marker, 134–38; pronouns, 59, 131–34; reconstruction of protolanguage, 129–38; religion and mythology, 51, 61f, 67–85, 118–21; stop consonants, 18, 190–91; velar consonants, 189–90; vowels, 190
Indo-Hittite, 49, 54–66 *passim*
Indo-Iranian, 191
Indonesian, 209, 224, 226ff
Indo-Pacific, 180
Indo-Uralic, 130, 397–402
Interlanguage influence. *See* Diffusion
Internal reconstruction, 17, 138; for Japanese, 270; for Korean, 270

Iranian, 31, 55, 356, 360. *See also* Persian
Isolated languages, 7
Italian, 394–97
Italic, 135
Ivanov, Vyacheslav V., 79–85, 124, 186, 190–91

Jacobsen, W. H., Jr., 384
Japanese, 137–38, 184, 207, 210ff, 225, 229, 269–89, 303n, 317–23 *passim*; as possible mixed language, 217; compared with Korean, 269–89; morphology, 282–89; proposed external relationships, 123f, 129–30, 202, 217, 269–89, 304f, 359; syntax, 221, 281
Jefferson, Thomas, 52
Jespersen, Otto, 36
Johnson, Dr. S., 26, 33
Jones, Sir William, 1, 9–12, 23–45, 51–52; portrait, 24; Third Anniversary Discourse (1786), 1–2, 5f, 9–10, 23–45, 51, 67, 126–27, 178, 293, 318
Jung, Carl G., 72
Jungraithmayr, H., 142

Kabardian, 234, 236–39 *passim*, 246ff, 252, 256, 262, 264
Kamchadal, 132–33
Karenic, 207–8, 211, 223. *See also* Tibeto-Karenic
Kartvelian, 201, 233–36, 242, 248f, 251–55 *passim*; proposed external relationships, 123, 179–184, 189, 258, 265, 359
Keresiouan, 349
Ket, 265, 331. *See also* Yeniseian
Khmer, 216, 227. *See also* Mon-Khmer
Khoisan, 180
Klimov, G. A., 259
Klokeid, T. J., 384
Korean, 123, 129–38 *passim*, 202, 207, 211, 269–89, 304, 317–23 *passim*, 359; compared with Japanese, 269–89; morphology, 282–89; syntax, 281
Koryak, 132–33. *See also* Chukotian
Krishnmurti, Bh., 369–70
Kroeber, Alfred, 366–68
Kuhn, Adelbert, 67
Kühner, Raphael, 15
Kuipers, A., 262
Kurgan, 118

Kuryłowicz, J., 17, 53, 190
Kutenai, 350

Lafon, R., 265
Lang, Andrew, 68
Language description, 10, 37
Lapp, 354ff
Laryngeal consonants, of IE, 17, 144–62
    passim, 168–70, 190; of Nostratic, 189f
Lass, Roger, 19
Latham, Robert G., 13
Latin, 31, 380–82; word order, 16
Lehmann, Winfred P., 39
Lepsius, R., 141
Lexicostatistics, 235–36, 296n, 365–87;
    fully parameterized, 376. *See also*
    Glottochronology
Lincoln, Bruce, 74, 84
Linguistic areas, 213. *See also* Diffusion
Linguistic diversity, development of, 362
Linnaeus, 32f, 42
Lislakh, 143
Lisramic, 141
Lithuanian, 55, 127, 174
Long-range relationships. *See* Distant
    genetic relationships
Luorawetlan, 359. *See also* Chukotian
Luwian, 190

Macro-Carib, 332–50
Macro-Ge, 332–50
Macro-Panoan, 332–50
Macro-Tucanoan, 332–50
Mahābhārata, 10, 37
Malay, 226
Malayo-Polynesian, 209–10, 215f, 223,
    228, 269
Male deities of Old Europe, 116–17
Mana, 68–72 *passim*
Manchu, 137, 207, 211, 221, 359–60. *See
    also* Tungus
Maori, 226f
Maranao, 225
Marlow, Elli, 4
Martin, Samuel, 130
Masai, 135
Mass comparison. *See* Multilateral com-
    parison
Matthews, Peter, 19
Meillet, Antoine, 17, 69

Merton, R. K., 324
Miao-Yao, 209–11, 214
Michael of Lithuania, 318
Mixed language, 202, 217
Monboddo, Lord, 23, 25, 27, 33f, 43
Mongolian, 40, 129–38 *passim*, 179, 184,
    207, 211, 293–325 *passim*, 359–60
Mon-Khmer, 209, 211, 215f, 223, 228
Monogenesis of language, 363
Monosyllabic languages, 210, 213, 229
Morpheme decay, 373
Mosan, 350
Moses, L., 369–70
Mother goddesses, 114, 119
Mountain of tongues, 233
Multidimensional scaling, 372
Multilateral comparison, 127, 129, 189,
    329, 403–4
Muṇḍa, 209–11, 217, 219
Murayama, Shichirō, 278–80
Myrkin, V. Ja., 132

Na-Dene, 180, 187, 265, 329–31, 333, 344
Neogrammarians, 12, 14, 128
New World, peopling of, 328, 331, 344
Nikolaev, S., 179–80, 262–66
Nilo-Saharan, 123, 135f
Nivhk. *See* Gilyak
Nootka, 362, 383
North Caucasian, 124, 179, 184–87, 192–
    93, 233–66; classification, 236; map,
    238; proposed external relationships,
    265–66, 331; reconstruction, 258–65
Northern Amerind, 335, 337, 339–49
    passim
Nostratic, 123f, 130n, 178–84, 188f, 202,
    236, 254, 265, 357–60; homeland, 183;
    proposed external relationships, 191–
    95; velars, 190; vowels, 190. *See also*
    Eurasiatic
Noun classification in Caucasian lan-
    guages, 250

Ob-Ugric, 354, 356
Oceanic, 209–11, 217, 226, 229
Odyssey, 10
Old Europe, 89–121, 168; defined, 121.
    See also Female deities of Old Europe;
    Male deities of Old Europe; Symbols of
    Old Europe

Old Iranian/Persian, 31. *See also* Avestan
Omotic, 143–62
Orkhon inscriptions, 138
Otto, Rudolph, 71

Paleosiberian, 207, 265
Pāṇini, 10, 30, 37
Pedersen, Holger, 36, 124, 130n, 179, 398
Penutian, 4, 332–50
Persian, 23, 26ff, 30f. *See also* Avestan;
  Iranian
Phonological correspondences, 5–6, 127,
  141, 185, 205–7, 302; difficulties in
  North Caucasian, 262; resulting from
  massive borrowing, 205
Pliny, 232
Polynesian, 209, 225, 227f. *See also* Mal-
  ayo-Polynesian; Oceanic
Polysyllabic languages, 210, 213, 215, 229
Poppe, Nikolaus N., 297–300, 302–6,
  309–17 *passim*, 322
Potlach relationships, 383
Pott, A. F., 166
Prayer, IE terms for, 78, 80–81
Pregnant goddess, 113–14, 116

Ramstedt, G. J., 298ff, 305f, 308–16
Rape, 64–66
Rask, Rasmus, 35, 39, 126f, 329
Reconstruction, 128–29; difficulty in
  Uralic, 128; methodology, 311–20,
  323–24; use of typology in, 17f, 129
Regeneration, goddess, 102–12; symbols,
  104–9, 120
Regular sound change, 12–14, 127f. *See
  also* Phonological correspondences
Remote relationships. *See* Distant genetic
  relationships
Rice University, 11, 20f
Ritwan, 350
Robins, R. H., 39
Romance languages, 370–72, 380–82
Romany, 41
Ross, Alan S. C., 367–68
Russian, 398–99, 401

Salishan, 383
Samoan, 226f
Samoyed, 134, 354, 356, 397–98

Sankoff, D., 376f, 385
Sanskrit, 9–10, 23–45 *passim*; grammar,
  10, 36
Sapir, Edward, 180, 331, 384
Saussure, Ferdinand de, 17, 36, 190
Saussure's law, 176
Savchenko, A. N., 131f
Sawyer, L., 384
Schlegel, F. von, 34ff, 53
Schleicher, August, 13–14, 15ff, 32, 129
Schmidt, Johannes, 317
Schmidt, Wilhelm, 68
Scriptures, chanting of, 169
Scythian, 293, 401
Secret History of the Mongols, 294n
Semantic change/shift, 4, 402–3
Semitic, 41f, 124, 130, 143–62, 166–76,
  359. *See also* Afro-Asiatic
Serpent goddess, 94–96, 119–20
Sexual relations, illegal, 64–66
Shimizu, K., 142
Sinitic. *See* Chinese
Sino-Caucasian, 124, 179–80, 183, 184–87,
  192–95, 254, 265
Sinor, D., 299
Sino-Tibetan, 124, 179, 184–87, 192–93,
  207–29, 265, 331
Slavic, 127, 356
Snake goddess. *See* serpent goddess
Soma, 74f
Sound correspondences. *See* Phono-
  logical correspondences
South Caucasian. *See* Kartvelian
Southern Amerind, 339f, 342–49 *passim*
Stable vocabulary, 188–89
Starostin, S., 179, 184–87, 192–93,
  262–66
Strabo, 232f, 235
Stralenberg, Philip J. T. von, 293
Sturtevant, Edgar, 54
Sudanic, 135f
Sumerian, 265
Swadesh, Morris, 365, 370–76, 384
Swadesh list, 372f, 390
Symbols of Old Europe: bee, 110f; blood,
  104; bucranium, 104, 111, 119; bulls, 104,
  109, 111, 118–19; butterfly, 110f; but-
  tocks, 115; centaurs, 108–9; crescent,
  108; double ax, 111; eggs, 104, 109, 115;

eyes, 106–7; female 90–115; fertility, 114–15; four-corner designs, 108–9; hills, 114; horns, 108; labyrinths, 106; life column, 110; lightning, 110; lozenges, 111–12; mounds, 114; nets, 106–7; ovens, 114; phallus, 110; pregnancy, 113–15; regeneration, 102; snake, 110, 119; sun, 106; three, 94; tombs, 104–5; tree of life, 110; triangle, 111; two, 115; whirls, 108; womb, 104, 115, 119; zigzags, 110

Szemerényi, Oswald, 17, 132

Tai, 209–11, 214, 216, 223, 226ff
Tartar, 293
Tartarian. *See* Altaic
Thai, 216. *See also* Tai
Thieme, Paul, 73
Thomsen, Vilhelm, 398
Three as symbol, 94
Thunder god, 118f
Tibetan, 217f, 221, 254
Tibeto-Burman, 207–8, 211, 217f, 221–24, 226ff
Tibeto-Karenic, 207–8, 211, 223
Time depth, 365; Afro-Asiatic, 141; Germanic, 378–80; Romance, 380–82; Wakashan, 383–84
Timosthenes, 232
Tocharian, 53, 55, 135
Tok Pisin, 378–80
Tombs in Old Europe culture, 104–5
Tones, 210, 212f, 215, 229, 275–80
Trombetti, A., 357–58
Tungus, 129–38 *passim*, 179, 207, 211, 293–325 *passim*, 359–60
Turkic, 136ff, 184, 211, 240, 293–325 *passim*, 356; proposed external relationships, 129, 179, 207, 293–325 *passim*, 359–60
Turkish, 16, 40, 136
Tylor, Edward Burnett, 68
Typological classification, 210–15, 219–29
Typological relationship, 205f
Typologically based reconstruction, 17f
Typology, 201, 227–29; of Caucasian languages, 241–55. *See also* Typological classification

Ubykh, 234, 238f, 242, 244, 248, 256, 264
Ugric, 134, 354, 356, 361
Uighur, 211
Ural-Altaic, 401–2
Uralian. *See* Uralic
Uralic, 3f, 123f, 128–38 *passim*, 179–84, 189, 211, 217, 353–62, 397–402; family tree, 354. *See also* Finno-Ugric
Urartean, 179, 186–87, 265
Uslar, Baron Pjotr K., 241

van der Leeuw, G., 71
Verner, G. K., 192–93
Verner, Karl, 6, 12f, 35
Verner's law, 6, 12f, 138, 302
Viet-Muong, 209, 211, 214, 216, 223
Vietnamese, 216. *See also* Viet-Muong
Virgin Mary, 119–20
Voegelin, C. F. and F. M., 362
Vogul, 134
Vowel harmony, 212, 214f

Wakashan, 383–84
Wave theory, 317
Weil, Henri, 16
Whitman, John, 270–75, 277, 280n
Whitney, William Dwight, 13, 32, 401
Wilamowitz-Moellendorff, U. von, 71
Wilkins, Charles, 27f, 33
Wittgenstein, Ludwig, 20
Word order, 16; in Far Eastern languages, 220–27
Wundt, Wilhelm, 71–72

Yeniseian, 179, 184–87, 192–93, 265
Yue, 208, 214
Yukaghir, 123f, 129, 137, 359, 361
Yurak, 397–98, 400. *See also* Samoyed

Zeus, 62, 118
Zeuss, Caspar, 52
Zimmer, H., 135
Zoroastrianism, 74–75
Zulu, 217